To Gianni

[signature]

God bless you -
Paul L. Williams

KILLING THE
PLANET

KILLING THE PLANET

HOW A FINANCIAL CARTEL DOOMED MANKIND

RODNEY HOWARD-BROWNE *and* PAUL L. WILLIAMS

REPUBLIC

BOOK PUBLISHERS

KILLING THE PLANET
FIRST EDITION

Scripture quotations are taken from the Holy Bible, King James Version (public domain).

For inquiries about volume orders, please contact:
Republic Book Publishers
501 Slaters Lane #206
Alexandria VA 22314
editor@republicbookpublishers.com

ISBN: 9781645720003

Published in the United States by Republic Book Publishers

Distributed by Independent Publishers Group
www.ipgbook.com

Printed in the United States of America

In talking to my coauthor about the dedication, he and I both felt that we should dedicate this book to my mother, Lorna May Howard-Browne, who went home to be with Jesus in June 2018, at the age of ninety. She was an amazing woman, wife, and mother, who set an example of a strong faith, a tremendous work ethic and perseverance in the face of every obstacle. She said what she meant, and she meant what she said. She loved people and she loved to help people. She taught me the Word of God, and when I was about twelve, she gave me the book *None Dare Call It Conspiracy*. Over the years, my eyes have been opened, more and more, to see and understand that people have a right and a need to hear and experience the truth. "You will know the truth, and the truth will set you free!" Thank you, Mom, for your life. We love you so much, and we will see you soon!

CONTENTS

For the love of money is the root of all evil:
which while some coveted after,
they have erred from the faith,
and pierced themselves through with many sorrows.

—1 TIMOTHY 6:10

A MESSAGE TO THE READER

THIS WELL-RESEARCHED and documented sequel to *The Killing of Uncle Sam, Killing the Planet*, picks up the thread with a recap for all those who have not read the first book.

In case you have not realized it yet, the majority of world events that affect our daily lives are not random but are planned and follow a preset agenda.

How did our current problems start? Well, a large branch of it started in South Africa, the country of my birth. "For the furtherance of the British empire, and the recovery of the United States"—this came straight from the manifesto of Cecil John Rhodes.

From the secret society, birthed and funded from the world's financial capital, London, England, to New York, by way of the private central banks. The foundation of the Council on Foreign Relations and the Trilateral Commission. The forming of the League of Nations, which would eventually become the United Nations. The parallel rise of the

Rothschild and Rockefeller empires—birthed by the great-grandfather, a snake oil salesman and con man. Then, following the money trail through his transition into the oil business as he took control of energy, created the derivatives that followed, all which ultimately became about the control of the planet.

Out of oil came medicine and the control of the medical field: medicines, hospitals, doctors, and medical schools.

They took control of the judiciary—the control of the courts from the lower court, to the state court, all the way to the Supreme Court—controlling law schools, the narrative, the language, and the bar. This resulted in an outcome that was less about justice and more about their agenda. The trials, the sentencing—all rigged with false weights and balances. No blind justice at all. The scales tipped, not in favor of humanity but in the favor of the private central banking system.

At one time, the Rothschilds' wealth was $500 trillion. That never changed. It has morphed, hidden behind hundreds of Delaware corporations. Companies bought out, names changed, but the show goes on. Remember that they made their money through the exploitation of capitalism and then funded communism—a top-down system of control. You have the appearance of opposing teams, but when you own both sides, who cares who wins or loses?

On the governmental side, Republicans and Democrats are funded by/work for the same people. The ones who own the private central banks of the world, run the planet. Not the 1 percent but the 1 percent of the 1 percent. Their wealth is hidden in foundations and influences every area of human life. They fund population control and eugenics; wars and death—as millions die in in the machinations of this monster of destruction.

Death rides—here comes the pale horse of the apocalypse. Everything racing towards Armageddon. The rise of a world leader—an Antichrist—a one-world government, a one-world religion, and one money system. The Constitution of America was surreptitiously rewritten in each state, not favoring people but the corporations. Each new law favoring the machine and legalizing corruption. An intricate web of lies and deceit, hiding behind religion, world peace, save the planet, the trees, etc., etc., while millions of babies are murdered in and out of the womb.

Money must be made. Every blockage must be moved. The result is assassinations, murder, or slow death. Collusion to defraud—from character assassination, stealing inventions, and stopping innovation. Cures for diseases hidden, available only for the few. The concoction of conspiracies and the control of the news narrative—through misinformation, disinformation, lies, obfuscation.

The masses distracted through movies, music, entertainment and sports—while the takeover occurs. Co-opting education, agriculture, food, medicine, the judiciary, controlling the weather, controlling people, from the cradle to the grave. "Insurance, you need insurance; your retirement; your future"—keeping the narrative going. By hook or by crook, it's accomplished. Flatulent cows are made to be the world's biggest problem even as the "ice caps are melting and the polar bears are dying" because the earth is warming.

The whole agenda is not motivated by the desire to save the earth— it is really about extracting a carbon tax of $1.5 trillion a year and the creation of an overarching organization that will have control over every nation and its resources.

The earth has always gone through great fluctuations of weather— from season to season; from year to year; from decade to decade; from century to century. Right now, we are experiencing a Grand Solar Minimum, causing earthquakes and volcanoes. A mini ice age is now in effect across the planet. But you would never know that by watching, or listening to, the news or reading the newspaper. Any natural phenomena is proof—apparently—only of global warming and climate change.

Data is falsified, so scientists can continue to receive research funding. They are funded as long as they adhere to the narrative. Any attempt at independent thought, or asking questions, or actually following the numbers and the science to the truth, is not tolerated. If you dare to seek the truth, you are censored, silenced and/or discredited.

That which has been perpetrated over the past 200 years could only have been spawned in the bowels of hell. It is evident that the planet is run by Lucifarians who hate God, the Creation, and all humanity. They have an insatiable love for money and power. They would kill their own family members for a quick buck. It is evident that they have no fear of God or eternity; rather, they have set themselves up as God—to decide who lives and who dies.

They plan to do away with humans and merge with machines—to live forever. They try to find life on other planets, while life is exterminated here on Earth. The masses, kept as hamsters in a wheel, going round and round. Useful idiots—just cannon fodder—human mice to be used to experiment on.

Those who break free, and rise above, are paid a visit. If they comply, they become part of the elite club, because if they don't, they die. This scenario is as old as the earth—Lucifer taking Jesus to a high mountain and offering him the kingdoms of this earth if He would just bow. This is repeated over and over, throughout history, as men choose to sell their souls to the highest bidder. History repeats itself over and over again.

As you read this book, we trust your eyes will be opened to see the truth. Take note as you read—see if you can connect the dots. It's like a 3D picture—once you see it, once it pops out, you cannot unsee it. Then, when you watch the news, when you listen to people talk—you will know and understand the agenda immediately. It will be plain to you—because the difference is like night and day.

Remember this: a conspiracy is a secret plot to do something. A conspiracy theory is a suspicion that there is a conspiracy. But when it's uncovered and revealed, you know it's a fact. This book is not full of theories but full of historically documented facts. As we tell readers: if you find any mistakes in this book, or the previous, contact us. We will be happy to correct it in the reprint.

Neither I nor my co-author receive a royalty. All the proceeds go toward the River School of Government—raising up a new generation of servant leaders—endeavoring to set the standard and stand up for righteousness and truth.

May your eyes be opened to the truth. May you be inspired to do everything you can to help your fellow man before you take your final breath.

—DR. RODNEY M. HOWARD-BROWNE

TAMPA, FLORIDA, USA

While the earth remaineth,
seedtime and harvest,
and cold and heat,
and summer and winter,
and day and night shall not cease.

—GENESIS 8:22

PROLOGUE

AFRICAN GENESIS

(The Society should inspire and even own portions of the press for the press rules the mind of the people. The Society should always be searching for members who might by their position in the world by their energies or character forward the object but the ballot and test for admittance should be severe).

Once make it common and it fails. Take a man of great wealth who is bereft of his children perhaps having his mind soured by some bitter disappointment who shuts himself up separate from his neighbors and makes up his mind to a miserable existence. To such men as these the society should go gradually disclose the greatness of their scheme and entreat him to throw in his life and property with them for this object. I think that there are thousands now existing who would eagerly grasp at the opportunity. Such are the heads of my scheme.

—CECIL JOHN RHODES, "CONFESSION OF FAITH," JUNE 2, 1877

THE STORY STARTS IN AFRICA, where an elite society of English Masons initiated a plan to forge a one-world government. The society was imbued with a belief in the superiority of the Anglo-Saxon race and the need to bring all of mankind under British rule. The members of the society had journeyed from England to seek their fame and fortune within the diamond pits of Kimberley on the Vaal River. The leader was Cecil John Rhodes, the son of an Anglican vicar. At 6' 3" and 200 pounds, Rhodes was an imposing figure. He had a leonine head, light blue eyes, wavy brown hair, a carefully groomed mustache, and a ruddy complexion. The forcefulness of Rhodes's appearance was offset only by his tinny voice. Still and all, he possessed so much charisma that one contemporary claimed that "belief in Rhodes was a substitute for religion."[1] Rhodes was a Social Darwinist, an avowed agnostic, a practitioner of the occult, a homosexual, and a pederast, who surrounded himself with a stable of "angels and lambs" (young boys to furnish his sexual needs).[2]

The idea of the society came to Rhodes on June 2, 1877, the day he became a lifetime member of the Oxford University Apollo Chapter of the Masonic Order. Rhodes immediately put the revelation to paper in a document that he called his "Confession of Faith": "The idea gleaming and dancing before one's eyes like a will-of-the-wisp at last frames itself into a plan. Why should we not form a Secret Society with but one object the furtherance of the British Empire and the bringing of the whole uncivilized world under British rule for the recovery of the United States for the making the Anglo-Saxon race but one Empire."[3]

The religious, political, and economic unification of the world, Rhodes realized by his vision, was an achievable goal. The process, in fact, had already begun. Almost overnight, England had been industrialized by a revolution that gave birth to spinning machines and high-pressure steam engines that could be used not only in mining and manufacturing but also to power locomotives and cargo ships. Huge foundries, munitions plants, canneries, and silk mills had sprouted up

---

1   Sidney Low, "Some Conversations in London," in *The Nineteenth Century and After* (New York: Leonard Scott, 1902), 51:840.

2   "Cecil Rhodes, the Omnipotent," *Sunday Tribune* (South Africa), November 8, 2015, https://www.pressreader.com/, accessed February 13, 2019.

3   Cecil John Rhodes, "Confession of Faith," June 2, 1877, http://pages.uoregon.edu/kimball/Rhodes-Confession.htm, accessed February 13, 2019.

in cities throughout England all because of this newborn concept of financial capitalism. Raw material was being shipped to English plants and factories from the four corners of the globe. Goods were being created in such quantity that the surplus could be shipped out to ports throughout the world, and the English banking system came to the fore as the leading force in international affairs and economics.[4]

The population of England soared from 8.3 million in 1801 to 30.1 million at the time of Rhodes.[5] Wealth became confined to those who controlled the means of production and finance. The industrial merchant became replaced by the industrial millionaire. Marx and Engel, in their *Communist Manifesto,* explained: "All old-established national industries have been destroyed or are daily being destroyed. They are dislodged by new industries, whose introduction becomes a life and death question for all civilized nations, by industries that no longer work up indigenous raw material, but raw material drawn from the remotest zones; industries whose products are consumed, not only at home, but in every quarter of the globe. In place of the old wants, satisfied by the production of the country, we find new wants, requiring for their satisfaction the products of distant lands and climes. In place of the old local and national seclusion and self-sufficiency, we have intercourse in every direction, universal inter-dependence of nations."[6] The thought of Cecil Rhodes was inexorably bound to these changes in material productivity.

In September 1877, Rhodes returned to Kimberley and his "very small two roomed corrugated iron house with a wooden floor . . . iron

---

4   Geraldine Corrodus, et al., *Oxford Big Ideas—Geography, History* (South Melbourne, Australia: Oxford University Press, 2013), pp. 272–275.

5   E. A. Wrigley, ed., *Nineteenth-Century Society: Essays in the Use of Quantitative Methods for the Study of Social Data* (Cambridge: Cambridge University Press, 2008), pp. 32–36.

6   Karl Marx and Frederick Engels, "Manifesto of the Communist Party," February 1848, Creative Commons Attribution—Share—Alike License, p. 16, https://www.marxists.org/archive/marx/works/download/pdf/Manifesto.pdf, accessed February 13, 2019.

walls and roof."[7] To this humble dwelling, he invited his closest friends and confidants for a dinner meeting. The guests included Joseph Orpen, who would become an influential administrator for the British Crown in South Africa; Henry Caesar Hawkins, son of the resident magistrate of the Umkomaas Valley; Alfred Beit, a German Jew, who dealt in diamonds; Leander Starr Johnson, a youthful physician; Charles Rudd; Shippard; and Lewis Michell, a prominent South African banker, who recorded the words of Rhodes to the gathering as follows:

> Gentlemen I have asked you to dine . . . because I want to tell you what I want to do for the remainder of my life. I think that if a man when he is young determined to devote his life to one worthy object and persists in that he can do a good deal during that life even if it is to be a short one as I know my life will be. . . . The object of which I intend to devote my life is the defence and the extension of the British Empire. . . . The British Empire stands for the protection of all the inhabitants of a country in life, liberty, fair play and happiness and it is the greatest platform the world has ever seen for these purposes. . . . It is mainly the extension of the empire northward that we have to watch and work for in South Africa.[8]

The men in attendance were so moved by these remarks that they agreed to join with Rhodes in devoting their lives and wealth to the secret society. Their commitment was to be without personal reservation. For this reason, Rhodes urged his "band of brothers" to avoid all emotional entanglements, including marriage. "I hate people getting married," he said, "because they simply become machines and have no

---

7   Robert I. Rotberg, *The Founder: Cecil Rhodes and the Pursuit of Power* (New York: Oxford University Press, 1988), p. 103.

8   Sir Lewis Michell, *The Life of Rt. Hon. C. J. Rhodes, 1853–1902*, vol. 1 (London: Edward Arnold, 1910), p. 223, https://archive.org/stream/lifeofrthoncecil01michuoft/lifeofrthoncecil01michuoft_djvu.txt, accessed February 13, 2019.

ideas beyond their respective spouses and offspring."[9] The new initiates to the "Kimberley Club" took this advice to heart, thereby granting a hint of monasticism to their society, which would evolve into a hotbed of homosexuals and pederasts.

The first step toward a new world order, Rhodes maintained, was the conquest of Africa, with its vast reserves of diamonds, gold, iron ore, coal, and timber. "Africa is still lying ready for us; it is our duty to take it," he wrote in his Confession. "It is our duty to seize every opportunity of acquiring more territory and we should keep this one idea steadily before our eyes: that more territory simply means more of the Anglo-Saxon race, more of the best, the most human, most honorable race the world possesses."[10]

Throughout his life, Rhodes's belief in the necessity of the British conquest of Africa remained unswerving. Fifteen years after penning his Confession, he confided the following to William H. Stead, one of his most ardent disciples: "If there is a God, it is clear that He would like me to do what He is doing Himself. And He is manifestly fashioning the English-speaking race as the chosen instrument by which He will bring in a state of society based upon Justice, Liberty, and Peace. He would like me to paint as much of the map of Africa British red as possible, and to do what I can elsewhere to promote the unity and extend the influence of the English-speaking race."[11]

To initiate the conquest, Rhodes and members of his society entered politics and became elected to the Parliament of the Cape Colony. By 1891, Rhodes became the Prime Minister, a position he would hold for the next five years. Addressing the Cape Parliament, Rhodes said: "If you were to sleep for five and twenty years, you might find a gentleman

---

9   Cecil John Rhodes, "Letter to Charles Rudd," October 1876, in *Diamonds Fields Advertiser*, December 25, 1906.

10   Rhodes, "Confession of Faith."

11   William T. Stead, *The Last Will and Testament of Cecil John Rhodes* (London: Review of Reviews Office, 1902), pp. 97–98.

called your prime minister sitting in Cape Town and controlling the whole, not only to the Zambezi, but to Lake Tanganyika."[12] Now known as the "Colossus," he initiated railway systems that ran from the Cape through the Orange State of the Boers and onto Johannesburg, and from southern (Matabeleland) to northern (Mashonaland) Rhodesia.

The dream that Rhodes expressed in his "Confession of Faith" was coming to fruition. Tens of thousands of British immigrants lured by reports of gold, including the location of the fabled "King Solomon's mines," and the offer of free land moved from the overpopulated cities of England to the lands owned and controlled by Rhodes in South Africa. Within the new country that Rhodes called Zambezi,[13] the new settlers came to produce more wheat, maize, and tobacco than anywhere else save America.[14] Beef cattle thrived in the lowlands north of Bulawayo, and fruit—apples, oranges, lemons, pears, peaches, apricots, pineapples, strawberries, coconuts, and melons—grew in such prodigious quantity that the highly profitable Rhodes Fruit Farms came into existence.[15]

To unify the vast continent into one enormous country, Rhodes laid plans for a Cairo-to–Cape Town railroad, a train that would traverse the Zambezi with its mighty falls; run through the meandering Congo; scale massive mountains, like Kilimanjaro and Mount Kenya; stretch boundless savannahs and vast deserts; and circle lakes the size of small seas. The jungles would be cleared. The timber would be transported on railroad cars to the cities, which would sprout up at the railroad stations. The natives would be pushed from their lands in accordance with the Glen Gray Act (legislation initiated by Rhodes) and sent to work on the farms, factories, and industrial plants. This work, Rhodes

---

12   Robin Brown, *The Secret Society: Cecil John Rhodes's Plan for a New World Order* (Cape Town, South Africa: Penguin Books, 2015), p. 129.

13   Robert Blake, *A History of Rhodesia* (London: Eyre Methuen, 1977), p. 114.

14   Brown, *The Secret Society*, p. 174.

15   Robert I. Rotberg, *The Founder: Cecil Rhodes and the Pursuit of Power* (New York: Oxford University Press, 1988), p. 640.

believed, would assist the black natives in shedding their slovenly habits. "It must be brought home to them," Rhodes said, "that, in the future, nine-tenths of them will have to spend their lives in manual labor, and the sooner that is brought home to them the better."[16] The inexhaustible minerals—iron ore, coal, copper, nickel, lead, bauxite, and gold—of Africa would be mined by the black labor force. Riches beyond measure would be added to the British Empire. And it all seemed well within the grasp of Cecil Rhodes in 1895, when Zambesia was renamed Rhodesia in his honor.

During this time, Rhodes made frequent visits to England, where he attracted a host of influential aristocrats to his secret society, now dubbed "the Society of the Elect." The list of his new recruits included Lord Reginald Baliol Brett, Queen Victoria's closest advisor; Lord Archibald Primrose, the 5th Earl of Roseberry and Rothschild's son-in-law, who would serve as Britain's prime minister from 1894 to 1895; and Arthur James Balfour, 1st Earl of Balfour, who would become the British prime minister from 1902 to 1905. Rhodes's ties to these three men would become tightened by their shared homosexuality and their preference for "burly, blue-eyed boys."[17] Among the other recruits were Albert Lord Grey and Robert Armstrong Yates, two prominent members of the British Parliament; William Palmer, the 2nd Earl of Selborne; Cardinal Henry Edward Manning, the leading Roman Catholic prelate in England; (General) William Booth, the founder of the Salvation Army; William Stead, Britain's most prominent journalist; "Little" Harry Johnson, head of the British consular service in West Africa; and Alfred Milner, undersecretary of finance in Egypt.[18] Milner, who was also of questionable sexual orientation, merits special mention. Rhodes recognized in him the kind of steel that was required to pursue

---

16 Martin Meredith, *Diamonds, Gold, and War: The British, the Boers, and the Making of South Africa* (New York: Public Affairs, 2008), p. 265.

17 Ibid., p. 36.

18 Ibid., pp. 83–86.

the dream of world domination, "I support Milner absolutely without reserve. If he says peace, I say peace; if he says war, I say war. Whatever happens, I say ditto to Milner."[19]

But the most important recruit was Lord Nathan Rothschild, who had gained complete control of the Bank of England. Lord Rothschild was the leading member of the world's most influential banking families. The Rothschilds had established financial ties to such countries as Austria, Germany, Russia, Italy, France, Egypt, China, South Africa, China, India, New Zealand, and Australia. In the process, they established close relations with other Jewish banking families, including the Cohens, Warburgs, Schiffs, Kuhns, Loebs, Lazards, Lehmans, and Goldmans. These families worked together, shared resources, and engaged in joint business ventures. They shared a common Jewish heritage, maintained close social ties, and often intermarried.[20] "Natty" Rothschild married the oldest daughter of Levi Barent Cohen, a prominent London financier. Jacob Schiff, who had lived with the Rothschilds, moved to America and married the daughter of Solomon Loeb, the head of the Kuhn Loeb banking dynasty. The two daughters of Marcus Goldman married the sons of Samuel Sachs to form Goldman Sachs. Paul Warburg left Hamburg for New York, where he married Nina Loeb, the daughter of Solomon Loeb.[21] United by blood, marriage, and ethnicity, they provided funding to American businessmen and industrialists, including Andrew Carnegie, John D. Rockefeller, and J. P. Morgan.[22] In this way, they created a money cartel that became the most powerful force on planet Earth.

---

19   Stead, *The Last Will and Testament of Cecil John Rhodes*, 108.

20   Dean Henderson, "The Federal Reserve Cartel: The Eight Families," *Global Research,* June 1, 2011, http://www.globalresearch.ca/the-federal-reserve-cartel-the-eight-families/25080, accessed February, 13, 2019.

21   Ibid.

22   Eustace Mullins, "Mayer Rothschild and the Five Arrows," *Modern History Project*, 1984, http://modernhistoryproject.org/mhp?Article=WorldOrder&C=1.1, accessed February 13, 2019.

The members of the Society of the Elect met regularly at the Mowbray House in London. The Society's original members shared much in common. Apart from Stead, they were personages of means who had been educated at Oxford or Cambridge. They were Masons, most members of the Apollo Chapter; even Manning, prior to receiving Holy Orders, had been a lodge member. They were imperialists, who had been influenced by the thoughts of John Ruskin and his belief that the world must be reshaped into an aesthetically pleasing whole. They were Social Darwinists who believed that the British people, through the process of natural selection, had evolved into the master race. With the exception of Stead, they held positions of political power that would impact the course of British affairs. They all had cultivated strong ties to the Rothschild family, who had served as the governor of the Bank of England before becoming a prelate.[23] And they all shared a deep interest in the occult, including theosophy.[24]

Still focused on Africa and its vast riches, the Society plotted the Second Boer War, which raged from 1899 to 1902. As a result of this conflict, the Transvaal and the Orange Free State became incorporated into the British Empire. Six thousand Boers were killed in action, while 26,000 white civilians and 17,182 African natives died of disease and starvation in concentration camps that had been set up in territories previously ruled by the Boers.[25] In a letter to Lord Frederick Roberts, Alfred Milner wrote: "I precipitated the crisis, which was inevitable, before it was too late. It is not very agreeable, and in many eyes, not very creditable piece of business to have been largely instrumental in bringing about a big war."[26] However, the 20,000 children who had died

---

23   Ibid.

24   Brown, *The Secret Society*, p. 110.

25   Owen Coetzer, *Fire in the Sky: The Destruction of the Orange Free State* (Johannesburg: Covos Day, 2000), pp. 82–83.

26   Milner, quoted in Thomas Pakenham, *The Boer War* (New York: Random House, 1979), p. 115.

in the British concentration camps were of little consequence to Milner. When faced with criticism about the atrocities, Milner responded: "If we are to build up anything in South Africa, we must disregard, and absolutely disregard, the screamers."[27]

The second objective of the Society of the Elect toward a New World Order was the restoration of America to the imperial fold of Great Britain. In his Confession, Rhodes wrote:

> I once heard it argued by a fellow in my own college, I am sorry to own it by an Englishman, that it was good thing for us that we have lost the United States. There are some subjects on which there can be no arguments, and to an Englishman this is one of them, but even from an American's point of view just picture what they have lost, look at their government, are not the frauds that yearly come before the public view a disgrace to any country and especially theirs which is the finest in the world. Would they have occurred had they remained under English rule great as they have become how infinitely greater they would have been with the softening and elevating influences of English rule, think of those countless number of Englishmen that during the last 100 years would have crossed the Atlantic and settled and populated the United States. Would they have not made without any prejudice a finer country of it than the low class Irish and German emigrants? All this we have lost and that country loses owing to whom? Owing to two or three ignorant pig-headed statesmen of the last century, at their door lies the blame. Do you ever feel mad? Do you ever feel murderous? I think I do with those men.[28]

During his final years, the thoughts of Cecil John Rhodes turned more and more to the United States. William Stead observed: "He [Rhodes] was devoted to the old flag [the Union Jack] but in his ideas he was an

27   Ibid., p. 483.

28   Rhodes, "Confession of Faith."

American, and in his latter years he expressed to me his unhesitating readiness to accept the reunion of the [English] race under the Stars and Stripes if it could not be obtained in any other way. Although he had no objection to the monarchy, he unhesitatingly preferred the American to the British Constitution, and the textbook which he laid down for his novitiates was a copy of the American Constitution."[29] Rhodes believed that the unification of Britain and the United States would secure "the peace of the world for all eternity" and the creation of a "universal language."[30]

This merger could be effected, Rhodes argued, by the strengthening of economic trade between the two nations. Trade would be unencumbered by tariffs; by the planting of "Pilgrim Societies" in London and New York, where American and British bankers, businessmen, and industrialists could meet in private to outline their joint goals and objectives; and by the awarding of Rhodes Scholarships to Oxford University for the best and brightest American students so that they could play an integral part in the formation of the New World Order.[31] Once sufficient support for the merger was achieved, he believed, the British House of Commons would unite with the U.S. Congress

Rhodes believed that the unification of Britain and the United States would secure "the peace of the world for all eternity" and the creation of a "universal language." Image © Acabashi, Creative Commons CC-BY-SA 4.0, Wikimedia Commons

---

29   William T. Stead, *The Last Will and Testament of Cecil John Rhodes* (London: Review of Reviews Office, 1902), p. 63.

30   Ibid., p. 73.

31   Ibid., pp. 23–45.

for the formation of an "Imperial Parliament," the members of which would remain seated for five-year terms, alternating their location between London and Washington, D.C.[32]

To effect this alliance, Rhodes dispatched leading members of his society, including Stead and Lord Roseberry, to travel to America in order to meet with the country's leading industrialists, including Andrew Carnegie and J. P. Morgan. As a result of these meetings, the American branch of the Rhodes Society was established at the Waldorf Astoria Hotel in New York. This group would give birth to the Federal Reserve System, which would govern the American economy. It would also bring its own candidates to political power, including Woodrow Wilson and Franklin Delano Roosevelt. It would drag the United States into World War I, create the Great Depression, and establish the Council on Foreign Relations, which would gain complete control of the U.S. State Department.

All of these developments took place according to plan. But something went haywire. The forger of this global government was supposed to be an international banker or a well-heeled aristocrat. But what happened, in actual fact, was incredible. The control of the world and the fate of mankind would fall into the hands of the hairless and humorless son of a horse thief.

His name was John D. Rockefeller.

---

32   Ibid., p. 73.

PART ONE

THE CARTEL

The nation-state as a fundamental unit of man's organized life has ceased to be the principal creative force: "International banks and multinational corporations are acting and planning in terms that are far in advance of the political concepts of the nation-state."
—ZBIGNIEW BRZEZINSKI, *BETWEEN TWO AGES: AMERICA'S ROLE IN THE TECHNETRONIC ERA*, 1971

There exists a shadowy government, with its own Air Force, its own Navy, its own fundraising mechanism, and the ability to pursue its own ideas of national interest, free from all the checks and balances, and free from the law itself.
—DANIEL K. INOUYE, U.S. SENATOR, 1977

Some even believe we [Rockefeller family] are part of a secret cabal, working against the best interests of the United States, characterizing my family and me as "internationalists," and of conspiring with others around the world to build a more integrated global political and economic structure—one world, if you will. If that's the charge, I stand guilty, and I am proud of it.
—DAVID ROCKEFELLER, *MEMOIRS*, 2002

1

SNAKE OIL

If thou, Columbia, dost from this, thy son—
The condor beak and python eyes—recoil,
Bethink thee of the years that Freedom's soil
Was husbanded by devil-feet which run
To scatter lies and wrongs; until thereon
Huge growths do thrive, once meadow, by the toil
Of pioneers; where now resort for spoil
The mouths and beaks that hunt for carrion.
In years to come, if men mid the debris
Of this republic shall explore the cause
Of vast decay, two faces will appear:
The perjured Marshall, who with sorcery
Planted the jungle of unequal laws,
And this huge reptile, now a nation's Fear!
—EDGAR LEE MASTERS, "ON A PICTURE OF JOHN D. ROCKEFELLER"

IN THE MIDST OF THE 19TH CENTURY, Dr. William (Bill) Levingston traveled throughout the Northeast states, peddling "Seneca Oil," which he claimed was a surefire cure for cancer. The medicine was his homemade concoction of liquid paraffin, calomel, Epsom salts, and petroleum. The oil came from a salt well in Tarentum outside of

Pittsburgh, Pennsylvania.[1] He named his product Seneca after a group of Iroquoian-speaking Indians who lived in upper New York State before the American Revolution.

At $25 a pint, the concoction was incredibly pricey in that time, when the wages for an average American laborer were less than six dollars a week.[2] But Dr. Levingston assured all those who gathered to listen to him at his medical show that the cost was well worth the result. "A single bottle," he claimed, "can cure all cases of cancer unless they are too far gone."[3]

A SMALL SIDE EFFECT

But Dr. Bill warned that the concoction should not be administered to pregnant women since a few spoonfuls would likely cause an instantaneous abortion. "As a physician," Levingston said, "I am duty bound to warn you of this side effect." This side effect was always of interest to a few of the young men in the audience, who were willing to empty their pockets for a small sampling of the medicine.

A towering figure with a thick auburn beard, Dr. Bill, wearing a top hat and black waistcoat, spoke with a sonorous voice and possessed a pleasing appearance and a magnetic charm that evoked confidence from his listeners. His medical show was successful enough for him to keep two wives, eight children, two separate households, and a stable of mistresses.

A HORSE THIEF AND CHILD MOLESTER

Everything, however, about the charismatic doctor was bogus. He was not a physician. He had never received any medical training, not even as

---

1   Robert Gates Jr., *The Conspiracy That Will Not Die: How the Rothschild Cartel Is Driving America into One World Government* (Oakland, Oregon: Red Anvil Press, 2011), p. 136.

2   "Typical Wages in 1860 through 1890," *Outrun Change*, June 14, 2012, https://outrunchange. com/2012/06/14/typical-wages-in-1860-through-1890/, accessed January 16, 2019.

3   William Livingston, quoted in Gates, *The Conspiracy That Will Not Die*, p. 135.

an orderly in a rural hospital. The medicine that he sold from the back of his black wagon could not cure cancer, but it could produce such severe abdominal cramping in women that abortions often occurred.[4] And his name was not William Levingston but rather William Avery Rockefeller.

In addition to the fleecing marks far and wide of their hard-earned cash, Dr. Bill, also known as "Devil Bill," was a horse thief who often tied an unattended stallion to the back of his wagon before leaving town.[5] He was a gifted card shark and notorious child molester. The good doctor avoided prosecution in Cayuga County, New York, for raping a 15-year-old girl by hightailing it for Cleveland.[6]

A FATHER'S LESSON

When he wasn't absent from his first wife and children, peddling his "medicine" or running away from the law, Devil Bill taught his kids the fine art of cheating. "I cheat my sons every chance I get," he bragged of his parenting technique. "I want to make 'em sharp. I trade with the boys and skin 'em, and I just beat 'em every time I can. I want to make 'em sharp."[7]

Even as a boy, John D., the eldest of Devil Bill's sons, represented a perfect example of *homo economicus.* He kept his weekly allowance so that he could buy candy by the pound. He divided the candy into small portions that he sold to his siblings and classmates.[8] By age seven, he was dropping gold, silver, and copper coins into a blue china bowl on the mantel. By this time, he had developed his own business coup by

---

4   Ron Chernow, *Titan: The Life of John D. Rockefeller, Sr.* (New York: Vintage Books, 1998), p. 11.

5   Gates, *The Conspiracy That Will Not Die*, p. 137.

6   Gary Allen, *The Rockefeller File* (Seal Beach, CA: '76 Press, 1976), p. 20.

7   William Rockefeller, quoted in Grant Segall, *John D. Rockefeller: Anointed with Oil* (New York: Oxford University Press, 2001), pp. 15–16.

8   Ibid., p. 17.

shadowing turkeys as they waddled into the woods, raiding their nests, and raising the chicks for sale.[9]

To the residents of Moravia, New York, where John D. spent his childhood, he always seemed abstracted. They remembered him with a deadpan face, trudging along the country roads, lost in thought.

NAKED AMBITION

In early photos, John D. appears grim and expressionless, lacking any sense of boyish joy or animation. His skin is drawn, and his small, dark eyes appear blank and lusterless. To the residents of Moravia, New York, where John D. spent his childhood, he always seemed abstracted. They remembered him with a deadpan face, trudging along the country roads, lost in thought.[10] And his thought, even as a child, was set. He wanted to become the world's wealthiest man and to live 100 years.[11]

At 16, John D. dropped out of school to become a bookkeeper for Hewitt & Tuttle, a Cleveland brokerage firm that specialized in the importing of iron ore. Two years later, he established his own business with Maurice Clark, an Englishman who worked at a produce house. The firm called Clark and Rockefeller specialized in the sale of commodities, including meat

---

9   Ibid.

10   Chernow, *Titan*, p. 17.

11   Carl O'Donnell, "The Rockefellers: The Legacy of History's Richest Man," *Forbes,* July 11, 2014, https://www.forbes.com/sites/carlodonnell/2014/07/11/the-rockefellers-the-legacy-of-historys-richest-man/#a4510473c266, accessed January 16, 2019.

and grain.[12] The outbreak of the Civil War proved to be a great boon for the new business, which secured a contract to provide produce to the Union army. By the war's end, Rockefeller had amassed a tidy fortune of $250,000.[13]

DRAKE'S FOLLY

A new commodity arising from the farming backwoods of western Pennsylvania now attracted John D.'s attention. Colonel Edwin Drake, who was not really a colonel, erected a tall wooden structure known as a derrick and began drilling for oil with equipment used in salt wells. His notion of drilling for oil made him the laughingstock of the small town Titusville. But

Colonel Edwin Drake, who was not really a colonel, erected a tall wooden structure known as a derrick and began drilling for oil with equipment used in salt wells. His notion of drilling for oil made him the laughingstock of the small town Titusville. But the laughter stopped on August 28, 1859, when oil began to gush from the ground and to fill the pails that Drake had placed within the derrick.

the laughter stopped on August 28, 1859, when oil began to gush from the ground and to fill the pails that Drake had placed within the derrick. A whole new industry was born overnight. Drake proved that through drilling, oil could be found in abundance and produced cheaply.[14]

12   Chernow, *Titan*, p. 60.

13   Rob Wile, "The Rockefellers: How a Few Poor Germans Became an Immortal American Dynasty," *Business Insider*, April 29, 2012, https://www.businessinsider.com/a-history-of-the-rockefellers-2012-4, accessed January 16, 2019.

14   James Corbett, "How & Why Big Oil Conquered the World," *The Corbett Report*, October 14, 2017, https://www.corbettreport.com/bigoil/, accessed January 17, 2019.

Before 1850, oil was not a precious commodity. Quacks like Devil Bill used it to treat a variety of diseases, including consumption and diphtheria, and paraffin, developed in 1830, was used to make candles and to lubricate machinery. Kerosene was invented by Dr. Abraham Gesner in 1848, by distilling coal to produce a clear fluid. But this method of making kerosene was expensive and kept kerosene lamps from use in average households.[15]

In 1853, a new method of producing kerosene was discovered by "washing" crude oil with sulfuric acid.[16] The possibility now loomed that oil could be used to light the lamps of the world. By the end of the decade, thanks to "Drake's folly," the oil rush began.

A whole new industry was born overnight. Drake proved that through drilling, oil could be found in abundance and produced cheaply. "Drake Well, June 2012" by Niagara is licensed under CC BY-SA 3.0

A GRANDIOSE SCHEME

Realizing that the potential of incredible wealth was at stake, John D. approached the directors of the Bank of Cleveland for a multimillion-dollar loan to build a refinery. The site he had chosen was a mile and a half from downtown Cleveland on a narrow waterway called Kingsbury Run.[17] If Rockefeller had not included two carrots to his proposal, the bank directors

15 "History of Kerosene Lamps," History of Lamps, 2018, http://www.historyoflamps.com/lamp-history/history-of-kerosene-lamp/, accessed January 16, 2019.

16 C. C. Opara, Alex Igiri Oyom, and Moses C. Okonkow, "Deodorization of Kerosene Using Activated Carbon as Absorbent," *Greener Journal of Physical Sciences* 3, February 2013, http://gjournals.org/GJPS/GJPS%20PDF/2013/February/Opara%20et%20al.pdf, accessed January 16, 2019.

17 Chernow, *Titan*, p. 78.

certainly would have scoffed at his request for a loan since twenty-seven other refineries were being built in Cleveland. The first carrot was the fact that the Erie Railroad planned to lay track next to Rockefeller's proposed site. This development meant that John D. would have little difficulty in transporting the oil from his refinery to locations throughout the country.[18] The second carrot resided in Rockefeller's rebate scheme. If the Bank of Cleveland provided him a promissory note of unlimited funding, he intended to secure rebates from the owners of Erie for every barrel of oil that was carried on their freight cars.

The scheme was not complicated. Rockefeller would guarantee Jim Fisk and Jay Gould, the owners of Erie, massive daily shipments of refined oil on their railroad line. Such a guarantee would be tanta-lizing to the two railroad barons since the freight business had become incredibly competitive. In exchange, Fisk and Gould would provide Rockefeller with a rebate on all his shipments.[19] It was a grandiose scheme that involved a clandestine kickback. It reeked of grave illegality since it threatened to eliminate any possibility of fair and equitable competition.

With the possibility of incredible wealth at stake, John D. approached the directors of the Bank of Cleveland for a multimillion-dollar loan to build a refinery. "Drake Well petroleum" by Niagara is licensed under CC BY-SA 3.0

---

18   Ibid.

19   Michael Reksulak and William F. Shughart II, "Of Rebates and Drawbacks: The Standard Oil (N.J.) Company and the Railroads," *Review of Industrial Organizations* 38, May 2011, https://www. jstor.org/stable/23884928?seq=1#page_scan_tab_contents, accessed January 16, 2019.

THE ROTHSCHILD BANK

But the scheme ran far deeper than a simple kickback. John D. would also demand from Fisk and Gould a rebate on every barrel of oil shipped by his competitors. No other refinery could hope to remain in business under such conditions. His competitors would be forced to sell their holdings to Rockefeller at rock-bottom prices. Regarding the scheme, prominent Rockefeller critic Ida M. Tarbell wrote:

> Men generally held then, as now, that it was not fair for the railroads to allow one shipper a better rate than another. The common law was known to disapprove the practice. The theory that the railroad held its right of way from the people, and therefore must be just to the people, treating them without discrimination, was familiar enough, so familiar that the railroads never dared show favoritism save secretly. But under threats of loss of business, under promise of larger or more regular shipments, under chances of sharing in the profits of the enterprises they favored, they did do it secretly. That is, rebate giving then, as now, was regarded as one of those lower business practices which characterize commerce at all periods, and against which men of honor struggle, and of which men of greed take advantage. Naturally, one would expect Mr. Rockefeller to spurn such an advantage. The one thing for which he was conspicuous outside of his zeal for business was his devotion to the church, one of whose cardinal teachings is "whatsoever ye would that men do to you do ye even so to them." Naturally, one demands a man of his profession to be keenly alive to degrading business practices and keen to overthrow them. But, although Mr. Rockefeller no doubt heard weekly from the pulpit that the "law and the prophets" were all summed up in doing as you would be done by, it is quite probable he had never seen any connection between the doctrine and railroad rebates. He was not an educated man. He had evidently never thought seriously of anything but making money. His religious training seems to have been purely formal, awakening him merely to the duty of attending to devotional exercises and giving to the church. So, when he realized

that the rebate was the means by which he could gain control of the oil industry in Cleveland, he went after it, ignorant of, or indifferent to the ethical quality of the act.[20]

The brashness of the concept was breathtaking, and John D.'s scheme would have been repellent to any banker with a modicum of integrity. But by happenstance, the young Rockefeller had walked into one of the three banks in the United States that would have been open to such a deal. This bank was owned by the Rothschilds.

---

20   Ida M. Tarbell, "John D. Rockefeller: A Character Study," Part One, *McClure's Magazine*, August 1906, http://www.reformation.org/john-d-rockefeller.html, accessed January 16, 2019.

2

THE OIL WAR

He [John D. Rockefeller, Sr.] was simple and frugal in his habits. He never went to the theater, never drank wine. He was a devoted husband, and he gave much time to the training of his children, seeking to develop in them his own habits of economy and of charity. Yet he was willing to strain every nerve to obtain for himself special and illegal privileges from the railroads which were bound to ruin every man in the oil business not sharing them with him.

—IDA TARBELL, "THE OIL WAR OF 1872," *MCCLURE'S MAGAZINE*,

JANUARY 1903

WITH THE BORROWED CASH from the Bank of Cleveland, Rockefeller dissolved his partnership with Maurice Clark for $72,000 and formed a company that would become known as Standard Oil.[1] As soon as the company was formed, he met in secret with Jay Gould, who granted him a whopping 75 percent on transportation cost in exchange for a guarantee of shipments of 60 railroad cars filled with oil from Rockefeller's new refinery. Gould, as John D. had planned, also agreed

---

1   Robert Gates Jr., *The Conspiracy That Will Not Die: How the Rothschild Cartel Is Driving America into One World Government* (Oakland, OR: Red Anvil Press, 2011), p. 40.

to provide a 25 percent rebate on all the oil shipped by Rockefeller's competitors on the Erie Railroad.[2]

Due to unlimited finances, John D. was able to construct a refinery that was larger and better planned and equipped than the other oil operations. He also purchased his own barrel-making plant, which contained timber-drying facilities. He manufactured his own sulfuric acid and came up with a means to recover it for reuse.[3]

WEALTH FROM WASTE

The enormous size of his new refinery permitted Rockefeller to handle all the "waste" products from the burning of kerosene. He began manufacturing high-quality lubricating oil that quickly replaced lard oil as a lubricant for machinery. And the gasoline, which other refiners surreptitiously dumped into the Cuyahoga River at night (the river often caught fire), Rockefeller used as fuel.[4]

Within a few months of the opening of his refinery, John D. was able to manufacture benzene (used as a cleaning fluid; a solvent for fat, gums, and resin; and to make varnish), paraffin (insoluble in water, used for making candles, waterproofing paper, preservative coatings, etc.), and petrolatum (used as a basis for ointments and as a protective dressing; as a local application in inflammation of mucous membrane; as an intestinal lubricant, etc.; and white petrolatum, later marketed under the brand name *Vaseline*).[5]

In 1871, one year after it was incorporated, Standard Oil declared a

---

2   Charles Rivers, *Robber Barons: The Lives and Careers of John D. Rockefeller, J. P. Morgan, Andrew Carnegie, and Cornelius Vanderbilt* (Scotts Valley, CA: CreateSpace Independent Publishing Platform, 2016), pp. 128–29.

3   Keith Poole, "Biography: John D. Rockefeller, Senior," *American Experience,* Public Broadcasting System (PBS), n.d., http://www.pbs.org/wgbh/americanexperience/features/rockefellers-john/, accessed January 17, 2019.

4   Ibid.

5   Ibid.

40 percent dividend to shareholders. Millions of dollars began to pour into the coffers of the new oil company from Wall Street bankers and speculators to stake John D.'s mission of obtaining more and more volume-based shipping rebates from the railroads in order to gain sole control of America's burgeoning oil industry.[6]

Ida Tarbell, the daughter of a Cleveland refinery owner, later recalled how her father attempted to understand the events that produced a sudden and devastating impact on his business.

THE REBATE PLAN UNLEASHED

By this time, Rockefeller had cemented a deal for rebates with other railroads, including Pennsylvania Central, with the help of Jacob Schiff, a Rothschild lackey who had become a partner in Kuhn, Loeb & Company, one of America's largest banks.[7] John D. now set up the South Improvement Company. This company was used to funnel the rebates to Standard Oil and to pressure the railroad owners to raise the rates for Rockefeller's competitors so that he could receive a kickback from all their shipments.

Ida Tarbell, the daughter of a Cleveland refinery owner, later recalled how her father attempted to understand the events that produced a

---

6   Anton Chaitkin, "America's Former Greatness and the World's Future," *Executive Intelligence Review*, January 2, 2015, https://larouchepub.com/other/2015/4201us_former_greatness_1870.html, accessed January 17, 2019.

7   H. D. Lloyd, "Story of a Great Monopoly," *Atlantic Monthly*, March 1881, https://ehistory.osu.edu/exhibitions/1912/trusts/lloyd_article, accessed January 17, 2019.

sudden and devastating impact on his business. "On the morning of February 26, 1872," she wrote, "the oil men read in their morning papers that the rise [in freight rates] which had been threatening had come; moreover, that all members of the South Improvement Company were exempt from the advance. At the news all Oildom rushed into the streets. Nobody waited to find out his neighbor's opinion. On every lip there was but one word, and that was 'conspiracy.'"[8]

"THE MEPHISTOPHELES OF CLEVELAND"

In accordance with his backdoor deal, the rate of freight from the Oil Regions increased 100 percent. Standard Oil shipped its own oil at a dollar a barrel cheaper than anyone else and received a dollar a barrel "rake-off" from every barrel shipped by its competitors.[9] A wave of backlash arose against Rockefeller. The press began to depict him as "the Mephistopheles of Cleveland."[10] Effigies of John D. were burned in public squares. Drillers who were caught selling to Rockefeller were assaulted by mobs and beaten senseless. Saboteurs attacked Standard Oil shipments and destroyed railroad track. Hate mail and death threats flowed into Rockefeller's office. He hired a team of private security guards and slept with a loaded revolver in reach.[11]

The Petroleum Producer's Union was formed to combat the South Improvement Company. The union organized strikes to stop the drilling of new oil wells and petitioned state legislators to

---

8   Ida Tarbell, "The Oil War of 1872," *The History of the Standard Oil Company*, chap. 3, in *McClure's Magazine*, January 1903, http://nebula.wsimg.com/1400148e21a78fa142307881891b7342?Access KeyId=94861742399A59C7B18A&disposition=0&alloworigin=1, accessed January 17, 2019.

9   Ibid.

10   Ibid.

11   Dan Bryan, "The 'Cleveland Massacre'—Standard Oil Makes Its First Attack," *American History USA*, April 15, 2012, https://www.americanhistoryusa.com/cleveland-massacre-standard-oil-makes-first-attack/, accessed January 17, 2019.

revoke the company's charter.[12] Such efforts were successful, and the Commonwealth of Pennsylvania revoked the charter for the South Improvement Company on April 8, 1872.[13] To all outward appearance, Rockefeller had been routed.

"TAKE THE STOCK"

But appearance was deceptive. The day after the charter was revoked in Pennsylvania, John D. began to make visits to the owners of the other refineries in Cleveland with an offer no sensible businessman could refuse. Standard Oil, he assured them, still possessed the power and influence to manipulate shipping rates. What's more, he said that his refinery was making millions while their operations were on the brink of bankruptcy. John D. was willing to offer them Standard Oil stock in exchange for their operations. "Take the stock," he said, "and your family will never know want."[14]

To prove his point, he showed them Standard Oil's accounting books. The books, which presented an account of enormous profit and tremendous cash reserves, were enough to cower the owners of the other refineries into submission. They signed on the dotted line, handed over their refineries to Rockefeller, and took the stock. Most who took the deal became rich men; a few even received executive positions within the financial headquarters of Standard Oil. Of the four firms that rejected the proposal, Grant, Foote, and Company was the largest. This firm struggled for two years to compete against Rockefeller before falling into insolvency.[15]

12   "South Improvement Company: Start of a Monopoly," *Searching in History*, March 30, 2014, https://searchinginhistory.blogspot.com/2014/03/south-improvement-company-start-of.html, accessed January 17, 2019.

13   Bryan, "The Cleveland Massacre."

14   John D. Rockefeller, quoted in ibid.

15   Ibid.

THE PERSUASIVE USE OF DYNAMITE

Throughout the next decade, when a new oil company opened and attempted to compete with Standard Oil, John D. resorted to violence, dispatching his henchmen to make use of the modern weapon of dynamite. In *The Robber Barons,* Matthew Josephson writes:

> In Buffalo, the Vacuum Oil Company, one of the "dummy" creatures of the Standard Oil system, became disturbed one day by the advent of a vigorous competitor who built a sizable refinery and located it favorably upon the water front. The offices of Vacuum conducted at first a furtive campaign of intimidation. Then emboldened or more desperate, they approached the chief mechanic of the enemy refinery, holding whispered conferences with him in a rowboat on Lake Erie. He was asked to "do something." He was urged to "go back to Buffalo and construct the machinery so it would bust up . . . or smash up," to fix the pipes and stills "so they cannot make a good oil. . . . And then if you would give them a little scare, they not knowing anything about the business. You know how . . ." In return the foreman would have a life annuity which he might enjoy in another part of the country. So in due time a small explosion took place in the independent plant.[16]

PEOPLE AS COMMODITIES

To maintain control of America's oil industry, John D. employed an army of agents who labored among competitors, politicians, and the media. He came to believe that everyone has a price and can be bought. "The ability to deal with people is as purchasable a commodity as sugar and coffee," he said and added, "I pay more for that ability than any under the sun."[17] After the oil war of 1872, Rockefeller's industrial espionage system became the most elaborate, most successful, and most sophisticated in the country. In *The Rockefeller Family Portrait,* biographer William Manchester writes:

16 Matthew Josephson, *The Robber Barons* (San Diego: Harvest Books, 1934), http://www.yamaguchy.com/library/josephson/baron_12.html, accessed January 17, 2019.

17 John D. Rockefeller, quoted in Allen, *The Rockefeller File*, p. 23.

John D. now set up the South Improvement Company. This company was used to funnel the rebates to Standard Oil and to pressure the railroad owners to raise the rates for Rockefeller's competitors so that he could receive a kickback from all their shipments.

The trouble with fighting John D. was that you never knew where he was. He ran his company as though it were a branch of the CIA. All important messages were in code—Baltimore was "Droplet," Philadelphia "Drugget"; refiners were "Douters," the Standard itself "Doxy." Shadowy men came and went by his front door; shadowy companies used his back door as a mailing address. For a long time the public didn't realize how powerful he was because he kept insisting he was battling firms that he secretly owned outright. His real rivals were forever discovering that their most trusted officers were in his pocket. The tentacles of the octopus were everywhere.[18]

"I AM MR. ROCKEFELLER"

To his competitors, John D. was a vampire, capable of draining the last ounce of oil from a competitor's business and willing to drive them into bankruptcy by any means possible—even force. This image of Rockefeller was intensified by his affliction with alopecia, a condition that resulted in the total loss of his body hair. The disease resulted in transforming John D. from a dapper,

---

18   William Manchester, *A Rockefeller Family Portrait: From John D. to Nelson* (New York: Little Brown, 1959), p. 72.

mustachioed figure with brown hair and long sideburns into a bald ogre. The change in Rockefeller's appearance was drastic and startling. Soon after losing his hair, John D. attended a dinner hosted by J. P. Morgan and sat down next to Charles Schwab, the owner of Bethlehem Steel. "I see you don't know me, Charley," he said. "I am Mr. Rockefeller."[19]

A JEKYLL AND HYDE PERSONALITY

But like Mr. Hyde, Rockefeller was capable of transforming into a benign Dr. Jekyll. On Sunday mornings, he assumed his place as a parishioner at the Euclid Street Baptist Mission Church, where he provided half of its annual budget.[20] As the superintendent of the church's Sunday school, he railed against such "unholy" activities as smoking, dancing, card-playing, billiards, and attending the theater. He labeled liquor "the devil's brew" and was a founding father of the Anti-Saloon League.[21]

John D.'s religiosity enabled him to believe that he was singled out by Almighty God to acquire enormous wealth and to preside over the oil empire. "God gave me my money," he proclaimed on many occasions.[22] This belief was not a pious claim but rather an unshakable conviction. Since Standard Oil was God's favored company just as assuredly as Israel was God's Promised Land, anyone who dared to challenge Rockefeller's monopoly was acting against the will of Almighty God. "Competition is a sin," John D. said.[23]

---

19   John D. Rockefeller, quoted in Ron Chernow, *Titan: The Life of John D. Rockefeller, Sr.* (New York: Vintage Books, 1998), p. 408.

20   Ibid., p. 189.

21   Ibid., p. 637.

22   John D. Rockefeller, quoted in David L. Stern, *Rockefeller Philanthropy and Modern Science* (Abingdon, UK: Routledge, 2015), p. 4.

23   John D. Rockefeller, quoted in Allen, *The Rockefeller File*, p. 19.

3

THE GATHERING STORM

However much of the Rockefeller wealth may be attributed to old John D.'s rapacity and ruthless-ness, its origins are indubitably based in his initial financing from the National City Bank of Cleveland, which was identified in Congressional reports as one of the three Rothschild banks in the United States and by his later acceptance of the guidance of Jacob Schiff of Kuhn, Loeb & Company, who had been born in the Rothschild house in Frankfort and was now the principal Rothschild representative (but unknown as such to the public) in the United States.

—EUSTACE MULLINS, "ROCKEFELLERS SECONDARY TO ROTHSCHILDS,"
THE *JOURNAL OF HISTORY*, FALL 2009

BY 1880, the American oil industry was the Standard Oil Company. And Standard Oil was John D. Rockefeller. He owned a third of all the world's oil wells and 90 percent of the oil refining. The product he produced lit the lamps of China and almost every household within the civilized world.[1] In an 1881 article for *Atlantic Monthly*, H. D. Lloyd wrote:

---

1   James Corbett, "How & Why Big Oil Conquered the World," *The Corbett Report*, October 6, 2017, https://www.corbettreport.com/bigoil/, accessed January 17, 2019.

Kerosene has become, by its cheapness, the people's light the world over. In the United States we used 220,000,000 gallons of petroleum last year. It has come into such demand abroad that our exports of it increased from 79,458,888 gallons in 1868, to 417,648,544 in 1879. It goes all over Europe, and to the far East. The Oriental demand for it is increasing faster than any other. . . . China and the East Indies took over 10,000,000 gallons in 1877, and nearly 25,000,000 gallons in 1878. After articles of food, this country has but one export, cotton, more valuable than petroleum. It was worth $61,789,438 in our foreign trade in 1877; $46,574,974 in 1878; and $18,546,642 in the five months ending November 30, 1879. In the United States, in the cities as well as the country, petroleum is the general illuminator. We use more kerosene lamps than Bibles.[2]

THE OIL BOOM

In 1876, the first internal combustion engine fed by gasoline was created by German engineer Nicholas Otto. Several years later, fellow German inventor Gottlieb Daimier strapped gasoline engines onto bicycles, tricycles, and other vehicles. In 1886, Karl Benz, yet another German, patented a three-wheeled automobile with a single engine.[3] In 1893, the Duryea brothers successfully tested their four-wheel motorcar on the streets of Springfield, Massachusetts.[4] By 1897, Henry Ford was producing "horseless carriages" for the general public. The number of automobiles leaped from 800 in 1898 to 8,000 in 1900.[5] Other developments quickly followed. When the Wright Brothers took off on an

2   H. D. Lloyd, "The Story of a Great Monopoly," *Atlantic Monthly*, March 1881, https://www.theatlantic.com/magazine/archive/1881/03/the-story-of-a-great-monopoly/306019/, accessed January 17, 2019.

3   Ron Chernow, *Titan: The Life of John D. Rockefeller, Sr.* (New York: Vintage Books, 1998), p. 335.

4   Mary Bellis, "The Duryea Brothers of Automobile History," *ThoughtCo*, September 6, 2017, https://www.thoughtco.com/duryea-brothers-automobile-history-1991577, accessed January 17, 2019.

5   Chernow, *Titan*, p. 430.

airplane at Kitty Hawk in 1903, their flight was powered by gasoline and brought to the beach by Standard Oil.[6] That same year, the British Navy began to outfit their battleships to use fuel oil rather than coal.[7]

The future of the world was set. It would be fueled by oil, and whoever controlled this commodity could set the course of human history. Aware of this fact, the Paris Rothschilds, led by Baron Alphonse de Rothschild, established the Caspian and Black Sea Petroleum Company and built refineries at Baku in the South Caucasus region of Imperial Russia, a land that became the modern-day Azerbaijan. The investment was lucrative, and the Baku refineries were producing more oil than any other country in the world. In 1891, Baron Rothschild teamed up with the M. Samuel and Company, a Far East shipping company headquartered in London, to build the world's first oil tanker, the *Murex*, which sailed through the Suez Canal in 1892 with a shipment of oil for Thailand.[8] The company that Rothschild created with Samuel became known as the Shell Transport and Trading Company in honor of Samuel's family-owned seashell box business.[9]

After Dutch drillers struck oil in North Sumatra and set up the Royal Dutch Petroleum Company of the Netherlands, Samuel and Rothschild united with the Dutch to form the Royal Dutch Shell Company.[10] The headquarters of this new firm was established at The Hague, a site that would become of strategic importance in the formation of the New World Order. The Rothschilds were now tied to the Dutch Royal Family, a development that would result in the creation of the Bilderberg Group.

---

6   Ibid.

7   Ibid.

8   David B. Green, "1927: The Jew behind the 'Hebrew' Part of Royal Dutch Shell Dies," *Haaretz*, January 17, 2016, https://www.haaretz.com/jewish/1927-the-jew-behind-shell-oil-dies-1.5390785, accessed January 17, 2019.

9   Chernow, *Titan*, p. 249.

10   Ibid.

THE SOCIETY OF THE ELECT

The Bilderbergs would not be the only secret society that would come into being from the Rothschild family and the Illuminati. In 1888, Lord Nathan Rothschild had united with Cecil John Rhodes to create the Society of the Elect, an organization that sought to bring all mankind under the rule of a synarchy, i.e., an elite group of bankers, businessmen, and industrialists who would meet in secret to chart global events.[11]

In 1888, Lord Nathan Rothschild had united with Cecil John Rhodes to create the Society of the Elect, an organization that sought to bring all mankind under the rule of a synarchy, i.e., an elite group of bankers, businessmen, and industrialists who would meet in secret to chart global events.

Like the Illuminati, the Society of the Elect has its roots in Freemasonry. The founding members of this secret society included Lord Reginald Baliol Brett, Queen Victoria's closest advisor; Lord Archibald Primrose, the 5th Earl of Roseberry and Rothschild's son-in-law, who would serve as Britain's prime minister from 1894 to 1895; and Arthur James Balfour, 1st Earl of Balfour, who would become the British prime minister from 1902 to 1905. Rhodes's ties to these three men would become tightened by their shared homosexuality and their preference for "burly, blue-eyed boys."[12] Among the other recruits were Albert Lord Grey and Robert Armstrong Yates, two prominent members of the British Parliament; William Palmer, the 2nd Earl of Selborne; and Alfred Milner, under-secretary of finance in Egypt.[13]

---

11   Robin Brown, *The Secret Society: Cecil John Rhodes's Plan for a New World Order* (Cape Town, South Africa: Penguin Books, 2015), p. 80.

12   Ibid.

13   Ibid.

COMMON INTERESTS

The members of the Society of the Elect were cut from the same cloth. They were rich, aristocratic, Oxford or Cambridge educated, and freemasons. They were disciples of John Ruskin and ardent imperialists, who believed the British were the master race. They shared a deep interest in the occult, including theosophy, Satanism, and communication with the spirit world. In addition, many, including Lord Brett, Lord Roseberry, and Lord Balfour, were pederasts. Rhodes, throughout his life, kept a stable of "angels and lambs" (young boys) to satisfy his sexual needs.[14]

Of equal importance was their interest in the occult. Rhodes and Rothschild shared an interest in the Jewish cabala, a mystical interpretation of Scripture based on the concealed meaning in its letters and words, and the mystery religions that flourished at the time of Christ. This interest resulted in Rhodes's belief in pre-existence and reincarnation.[15] Arthur Balfour established the Society for Psychical Research in 1882 and the Synthetic Society in 1890. Both groups espoused the doctrine that "departed spirits" can communicate "great truths." These revelations from the grave, they maintained, would be used to form the basis of a "one world religion."[16]

A VISIT FROM ALPHONSE

In July 1892, Baron de Rothschild visited John D. in New York. The two moguls cut a deal. Rockefeller would retain his monopoly over the oil industry in the United States and the lion's share of the European

---

14   Ibid., p 161.

15   Brown, *The Secret Society*, p. 81.

16   James Bruggeman, "The Political and Occult Connections of Wescott and Hort," *The Great Controversy*, n.d., http://thegreatcontroversy.info/the-political-occult-conne.html, accessed January 17, 2019.

market, while the Rothschilds would control the Asian oil industry.[17] The meeting was of crucial importance to the Rothschilds, who sought to use Rockefeller and Standard Oil to regain their footing on American soil.

THE ROTHSCHILD AGENT

Jacob Schiff was dispatched by the Rothschilds to serve as John D.'s financial advisor. He had been born and raised at 148 Judengasse, Frankfort, a residence that the Schiffs shared with the Rothschilds. In 1865, he arrived in America to further the Rothschilds' interests. Schiff brought such a large amount of Rothschild capital to the financial firm of Kuhn-Loeb that the firm was able to expand tenfold within a matter of months. After becoming a full-fledged partner in Kuhn-Loeb, he married Loeb's daughter.[18]

Schiff's place in American history has often been underestimated. Few historians take note that Schiff was the Rothschild family's representative in New York. Through his efforts, the banking firm of Kuhn-Loeb became inextricably bound to the House of Rothschild. He became the founding father of the Hebrew Free Loan Society, which provided interest-free loans to Jewish immigrants, and the National Association for the Advancement of Colored People (NAACP). He also served with Paul Warburg, his brother-in-law and fellow Rothschild operative, to set the stage for the creation of the Federal Reserve System.[19]

Under Schiff's guidance, John D. gobbled up shares in prominent New York banks, including National City Bank, First National, and Bankers Trust. With Schiff as a partner, Rockefeller acquired the Equitable Trust Company, which would become the eighth largest

---

17   Chernow, *Titan*, p. 248.

18   Eustace Mullins, "Chapter 1.1, Mayer Rothschild and the Five Arrows," *The World Order: A Study in the Hegemony of Parasitism*, 1984, *Modern History Project*, https://www.bibliotecapleyades.net/sociopolitica/world_order/WorldCh01-1.htm, accessed January 17, 2019.

19   Mike King, "Jacob Schiff: The Most Powerful Man in U.S. History" *Tomato Bubble*, n.d., http://www.tomatobubble.com/id695.html, accessed January 17, 2019.

bank in the country. Equitable Trust would eventually merge with the Chase Bank to become Chase Manhattan, a bank with strong ties to the House of Rothschild and the Bank of England.[20]

ANOTHER ROTHSCHILD LACKEY

Rockefeller also purchased massive issues of stock in the Erie, the Southern Pacific, the Union Pacific, and the Pennsylvania Railroad. These interests brought Rockefeller into a close relationship with John Pierpont (J. P.) Morgan, who controlled more than 5,000 miles of railroad track in America.[21] Morgan granted preferential shipping rates to Rockefeller on his railroads and Rockefeller, in exchange, purchased a major stake in Morgan's New York Central.[22]

J. P. Morgan, like Schiff, was a Rothschild agent. In 1854, the Morgan Bank had been established in London by two American financiers: George Peabody and Junius Morgan. The Rothschilds developed a close relationship with Peabody and Morgan, and following a financial crash in 1857, they saved the Morgan Bank by organizing a bailout from the Bank of England.[23] The Morgan Bank, with unlimited funding from the Rothschilds, became the driving force behind western expansion in the United States. It financed and controlled westbound railroads through voting trusts.[24]

In 1888, William Rockefeller, John D.'s younger brother, joined with Morgan in establishing the Jekyll Island Club—a posh resort for millionaires off the coast of Georgia. The island, which boasted

20 Chernow, *Titan*, p. 377.

21 Editors of Encyclopedia Britannica, "J. P. Morgan: American Financier," *Encyclopedia Britannica*, last updated April 29, 2019, https://www.britannica.com/biography/J-P-Morgan, accessed January 17, 2019.

22 Dean Henderson, "The Federal Reserve Cartel: The Eight Families," *Global Research*, January 31, 2018, https://www.globalresearch.ca/the-federal-reserve-cartel-the-eight-families/25080, accessed January 17, 2019.

23 Mullins, "Mayer Rothschild and the Five Arrows."

24 Ibid.

such walkways as Morgan's Road and the Rockefeller Path, became the site where the plans for the Federal Reserve System were drafted.

INTERLOCKING INTERESTS

In 1900, when Morgan bought Carnegie Steel for $480 million—the highest price ever paid for a business at the time—Rockefeller invested heavily in the new company dubbed U.S. Steel. By 1904, the financial holdings of Rockefeller and Morgan had become so intertwined that John Moody, founder of Moody's Investment Services and America's leading economic analyst, said that it was impossible to separate the interests of Rockefeller from the interests of Morgan.[25] Although they bristled in each other's company, the alliance was inevitable since their financial empires remained grounded in the House of Rothschild.[26]

John Pierpont Morgan controlled more than 5,000 miles of railroad track in America.

25 John H. Bodley, *Cultural Anthropology: Tribes, States, and the Global System* (Lanham, MD: Rowan and Littlefield, 2016), p. 309.

26 Henderson, "The Federal Reserve Cartel."

A cartel, consisting of Rockefeller, Carnegie, Morgan, Schiff, and Rothschild, came into being. In time, this cartel would come to control not only the world's economy but also its systems of education, politics, medicine, and religion. The planet was doomed.

4

THE PILGRIM

Rockefeller's story was perfectly mirrored by the story of Colonel Edwin Drake. Having struck oil in Titusville and given rise to a billion-dollar global industry, Drake had not had the foresight to patent his drilling technique or even to buy up the land around his own well. He ended up in poverty, relying on an annuity from the Commonwealth of Pennsylvania to scrape together a living and dying in 1880.

—JAMES CORBETT, "HOW AND WHY BIG OIL CONQUERED THE WORLD,"

THE CORBETT REPORT, JUNE 10, 2017

IN 1903, the cartel created the Pilgrim Society with chapters in New York and London. The purpose of the new clandestine organization was to further the plans of a New World Order as conceived by Cecil Rhodes. Lord Nathan Rothschild was a member of the Society of the Elect, which had been created by Rhodes to bring the globe under the control of a group of elitists who would decide the future of the world in secret.[1]

---

1   Robin Brown, *The Secret Society: Cecil John Rhodes's Plan for a New World Order* (Cape Town, South Africa: Penguin Books, 2015), p. 80.

THE LONDON CHAPTER

The London chapter of the Pilgrim Society, which was established under Lord Alfred Milner, was composed almost entirely of members of the Society of the Elect, the secret society created by Cecil Rhodes and Nathan Rothschild to forge a New World Order. Lord Milner had risen in rank and privilege to become the first governor of the Transvaal and the Orange Free State in South Africa and the administrator of the Rhodes Scholarships. The pilgrims included Lord Rosebery, Lord Robert Brand, Lord Reginald Brett, Arthur Lord Balfour, Albert Lord Grey, and Lord Rothschild, along with John Jacob Astor, the New York real estate magnate; Alfred Beit, Rhodes's partner in the diamond business; Sir Arthur Conan Doyle, the author of *Sherlock Holmes*; Philip Henry Kerr, 11th Marquess of Lothian and the British ambassador to the United States; H. G. Wells, noted novelist and historian; and Jan Smuts, legal advisor to Cecil Rhodes and future prime minister of the Union of South Africa; and Lord Nathan Rothschild.[2] The elite group met monthly at the Carlton Hotel.[3]

THE NEW YORK CHAPTER

The New York branch, which met at the Waldorf Astoria, was established by J. P. Morgan. It boasted such members as John D. Rockefeller, Andrew Carnegie, Jacob Schiff, former U.S. president Grover Cleveland, future U.S. president William Howard Taft, Mark Twain, Elihu Root, Thomas W. Lamont, Percy Rockefeller, William Rockefeller, Ogden Mills Reid, Otto Kahn, Andrew Mellon, W. B. Whitney, Cornelius Vanderbilt, Vincent Astor, Mortimer I. Schiff, Frank Vanderlip, Henry Davison, Charles D. Norton, Benjamin Strong, Nelson Aldrich, and Paul Warburg. The fact that the pilgrims were controlled by the

---

2   Joel van der Reijden, "Pilgrim Society: U.S.- British Historical Membership List," Institute for the Study of Globalization and Covert Politics, 2017, https://isgp-studies.com/pilgrims-society-membership-list, accessed January 17, 2019.

3   Ibid.

Rothschild money cartel was verified by the presence of Jacob Schiff and Paul Warburg at the monthly gatherings. Warburg, a prominent member of the Warburg banking consortium in Germany which was allied to the House of Rothschild, had married Nina Loeb, the daughter of one of the founders of Kuhn, Loeb & Company, a financial firm tightly connected to Rothschild.[4]

The incredible importance of this exclusive "dining club" to the future of America became clear in 1910, when prominent pilgrims, including Warburg, Vanderlip, Davison, Norton, Strong, and Aldrich, set off for Jekyll Island off the coast of Georgia to plan the formation of the Federal Reserve System.[5]

AN ELITE SOCIETY

The pilgrims from the London and New York societies were welcomed guests at each other's clubs and shared in each other's efforts to advance a concept that they called "the New World Order." The meaning of this phrase was clarified by William Lyon Mackenzie King, the premier of Canada, in his dinner address to New York pilgrims in 1912. King envisioned a future in which the world would be united in peace and harmony under an Anglo-American alliance. "When victory and peace came," he prophesied, "the peoples of the British Commonwealth and of the United States would be united more closely than ever—as all the nations who have united in the defense of freedom would remain united in the defense of mankind."[6]

The meetings were held in secret. No guests were allowed to attend. No minutes were kept. No financial records were disclosed. Proof of the commitment of members to the cause of their society came in 1919,

---

4   Joel van der Reijden, "The Pilgrim Society," *Journal of History,* September 21, 2005, http://www .truedemocracy.net/hj31/37.html, accessed January 17, 2019.

5   G. Edward Griffin, *The Creature from Jekyll Island,* 5th ed. (Westlake Village, CA: American Media, 2014) p. 5.

6   William Lyon Mackenzie King, quoted in Brown, *The Secret Society,* 279.

when U.S. pilgrim Irving T. Bush plunked down the funding for the Bush House in downtown London. Cut from Portland stone at a cost of $20 million, it was at the time the most expensive building in the world. To dispel any doubts about the purpose of the building, Bush commissioned the erection of a large statue at its entrance of two semi-naked men holding aloft the torch of liberty while brandishing two swords. One sword was emblazoned with lions and the other with eagles. The inscription read: "To the friendship of English-speaking peoples."[7]

FOR MEMBERS ONLY

Thirty-seven years after its founding, an obscure American journalist took notice of the clandestine club. In 1940, *Sir Uncle Sam: Knight of the British Empire*, a book that sold fewer than 500 copies, John Whiteford wrote:

> There are several curious things about these Pilgrim functions. In the first place, there is present at these dinners an array of notables such as it would be impossible to bring together under one roof for any other purpose and by any other society. . . . Among the guests were John D. Rockefeller and J. P. Morgan, Thomas W. Lamont and other members of the House of Morgan. . . . We are entitled to know what the Pilgrim Society is, what it stands for, and who these powerful Pilgrims are that can call out the great to hear a British Ambassador expound to Americans the virtues of a united democratic front.[8]

The lack of public awareness of the workings of the Pilgrim Society through the years remains mind-boggling, since its members would come to include Harry Truman, John Foster Dulles, Allen Dulles, General George Marshall (of the Marshall Plan), W. Averill Harriman,

---

7   Brown, *The Secret Society*, 282.

8   John T. Whiteford, *Sir Uncle Sam: Knight of the British Empire*, 1940, https://www.scribd.com/document/203056279/Whiteford-Sir-Uncle-Sam-Knight-of-the-British-Empire-1940, accessed February 2, 2019.

Joseph P. Kennedy, Henry Luce (founder of *Time* magazine), Henry Kissinger, Gerald Ford, Winston Churchill, Zbigniew Brzezinski, General Alexander Haig, William Paley (CBS president), Walter Cronkite, Sandra Day O'Connor, Elliot Richardson, George H. W. Bush, Paul Volker, George W. Bush, and David Rockefeller.[9]

THE ROCKEFELLER TRANSFORMATION

John D. may have been a reluctant pilgrim. Unlike the other members, he was neither a freemason nor an ardent Anglophile. He was neither a socialist nor an advocate of free trade. He possessed little knowledge of the thought of John Ruskin or the writings of Helena Petrovna Blavatsky. But as soon as he joined the society, John D. began to undergo a mental and spiritual transformation that was just as dramatic as the change that the onset of alopecia had produced in his physical appearance. He turned his attention to global affairs and, together with Schiff, financed the Russo-Japanese War of 1904 to 1905.[10] The funding permitted Imperial Japan to mount an attack against the Russians at Port Arthur and, within a year, to decimate the

As soon as he joined the society, John D. began to undergo a mental and spiritual transformation that was just as dramatic as the change that the onset of alopecia had produced in his physical appearance.

---

9   Van der Reijden, "The Pilgrim Society."

10   Ron Chernow, *Titan: The Life of John D. Rockefeller, Sr.* (New York: Vintage Books, 1998), p. 373.

Russian Navy.[11] The purpose of the war was not to prop up the Japanese Emperor but rather to weaken Czarist Russia.

After the war, Rockefeller and the Rothschilds offered the Czar $200 million for the control of the Russian oil fields and the concession for railroads from Tashkend to Tomsk and from Tehita to Polamoshna and a grant of land on both sides of the prospective lines.[12] When the Czar declined the offer, Rockefeller and the Rothschilds began funding the Bolsheviks to mount a revolution.[13] Rockefeller went on to fund the rebellion in China that led to the fall of the Qing Dynasty in 1911.[14]

OIL FOR THE LAMPS OF CHINA

Because of this funding, John D. gained the right to erect refineries and distribution centers so that Standard Oil came to light the lamps of China.[15] These developments ominously provided a portent for the events of the twentieth century. Rockefeller now realized that war could be created to serve his own economic ends. Millions of soldiers and civilians throughout the world would now die not for the sake of their native lands but rather for the financial interests of Standard Oil and the Rockefeller empire.

11   Ibid, p. 263.

12   Andrew Gavin Marshall, "Origins of the American Empire: Revolution, World Wars, and World Order," *Global Research,* July 28, 2009, https://www.globalresearch.ca/origins-of-the-american-empire-revolution-world-wars-and-world-order/14552, accessed January 17, 2019.

13   Ibid.

14   "United States Relations with China: Boxer Uprising to the Cold War (1900–1949)," U.S. Department of State, January 29, 2009, https://2001-2009.state.gov/r/pa/ho/pubs/fs/90689.htm, accessed January 17, 2019.

15   Ariel Burde, "The Danger of Assumed Sovereign Power: The Standard Oil Trust in China," Seminar on Corporations and International Law, Duke University, January 20, 2018, https://sites.duke.edu/corporations/2018/01/20/the-danger-of-assumed-sovereign-power-the-standard-oil-trust-in-china/, accessed January 17, 2019.

THE ROCKEFELLER BLESSING

Like his fellow pilgrims, John D. now espoused the doctrine of Social Darwinism. "The growth of a large business is merely a survival of the fittest," he maintained when questioned about his success.[16] Although he purportedly never joined a Masonic lodge, John D.'s luxurious summer estate in Forest Hills, Ohio, became transformed into a Masonic Temple.[17]

In 1906, John D. suddenly decided to reshape his image by hiring Ivy Ledbetter Lee as a publicist. Lee came up with the gimmick of having the old skinflint shell out dimes to adults and nickels to children whenever he appeared in public. After passing out the coins, Lee encouraged Rockefeller to say, "Bless you" to each recipient of his largesse.[18] In this way, it came to appear that John D. was a saintly figure who was dispersing communion wafers for the sake of human redemption.

ONCE A SCOUNDREL

Yet, despite Rockefeller's abandonment of his parochialism and the changes in his outlook and appearance, he remained the same ruthless oligarch he had been at the time of the great oil war of 1872. In addition to his oil refineries and distribution companies, John D. owned coal mines throughout the country. When 9,000 of Rockefeller's miners went on strike in Ludlow, Colorado, to protest the onerous prices at the company stores and the $1.68 wages for a 12-hour workday, John D. called in the state militia to mow down the strikers with machine guns. Nineteen miners were killed by the gunfire, while four women and 11 children burned to death in tents that had been soaked by Rockefeller's

16 John D. Rockefeller, quoted in Richard Hofstadter, *Social Darwinism and American Thought, 1860–1915* (Philadelphia: University of Pennsylvania Press, 1992), p. 45.

17 "Our History," Forest Hills Homeowners, Inc., July 2018, http://www.fhho.org/rockefeller-and-forest-hill/, accessed January 17, 2019.

18 Chernow, *Titan*, pp. 612–614.

In 1906, John D. suddenly decided to reshape his image by hiring Ivy Ledbetter Lee as a publicist. Lee came up with the gimmick of having the old skinflint shell out dimes to adults and nickels to children whenever he appeared in public.

henchmen with kerosene.[19]

There was an immediate public outcry. John D.'s publicists now went into overtime. Publishers were paid to run stories in which Rockefeller became depicted as a warm-hearted and incredibly generous employer who looked over his workers with paternalistic affection. Accounts were circulated of John D. redressing grievances from his workers, establishing state-of-the art working conditions, and caring for widows and orphans.[20] It was all hype, but it was gobbled up by millions of Americans who came to equate Rockefeller with model Christian ethics.

Accepting semblance as reality, few Americans expressed alarm with Rockefeller proceeding to gain control of the nation's systems of finance, education, medicine, and government to pave the way for the New World Order and the reign of his son John Jr.

19   Mike Lee, "Ivy Lee Was Decades Ahead of His Contemporaries," On-Line Readings in Public Relations, 2015, https://www.nku.edu/~turney/prclass/readings/3eras2x.html, accessed January 17, 2019.

20   Ibid.

5

THE OCTOPUS

In order to scrub up his image (and possibly assuage his conscience), John D. hired Ivy Lee, the nation's most prestigious ad man of the day. Lee suggested that the aging gentleman offset his skinflint image by starting to give away money. Scrooge was to be turned into an instant Santa Claus. To begin with, Lee (the original Madison Avenue truth-twister) had Mr. Standard Oily carry around a pocketful of dimes which he would strew before deliriously happy and grateful kiddies whenever he made one of his infrequent public appearances. Cynics observed that St. John ripped off money by the millions and doled it back a dime at a time.

—GARY ALLEN, *THE ROCKEFELLER FILE*, 1976

The real menace of our Republic is the invisible government, which like a giant octopus sprawls its slimy legs over our cities, states, and nation.

—JOHN F. HYLAN, MAYOR OF NEW YORK CITY, 1922

IN 1909, THE Department of Justice filed a lawsuit charging that Standard Oil represented an illegal monopoly by violating the 1890 Sherman Antitrust Act in a variety of ways, including "rebates, preferences, and other discriminatory practices by railroad companies; restraint and monopolization by control of pipe lines, and unfair practices against competing pipe lines; contracts with competitors in restraint of trade; unfair methods of competition, such as local price cutting at the points where necessary to suppress competition; [and] espionage of the business of competitors, the operation of bogus independent companies, and payment of rebates on oil, with the like intent."[1]

THE CASE AGAINST STANDARD OIL

The suit maintained that these offenses took place not only during the Oil War of 1872 but also within the past four years (1905–1909). It charged the following: "The general result of the investigation has been to disclose the existence of numerous and flagrant discriminations by the railroads in behalf of the Standard Oil Company and its affiliated corporations. With comparatively few exceptions, mainly of other large concerns in California, the Standard has been the sole beneficiary of such discriminations. In almost every section of the country that company has been found to enjoy some unfair advantages over its competitors, and some of these discriminations affect enormous areas."[2]

The Justice Department singled out four illegal patterns: (1) secret and semisecret railroad rates; (2) discriminations in the open arrangement of rates; (3) discriminations in classification and rules of shipment; (4) discriminations in the treatment of private tank cars. The suit alleged:

> Almost everywhere the rates from the shipping points used exclusively, or almost exclusively, by the Standard are relatively lower than the rates from the shipping points of its competitors. Rates have been made low to let the Standard into markets, or they have been made high to keep its competitors out of markets. Trifling differences in distances are made an excuse for large differences in rates favorable to

---

1   Leslie D. Manns, "Dominance in the Oil Industry: Standard Oil from 1865 to 1911," in *Market Dominance: How Firms Gain, Hold, or Lose It and the Impact on Economic Performance*, ed. David I. Rosenbaum (New York: Praeger, 1998), p. 11.

2   Eliot Jones, *The Trust Problem in the United States* (New York: The Macmillan Company, 1923), pp. 89–90.

the Standard Oil Co., while large differences in distances are ignored where they are against the Standard. Sometimes connecting roads prorate on oil—that is, make through rates which are lower than the combination of local rates; sometimes they refuse to prorate; but in either case the result of their policy is to favor the Standard Oil Co. Different methods are used in different places and under different conditions, but the net result is that from Maine to California the general arrangement of open rates on petroleum oil is such as to give the Standard an unreasonable advantage over its competitors."[3]

"AN OPEN AND ENDURING MENACE"

The government concluded its case against Standard Oil by saying: "The evidence is, in fact, absolutely conclusive that the Standard Oil Co. charges altogether excessive prices where it meets no competition, and particularly where there is little likelihood of competitors entering the field, and that, on the other hand, where competition is active, it frequently cuts prices to a point which leaves even the Standard little or no profit, and which more often leaves no profit to the competitor, whose costs are ordinarily somewhat higher.[4]

On May 15, 1911, the United States Supreme Court agreed that Standard Oil was "an open and enduring menace to all freedom of trade and a byword and reproach to modern economic methods."[5] John D. was now compelled to break down his monopoly into a host of smaller, independent companies. Strange to say, what should have been a setback for Rockefeller was actually an enormous stroke of good fortune. The antitrust decision turned him into the world's first billionaire.[6] His

---

3   Ibid, pp. 75–76.

4   Ibid., p. 80.

5   *United States vs Standard Oil*, Legal Information Institute, Cornell University, https://www.law. cornell.edu/supremecourt/text/221/1, accessed January 17, 2019.

6   James Corbett, "How and Why Big Oil Conquered the World," *The Corbett Report*, October 6, 2017, https://www.corbettreport.com/bigoil/, accessed January 17, 2019.

On May 15, 1911, the United States Supreme Court agreed that Standard Oil was "an open and enduring menace to all freedom of trade and a byword and reproach to modern economic methods."

companies would become omnipresent. Standard Oil of New Jersey became Exxon; State Oil of New York—Mobil; State Oil of Indiana—Amoco; Standard Oil of California—Chevron; Atlantic Refining—ARCO and eventually Sunoco; and Continental Oil—Conoco.[7]

"THE FUTURE IS FRUIT"
When the Supreme Court decision was made, it remained somewhat

---

7   Ron Chernow, *Titan: The Life of John D. Rockefeller, Sr.* (New York: Vintage Books, 1998), pp. 558–59.

doubtful that automobiles would become a mainstay of the oil industry. Ethyl alcohol had been used as a fuel source since the early years of the 19th century, and Henry Ford believed that the Model T, which he was mass-producing in Detroit, would prove to be an enormous boon for farmers. Ford said to a reporter from the *New York Times:* "The fuel of the future is going to come from fruit like that sumach *[sic]* out by the road, or from apples, weeds, sawdust—almost anything. There is fuel in every bit of vegetable matter that can be fermented."[8]

When Ford made this prediction, the Model T was manufactured in a variation that allowed drivers to switch the carburetor to run the engine on ethanol. This modification allowed drivers to stop at local farms, equipped with stills, to refuel their cars during trips through the country.[9]

NO ALCOHOL TAX

Believing Ford that crops could provide America's fuel for the future, farmers throughout the country lobbied Congress to repeal the $2.08 per gallon tax on alcohol that had been in effect since the Civil War. In support of the repeal, President Teddy Roosevelt addressed Congress and said: "The Standard Oil Company has, largely by unfair or unlawful methods, crushed out home competition. It is highly desirable that an element of competition should be introduced by the passage of some such law as that which has already passed the House, putting alcohol used in the arts and manufactures upon the free list."[10]

The alcohol tax was repealed, and corn ethanol at 14 cents a gallon

---

8   Henry Ford, quoted in Corbett, "How and Why Big Oil Conquered the World."

9   "The Great Scheme: Alcohol-Based Fuels, Ford, Rockefeller, and Prohibition," *Serendipity*, June 26, 2007, dgrim.blogspot.com/2007/06/great-scheme-alcohol-based-fuels-ford.html, accessed January 17, 2019.

10   Teddy Roosevelt, quoted in Corbett, "How and Why Big Oil Conquered the World."

became considerably cheaper than a gallon of gasoline at 22 cents.[11] The promise of a new, inexpensive fuel that could be produced from raw vegetables electrified the agricultural industry. Throughout the country, farmers allocated more and more of their fields for corn that could be fermented into fuel for cars and trucks that were rapidly becoming omnipresent.

ROCKEFELLER INAUGURATES PROHIBITION

Alarmed by these developments, Rockefeller pumped the equivalent of $60 million into groups supporting Prohibition, including the Women's Christian Temperance League, and thereby became the driving force behind the movement to ban the production and sale of alcohol.[12]

When the Eighteenth Amendment went into effect on January 16, 1920, farmers were compelled to add poison to their alcohol, and their stills fell under the surveillance of the 1,520 Prohibition officers.[13] Ethanol became too expensive and troublesome to produce, and Rockefeller had managed to secure his monopoly.

RICHER THAN CRESSUS

The fortune of the Rockefeller family expanded throughout the 20th century beyond the wildest imagination of Ida Tarbell or any of John D.'s critics. By 1976, when America celebrated its bicentennial, the Rockefellers owned 25 percent of all the assets of the world's 50 largest commercial banks and 30 percent of the assets of all the insurance companies. In addition, the family held controlling interest in Exxon, Mobil Oil, Standard Oil of California (ChevronTexaco), Standard Oil

---

11   Ibid.

12   "Prohibition Sponsored by Standard Oil," Snopes, November 29, 2008, message.snopes.com/showthread.php?t=38995, accessed January 17, 2019.

13   Benjamin Elisha Sawe, "What Was Prohibition in the United States?" *World Atlas*, April 25, 2017, https://www.worldatlas.com/articles/what-was-prohibition-in-the-united-states.html, accessed January 17, 2019.

When the Eighteenth Amendment went into effect on January 16, 1920, farmers were compelled to add poison to their alcohol, and their stills fell under the surveillance of the 1,520 Prohibition officers.

of Indiana (Amoco), International Harvester, Inland Steel, Marathon Oil, Quaker Oats, Wheeling-Pittsburgh Steel, Freeport Sulfur, and International Basic Economy Corporation.[14]

Through trust departments and the Rockefeller Foundation, the family held the single largest block of stock in United Airlines, Northwest Airlines, Long Island Lighting, Atlantic Richfield, National Airlines, Delta, Braniff, Consolidated Freightways, IBM, IT&T, Westinghouse, Boeing, International Paper, Minnesota Mining and Manufacturing, Sperry Rand, Xerox, National Cash Register, National Steel, American

14   Gary Allen, *The Rockefeller File* (Seal Beach, CA: '76 Press, 1976), pp. 31–32.

Home Products, Pfizer, Avon, and Merck. Other corporations in which the Rockefellers possessed significant shares were AT&T, Motorola, Safeway, Honeywell, General Foods, Hewlett-Packard, and Burlington Industries.[15] Corporations that maintained interlocking directorates with the Rockefeller Group included Allied (Chemical), Anaconda Cooper, DuPont, Monsanto, Olin Matheson, National Distillers, Shell, Gulf, Union Oil, Dow Chemical, Celanese, Pittsburgh Plate Glass, Cities Service, Stauffer Chemical, Continental Oil, Union Carbide, American Cyanamid, Chrysler, C.I.T. Financial, S. S. Kresge, and R. H. Macy.[16]

POWER UNLIMITED

These holdings were discovered in 1975. At present, it is impossible to discern the full extent of the Rockefellers' control of major banks, and corporations throughout the world since the holdings of the family are held in trust with "street names" that are totally fictitious.

In addition to the monumental control that the Rockefellers wielded over America's private-sector banks and businesses, the family, according to economist Eustace Mullins, held the lion's share of stock in the Federal Reserve System.[17] This development occurred as a result of John D.'s association with J. P. Morgan, his ties to the House of Rothschild, and his membership in the Pilgrim Society. Only by the House of Rockefeller's acquisition of such power and might could the killing of the planet get underway.

---

15   Ibid., pp. 32–33.

16   Ibid., p. 34.

17   Eustace Mullins, *The Secrets of the Federal Reserve* (New York: Kasper and Horton, 1982), http://www.jrbooksonline.com/PDF_Books/SecretsOfFedReserve.pdf, accessed January 17, 2019.

PART TWO

THE RISE TO POWER

6

THE PLUTOCRAT

The rich will strive to establish their dominion and enslave the rest. They always did. They always will. . . . They will have the same effect here as elsewhere, if we do not, by such a government, keep them within their proper spheres. We should remember that the people never act from reason alone. The rich will take the advantage of their passions, and make these the instruments for oppressing them. The result of the contest will be a violent aristocracy, or a more violent despotism.

—GOVERNEUR MORRIS, DELEGATE FROM NEW YORK,

FEDERAL CONVENTION OF 1787

THE FEDERAL RESERVE SYSTEM was hatched by members of the Pilgrim Society who believed that a new central bank in the United States could be joined to the Bank of England to forge in iron an Anglo-American Alliance that would be almost impossible to dissolve. Such a bank became the primary focus of the pilgrims' attention when they gathered to meet each month in London and New York.

AMERICA'S FIRST CENTRAL BANK
The establishment of a centralized bank in the United States would be met, as the pilgrims well knew, with formidable resistance. After

the Revolutionary War, Alexander Hamilton became an agent for the Rothschilds. His association with the prominent Jewish banking family most likely began when he joined forces with Robert Morris, a member of the Continental Congress, to establish the Bank of

North America. Modeled after the Bank of England, the bank, which was chartered in 1781, was authorized to issue paper promissory notes that became the new nation's currency.

The purpose of the Bank of the United States was to provide the federal government a steady supply of loans. The government, in turn, would pledge that the notes they received from the new central bank were valid for payments to the United States. "First Bank of the United States from north" by Beyond My Ken is licensed under CC BY-SA 4.0

From the start, the Bank of North America was riddled with fraud. Unable to secure the requisite $400,000 for the initial subscription of bank-up funds, Morris used his political influence to secure the gold that had been lent to the United States from France and to deposit it in the bank. With these funds as fractional reserve, he created millions of dollars in paper money (then known as *scrip*), which he lent to himself and his associates.[1] The inflated notes, which Morris and Hamilton would not redeem for gold, quickly became subjected to depreciation. The bank lost its charter and was forced to close after a year of operation.[2]

THE ROTHSCHILD FACTOR

During the Revolutionary War, the Rothschilds secured a firm footing in the United States. Nathaniel M. Rothschild, in addition to his banking business, operated a textile mill in Manchester, England,

1   Murray N. Rothbard, *Conceived in Liberty: The Revolutionary War, 1775–1784* (New Rochelle, NY: Arlington House, 1979), 4:392.

2   G. Edward Griffin, *The Creature from Jekyll Island*, 5th ed. (Westlake Village, CA: American Media, 2014), p. 326.

and purchased cotton from American farmers in Virginia, North and South Carolina, and Georgia.[3] Along with his brother Amschel, Nathan provided loans to various state governments and loans to England for the hiring of German mercenaries.[4] The agents of the Rothschilds were omnipresent throughout colonial America and assisted Hamilton in establishing the Bank of North America.[5]

Upon becoming America's first Secretary of the Treasury, Hamilton relied on the Rothschilds to establish the Bank of the United States, the country's second central bank. This new creation was modeled after the Bank of England,

ALEXANDER HAMILTON,

After the Revolutionary War, Alexander Hamilton became an agent for the Rothschilds. His association with the prominent Jewish banking family most likely began when he joined forces with Robert Morris, a member of the Continental Congress, to establish the Bank of North America.

which remained solely in the control of the House of Rothschild. The purpose of the Bank of the United States was to provide the federal government a steady supply of loans. The government, in turn, would pledge that the notes they received from the new central bank were valid for payments to the United States.[6]

---

3   Ibid., p. 331.

4   William Guy Carr, *Pawns in the Game*, 3rd ed. (Willowdale, ON: Federation of Christian Laymen, 1958), chap. 5, http://www.lovethetruth.com/books/pawns/05.htm, accessed January 17, 2019.

5   Griffin, *The Creature from Jekyll Island*, p. 331.

6   Gordon S. Wood, "The Birth of American Finance," *New Republic*, December 7, 2012, https://newrepublic.com/article/110824/the-birth-american-finance, accessed January 17, 2019.

FRACTIONAL RESERVES

Like the Bank of England, the Bank of the United States regulated America's currency by the process of printing or burning the paper money. It could increase the money supply to produce prosperity or decrease the supply to cause recession. These manipulations were based on the distinction between money and goods. Goods were the real wealth that a person possessed, while money remained only a person's claim on the wealth that was being retained by someone or something (i.e., a bank) else. Goods were tangible assets, while money

Like the Bank of England, the Bank of the United States regulated America's currency by the process of printing or burning the paper money.

represented a statement of the debt that was owed to the holder.[7] The use of money rather than goods as payment for a transaction dated back to the creation of the Bank of England by William Paterson, a retired pirate, in 1694.[8] Paterson alleviated his customers of the burden of transferring heavy bags or chests of gold for business transactions by producing paper certificates, which entitled the bearers to exchange them for gold upon demand.[9]

Due to the convenience of paper, only a small fraction of certificate holders ever sought redemption in the precious metal. Paterson quickly realized that they only needed to keep enough gold in hand to cover the fraction of certificates presented as payment. The rest of the gold could be used to mount a myriad of public and private ventures, including the building of ships and the waging of war. The excess volume, which rose to 90 percent, of the paper claims against reserves became known as "bank notes." An economic miracle had been performed. The issuance of paper claims greater than the gold at hand meant that the Bank of England was creating most of its money out of nothing. This practice, known as fractional reserves, became adopted by the Rothschilds, who took over the Bank of England, and the other central banks in existence at the time of the creation of the Bank of the United States, Swedish Riksbank, Banco de

The use of money rather than goods as payment for a transaction dated back to the creation of the Bank of England by William Paterson, a retired pirate, in 1694.

---

7   John Cooper, *The Unexpected Story of Nathaniel Rothschild* (New York: Bloomsbury Publishing, 2015), p. 44.

8   Ibid., p. 46.

9   Ibid.

España, Banque de France, Bank of Finland, De Nederlandsche Bank, Norges Bank, Osterreichische Nationalbank, Danmarks Nationalbank, Banco de Portugal, National Bank of Belgium, Bank of Indonesia, German Reichsbank, Bulgarian National Bank, National Bank of Romania, Bank of Japan, and the National Bank of Serbia.[10]

AMERICA'S SECOND NATIONAL BANK

The Bank of the United States was not established without formidable opposition. Thomas Jefferson pointed out that the creation of such an economic animal was unconstitutional. Only Congress, Jefferson argued, possessed the right to manufacture and control the nation's currency. "To take a single step beyond the boundaries thus specially drawn around the power of Congress," he said, "is to take possession of a boundless field of power, no longer susceptible of any definition."[11] After a year of debate, Hamilton's views prevailed, and, in 1791, Congress granted a 20-year charter to the new central bank.[12]

The Bank of the United States was capitalized at $10 million; $8 million came from private investors, including the Rothschilds; and $2 million came from the federal government.[13] The latter investment was deemed necessary to safeguard the country's interest and to ensure that the new central bank was not used for personal gain. As soon as it was established in Philadelphia, the Bank of the United States opened branches in Baltimore, Boston, Charleston, and New York.

THE BIRTH OF BIG GOVERNMENT

In accordance with Hamilton's plans, the new central bank instituted a

---

10   Stephen Mitford Goodson, *A History of Central Banking and the Enslavement of Mankind* (London: Black House, 2014), p. 92.

11   Jefferson, quoted in Griffin, *The Creature from Jekyll Island*, p. 329.

12   Ibid.

13   David Cowen, "Birth of the Bank," Economic History Association, March 16, 2008, https://eh.net/encyclopedia/the-first-bank-of-the-united-states/, accessed January 17, 2019.

federal tax system to further the nation's debt. This was essential since the shareholders of the Bank of the United States obtained interest from the government at the rate of 6 percent for every dollar it produced. With its ability to secure unlimited loans, the federal government grew by leaps and bounds with enough revenue to sustain a standing army and navy and to create a bureaucracy. This, too, took place according to the blueprint. Hamilton believed the republican government would evolve within a matter of decades into a fiscal-military state. By means of this evolution, America would become increasingly less egalitarian as it matured and more monarchial.[14] The final result would be the creation of a plutocracy, a group of elite bankers who would rule the country.[15] But in order for that to take place, the creators of the new central bank would have to gain complete control of its operations without any interference from the government or any elected official.

THE DELIGHTS OF DEBT

By 1796, the Bank of the United States had shelled out $68.2 million to the federal government so that it could go on a spending spree and fall into insurmountable debt. In tandem with this development, the prices on consumer goods increased by 72 percent.[16] Now, the directors of the central bank demanded a payment of one-third of its loans, knowing that the government would be unable to come up with the necessary cash. The only solution to this situation was for the government to sell its share of the bank. While Jefferson and other opponents of the bank watched in horror, the Bank of the United States became 100 percent privately owned and most of the shares were in the hands of the Rothschilds and their associates.[17]

---

14 Wood, "The Birth of American Finance."

15 Ibid.

16 Goodson, *A History of Central Banking*, p. 61.

17 Ibid.

Through the first decade of the nineteenth century, inflation continued to ravage the country because of the central banks' churning out
of paper dollars as quickly as the government could swallow them. By
1811, when the charter for the bank was up for renewal, the American
people had lost 42 percent of the value of their money due to the
unchecked rise in prices for goods and services. The only individuals
profiting from this development were the bank's shareholders, who
received interest on every dollar that their institution made out of nothing.[18] By design, the rampant inflation had little effect on the wealthy,
who possessed tangible assets.[19] The plutocracy Hamilton envisioned
for America was coming to fruition at an alarming rate.

THE BATTLE LINES
By 1811, when the charter for the Bank of the United States came up
for renewal, the battle lines were sharply drawn between those who supported the bank and those who sought its demise. When the dust of the
battle settled, the charter for renewal had been defeated by one vote in
the House of Representatives and one vote in the Senate.[20] The central
bank was forced to close its doors on January 24, 1811.[21] Jefferson
uttered a sigh of relief, not knowing that the creature that had been
created by Hamilton and the Rothschilds was far from dead.

---

18   Griffin, *The Creature from Jekyll Island*, p. 332.

19   Ibid., p. 335.

20   Ibid., p. 336.

21   Ibid.

7

THE ROUT

Is there no danger to our liberty and independence in a bank that in its nature has so little to bind it to our country? The president of the bank has told us that most of the State banks exist by its forbearance. Should its influence become concentered, as it may under the operation of such an act as this, in the hands of a self-elected directory whose interests are identified with those of the foreign stockholders, will there not be cause to tremble for the purity of our elections in peace and for the independence of our country in war? Their power would be great whenever they might choose to exert it; but if this monopoly were regularly renewed every fifteen or twenty years on terms proposed by themselves, they might seldom in peace put forth their strength to influence elections or control the affairs of the nation. But if any private citizen or public functionary should interpose to curtail its powers or prevent a renewal of its privileges, it can not be doubted that he would be made to feel its influence.

Should the stock of the bank principally pass into the hands of the subjects of a foreign country, and we should unfortunately become involved in a war with that country, what would be our condition? Of the course which would be pursued by a bank almost wholly owned by the subjects of a foreign power, and managed by those whose interests, if not affections, would run in the same direction there can be no doubt. All its operations within would be in aid of the hostile fleets and armies without. Controlling our currency, receiving our public moneys, and holding thousands of our citizens in dependence, it would be more formidable and dangerous than the naval and military power of the enemy.

—ANDREW JACKSON, "VETO MESSAGE REGARDING THE BANK OF THE
UNITED STATES," JULY 10, 1832

DESPITE THE DISSOLUTION of the Bank of the United States and the need for some regulation over America's burgeoning economy, Congress refused to assert the power granted to them by Article I, Section 8 of the Constitution "to coin money and regulate the value thereof."[1] To make matters worse, they granted this power to state-chartered corporations, who proceeded to produce as much paper currency as a colonial press could produce. The glut of money flowed from the fact that these corporations charged interest on every dollar that they produced. Since the States were not actually producing currency, but rather chartering companies to perform the task, the state and federal legislations managed to skirt the implicit Constitutional provision (Article I, Section 10) that prohibited state governments from coining money, emitting bills of credit, or making anything but gold and silver coin a legal tender for the payment of debts.[2]

THE WAR OF 1812

The grim financial situation was worsened by the War of 1812. This conflict erupted because of Britain's attempts to restrict trade between the United States and France and the impression of American seamen into British service. By the time that war had been declared, 400 U.S. ships had been impounded by the British fleet; their cargo was impounded; and 6,000 sailors were declared to be British subjects and forced into the service of the Royal Navy.[3]

With the war raging, the banks continued to churn out as much paper money as they could print to purchase government bonds. These bonds

1   George Leef, "After a Century of the Fed, It's Time to Return to Constitutional Money," *Forbes*, February 11, 2014, https://www.forbes.com/sites/georgeleef/2014/02/11/after-a-century-of-the-fed-its-time-to-return-to-constitutional-money/#166f987a7a0f, accessed January 17, 2019.

2   Ibid.

3   Lonnae O'Neal Parker, "Maryland's Historical Society's 1812 Exhibit Captures a War's Ambiguities," *Washington Post*, June 7, 2012, https://www.washingtonpost.com/entertainment/museums/maryland-historical-societys-1812-exhibit-captures-a-wars-ambiguities/2012/06/07/gJQASXowLV_story.html?noredirect=on&utm_term=.5fb68e865f7d, accessed January 17, 2019.

were used to purchase war munitions, including ships and cannons. The national debt soared from $45 million to $127 million, a crippling sum for the new nation. Tripling the money supply without an appreciable increase in goods meant that the dollar lost more than one-third of its purchasing power. This devaluation caused a massive run on the banks as more and more Americans sought to redeem their paper certificates for gold or silver. Since the banks lacked the reserves to meet the demand for *specie* (tangible assets), armed guards were hired to protect bank officials from angry crowds in cities throughout the country.[4]

THE ROTHSCHILD THREAT

In 1811, when the charter for First National was set to expire, "Natty" Rothschild, the new head of the family, issued this order: "Either the application for renewal of the charter is granted, or the United States will find itself in a disastrous war."[5] While the actual role of the banking family in instigating the war remains unknown, the Rothschilds provided the British government with loans without interest for the war effort.[6] They also had solicited the services of Nicholas Biddle, who had acted as secretary to John Armstrong, the U.S. Ambassador to France from 1804 to 1810. In France, Biddle, who was a financial prodigy, gained the attention of James de Rothschild, who made him the family's new point man in America.[7] When he returned to the States, Biddle became a close advisor to President Madison and pressed for the war with England. His influence with the Madison administration intensified when Armstrong became Secretary of War in 1812.[8]

---

4   G. Edward Griffin, *The Creature from Jekyll Island*, 5th ed. (Westlake Village, CA: American Media, 2014), p. 338.

5   Andrew Hitchcock, "The History of the House of Rothschild," *Rense.com*, October 31, 1999, http://rense.com/general88/hist.htm, accessed January 17, 2019.

6   Ibid.

7   Patrick Carmack and William Still, *The Money Masters: How International Bankers Gained Control of America* (video, 1998), https://www.imdb.com/title/tt1954955/, accessed January 17, 2019.

8   Ibid.

At the end of the struggle, America may have won its second war of independence, but the country was left with a huge war debt of $105 million relative to a population of eight million.[9] Faced with this financial burden, Congress approved the creation of the Second Bank of the United States in 1816. To no one's surprise, the Rothschilds emerged as the major shareholders.[10]

THE THIRD NATIONAL BANK

Nicholas Biddle, at the instigation of the Rothschild family, was appointed president of Second National, which opened a string of branches in every major city. These branches extended loans to businessmen, banks, farmers, and settlers who wished to purchase land in the American West. In 1819, the Second Bank drastically reduced the money supply. Loans were no longer available. Thousands of Americans suddenly discovered that they were unable to pay off their bank debts. Farmers were forced into foreclosure. Businesses went belly up. Speculators and settlers lost their land and savings. The widespread financial disaster and depression, which provoked popular resentment against banking and business enterprise, enabled the shareholders of Second National, namely the Rothschilds, to purchase enormous assets at greatly depressed prices.[11]

In 1828, Andrew Jackson ran for president with the slogan, "Jackson and No Bank." The slogan was in keeping with his plan to seize control of the currency and to end the profiteering of the Rothschilds. As soon as he assumed the oath of office, Jackson began to withdraw government money from the Second Bank to deposit it in state banks. This action prompted the Rothschilds to contract the money supply and to create another depression. Jackson, who was known for his fiery temper, responded by swearing: "You are a

9   Hitchcock, "The History of the House of Rothschild."

10   Ibid.

11   Bray Hammond, "Jackson's Fight with the Money People," *American Heritage* 7, no. 4, June 1956.

den of thieves and vipers, and I intend to rout you out. If the people understood the rank injustices of our money and banking system, there would be a revolution before morning."

ROUTING THE ROTHSCHILDS
Rout the Rothschilds, Jackson did. On September 10, 1833, he revoked the charter for the Second Bank five years before it was set to expire. In defense of his action, Jackson condemned the legislation that brought the bank into existence by saying:

> The Act seems to be predicated on an erroneous idea that the present shareholders have a prescriptive right to not only the favor, but the bounty of the government...for their benefit does this Act exclude the whole American people from competition in the purchase of this monopoly. Present stockholders and those inheriting their rights as successors be established a privileged order, clothed both with great political power and enjoying immense pecuniary advantages from their connection with government. Should its influence be concentrated under the operation of such an Act as this, in the hands of a self-elected directory whose interests are identified with those of the foreign stockholders, will there not be cause to tremble for the independence of our country in war...controlling our currency, receiving our public monies and holding thousands of our citizens independence, it would be more formidable and dangerous than the naval and military power of the enemy. It is to be regretted that the rich and powerful too

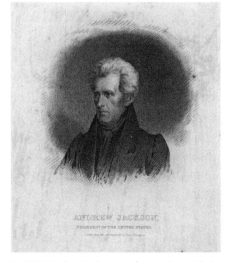

In 1828, Andrew Jackson ran for president with the slogan, "Jackson and No Bank."

often bend the acts of government for selfish purposes…to make the rich richer and more powerful. Many of our rich men have not been content with equal protection and equal benefits, but have besought us to make them richer by acts of Congress. I have done my duty to this country.[12]

THE ROTHSCHILDS' HIT MAN

On January 30, 1835, Richard Lawrence, an English immigrant, attempted to shoot President Jackson in front of the Capitol building. His pistols misfired, and the President clubbed Lawrence to the ground with his cane. The would-be assassin was deemed mentally unsound and confined to an asylum for the criminally insane. Jackson said that the Rothschilds were responsible for the attempt on his life, and Lawrence insisted that he had been commissioned to commit the murder by a group of "powerful people in Europe."[13]

THE SECRET SOCIETY

The Rothschilds may have been routed, but they still cast their greedy eyes on the expanding new nation that was beginning to emerge as a leading industrial power. Their desire grew when Nathan Rothschild joined with Cecil John Rhodes to form the Society of the Elect. The notion of this secret society came from a brainstorm that struck Rhodes on June 2, 1877, the day he became a lifetime member of the Oxford University Apollo Chapter of the Masonic Order. Rhodes recorded his revelation as follows in his "Confession of Faith": "The idea gleaming and dancing before one's eyes like a will-of-the-wisp at last frames itself into a plan. Why should we not form a Secret Society with but one object the furtherance of the British Empire and the bringing of the

12   Andrew Jackson, quoted in Dean Henderson, "The Federal Reserve Cartel: Freemasons and the House of Rothschild," *Global Research*, June 8, 2011, http://www.globalresearch.ca/the-federal-reserve-cartel-freemasons-and-the-house-of-rothschild/25179, accessed January 17, 2019.

13   Hitchcock, "The History of the House of Rothschild."

An 1833 lithograph by Edward W. Clay, published by H. R. Robinson, N.Y.

As soon as he assumed the oath of office, Jackson began to withdraw government money from the Second Bank to deposit it in state banks. This action prompted the Rothschilds to contract the money supply and to create another depression.

whole uncivilized world under British rule for the recovery of the United States for the making the Anglo-Saxon race but one Empire."[14]

After recruiting the most influential and wealthy individuals in England, Rothschild and Rhodes set out to forge this New World Order by initiating the Second Boer War in South Africa. By the time this bloody conflict came to an end in 1902, 7,582 British soldiers had been killed in action, 13,139 died of disease, 40,000 were wounded, and one had been eaten by a crocodile.[15] Six thousand Boers were killed in action, while 26,000 white civilians and 17,182 African natives died of

---

14 Cecil John Rhodes, "Confession of Faith," June 2, 1877, http://pages.uoregon.edu/kimball/Rhodes-Confession.htm, accessed January 17, 2019.

15 Megan French, "Boer War Soldiers' Records Published Online," *Guardian*, June 24, 2010, https://www.theguardian.com/uk/2010/jun/24/boer-war-soldiers-records-online, accessed January 17, 2019.

After recruiting the most influential and wealthy individuals in England, Rothschild and Rhodes set out to forge this New World Order by initiating the Second Boer War in South Africa.

Rhodes and Rothschild gained complete control of the gold and diamond mines in South Africa, and the Transvaal and the Orange Free State became incorporated into the British Empire under Alfred Milner, who became the Society's new leader. "De Kaap Gold Fields, South Africa: miners of the Republic Go" is licensed under CC BY 4.0

disease and starvation in concentration camps that had been set up in the Cape and Orange River colonies.[16]

The war for the Society of the Elect produced salubrious efforts. Rhodes and Rothschild gained complete control of the gold and diamond mines in South Africa, and the Transvaal and the Orange Free State became incorporated into the British Empire under Alfred Milner, who became the Society's new leader.[17]

The next step in achieving the Society's objective was the reestablishment of a new centralized bank in America that would be yoked to the Bank of England. This would be accomplished by the Pilgrim Societies that had been established in London and New York and the alliance that had been forged by the Rothschilds' creation of the great industrial empires of Andrew Carnegie, J. P. Morgan, and John D. Rockefeller.

---

16 Owen Coetzer, *Fire in the Sky: The Destruction of the Orange Free State* (Johannesburg: Covos Day, 2000), pp. 82–83.

17 Philip Ziegler, *Legacy: Cecil Rhodes, The Rhodes Trust, and Rhodes Scholarships* (New Haven, CT: Yale University Press, 2008), p. 12.

8

THE EXPEDITION

Picture a party of the nation's greatest bankers stealing out of New York on a private railroad car, hieing hundreds of miles south to an island deserted by all but a few servants, and living there a full week under such rigid secrecy that the name of not one of them was once mentioned lest the servitors learn their identity and disclose to the world this historic episode in American finance.

—B. C. FORBES, *MEN WHO ARE MAKING AMERICA*, 1917

TO CONVINCE THE AMERICAN PEOPLE of the need for a new central bank, the pilgrims, under J. P. Morgan, staged the Panic of 1907. Stories were circulated in the newspapers under Morgan's control that the Knickerbocker Trust Company, one of America's leading financial institutions, was on the brink of insolvency. The stories prompted the customers of the bank en masse to withdraw their savings. Knickerbocker crashed, causing the hundreds of banks linked to it to fall like dominoes. Depositors were left with no means of recovering their savings; Wall Street brokers could not obtain the loans required for their daily transactions; the stock market declined by 50 percent; and no central agency existed to clean up the mess.[1]

---

1   Finra Staff, "Born of Panic: The Federal Reserve and the Panic of 1907," Part 2, *The Alert Investor*, April 8, 2016, https://www.finra.org/investors/born-panic-federal-reserve-and-panic-1907-part-2, accessed February 6, 2019.

THE MORGAN KINGDOM

After creating the crisis, Morgan came to the rescue. He dispatched an army of clerks to troubled banks to look into their vaults and verify their assets. If the banks were solvent, he sent more clerks with satchels of gold coins, which he imported from Europe, to the banks to place them on display, so that depositors would be assured of the safety of their money. On Wall Street, Morgan convinced several of his fellow bankers, including Rockefeller and Schiff, to offer $25 million in loans to brokers in order to keep the stock market afloat.[2] He also met with U.S. Treasury Secretary George Cortelyou, who placed $25 million of Treasury funds in national banks and provided $36 million in small bills to meet the bank runs. By the middle of November, the working capital of the U.S. Treasury had dwindled down to $5 million.[3]

To convince the American people of the need for a new central bank, the pilgrims, under J. P. Morgan, staged the Panic of 1907. Stories were circulated in the newspapers under Morgan's control that the Knickerbocker Trust Company, one of America's leading financial institutions, was on the brink of insolvency.

Morgan's "rescue" measures resulted not only in averting a financial meltdown but also in producing sizable interest payments on all the loans the House of Morgan provided to the nation's banks and to Wall Street. The measures also served to solidify Morgan's position as the

---

2   Ibid.

3   Jon Moen, "The Panic of 1907," *Economic History Association*, August 4, 2001, https://eh.net/encyclopedia/the-panic-of-1907/, accessed January 17, 2019.

leader of the American money trust and the driving force behind the emergence of the shadow government. As Morgan biographer Frederick Lewis Allen pointed out: "Where there had been many principalities, there was now one kingdom, and it was Morgan's."[4]

THE NATIONAL MONETARY COMMISSION

In 1908, President Theodore Roosevelt brought into being the National Monetary Commission to study the cause of the economic disaster and to suggest remedies. This, too, was a result of orchestration.

Schiff now appeared before the Chamber of Commerce in Washington, D.C., to say: "Unless we have a central bank with control of credit resources, this country is going to undergo the most severe and far reaching panic in its history."[5] One year later, President Theodore Roosevelt brought into being the National Monetary Commission to study the cause of the economic disaster and to suggest remedies. This, too, was a result of orchestration. Senator Nelson Aldrich, who received the appointment to head the Commission, was "J. P. Morgan's floor broker in the Senate."[6] For two years, Aldrich and his entourage visited Europe's central banks, most of which were run by the Rothschilds, at the cost of $300,000 to U.S. taxpayers. It was all

---

4   Frederick Allen Lewis, *The Lords of Creation* (New York: Harper and Brothers, 1935), p. 142.

5   Jacob Schiff, quoted in T. D. Madmin, "The Panic of 1907 & the History of the Banking System," *Global Movement*, December 3, 2013, http://www.theglobalmovement.info/wp/the-panic-of-1907-the-history-of-the-banking-system, accessed January 17, 2019.

6   Ferdinand Lundberg, *America's Sixty Families* (New York: Vanguard Press, 1938), p. 69.

a ruse to cause Congress to believe that the commission was engaged in a massive study to prevent a future financial crisis. The final report of the commission maintained that the United States must waste no time in creating a new central bank on the model of the Bank of England.[7]

THE DUCK-SHOOTING PARTY

On November 22, 1910, shortly after the return of the commission members to America, Davison, at Morgan's command, invited Aldrich and a small group of Wall Street bankers to a "duck-shooting party" on Jekyll Island, off the coast of Georgia. The group included Frank A. Vanderlip, president of the National City Bank of New York, a Rockefeller firm in which Morgan was a principal shareholder; Abraham Platt Andrew, Assistant Secretary of the Treasury; Benjamin Strong, president of J. P. Morgan's Bankers Trust Company; and Paul Warburg.[8]

Many of these men were founding fathers of the Pilgrim Society and in addition to their ties to Morgan, were also allied with John D. Rockefeller. Vanderlip, as noted, was the president of the National City Bank of New York, which oversaw the interests of Standard Oil.[9] Benjamin Strong became closely associated with Rockefeller, since the oil tycoon had purchased a lion's share of Baker's Trust.[10] Paul Warburg was a partner in Kuhn, Loeb & Company, along with Jacob Schiff, his brother-in-law and John D. Rockefeller's financial advisor.[11] Henry Davison, as Morgan's partner, was instrumental in acquiring

7   Murray N. Rothbard, "Origins of the Federal Reserve," Mises Institute (Australia), November 13, 2009, https://mises.org/library/origins-federal-reserve, accessed January 17, 2019.

8   G. Edward Griffin, *The Creature from Jekyll Island* (New York: American Media, 2008), p. 5.

9   Priscilla Roberts, "Frank A. Vanderlip and the National City Bank during the First World War," *Essays in Economic & Business History,* University of Hong Kong, 2002.

10   Henry H. Klein, *Dynastic America and Those Who Own It* (New York: Henry Klein, 1921), p. 106.

11   "Paul Warburg," *National Cyclopaedia of American Biography* (New York: James T. White and Company, 1937), pp. 151–52.

Rockefeller's iron ore and steamship properties for U.S. Steel.[12] Nelson Aldrich's daughter, Abby, was married to John D. Rockefeller Jr. His grandson Nelson Aldrich Rockefeller would become the vice president under Gerald Ford in 1974, while his grandson David Rockefeller would serve as the chief executive officer of the Chase Manhattan Corporation and the founder of the Trilateral Commission.[13]

The meeting, G. Edward Griffin argues in *The Creature from Jekyll Island,* was "a classic example of cartel structure." A cartel, he maintains, is a group of independent businesses who join together to create "a shared monopoly," which forces the public to pay higher prices for their goods or services. Griffin writes: "Here were the representatives of the world's leading banking consortia: Morgan, Rockefeller, Rothschild, Warburg, and Kuhn-Loeb. . . . They were driven together by one overriding desire to fight their common enemy. The enemy was competition."[14]

Vanderlip described how the participants came together as follows:

> Despite my views about the value to society of greater publicity for the affairs of corporations, there was an occasion, near the close of 1910, when I was as secretive—indeed, as furtive—as any conspirator. . . . I do not feel it is any exaggeration to speak of our secret expedition to Jekyll Island as the occasion of the actual conception of what eventually became the Federal Reserve System. . . . We were told to leave our last names behind us. We were told, further, that we should avoid dining together on the night of our departure. We were instructed to come one at a time and as unobtrusively as possible to the railroad terminal on the New Jersey littoral of the Hudson, where Senator Aldrich's private car would be in readiness, attached to the rear end

---

12   Ron Chernow, "The Deal of the Century," *American Heritage,* July/August 1998.

13   "Biography: Nelson A. Rockefeller," *American Experience,* Public Broadcasting System, n.d., https://www.pbs.org/wgbh/americanexperience/features/rockefellers-nelson/, accessed January 17, 2019.

14   Griffin, *The Creature from Jekyll Island,* pp. 11–12.

of a train for the South. . . . Once aboard the private car we began to observe the taboo that had been fixed on last names. We addressed one another as "Ben," "Paul," "Nelson," and "Abe." Davison and I adopted even deeper disguises, abandoning our own first names. On the theory that we were always right, he became Wilbur and I became Orville, after those two aviation pioneers, the Wright brothers. . . . Discovery, we knew, simply must not happen, or else all our time and effort would be wasted.[15]

THE PURPOSE OF THE PARTY

The gathering was to serve the following purposes: (1) to ensure that the money trust would gain complete control over the nation's financial resources; (2) to make the money supply elastic in order to reverse the trend of private capital formation and to recapture the industrial loan market; (3) to pool the resources of the nation's banks into one reserve that would serve to protect a few of them from currency drains and bank runs; and (4) to shift inevitable financial losses from the money trust to the U.S. taxpayers.[16] It had been instigated by the problem of competition. In 1910, the number of banks in America had doubled to over 20 thousand within a decade. Most of these banks were in the South and West, causing the New York banks to suffer a steady decline of market share. Forty percent of the institutions were national banks that had been chartered by the federal government. These banks, which were located in every major American city, were allowed to issue their own currency in the form of bank notes.[17] This ability served as a safeguard to financial independence, since it prevented a single, centralized agency from gaining control of the nation's economy.

---

15   Frank Vanderlip, "U.S. Farm Boy to Financier," *Saturday Evening Post*, February 9, 1936.

16   Griffin, *The Creature from Jekyll Island*, p. 437.

17   Ibid., p. 12.

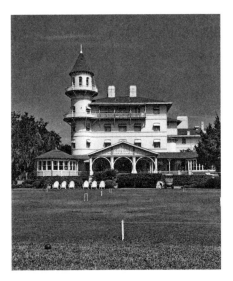

At the Jekyll Island Hunt Club—a property owned by Morgan and William Rockefeller—Warburg told the group that the bill they would compose for Congress must avoid any reference to a "central bank," since several American presidents, including Thomas Jefferson and Andrew Jackson, had railed against the establishment of such an entity. "Jekyll Island Historic Club Resort, Jekyll Island, Glynn County, Georgia" by Farrargirl is licensed under CC BY-SA 4.0

THE WARBURG WARNING

At the Jekyll Island Hunt Club—a property owned by Morgan and William Rockefeller—Warburg told the group that the bill they would compose for Congress must avoid any reference to a "central bank," since several American presidents, including Thomas Jefferson and Andrew Jackson, had railed against the establishment of such an entity.[18] It was sound advice. In 1910, America was the only major economic power without a central bank. Throughout its history, the country had deep suspicion against the very idea of central banking. East Coast bankers with ties to the House of Rothschild pressed the case for centralizing control over the nation's monetary system in a single overarching bank. Their efforts met with resistance from average citizens, who maintained, in the spirit of Jackson, that granting such power to one institution was blatantly un-American. The commoners had prevailed for 77 years.[19]

---

18   G. Vance Smith and Tom Gow, *Masters of Deception: The Rise of the Council on Foreign Relations* (Colorado Springs: Freedom First Society, 2012), p. 20.

19   Liaquat Ahamed, *Lords of Finance: The Bankers Who Broke the World* (New York: Penguin Books, 2009), p. 52.

AN ECONOMIC COUP D'ETAT

Warburg further advised the group that legislation for a central bank must create an illusion that control of the system would reside with the government, since the chairman of the Federal Reserve in Washington, D.C., would be appointed by the president and would remain answerable to Congress. For further camouflage, Warburg insisted that the legislation must be presented as a regional system, with the 15 branches responsible for overseeing the financial conditions within their jurisdiction.[20] Such measures were necessary since the cabal of millionaires at Jekyll Island were plotting the greatest financial and political coup d'état in American history: the usurpation of Congress's authority, as provided in the Constitution, to create and control the country's money supply.

THE FINAL REPORT

After spending 10 days on the island, the final draft for the new banking system was written by Vanderlip from Warburg's notes. Aldrich, upon returning to Washington, inserted the draft within the pages of the report, a work of 23 volumes replete with copious analytical data, which was being prepared for Congress by the National Monetary Commission.[21] In 1911, when asked by his fellow Republicans to prepare a bill for financial and monetary reform, Aldrich merely plucked the draft from the voluminous report and presented it to Congress as though the legislation had sprung from three years of travel, study, and work by diligent members of the Commission and was not the product of a clandestine meeting on Jekyll Island.[22]

---

20 Ibid.

21 N. A. Weston, "Studies of the National Monetary Commission," *Annals of the American Academy of Political and Social Science* 99 (January 1922), https://www.jstor.org/stable/1014505?seq=1#page_scan_tab_contents, accessed January 17, 2019.

22 Nathaniel Wright Stephenson, *Nelson W. Aldrich: A Leader in American Politics* (Port Washington, NY: Kennikat Press, 1971), pp. 129–30.

9

THE VAMPIRES

Mr. Chairman, we have in this Country one of the most corrupt institutions the world has ever known. I refer to the Federal Reserve Board and the Federal Reserve Banks, hereinafter called the Fed. The Fed has cheated the Government of these United States and the people of the United States out of enough money to pay the Nation's debt. . . .

This evil institution has impoverished and ruined the people of these United States, has bankrupted itself, and has practically bankrupted our Government. It has done this through the defects of the law under which it operates, through the maladministration of that law by the Fed and through the corrupt practices of the moneyed vultures who control it.

Some people think that the Federal Reserve Banks are United States Government institutions. They are private monopolies which prey upon the people of these United States for the benefit of themselves and their foreign customers; foreign and domestic speculators and swindlers; and rich and predatory money lender. In that dark crew of financial pirates there are those who would cut a man's throat to get a dollar out of his pocket; there are those who send money into states to buy votes to control our legislatures; there are those who maintain International propaganda for the purpose of deceiving us into granting of new concessions which will permit them to cover up their past misdeeds and set again in motion their gigantic train of crime.

—THE HONORABLE LOUIS MCFADDEN, REMARKS IN CONGRESS, 1934

THE FEDERAL RESERVE System was brought into being on December 23, 1913, by an act of Congress. The House vote was 298 to 60; the Senate 43 to 25. The timing was propitious for passage since the members of both houses of Congress were most anxious to adjourn for the Christmas holidays. The fact that the legislation cleared the Senate with a minority vote was due to the fact that 27 Senators refused to vote, and five were absent.[1] Upon its passage, Senator Charles A. Lindbergh (R-MN), father of the famous aviator, said:

> This Act establishes the most gigantic trust on earth. . . . When the President signs this Act, the invisible government by the Money Power, proven to exist by the Money Trust Investigation, will be legalized. . . . The money power overawes the legislative and executive forces of the Nation and of the States. I have seen these forces exerted during the different stages of this bill. The new law will create inflation whenever the trusts want inflation. It may not do so immediately, but the trusts want a period of inflation, because all the stocks they hold have gone down. . . Now, if the trusts can get another period of inflation, they figure they can unload the stocks on the people at high prices during the excitement and then bring on a panic and buy them back at low prices. . . . The people may not know it immediately, but the day of reckoning is only a few years removed.[2]

THE SHAREHOLDERS

A partial listing of the 1914 principal shareholders in the Fed's district banks contains the names of N. M. Rothschild, London; Lord Montagu Norman, London; Brown, Shipley, and Company, London; Alex Brown and Sons, Baltimore; Brown Brothers Harriman, New York; Morgan et Cie, Paris; Morgan, Grenfell and Company, London; J. P.

---

1   Stephen Mitford Goodson, *A History of Central Banking and the Enslavement of Mankind* (London: Black House, 2014), p. 75.

2   Charles A. Lindbergh Sr., *Congressional Record* 51, December 22, 1913, p. 1446.

PRESIDENT'S SIGNATURE ENACTS CURRENCY LAW

Wilson Declares It the First of Series of Constructive Acts to Aid Business.

Makes Speech to Group of Democratic Leaders.

Conference Report Adopted in Senate by Vote of 43 to 25.

Banks All Over the Country Hasten to Enter Federal Reserve System.

Gov-Elect Walsh Calls Passage of Bill A Fine Christmas Present.

WILSON SEES DAWN OF NEW ERA IN BUSINESS

Aims to Make Prosperity Free to Have Unimpeded Momentum.

HOME VIEWS OF CURRENCY ACT — FOUR PENS USED BY PRESIDENT

The Federal Reserve System was brought into being on December 23, 1913, by an act of Congress. The House vote was 298 to 60; the Senate 43 to 25.

Morgan Company, New York; Morgan Guaranty Company, New York; Morgan Stanley Company, New York; Lazard Brothers, London; Lazard Freres, Paris; Lazard Brothers, New York; J. Henry Schroder Banking Corporation, New York; Schroder Bank, Hamburg, New York, and Montgomery, Alabama; Lehman-Stern, New Orleans; Drexel and Company, Philadelphia; National City Bank, New York; William Rockefeller; J. P. Morgan; Percy Rockefeller; New York Trust; New York Edison; Sherman and Sterling; National Bank of Commerce (later identified as Morgan Guaranty Trust Company); New York Equitable Life (J. P. Morgan); H. P. Davison (J. P. Morgan; North British Mercantile Insurance, London; Levi P. Morgan, New York; First National Bank of New York; Goldman Sachs Bank of New York; Israel Moses Seif Bank of Italy; Royal Bank of Scotland; Bank of Nova Scotia; First National Bank of Boston; First National Bank of Cincinnati; Philadelphia National Bank; First National Bank of Minneapolis; First National Bank of Kansas City; and the American Foreign Banking Corporation, New York.[3] The largest shareholder was the Rockefeller-controlled National City Bank with 30,000 shares.[4]

3   Eustace Mullins, *Secrets of the Federal Reserve* (New York: Kasper and Horton, 1982), http://www.jrbooksonline.com/PDF_Books/SecretsOfFedReserve.pdf, accessed January 17, 2019.

4   Ibid.

THE POWER BASE

The Federal Reserve Bank of New York quickly emerged as the fountainhead of the system, since Manhattan remained the financial capital of the nation. The other 11 banks, in the words of Frederick Lundberg, became "so many expensive mausoleums erected to salve the local pride and quell the Jacksonian fears of the hinterland."[5] These banks were set up in Boston, Philadelphia, Cleveland, Richmond, Atlanta, Chicago, St. Louis, Minneapolis, Kansas City, Dallas, and San Francisco.

Benjamin Strong, president of the [Morgan] Bankers Trust Company, served as the first Governor of the New York Fed. Under Strong's leadership, the Federal Reserve of New York, unsuspected by the nations, became interlinked with the Bank of England and

The Federal Reserve Bank of New York quickly emerged as the fountainhead of the system, since Manhattan remained the financial capital of the nation. The other 11 banks, in the words of Frederick Lundberg, became "so many expensive mausoleums erected to salve the local pride and quell the Jacksonian fears of the hinterland."

---

5   Lundberg, *America's 60 Families*, p. 122.

the Banque de France.[6] It alone became authorized to receive massive deposits of gold from other central banks. By 1924, a massive vault, half the size of a football field, was built 86 feet beneath the Federal Reserve Bank on the corner of William and Nassau Street in lower Manhattan. Three years later, the vault contained 10 percent of world's entire supply of monetary gold.[7]

ROCKEFELLER'S CONTROL

Strong was closely related to the Rockefellers, since they gained controlling interest in Bankers Trust, where he had served as president.[8] When Strong retired, he was replaced by George L. Harrison, another Rockefeller associate, who later became the president of New York Life, a firm controlled by the Rockefeller banking group.[9] Allan Sproul, Harrison's successor, was an associate of the Rockefellers. His brother, Robert, served as a director of the Rockefeller Foundation.[10]

Alfred Hayes, the next president of the New York Fed, was a Rhodes scholar who became the director of the bond department of the National City Bank, where William Rockefeller, John D.'s brother, had gained controlling interest.[11] Paul Volcker, Hayes's successor, was also a Rhodes scholar and the financial economist for the Rockefeller-owned Chase Manhattan Bank. Volcker became a member of the Council on Foreign

---

6   Ibid.

7   "The Founding of the Fed," Federal Reserve Bank of New York, n.d., https://www.newyorkfed. org/aboutthefed/history_article.html, accessed January 17, 2019.

8   Henry H. Klein, *Dynastic America and Those Who Own It* (New York: Henry Klein, 1921), p. 106.

9   "George L. Harrison," *About the New York Fed*, Federal Reserve Bank of New York, n.d., https:// www.newyorkfed.org/aboutthefed/GHarrisonbio.html, accessed January 17, 2019.

10   Eustace Mullins, *The World Order: A Study in the Hegemony of Parasitism,* 1984, Modern History Project, n.d., http://modernhistoryproject.org/mhp?Article=WorldOrder&C=7.1, accessed January 17, 2019.

11   Wolfgang Saxon, "Alfred Hayes, 79, Retired Chief of the Reserve Bank of New York," *New York Times,* October 22, 1989, https://www.nytimes.com/1989/10/22/obituaries/alfred-hayes-79-retired-chief-of-the-reserve-bank-of-new-york.html, accessed January 17, 2019.

Relations or CFR (an organization controlled by the Rockefellers), the Trilateral Commission (an organization created by the Rockefellers), and the Bilderberg Group.[12]

THE PATTERN PERSISTED

The same pattern persisted when Anthony Solomon became the head of the New York Fed. Solomon was the founder of General Foods, a company that was seized by one of the tentacles of the Rockefeller octopus.[13] E. Gerald Corrigan, Solomon's successor, possessed similar strong ties to the Rockefellers. Following his tenure as the New York Fed president, Corrigan became the director of the CFR and the Trilateral Commission, the managing director of Goldman Sachs, which purchased the Rockefeller Center, and a member of the Group of Thirty, a think tank founded and funded by the Rockefeller Foundation.[14] William J. McDonough, the eighth president of the New York Fed, was another member of the Group of Thirty and CFR director. He had served as the Vice-Chairman of First Chicago Bank, a part of Chase Manhattan network.[15] Timothy Geithner, who served as Nelson Rockefeller's political advisor, became the next Rockefeller associate to ascend to the presidency of the New York Fed. He later became Secretary of the Treasury under Barack Obama, a distinguished fellow of the CFR, and a member of the Group of Thirty.[16]

---

12 "Paul A. Volcker," Federal Reserve Bank of New York, n.d., https://www.newyorkfed.org/aboutthefed/PVolckerbio.html, accessed January 17, 2019.

13 Raymond W. Bernard, *The Revolt against Chemicals* (Whitefish, MT: Kessinger Publishing, 2010), p. 60.

14 Laurence H. Shoup, *Wall Street Think Tank: The Council on Foreign Relations and the Empire of Neoliberal Geopolitics, 1976–2014* (New York: Monthly Review Press, 2014), p. 142.

15 Rich Miller and Brendan Murray, "William McDonough, N.Y. Fed Chief in Twin Crises, Dies at 83," *Bloomberg*, January 23, 2018, https://www.bloomberg.com/news/articles/2018-01-25/ex-new-york-fed-chief-mcdonough-dies-led-bank-during-ltcm-9-11, accessed January 17, 2019.

16 "Timothy F. Geithner," Group of Thirty, September 8, 2018, https://web.archive.org/web/20081009165354/http://www.group30.org/bios/members15.htm, accessed January 17, 2019.

Geither was succeeded by William C. Dudley, yet another member of Rockefeller's Group of Thirty. Prior to his appointment, Dudley served as a managing director at Goldman Sachs and the vice president of Morgan Guaranty Trust, another branch of Rockefeller's Chase Manhattan empire.[17] John C. Williams, who came to occupy the presidency of the New York Fed in 2018, has spent his entire career as a lackey within the Federal Reserve System.[18]

POWER OVER ALL

The Federal Reserve System represented the ultimate political and economic power in the country. It alone possessed the ability to manufacture currency, to establish interest rates, and to precipitate prosperity or depression. By its sole decision, money became available for industrial expansion and business growth, or it became withdrawn from circulation, making it impossible for entrepreneurs to launch new ventures, for couples to purchase houses, or for people to gain employment. No other agency is more formidable or important to the everyday lives of American citizens, although few are aware of its function.

Almost everything about the system, from the time of the Fed's creation, remained shrouded in mystery. The chairman was appointed by the president of the United States, thereby eluding the impression that the 12 branches of the central bank were under the control of the federal government. But the person really in charge remained the director of the Federal Reserve in New York. The very name of America's central bank was deceptive. It was not federal. The government owned no shares. It was

---

17 Patrick McGeehan and Andrew Ross Sorkin, "Banking's Big Deal: The Overview; Chase Is Reported on Verge of Deal to Obtain Morgan," *New York Times*, September 13, 2000, https:// www.nytimes.com/2000/09/13/business/banking-s-big-deal-overview-chase-reported-verge-deal-obtain-morgan.html?sq=j.p.morgan+chase+manhattan+merger&scp=12&st=nyt, accessed January 17, 2019.

18 "John C. Williams," Federal Reserve Bank of New York, n.d., https://www.newyorkfed.org/ research/economists/williams, accessed January 17, 2019.

a private, profit-making company.[19] The Reserve System had no reserves of gold or silver. The money deposited was used at the discretion of the shareholders, including the Rothschilds and the Rockefellers. Finally, the System was not a system but rather a syndicate of bankers whose interests were often at odds with the welfare of the American people.

THE WORKINGS OF THE SYNDICATE

When the government needed money, the Treasury Department issued bonds, which were sold by bond dealers. When the Fed wanted to expand the money supply, it purchased the Treasury bonds from the bond dealers by the transfer of newly issued dollars. The dollars were created *ex nihilo*—out of nothing—they weren't even printed. The dollars were made to materialize by the click of a mouse on the Fed computer. This practice was called "open market operations," because the Fed bought the bonds on an open market from the bond dealers.[20] The bonds, which the Fed owned, became the "reserves" to back up the banking establishment's loans. Through "fractional reserve lending," the same reserves were lent over and over again, thereby expanding the money supply and generating interest through each loan.[21] Every act within this process represented an illusion. No material wealth was exchanged. And the value of the dollar was determined by fiat, that is, by a mere declaration of its worth by the Fed's Board of Governors.

Louis McFadden, who chaired the House Committee on Banking and Currency from 1920 to 1931, said at the time of his retirement: "When the Federal Reserve Act was passed, the people of the United States did not perceive that a world banking system was being set up here, a super-state controlled by international bankers and international industrialists acting together to enslave the world for their own pleasure.

---

19   Ellen Brown, "Who Owns the Federal Reserve?" *Global Research*, October 8, 2008, http://www.globalresearch.ca/who-owns-the-federal-reserve/10489, accessed January 17, 2019.

20   Ibid.

21   Ibid.

Every effort has been made by the Fed to conceal its power, but the truth is—the Fed has usurped the government."[22]

THE ROTHSCHILD NETWORK

In addition to their holdings in the Federal Reserve, the Rothschild banking family became major shareholders of every centralized bank throughout the world, including Swedish Riksbank, Banco de España, Banque de France, Bank of Finland, De Nederlandsche Bank, Norges Bank, Osterreichische Nationalbank, Danmarks Nationalbank, Banco de Portugal, National Bank of Belgium, Bank of Indonesia, German Reichsbank, Bulgarian National Bank, National Bank of Romania, Bank of Japan, the National Bank of Serbia, and the Bank of England.[23] Their tentacles within these institutions were extended by their involvement of other Jewish banking families who also became shareholders in the central banks. The Rothschilds were united to these families not only by business but by blood. "Natty" Rothschild had married the oldest daughter of Levi Barent Cohen, a prominent London financier. Jacob Schiff, who had lived with the Rothschilds, moved to America, and married the daughter of Solomon Loeb, the head of the Kuhn Loeb banking dynasty. The two daughters of Marcus Goldman married the sons of Samuel Sachs to form Goldman Sachs. Paul Warburg left Hamburg for New York, where he married Nina Loeb, the daughter of Solomon Loeb.[24]

NATIONAL SPENDING AND NATIONAL DEBT

With leverage within the central banks, the Rothschilds and their associates, including the Rockefellers, could cause the rise and fall of nations, the conditions of prosperity or poverty, and the matter of war or peace.

---

22 Louis McFadden, quoted in A. Ralph Epperson, *The Unseen Hand: An Introduction to the Conspiratorial View of History* (Tucson: Publius Press, 1985), p. 182.

23 Stephen Mitford Goodson, *A History of Central Banking and the Enslavement of Mankind* (London: Black House, 2014), p. 92.

24 Ibid.

Every piece of paper created by these banks increased their wealth since the money was produced with interest. The paper currency—which was readily available—permitted governments to spend massive amounts of money to create bureaucracies, to beef up their militaries, and to expand their social programs. The greater the governments plunged into debt, the more revenue would come into the hands of the central bankers. As of 2015, 97 percent of wealth in the world was owed as debt.[25]

Since the central banks thrived on national spending and national debt, the cartel who ran the central banks became proponents of socialism and communism. Within such systems of government, the states operated the industries and provided comprehensive social services for all of their citizens. Therefore, the political leaders would become totally dependent upon the central bank to churn out an endless supply of fiat money.

THE COMMUNIST IDEAL

The Rothschilds were intrigued by the economic theories of Karl Marx and provided him with ongoing financial support. The relationship between the bankers and the father of Communism caused Mikhail Bakunin, the famous anarchist, to say: "This world is now, at least for the most part, at the disposal of Marx on the one hand, and of Rothschild on the other. This may seem strange. What can there be in common between

The Rothschilds were intrigued by the economic theories of Karl Marx and provided him with ongoing financial support.

25   Robert Howells, *The Illumanati: The Counterculture Revolution from Secret Societies to Wikileaks and Anonymous* (London: Watkins Publishing, 2016), p. 146.

socialism and a leading bank? The point is that authoritarian socialism, Marxist communism, demands a strong centralization of the state. And where there is centralization of the state, there must necessarily be a central bank, and where such a bank exists, speculating with the labor of the people, will be found."[26] Similarly, Jacob Schiff shelled out $20 million to the Bolsheviks to spark uprisings against the Czarist regime in 1905. [27]

The Rockefellers, too, became Communist supporters. They subsidized Communist publications, including the *Daily Worker*, the *Masses*, the *PM*, and the *Amerasia*. What's more, after the failed 1905 rebellion, the Rockefellers transported Leon Trotsky, who led the rebellion with Vladimir Lenin, to Bayonne, New Jersey, where he lived rent-free and without any visible means of subsistence in a property owned by Standard Oil.[28]

THE GOODNESS OF WAR

Since the growth of government and national debt was of pivotal importance to the money cartel, they became ardent proponents of war. Once war was declared, astronomical amounts of cash were needed to support military forces, to purchase munitions, and to build tanks, ships, and planes. Nations engaged in armed conflict ran deeper and deeper in debt and came to rely more and more on the central banks to keep churning out the paper money. War also broke down borders between nations so that new central banks could emerge for the further enslavement of mankind and the confiscation by the cartel of the earth's natural resources. The South African Reserve Bank, for example, was set up at the close of World War I as a replication of the U.S. Federal Reserve.[29]

---

26 Mikhail Bakunin, quoted in Fergus O'Connor, "The Left and Their Jewish Question," *New English Review*, April 2018, https://www.newenglishreview.org/Fergus_O%27Connor/The_Left_and_Their_Jewish_Question/, accessed January 17, 2019.

27 Griffin, *The Creature from Jekyll Island*, pp. 274–77.

28 "Trilateral Commission and the Communism," *Conscendo Sodalitas*, n.d., http://conscendo.org/eng/textos/sodalitas/texto121c.asp, access January 17, 2019.

29 Goodson, *A History of Central Banking*, p. 108.

10

THE GREAT WAR

Despite his immense loot, Rockefeller lived in fear of poverty. And he instilled this fear in his offspring in such intense degree that his fear of poverty has become a fixed, paranoid characteristic of the Dynasty. Rockefeller yearned, above all things, for "security" for himself in his piracy. This meant to him that he must loot and despoil everyone, enslave the world and rob everyone else of their possessions and security in order to make sure that no one more ruthless and criminal than himself could arise and rob him of his loot. Like an ugly and monstrous spider, John D. sat in the midst of a vast sea of conspiracy in which he had entrapped the U.S.A. and the rest of the world, ready to pounce on and devour his victims, mankind.

—EMANUEL M. JOSEPHSON, *THE "FEDERAL" RESERVE CONSPIRACY &*
ROCKEFELLERS, 1968

STUDENTS ARE TAUGHT IN SCHOOLS and universities throughout the United States that the cause of World War I was the assassination of Archduke Franz Ferdinand, the heir to the Austro-Hungarian Empire, by a Serbian nationalist on June 28, 1914. The murder, according to this scenario, prompted conflict between Russia, Serbia's ally, and Germany, the Austro-Hungarian protector. This conflict caused the various European countries to fall like dominoes into the abyss of war since they were bound by a network of alliances.

World War I, like all wars, was caused by economic interests, and plans for the global conflict were underway decades before the assassination of Archduke Ferdinand.

A MATTER OF OIL

But World War I, like all wars, was caused by economic interests, and plans for the global conflict were underway decades before the assassination of Archduke Ferdinand. The creation of the German empire under Bismarck had upset the "balance of powers" that existed in Europe for more than two centuries. England ruled supreme over the continent until 1871. This supremacy had been repeatedly challenged by Spain and by France, but England always remained victorious. Because Germany grew increasingly stronger by acquiring colonies in Africa and by building up its military force, it became a severe threat to the economic hegemony of England. The threat was intensified when the German government obtained a concession from Sultan Abdul Hamid to drill the Baghdad-Mosul oilfields and to build a Baghdad-to-Berlin railroad in 1904.[1]

The British government, by this time, was keenly aware that whoever controlled the oil controlled the future. As early as 1882, Admiral Lord Fischer stressed the importance of oil as the fuel for the Royal Navy by saying: "The use of oil adds 50 percent to the value of any fleet that uses it. The use of oil would increase the strength of the British Navy by 33 percent, because it can refuel at any enemy's harbor. Coal necessitates about one-third of the fleet being absent at the refueling of a base."[2]

---

1   Emanuel M. Josephson, *The "Federal" Reserve Conspiracy and the Rockefellers: Their "Gold Corner"* (New York: Chedney Press, 1968), p. 74.

2   Admiral Fischer, quoted in Emanuel M. Josephson, *Rockefeller "Internationalist:" The Man Who Misrules the World* (New York: Chedney Press, 1952), p. 187.

THE COMMITTEE OF 300

At that time, the international bankers, who were excluded from the economic development in Germany, sought for ways to limit and control Germany. Between 1894 and 1907, a number of international treaties were signed to have Russia, France, England, and other nations unite against Germany in the case of war. It was the task of the so-called Committee of 300 at the British Pilgrim Society to set the stage for World War. Members of the committee included Lord Albert Grey, Lord Arnold Toynbee, Lord Alfred Milner, and H. J. Mackinder, who became known as the father of geopolitics.[3] Edward Bernays, the so-called father of public relations, and Walter Lippmann, the founding editor of the *New Republic,* were the American "specialists" of the Committee. Lord Rothermere, aka Harold Harmsworth, used his newspaper the *Daily Mail* as a tool to try out their "social conditioning" techniques on his readers. After a test period of six months, they had found that 87 percent of the public had formed opinions without rational or critical thought processes. Thereupon the English working class became subjected to a constant onslaught of propaganda designed to convince them that they were obliged to send their sons by the millions to their deaths.[4] The experiment verified that human beings can be conditioned as easily as rats.

THE MONEY FACTORY

A war on the grand scale of World War I could not have been mounted without the establishment of the Federal Reserve System. The Fed, by churning out a seemingly endless supply of cash, could provide loans to foreign governments for the production of arms and munitions,

---

3   Jan Van Helsing, "Geheimgesellschaften und Ihre Macht in 20 Jahrhundert," n. d., http://www.
     bibliotecapleyades.net/sociopolitica/secretsoc_20century/secretsoc_20century.htm#Contents,
     accessed January 17, 2019.

4   Jan van Helsing, "Secret Societies and Their Power in the 20ᵗʰ Century," 1998, http://www.
     bibliotecapleyades.net/sociopolitica/secretsoc_20century/secretsoc_20century05.htm, accessed
     January 17, 2019.

chemicals, aircraft, tanks, submarines, and battleships. To make sure that the war would occur, Chase Manhattan and other Rockefeller banks, now flush with cash, provided Kaiser Wilhelm II with over $300 million.[5] By 1917, the British War Office had borrowed $2.5 billion from Chase Manhattan and other Wall Street banks.[6] Americans, without realizing it, were paying the bill for the massive produce of money through a hidden tax called inflation.[7]

THE POSSIBLE STALEMATE

But a grave problem arose. By 1915, the Germans were emerging as victorious. They had nearly captured Paris, crushed Serbia and Romania, bled the French Army until it mutinied, and vanquished the mighty Russian army.[8] Even if the Germans did not attain victory, the possibility existed that the war could result in a stalemate. Since tanks were not manufactured until 1916, the armies had to rely on the infantries alone to stage an advance. But such advances were easily repelled since both sides had dug trenches protected by machine guns, barbed war, mines, and other obstacles. By 1916, the trenches had stretched over 400 miles from the Swiss border to the North Sea.[9]

AMERICAN ISOLATIONISM

It was becoming imperative for the money cartel to drag the United States into the conflict. But America stood as an isolationist nation. This

5   Josephson, *The "Federal" Reserve Conspiracy and the Rockefellers*, p. 74.

6   Oliver Stone and Peter Kuznick, *The Concise Untold History of the United States* (New York: Gallery Books, 2014), p. 14.

7   G. Edward Griffin, *The Creature from Jekyll Island* (New York: American Media, 2008), p. 260.

8   Michael Peck, "How Germany Could Have Won World War I," *National Interest*, May 8, 2014, https://nationalinterest.org/feature/how-germany-could-have-won-world-war-i-10398, accessed January 17, 2019.

9   Mark John McCulloch, "How Long Were the World War I Trenches?" *Quora*, March 23, 2018, https://www.quora.com/How-long-were-World-War-1-trenches, accessed January 17, 2019.

was in keeping with the advice of George Washington, who said in his Farewell Address: "The great rule of conduct for us in regard to foreign nations is in extending our commercial relations, to have with them as little political connection as possible. So far as we have already formed engagements, let them be fulfilled with perfect good faith. Here let us stop. Europe has a set of primary interests which to us have none; or a very remote relation. Hence she must be engaged in frequent controversies, the causes of which are essentially foreign to our concerns. Hence, therefore, it must be unwise in us to implicate ourselves by artificial ties in the ordinary vicissitudes of her politics, or the ordinary combinations and collisions of her friendships or enmities."[10]

Similarly, Thomas Jefferson in his inaugural address pledged "peace, commerce, and honest friendship with all nations, entangling alliances with none."[11] This tradition of isolationism was fortified by the millions of immigrants who came to America to escape from oppression. During the 1800s, the United States spanned North America without departing from its stance of isolationism. It fought the War of 1812, the Mexican War, and the Spanish-American War without forming foreign alliances or fighting on European soil.[12]

A CREDITOR NATION

The problem of enticing the American government to the European slaughter was further compounded by the fact that Rockefeller, Morgan, and other members of the cartel were making a fortune by supporting both sides in the struggle. In 1915, Thomas W. Lamont, a partner of Morgan and Company, delivered the following speech to the American Academy of Political and Social Science in Philadelphia:

---

10   George Washington, "Farewell Address," 1796, http://avalon.law.yale.edu/18th_century/washing. asp, accessed January 17, 2019.

11   James Simon, "Isolationism," *U.S. History,* n. d., http://www.u-s-history.com/pages/h1601.html, accessed January 17, 2019.

12   Ibid.

We are turning from a debtor into a creditor…We are piling up prodigious export trade balance….Many of our manufacturers and merchants have been doing a wonderful business in articles relating to the war [WWI]. So heavy have been the war orders running into the hundreds of millions of dollars, that now their effect is beginning to spread to general business….

This question of trade and financial supremacy must be determined by several factors, a chief one of which is the duration of the war. If…the war should come to an end in the near future…we should probably find Germany, whose export trade is now almost wholly cut off, swinging back into keen competition very promptly.

[Another factor that] is dependent on the duration of the war, is as to whether we shall become lenders to foreign nations upon a really large scale…Shall we become lenders upon a really stupendous scale to these foreign governments?…If the war continues long enough to encourage us to take such a position, then inevitably we would become a creditor instead of a debtor nation, and such a development, sooner or later, would tend to bring about the dollar, instead of the pound sterling, as the international basis of exchange.[13]

The money began to flow in January 1915 when the House of Morgan signed a contract with the British Army Council and the Admiralty. At the advent of modern warfare, the first purchase, curiously, was for horses, and the amount tendered was $12 million. But that was but the first drop in the banker's bucket. Total purchases from the Allies eventually climbed to an astronomical $3 billion. Morgan's office at 23 Wall Street became mobbed by brokers and manufacturers seeking to cut a deal. Each month, Jack Morgan presided over purchases that equaled the gross national product of the entire world just one generation before.[14]

---

13   Thomas W. Lamont, quoted in F. William Engdahl, *Gods of Money: Wall Street and the Death of the American Century* (San Diego: Progressive Press, 2011), p. 67.

14   Ibid.

THE BRITISH CONCESSION

The problem of securing America's involvement in the struggle was solved by Winston Churchill, the First Lord of the Admiralty. Churchill persuaded David Lloyd George, the British Prime Minister, and other leading members of the government to yield to the money cartel's demand that the British concede their claims to the rich oil fields of Saudi Arabia, one of the Empire's vassal countries, to the Rockefellers. In exchange for this concession, the Rockefellers and other cartel members would participate in staging events that would bring America's doughboys to the killing fields of France.[15]

A MANUFACTURED ATROCITY

An incident had to be manufactured that would provoke the American people to abandon their stance of isolationism and to enter the fracas. It came with the sinking of the *Lusitania* by a German submarine on May 7, 1915. When the ship went down, 1,198 civilians, including 128 Americans, died, and the seemingly unprovoked act of aggression against a passenger ocean liner served to arouse anti-German sentiment throughout the country. Many of the 767 survivors popped up and down in the waves for three hours while seagulls swooped from the sky to peck out the eyes of the floating corpses.[16] Few Americans realized that the sinking and delayed rescue had been planned by Winston Churchill and that members of the British Admiralty were acting in tandem with Britain's Board of Trade, including Colonel Edward M. House of the Wilson Administration and American industrialists, along with J. P. Morgan, who had provided massive loans to Great Britain and the Allied forces.

The American public was not informed that the *Lusitania* was transporting six million rounds of ammunition and other military munitions to Britain. Upon the order of President Wilson, the ship's original manifest

---

15   Josephson, *The "Federal" Reserve Conspiracy and the Rockefellers,* p. 75.

16   Erik Larson, *Dead Wake: The Last Crossing of the* Lusitania (New York: Crown, 2015), p. 296.

Few Americans realized that the sinking and delayed rescue [of the *Lusitania*] had been planned by Winston Churchill and that members of the British Admiralty were acting in tandem with Britain's Board of Trade.

was hidden away in the archives of the Treasury Department.[17] Nor were they made aware that Churchill and other members of the Admiralty had directed the *Lusitania* to proceed at considerably reduced speed and without escort to the precise location within the Irish Sea where the German U-boat was lying in wait.[18] And the public, for the most part, remained oblivious that the Germans had placed large ads in the New York newspapers to dissuade Americans from boarding the ocean liner.[19]

FAKE NEWS

After the sinking of the *Lusitania*, stories about German atrocities began to capture headlines in U.S. newspapers, including the *New York Times*. One story reported that German soldiers were deliberately mutilating Belgian babies by cutting off their hands and, in some cases, even eating them. Another atrocity story involved a Canadian soldier who had supposedly been crucified with bayonets by the Germans. Many Canadians claimed to have witnessed the event, yet they all provided different versions of

17 Sam Greenhill, "Secret of the *Lusitania*: Arms Find Challenges Allied Claims It Was Solely a Passenger Ship," *Daily Mail*, December 19, 2008, http://www.dailymail.co.uk/news/article-1098904/Secret-Lusitania-Arms-challenges-Allied-claims-solely-passenger-ship.html, accessed January 17, 2019.

18 Gary Allen with Larry Abraham, *None Dare Call It Conspiracy* (San Diego: Dauphin Publications, 2013), p. 38.

19 Ibid.

After the sinking of the *Lusitania*, stories about German atrocities began to capture headlines in U.S. newspapers, including the *New York Times*. . . . Few realized that the news came from the British Pilgrim Society and was circulated by the Morgans and the Rockefellers, who had gained control of America's newspapers.

how it had happened. The Canadian high command investigated the matter, concluding that it was untrue. Other reports circulated of Belgian women, often nuns, who had their breasts cut off by the Germans. A story appeared in the *Times* about German corpse factories where bodies of British and French soldiers were supposedly turned into glycerin for weapons or food for hogs. The stories produced moral outrage throughout America and a hatred for the bloodthirsty "Hun."

Few realized that the news came from the British Pilgrim Society and was circulated by the Morgans and the Rockefellers, who had gained control of America's newspapers. On February 9, 1917, Congressman Oscar Callaway inserted this statement within the *Congressional Record* about Morgan's ability to control and manipulate the national news:

> In March, 1915, the J. P. Morgan interests, the steel, ship building
> and powder interests and their subsidiary organizations, got together
> 12 men high up in the newspaper world and employed them to select

the most influential newspapers in the United States and sufficient number of them to control generally the policy of the daily press in the United States.

These 12 men worked the problems out by selecting 179 newspapers, and then began, by an elimination process, to retain only those necessary for the purpose of controlling the general policy of the daily press throughout the country. They found it was only necessary to purchase the control of 25 of the greatest papers. The 25 papers were agreed upon; emissaries were sent to purchase the policy, national and international, of these papers; an agreement was reached; the policy of the papers was bought, to be paid for by the month; an editor was furnished for each paper to properly supervise and edit information regarding the questions of preparedness, militarism, financial policies and other things of national and international nature considered vital to the interests of the purchasers.

This contract is in existence at the present time, and it accounts for the news columns of the daily press of the country being filled with all sorts of preparedness arguments and misrepresentations as to the present condition of the United States Army and Navy, and the possibility and probability of the United States being attacked by foreign foes.

This policy also included the suppression of everything in opposition to the wishes of the interests served. The effectiveness of this scheme has been conclusively demonstrated by the character of the stuff carried in the daily press throughout the country since March, 1915. They have resorted to anything necessary to commercialize public sentiment and sandbag the National Congress into making extravagant and wasteful appropriations for the Army and Navy under false pretense that it was necessary. Their stock argument is that it is "patriotism." They are playing on every prejudice and passion of the American people.[20]

---

20 *Congressional Record*, February 9, 1917, p. 2947.

"SAFE FOR DEMOCRACY"

On April 6, 1917, the joint sessions of Congress approved President Wilson's request for a declaration of war against the German Empire. U.S. intervention in the conflict was justified by Wilson's belief that the war would make the world "safe for democracy." Six senators voted against the declaration, including Robert La Follette of Wisconsin, and fifty members of the House of Representatives opposed it, including Jeannette Rankin of Montana, America's first congresswoman.[21]

Despite government appeals for a million volunteers, only 63 thousand enlisted in the first six weeks, forcing Congress to institute compulsory military inscription. Under the 1917 Espionage Act, hundreds of Americans who opposed the draft were tossed into prison, including political activist Eugene Debs, who said: "Let the capitalists do their own fighting and furnish their own corpses and there will never be another war on the face of the earth."[22]

THE MILITARY-INDUSTRIAL COMPLEX

The war gave rise to modern warfare. Huge plants sprouted up throughout the United States to produce military aircrafts, submarines, battleships, aircraft carriers, tanks, portable machine guns, flamethrowers, and automatic rifles. Military spending rose until it constituted 22 percent of the GNP in 1918. The principal beneficiaries were U.S. Steel, Bethlehem Steel, DuPont Chemical, Kennecott, and General Electric—all of which were related to the money cartel.[23] Enterprising defense companies set up shop, including General Dynamics, which produced submarines, and Boeing, which produced aircraft. The military-industrial complex had come into existence.

---

21 Stone and Kuznick, *The Concise Untold History of the United States*, p. 15.

22 Eugene Debs, quoted in ibid., p. 17.

23 Dean Henderson, "The Federal Reserve Cartel: The Eight Families," *Global Research*, June 1, 2011, http://www.globalresearch.ca/the-federal-reserve-cartel-the-eight-families/25080, accessed January 17, 2019.

By the summer of 1914, the British Navy was fully committed to oil, and the British government had assumed the role of majority stockholder in the Anglo Persian Oil Company, now known as British Petroleum (BP).[24] But 80 percent of the oil that was used to fuel the Royal Navy and Army came from America, and 90 percent of the oil in America was owned by the Rockefellers.[25]

WAR'S END

On November 11, 1918, the long war came to an end. Of the two million Americans who took part in the struggle, 116,000 were killed and 204,000 wounded. The European losses were staggering. Eight million soldiers and 6 to 10 million civilians were dead. The civilian casualties

On November 11, 1918, the long war came to an end. Of the two million Americans who took part in the struggle, 116,000 were killed and 204,000 were wounded. The European losses were staggering. Eight million soldiers and six to 10 million civilians were dead. The civilian casualties were caused by disease and starvation. No country suffered more than Russia with 1.7 million dead and five million wounded.

---

24   Daniel Yergin, *The Prize: The Epic Quest for Oil, Money & Power* (New York: Free Press, 2008), pp. 138–40.

25   Daniel Yergin, "The Blood of Victory: World War I," *Modern History*, n.d., http://erenow.com/modern/theepicquestforoilmoneyandpower/10.html, accessed January 17, 2019.

were caused by disease and starvation. No country suffered more than Russia with 1.7 million dead and five million wounded.[26]

The survivors found themselves in a strange new world. Britain and France had been severely weakened and no longer represented a threat to the rising American political and economic hegemony. The German Empire had collapsed into financial shambles. The Austro-Hungarian Empire vanished, necessitating the restructuring of Eastern Europe. The Ottoman Empire, which had stood for six hundred years, no longer ruled over the Middle East and Central Asia. And the reign of the czars in Russia had been overthrown by Bolshevik revolutionaries, who pledged to inaugurate a world revolution.[27]

THE TREATY OF VERSAILLES

By the Treaty of Versailles, which was signed on July 28, 1919, exactly five years after the assassination of Archduke Franz Ferdinand, Germany lost one-tenth of her population and one-eighth of her territory. Germany's overseas empire, the third largest in the world, was torn apart and handed over to the victors. German citizens, who lived in these German colonies, were obliged to forfeit all of their personal property. Japan was given the German concession in Shantung and the German islands north of the Equator. The German islands south of the Equator were handed over to Australia and New Zealand. Germany's African colonies were shelled out to Britain, South Africa, and France. German waterways were now internationalized, and she was compelled to open her markets to Allied imports but denied access to Allied markets.[28] Germany was also required to cede to the Allies the city of Danzig and its hinterlands, including the delta of the Vistula River on

26   Stone and Kuznick, *The Concise Untold History of the United States*, p. 18.

27   Ibid.

28   Ibid., p. 74.

By the Treaty of Versailles, which was signed on July 28, 1919, exactly five years after the assassination of Archduke Franz Ferdinand, Germany lost one-tenth of her population and one-eighth of her territory. "Treaty of Versailles Newspaper Article" by Kallen2021 is licensed under CC BY-SA 4.0

the Baltic Sea.[29] This last stipulation would spark World War II, since the Germans, residing in Danzig, would call on Adolf Hitler to liberate them from the clutches of the League of Nations.

REPARATIONS AND REVENGE

But the loss of empire was only a part of the punishment. Germany was forbidden to build armored cars and tanks, to produce heavy artillery, and to maintain an air force. Her High Seas Fleet and merchant ships were confiscated as booty. And the German army was restricted to a force of 100,000 men.[30] And then there was the matter of finances. Germany was required not only to pay the pensions of the Allied soldiers but also to cough up 32 billion gold marks—an amount equivalent to the entire wealth of the country—in reparations.[31] This indemnity would be used to repay the international bankers for the loans with

---

29   Treaty of Versailles, Article 110, Section XI of Part III, June 28, 1919, Library of Congress, https://www.loc.gov/law/help/us-treaties/bevans/m-ust000002-0043.pdf, accessed January 17, 2019.

30   Buchanan, *Churchill, Hitler and the Unnecessary War*, p. 72.

31   Stephen Mitford Goodson, *A History of Central Banking and the Enslavement of Mankind* (London: Black House, 2014), p. 91.

interest that they had provided to Great Britain and France.[32]

By 1923, the reparation payments imposed upon Germany by the Treaty of Versailles had caused the Weimar Republic to print such an outrageous quantity of paper money that 100 million marks was not sufficient to buy a box of matches.[33] The hyperinflation was accompanied by an unemployment rate that soared to 33 percent. When Germany was no longer able to come up with the mandated annual payments of 132 billion gold marks to the Allies, French and Belgium forces took possession of the Ruhr Valley. As a result of the occupation, German miners in this area reduced coal production. This situation intensified the financial crisis and poised the possibility of a renewed outbreak of armed conflict.[34]

THE DAWES PLAN

Within these dire developments, the Rockefellers spotted an opportunity to increase its wealth and came up with the Dawes Plan. As implemented in 1924, this plan called for the provision of $1.5 billion in loans from Morgan and Rockefeller to spark the German economy and to stabilize the German currency.[35] Germany, at that time, represented carrion for the money vultures. The opportunities seemed limitless. Major German businesses could be bought for pennies on the dollar. The Daimler-Benz motor company, for example, could be had for the price of 227 of its cars.[36] Some of the money was used to build theaters, sports stadiums, and even opera houses. But the lion's share went for industrialization.[37]

---

32 Ibid.

33 James Perloff, *The Shadows of Power: The Council on Foreign Relations and the American Decline* (Appleton, WI: Western Islands, 2005), p. 46.

34 Jennifer Llewellyn, Jim Southey, and Steve Thompson, "The Ruhr Occupation," *Alpha History*, 2014, http://alphahistory.com/weimarrepublic/ruhr-occupation/, accessed January 17, 2019.

35 Perloff, *The Shadows of Power*, p. 46.

36 Liaquat Ahamed, *Lords of Finance: The Bankers Who Broke the World* (New York: Penguin, 2009), p. 283.

37 Ibid.

A GERMAN CHEMICAL COMPANY

The Dawes Plan was foolproof. It stipulated that the American bankers would be repaid with interest ahead of the reparation payments to France and Great Britain. And it met with immediate success. Businesses began to flourish, imports ballooned, and the austerity measures that had been imposed upon the German people were lifted. By 1926, the German government was back to running modest deficits of $200 million without inflation.[38]

A major beneficiary of the Plan was IG Farben, who received a $30 million loan from Rockefellers' National City Bank. This funding allowed Farben to grow into the largest chemical company in the world. It produced 100 percent of Germany's synthetic oil; 100 percent of its lubricating oil, and 84 percent of its explosives. German bankers on the Farben *Aufsichsrat* (the supervisory Board of Directors) included the Hamburg banker Max Warburg, whose brother Paul Warburg was a founder of the Federal Reserve System in the United States. Not coincidentally, in 1928, Paul Warburg became a director of American I. G., Farben's wholly owned U.S. subsidiary, whose holdings came to include the Bayer Company, General Aniline Works, Agfa Ansco, and Winthrop Chemical Company.[39] By 1933, Farben had become so wealthy that it could fund the Nazi Party's rise to power. The ties to Hitler greatly increased the chemical company's worth. By 1943, it was the leading producer of Zylon B gas, which was used in the concentration camps.[40]

---

38   Ibid.

39   Antony Sutton, "The Empire of I. G. Farben," Reformation.org, 2004, http://www.reformation.org/wall-st-ch2.html, accessed January 17, 2019.

40   Perloff, *The Shadows of Power*, p. 47.

PART THREE

THE ECONOMIC ENSLAVEMENT

11

THE CLUBHOUSE

On the first Feminian Sandstones we were promised the Fuller Life
(Which started by loving our neighbor and ended by loving his wife)
Till our women had no more children and the men lost reason and faith,
And the Gods of the Copybook Headings said: "The Wages of Sin is Death."

In the Carboniferous Epoch we were promised abundance for all,
By robbing selected Peter to pay for collective Paul;
But, though we had plenty of money, there was nothing our money could buy,
And the Gods of the Copybook Headings said: "If you don't work you die."

Then the Gods of the Market tumbled, and their smooth-tongued wizards withdrew
And the hearts of the meanest were humbled and began to believe it was true
That All is not Gold that Glitters, and Two and Two make Four
And the Gods of the Copybook Headings limped up to explain it once more.
—RUDYARD KIPLING, "THE GODS OF THE COPYBOOK HEADINGS"

BY THE END OF WORLD WAR I, the Rockefeller clan became convinced that they could only safeguard their vast financial empire by becoming the sole rulers of the world. Their first attempt to create a global government came with the attempt to establish a League of Nations under their control. The plan was drafted by Paul Warburg, the father of the Federal Reserve; John Foster Dulles, a Rockefeller lawyer, whose wife, Janet Pomeroy Avery, was John D.'s first cousin;[1] James T. Shotwell, president of Columbia University, whose work on internationalism was sponsored by the Rockefeller Foundation;[2] Lord Robert Cecil,

a leading member of the secret society of Cecil Rhodes and an agent of the Rothschilds; and Jan Smuts, the Prime Minister of South Africa, a member of the Committee of 300 and a Rothschild lackey.[3]

The League, as conceived by the trustees and espoused by President Wilson, was to establish a global forum to settle territorial disputes through arbitration and the power to enforce those settlements; to create a free trade regime to remove "all economic barriers" between nations; to promote regional integration on both political and economic levels (including the welding together of North and South America); and to allow the United States to lead the way in the formation of a new world order.

THE SETBACK

The League, as conceived by the trustees and espoused by President Wilson, was to establish a global forum to settle territorial disputes through arbitration and the power to enforce those settlements; to create a free trade regime to remove "all economic barriers" between nations; to promote regional integration on both political and economic levels (including the welding together of North and South America); and to allow the United States to lead the way in

---

1   James Perloff, *The Shadows of Power: The Council on Foreign Relations and the American Decline* (Appleton, WI: Western Islands, 2005), 38.

2   *The Rockefeller Foundation: A Digital History,* Rockefeller Foundation, n.d., https://rockfound. rockarch.org/social-science-research-council, accessed February 12, 2019.

3   "Members of the Committee of 300," *Truth Control,* September 26, 2009, https://www.truthcontrol. com/articles/members-committee-300, accessed February 12, 2019.

the formation of a new world order.[4]

When Wilson submitted the treaty for ratification in June 1919, the Senate balked. The establishment of the League, Senator Henry Cabot Lodge maintained, would make Wilson "the President of the World."[5] The setback was so personally devastating for Wilson that he suffered a severe stroke in October 1919 that prevented him from seeking a third term in office.[6]

THE MEETING AT THE MAJESTIC HOTEL

Undeterred from the plans to form a global government, the American and British members of the Pilgrim Society met on May 30, 1919, at the Majestic Hotel in Paris to create the Institute for International Affairs, which was to have two chapters: the Royal Institute of International Affairs (RIIA), also known as the Chatham House Study Group, as an advisory group to the British Government, and the Council on Foreign Relations as a think tank for the U.S. State Department. A subsidiary organization, the Institute of Pacific Relations, was formed to deal exclusively with Far Eastern affairs. Other organizations were set up in Paris and Hamburg.[7]

The Royal Institute, which opened in London in 1920, was simply the secret society of Cecil Rhodes writ large. Its founding fathers included Lionel Curtis, Philip Kerr, Lord Robert Cecil, Arnold Toynbee, Arthur Balfour, Robert Brand, and Geoffrey Dawson. Initial funding came from the Carnegie Corporation, the Rockefeller Foundation, and the Rhodes Trust. RIIA became known as the Chatham House on the basis of its address at No. 4, St. James in London. The property was

---

4   Will Banyan, "The Invisible Man of the New World Order: Raymond B. Fosdick (1883–1972)" *Conspiracy Archives*, March 8, 2015, http://www.conspiracyarchive.com/2015/03/08/the-invisible-man-of-the-new-world-order-raymond-b-fosdick-1883-1972/, accessed February 12, 2019.

5   Ibid.

6   G. Vance Smith and Tom Gow, *Masters of Deception: The Rise of the Council on Foreign Relations* (Colorado Springs: Freedom First Society, 2012), p. 36.

7   Jim Marrs, *Rule by Secrecy* (New York: HarperCollins, 2001), pp. 31–33.

purchased for the group by Colonel Reuben Wells Leonard, a Canadian businessman, who named it in honor of William Pitt, the 1ˢᵗ Earl of Chatham, "to whom Canadians owed their status as British subjects."[8] At the time of his death, Baron Edmond de Rothschild spoke of the RIIA as his "greatest creation."[9]

THE CHATHAM HOUSE RULE

RIIA functioned and continues to function under this policy: "When a meeting, or part thereof, is held under the Chatham House Rule, participants are free to use the information received, but neither the identity nor the affiliation of the speaker(s), nor that of any other participant, may be revealed."[10] This rule mirrored the manner in which Rhodes believed information should be shared and disseminated, clandestinely through an elite group of decision makers, and it intimated that the inner workings of the group operates on the Society of the Elect's original rings-within-rings model. RIIA members have included a host of British Prime Ministers, including Winston Churchill, Harold Macmillan, Harold Wilson, and John Major. The list of foreign dignitaries who have addressed the gatherings at the Chatham House includes the names of Mahatma Gandhi, Ronald Reagan, Mikhail Gorbachev, Nelson Mandela, Yasser Arafat, Vladimir Putin, Alan Greenspan, Kofi Annan, and Hillary Clinton.[11]

8   Robin Brown, *The Secret Society: Cecil John Rhodes's Plan for a New World Order* (Cape Town, ZA: Penguin Books, 2015), p. 327.

9   Eustace Mullins, "Summary of Rothschild Power," Ezra Pound Institute of Civilization, 1985, available at https://archive.org/details/SummaryOfRothschildPower.

10   James Corbett, "The Truth about the Royal Institute of International Affairs," *Corbett Report*, January 20, 2019, https://www.howestreet.com/2019/01/20/the-truth-about-the-royal-institute-of-international-affairs/, accessed February 12, 2019.

11   Brown, *The Secret Society*, p. 322.

THE BIRTH OF THE CFR

As the Rockefellers and Morgans took the lead in the creation of the Federal Reserve, the Pilgrim Society, and the American Round Table, they also spearheaded the formation of the Council on Foreign Relations (CFR) on July 29, 1921.[12] John W. Davis, the first president of the organization, was a trustee of the Rockefeller Foundation;[13] Paul Cravath, the vice president, headed the law firm that protected the Rockefeller family's interests;[14] Russell Leffingwell, who became the first chairman, was one of Morgan's banking business partners; Edwin Gay was president of the *New York Post*, a newspaper owned by the Morgan Company; Hamilton Fish Armstrong, another employee of the *Post*, became the first editor of *Foreign Affairs*, the CFR monthly publication; and Elihu Root, another of Morgan's private attorneys, was named "honorary president." Many of the founders also possessed strong ties to the Carnegie and Rockefeller Foundations, which provided the funding for the organization's headquarters at 58 East 68th Street in New York City, a property known as the Pratt House. John Foster Dulles, the lawyer for Standard Oil and the board chairman of the Carnegie Foundation for International Peace, numbered among the CFR's founding fathers. In later life, John Foster Dulles would become Secretary of State under President Dwight D. Eisenhower, while his younger brother Allen, also a CFR founding member and Morgan lawyer, would become director of the CIA.[15] Another founding father was Paul Warburg, who was also the founding father of the Federal Reserve System.[16] Warburg now served as the Chairman of the International Acceptance Bank, which he

---

12   Perloff, *The Shadows of Power*, 5.

13   *Wikipedia*, s.v. "John W. Davis," last edited January 29, 2019, 02:35, https://en.wikipedia.org/wiki/John_W._Davis, accessed February 12, 2019.

14   Ron Chernow, *Titan: The Life of John D. Rockefeller, Sr.* (New York: Vintage Books, 2004), p. 605.

15   Ibid., p. 38.

16   "History of the Council on Foreign Relations," CFR website, n.d., http://www.cfr.org/about/history/cfr/appendix.html, accessed February 12, 2019.

had organized to promote the postwar reconstruction of Europe with the Rothschilds.[17]

A SINISTER ORGANIZATION

The members of the CFR met in private and under a cloak of secrecy to establish political and economic strategies and to groom individuals for powerful governmental positions. Like the Pilgrim Society, it was an elite organization, and the recruits came from the upper echelons of society so that it would eventually constitute the heart of the American Establishment.[18] The subversive nature of the CFR was revealed in 1957 by a congressional investigative committee as follows: "In the international field, foundations, and an interlock among some of them and certain intermediary organizations, have exercised a strong effect upon our foreign policy and upon public education in things international. This has been accomplished by vast propaganda, by supplying executives and advisers to government and by controlling much research in this area through the power of the purse. The net result of these combined efforts has been to promote 'internationalism' in a particular sense—a form directed toward 'world government' and a derogation of American 'nationalism.' The CFR has become in essence an agency of the United States Government [and its] productions are not objective but are directed overwhelmingly at promoting the globalist concept."[19]

This subversive purpose has been verified by *Foreign Affairs,* the Council's own publication, which has been called "the most influential periodical in print" by *Time* magazine.[20] In its inaugural issue

---

17   Mira Williams, *The History of Foreign Investments in the United States, 1914 to 1945* (Cambridge, MA: Harvard University Press, 2004), p. 719.

18   G. Vance Smith and Tom Gow, *Masters of Deception: The Rise of the Council on Foreign Relations* (Colorado Springs: First Freedom Society, 2012), pp. 5–6.

19   *Hearings Before the Special Committee to Investigate Tax-Exempt Foundations and Comparable Organizations,* House of Representatives, Eighty-Third Congress, Second Session on H. Res. 217, Part 1, pp. 1–943. (Washington, D.C.: Government Printing Office, 1954).

20   Advertisement in *Foreign Affairs,* Summer 1986.

(September 1922), the journal condemned "the dubious doctrines expressed by such phrases as "safety first" and "America first.""[21] In its second issue, Philip Kerr, a member of the British Round Table, declared: "Obviously there is going to be no peace or prosperity for mankind so long as it remains divided into fifty or sixty independent states. Equally obviously there is going to be no steady progress in civilization or self-government among the more backward peoples until some kind of international system is created which will put an end to the diplomatic struggles of every nation to make itself secure. The real problem today is that of world government."[22] This same insistence has been resounded *ad nauseum* in nearly every issue of *Foreign Affairs*. In "Reflections on Our National Purpose," an article published in the April 1972 issue, Kingman Brewster Jr., the U.S. Ambassador to Great Britain and president of Yale University, said: "Our national purpose should be to abolish American nationality and to take some risks in order to invite others to pool their sovereignty with ours."[23] Two years later, former deputy assistant Secretary of State Richard N. Gardner penned a piece called "The Hard Road to World Order" in which he wrote: "We are witnessing an outbreak of shortsighted nationalism that seems oblivious to the economic, political and moral implications of interdependence . . . The 'house of world order' will have to be built from the bottom up rather than from the top down." He went on to say: "An end run around national sovereignty, eroding it piece by piece, will accomplish much more than the old-fashioned frontal assault."[24]

---

21   Perloff, *The Shadows of Power*, p. 10.

22   Ibid., p. 11.

23   Kingman Brewster Jr., "Reflections on Our National Purpose," *Foreign Affairs,* April 1972, https://www.foreignaffairs.com/articles/united-states/1972-04-01/reflections-our-national-purpose, accessed February 2, 2019.

24   Richard N. Gardner, "The Hard Road to World Order," *Foreign Affairs*, April 1974, https://www.foreignaffairs.com/articles/1974-04-01/hard-road-world-order, accessed February 2, 2019.

THE STRANGLEHOLD

Proof of the stranglehold the CFR possesses over the federal government resides in the fact that by 2017, 20 Secretaries of State, 19 Secretaries of the Treasury, 15 Secretaries of Defense, and hundreds of other federal department heads have been CFR members, along with 21 of the 24 CIA Directors, and every chairman of the Federal Reserve since 1951. The name of Rex Tillerson, who was appointed Secretary of State by President Donald Trump, does not appear on the official CFR membership list. But the omission doesn't mean that Tillerson is not a member since he may have exercised his right to keep his name from the organization's public disclosures. What's more, Tillerson served as chairman and chief executive officer of ExxonMobil (the Rockefeller oil company) from 2006 to 2017, and ExxonMobil is a leading corporate member and sponsor of the CFR.[25] Similarly, Mike Pompeo, who replaced Tillerson as Trump's Secretary of State, is the only Secretary of State within the past 85 years without any known ties to the CFR.

THE ROCKEFELLERS TRIUMPHANT

By the time of the Great Depression, the Rockefellers gained control of a lion's share of the holdings of the House of Morgan. The success of this coup, which toppled the House of Morgan, was due to an alliance that the Rockefeller family formed with such burgeoning American financial establishments as Harriman Brown and Company (which included George Herbert Walker and Prescott Bush as partners), Lehman Brothers, and Goldman Sachs, which had managed to push Kuhn, Loeb & Company into the background.[26]

The harbinger of this revolution was the Rockefeller's successful takeover of the Morgans' flagship commercial bank, Chase National

---

25 "Rex Tillerson—Trump's Former Top Diplomat," *BBC News*, March 13, 2018, https://www.bbc.com/news/world-us-canada-38281954, accessed February 12, 2019.

26 Murray N. Rothbard, *The Case against the Fed* (Auburn, AL: Ludwig von Mises Institute, 2007), p. 130.

Bank of New York. After the 1929 crash, Winthrop W. Aldrich, son of Senator Nelson Aldrich and brother-in-law of John D. Rockefeller Jr., engineered a merger of his Rockefeller-controlled Equitable Trust Company into Chase Bank. From that point on, Aldrich engaged in a titanic struggle within Chase. By 1932, he managed to oust the Morgans' Chase CEO, Albert Wiggin, from office and take his place as the head of the gigantic financial firm. Chase has remained the financial headquarters of the House of Rockefeller.[27]

THE STUDY GROUPS

The family of John D. Rockefeller now possessed control of the Federal Reserve, which they could manipulate to further their vast empire. They also obtained absolute dominance over the CFR so that governmental policies would coincide with their interests. The policies were prepared by study groups within the CFR for implementation by the U.S. State Department. Regarding these groups, Admiral Chester Ward, a former CFR member, wrote: "Once the ruling members of the CFR have decided that the U.S. Government should adopt a particular policy, the very substantial research facilities of CFR are put to work to develop arguments, intellectual and emotional, to support the new policy, and to confound and discredit, intellectually and politically, any opposition."[28] Indeed, the studies generated by the council have resulted in the establishment of such international institutions as the United Nations, the World Bank, and the International Monetary Fund.

Financing for the study groups comes from the Rockefeller, Carnegie, and Ford foundations, which are governed by boards of directors that are interconnected. The board members of the Rockefeller Foundation often pop up as trustees of the Rockefeller, Carnegie, and Ford Foundations and vice versa. For example, CFR president John W. Davis served as a trustee for the Rockefeller and Carnegie foundations, while

---

27   Ibid.

28   Phyllis Schlafly and Chester Ward, *Kissinger on the Couch* (New Rochelle, NY: Arlington House, 1975), p. 151.

running for president in a campaign heavily funded by Kuhn, Loeb & Company, the bank in which Paul Warburg, the founder of the Federal Reserve, was a partner. By 1960, many of the trustees of America's three leading foundations were executives from Bechtel Construction, Chase Manhattan, Kimberly-Clark, Monsanto Chemical, and other leading international business and banking firms.[29] Twelve of the 15 Rockefeller Foundation trustees, 10 of the 15 Ford Foundation trustees, and 10 of the 14 Carnegie Foundation trustees were members of the CFR.[30]

A BIRTHDAY PARTY

On July 8, 1929, John D. Rockefeller celebrated his 87th birthday at the Casements, his home in Ormond Beach, Florida. He was surrounded by his daughters Alta and Edith; his son, John D. Rockefeller Jr.; and his grandchildren, including David, who would become the CEO of Chase Manhattan; Nelson, who would become the governor of New York and vice president of the United States; and Winthrop, who would become the governor of Arkansas. Fearful of public retribution for his exposed acts of piracy, John D. had built underground tunnels that led from his residence to the Ormond Beach Hotel and the home of his physician.[31] But the old man's fear of poverty that he had passed on to his progeny remained far stronger than his fear of physical violence.[32] For this reason, he had plotted one of his final crimes against humanity—an event that became known as "the Great Depression."

---

29   Daniel Estulin, *The True Story of the Bilderberg Group* (Waterville, OR: Trineday, 2009), p. 87.

30   Ibid.

31   Emily Blackwood, "The Tunnels: One Girl's Search for Something Worth Discovering," *Ormond Beach Observer*, January 18, 2014, https://www.ormondbeachobserver.com/article/tunnels-one-girls-search-something-worth-discovering, accessed February 12, 2019.

32   Emanuel M. Josephson, *The "Federal" Reserve Conspiracy and the Rockefellers: Their "Gold Corner"* (New York: Chedney Press, 1968), p. 70.

12

HARD TIMES

When everything was ready, the New York financiers started calling 24 hour broker call loans. This meant that the stock brokers and the customers had to dump their stock on the market in order to pay the loans. This naturally collapsed the stock market and brought a banking collapse all over the country because the banks not owned by the oligarchy were heavily involved in broker call claims at this time, and bank runs soon exhausted their coin and currency and they had to close. The Federal Reserve System would not come to their aid, although they were instructed under the law to maintain an elastic currency.

—WILLIAM BRYON, *THE UNITED STATES' UNRESOLVED MONETARY AND POLITICAL PROBLEMS*

AFTER WORLD WAR I, America had become the world's largest creditor nation. The money that flowed into America from the $8 billion in war loans granted to France, Great Britain, and Italy was used to fund U.S. business and industry and to provide loans to American workers. While Europe remained in a state of stagnancy, perpetuated by the devastation of property and loss of population caused by the war, cars, highways, bridges, manufacturing plants, hotels, theaters, and department stores were being built throughout America at an unprecedented rate. Unemployment dropped to less than 5 percent. Almost every home in the country had electricity. By 1920, the national income of the United States was greater than the combined incomes of Britain, France, Germany, Japan, Canada, and seventeen smaller countries.[1] Within the next five years, Ford, General Motors, and Chrysler emerged as the "Big Three" auto companies, and over 15 million cars were on the road.[2] By 1926, over 200,000 gas stations had cropped up throughout the United States, and the personal fortune of John D. Rockefeller, who became the world's first billionaire in 1916, had doubled.[3]

FINANCIAL IMPERIALISM

The Federal Reserve remained wedded to the Bank of England, and Montagu Norman, the governor of England's central bank, made regular trips to the United States for meetings with Benjamin Strong, the head of the New York Fed. In one of his visits, Norman addressed the United States Bankers Association and spoke in glowing terms about a great depression that would cause millions of Americans to lose their homes and jobs. He said that such an event would make people easier to govern by the "imperialism" of bankers. Norman told the crowd:

> Capital must protect itself in every possible way, both by combination and legislation. Debts must be collected, mortgages foreclosed as rapidly as possible. When, through the process of law, the common people lose their homes, they will become more docile and more easily governed through the strong arm of government applied by a

1   David Jarmal, "American History: Foreign Policy during the 1920s," *Masking of a Nation*, February 2, 2011, http://learningenglish.voanews.com/a/american-history-foreign-policy-during-the-1920s-115124654/116037.html, accessed February 12, 2019.

2   "Automobile History," *The History Channel*, April 26, 2010, https://www.history.com/topics/inventions/automobiles, accessed February 12, 2019.

3   Carl O'Donnell, "The Rockefellers: The Legacy of History's Richest Man," *Forbes*, July 11, 2014, https://www.forbes.com/sites/carlodonnell/2014/07/11/the-rockefellers-the-legacy-of-historys-richest-man/#5e387a823c26, accessed February 12, 2019.

central power of wealth under leading financiers. These truths are well known among our principal men, who are now engaged in forming an imperialism to govern the world. By dividing the voters through the political party system, we can get them to expend their energies in fighting for questions of no importance. It is, thus, by discrete action, we can ensure for ourselves that which has been so well planned and so successfully accomplished.[4]

The dutiful audience gave him a standing ovation, heeded his words, and proceeded to institute a banking procedure known as the "twenty-four hour call."

THE TWENTY-FOUR HOUR CALL

The "twenty-four hour call" enabled investors to purchase securities on extended credit from their bankers. This meant that if someone wanted to purchase $1,000 in stock, he only had to shell out $100 in cash. The loan for the remaining $900 was immediate and readily available from every national bank in the country. If the stock increased 10 percent in value, an investor could double his money.[5] In addition to enhancing one's financial portfolio, the easy money could be used to purchase homes, automobiles, and modern appliances, like self-contained refrigerators that required no ice.

To fuel the market, Andrew Mellon, the Secretary of the Treasury, proceeded to make more and more cuts to the tax rate so that Americans had more and more expendable income. For those who earned $5,000 or less, the rate fell from 15.9 percent in 1920 to 1.1 percent in 1928. Those who earned $10,000 or less saw their rate dwindled from 9.1 percent in 1920 to 2 percent in 1928. And those who earned $25,000 or less witnessed a drop in their taxable income from 16.6 percent in 1920

4   Montagu Norman, quoted in Stephen Mitford Goodson, *A History of Central Banking and the Enslavement of Mankind* (London: Black House, 2014), p. 92.

5   James Perloff, *The Shadows of Power: The Council on Foreign Relations and the American Decline* (Appleton, WI: Western Islands, 2005), p. 56.

to 7.1 percent in 1928.[6] Mellon had close ties to John D. Rockefeller, who had purchased his oil company at the turn of the century. Between 1923 and 1929, the Federal Reserve added helium to the financial balloon by expanding the money supply by 62 percent. This money was used to build up the stock market to dizzying heights.[7]

"INSTANT RICHES"

With credit money readily available to every Tom, Dick, and Harry, the mass media began to ballyhoo tales of the instant riches to be made in the stock market. According to Ferdinand Lundberg: "For profits to be made on these funds the public had to be induced to speculate, and it was so induced by misleading newspaper accounts, many of them bought and paid for by the brokers that operated the pools."[8]

THE DEPLETION OF GOLD

A savvy individual could have discerned that a depression was in the works by the fact that Chase National was transporting large quantities of gold outside the country. In 1928, more than $500 million in gold bars was shipped by the Rockefeller bank to financial firms in England and France.[9] Since the dollar remained bound to the gold standard, the depletion of the precious metal was accompanied by a curtailment in the money supply. Everything was ripe for an economic collapse of epic proportion. On February 6, 1929, Montagu Norman arrived in

6   Veronique de Rugy, "1920s Income Tax Cuts Sparked Economic Growth and Raised Federal Revenues," CATO Institute, March 4, 2003, https://www.cato.org/publications/commentary/1920s-income-tax-cuts-sparked-economic-growth-raised-federal-revenues, accessed February 12, 2019.

7   Gary Allen, *None Dare Call It Conspiracy* (San Diego, CA: Dauphin Publications, 1971), p. 53.

8   Ferdinand Lundberg, quoted in Gary Allen, "How a Group of International Bankers Engineered the 1929 Crash and the Great Depression," *Friends of the American Revolution*, February 11, 2008, https://21stcenturycicero.wordpress.com/2008/02/11/how-a-group-of-international-bankers-engineered-the-1929-crash-and-the-great-depression/, accessed February 12, 2019.

9   Emanuel M. Josephson, *The "Federal" Reserve Conspiracy and Rockefellers: Their "Gold Corner"* (New York: Chedney Press, 1968), pp. 89–90.

Washington to confer with Treasury Secretary Mellon. Immediately after the mysterious meeting, the Federal Reserve Board began to cut the money supply and to raise the interest rate.[10]

EXCREMENT HITS THE FAN

The collapse began when the commercial banks no longer could receive a flow of greenbacks from the Federal Reserve. Desperate for cash to continue their operations, the banks initiated the "call" on their loans on October 24, 1929. The millions of simple-minded blokes who had received the money so easily from their friendly neighborhood bankers were now obliged to come up with full repayment in twenty-four hours.

Americans who believed that they were very rich suddenly discovered that they were very poor. By the end of 1929, five thousand banks had collapsed, and six million Americans had lost their jobs. President Herbert Hoover could only sit back and watch as the financial devastation took place. He possessed no control over the Federal Reserve and was unable to force it to adopt the necessary rescue measures.

---

10   Eustace Mullens, *The Secrets of the Federal Reserve* (Staunton, VA: Bankers Research Institute, 1983), p. 143.

The proverbial excrement hit the fan. Throughout the country, the stampede to sell stocks, insurance policies, and businesses began. The stock market crashed; banks throughout the country ran out of cash and closed up shop; and the Fed refused to come to the rescue with a printing of fresh currency.[11] On Tuesday, October 29th, the exchanges were crushed by a new avalanche of selling. For many securities, there were no buyers at all. By the end of the day, over 16 million shares had been dumped, in most cases, at any price that was offered. Millions of investors were wiped out. Within several months of continual decline, $40 billion of wealth had vanished. Americans who believed that they were very rich suddenly discovered that they were very poor.[12] By the end of 1929, five thousand banks had collapsed, and six million Americans had lost their jobs.[13] President Herbert Hoover could only sit back and watch as the financial devastation took place. He possessed no control over the Federal Reserve and was unable to force it to adopt the necessary rescue measures.[14]

THE VULTURES DESCEND

The crash may have devastated the average American investor but not the Rockefellers. They were either out of the market or had sold "short" so that they earned enormous profits as the Dow Jones plummeted. Following the crash, they swooped down on Wall Street like vultures to feast on ravaged companies. Shares that once sold for a dollar now could be bought for a few pennies.[15] The worth of John P. Kennedy, a smuggler and bootlegger, increased from $4 million to $100 million. Similarly, while businesses went belly-up throughout the country,

---

11   Allen, *None Dare Call It Conspiracy*, pp. 54–55.

12   G. Edward Griffin, *The Creature from Jekyll Island: A Second Look at the Federal Reserve* (New York: American Media, 2008), p. 499.

13   "1930s High Society," *History Detectives*, PBS, n.d., http://www.pbs.org/opb/historydetectives/feature/1930s-high-society/, accessed February 12, 2019.

14   Josephson, *The "Federal" Reserve Conspiracy*, p. 100.

15   Perloff, *The Shadows of Power*, p. 57.

the Rockefeller concerns, including Standard Oil and International Harvester, experienced enormous expansion.[16]

Economic collapse set the Rockefellers up to gain monopolistic control over every necessity of life and source of energy—oil, gas, coal, water, wind, and atomic energy. They had even succeeded in making the sun, the greatest of all sources of power, render them tribute.[17] In addition, the family began to gobble up real estate in major American cities. By 1935, they owned 3 percent of the property in New York City.[18] They became the largest holders of government securities, including the NYC and State of New York bonds, and public utility companies, including Consolidated Edison, the Manhattan Elevated Railroad Company, the Manhattan Transit Corporation, the Interborough Rapid Transit Company (NYC), the United Gas Improvement Company, Public Service of New Jersey, People's Gas of Chicago, Mountain Fuel Supply, Colorado Interstate Gas Company, Mutual Fuel Gas Company, Chicago Railways Company, the Philadelphia Company, et al.[19] They gained control not only of America's railroads, leading industrial corporations, and mines, but also of the nation's major food suppliers, including Armour and Company (one of the five leading firms in the meatpacking industry), the Corn Products Refining Company (which supplied the raw material for cornstarch and corn oil), Sheffield Farms (which represented the largest dairy in the world), Borden's (which was the world's largest producer of dairy and pasta products), and Monsanto, an agrochemical and agricultural biotech company that developed genetically modified organisms (GMOs).[20]

16   William P. Hoar, *Architects of Conspiracy: An Intriguing History* (Appleton, WI: Western Islands, 1985), p. 190.

17   Emanuel M. Josephson, *Rockefeller "Internationalist:" The Man Who Misrules the World* (New York: Chedney Press, 1952), p. 20.

18   Ibid., p. 25.

19   Ibid., p. 37.

20   Ibid, p. 26. See also Gary Allen, *The Rockefeller File* (Seal Beach, CA; '76 Press, 1976), p. 34.

THE WORLD AND ITS RICHES

The decisions of the corporate executives within the board rooms of the Rockefeller empire were made solely on the basis of self-perpetuation and expansion. No considerations of altruism, let alone national well-being, were superseded by profit. The end was gain, and the purpose of the holdings could only be fulfilled when the Rockefeller dynasty gained sole possession of the world's wealth.

THE PROTOCOLS OF ZION

With the gold that the Rockefellers exported to England and France, they purchased 69,020 shares of the Royal Dutch Shell Oil Company from the Rothschilds and 50 percent of the Nobel Oil Works.[21] In 1893, John D. had tried to forge a union with the Rothschilds and Nobel for control of the Russian oil fields, but that effort was thwarted by Sir Henry Deterding, the Royal Dutch director, who knew that Rockefeller was adept at backstabbing. The setback forced Rockefeller to adopt other measures. In *The "Federal" Reserve Conspiracy and Rockefellers,* Emanuel M. Josephson writes:

> The situation left only two methods open to the Rockefeller interests to gaining access to the Russian oilfields, other than the prohibitively expensive and futile attempt to purchase control of the Royal Dutch in the open stock market. Their first approach was to create a breach between the Czarist regime and the Royal Dutch management. The second was to oust the Czarist regime by financing, with the funds of American taxpayers derived through their tax-exempt foundations, a revolution in Russia. The [Rockefeller] conspirators adopted both approaches. For the purpose of attempting to create a breach between the Czarist regime and the Royal Dutch Co., there was effected the publication in Russia, and widespread distribution,

---

21 Josephson, *Rockefeller "Internationalist,"* p. 25.

under the name of a Captain Linus, a notorious forged document labeled The Protocols of Zion.[22]

The Protocols of Zion purportedly represents the minutes of 24 meetings held secretly by Jewish bankers and financiers who sought to control the world. The 12th Protocol says: "Literature and journalism are two of the most important educative forces, and therefore our government will become proprietor of the majority of the journals . . . . It will put us in possession of a tremendous influence upon the public mind." In accordance with the 17th Protocol, the Church will be annihilated "so that only years divide us from the moment of the complete wrecking of that Christian religion." The final takeover of the world, the 21st Protocol, will be achieved financially. The 21st Protocol states, "We shall replace the money markets by grandiose government credit institutions, the object of which will be to fix the price of industrial values in accordance with government views . . . . You may imagine for yourselves what immense power we shall thereby secure for ourselves."[23]

WAVES OF ANTI-SEMITISM
The work makes the Jews responsible for present and past disasters from the downfall of Christian monarchies to the French Revolution and the advancement of liberal and bourgeois ideas. The plotters are portrayed as poisonous snakes, spiders weaving their webs, and wolves ready to devour Christian sheep. The final protocols describe the future reign of the Jews, including the installation of a "King of the Jews," who will be "the real Pope of the Universe and the patriarch of an international Church."[24]

22   Emanuel M. Josephson, *The "Federal" Reserve and Conspiracy*, p. 72.

23   Brigitte Sion, "Protocols of the Elders of Zion: The Lie That Will Not Die," *My Jewish Learning*, n.d., https://www.myjewishlearning.com/article/protocols-of-the-elders-of-zion/, accessed February 12, 2019.

24   Ibid.

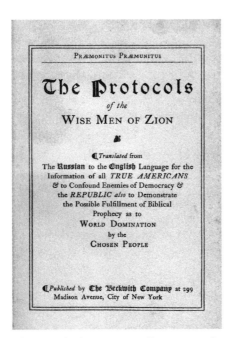

PRÆMONITUS PRÆMUNITUS

The Protocols
of the
WISE MEN OF ZION

❧

¶ *Translated* from
The **Russian** to the **English** Language for the
Information of all *TRUE AMERICANS*
& to Confound Enemies of Democracy &
the *REPUBLIC also* to Demonstrate
the Possible Fulfillment of Biblical
Prophecy as to
WORLD DOMINATION
by the
CHOSEN PEOPLE

¶ *Published* by **The Beckwith Company** at 299
Madison Avenue, City of New York

The Protocols of Zion purportedly represents the minutes of 24 meetings held secretly by Jewish bankers and financiers who sought to control the world. *The Protocols* appeared in Russia shortly after the Rothschilds and the Nobels joined forces to gain control of the Baku oil fields in 1886. The preparation and dissemination of the work, according to Josephson, was arranged by Rockefeller. The effects were immediate and devastating. A wave of anti-Semitism swept throughout Russia.

The Protocols appeared in Russia shortly after the Rothschilds and the Nobels joined forces to gain control of the Baku oil fields in 1886.[25] The preparation and dissemination of the work, according to Josephson, was arranged by Rockefeller.[26] The effects were immediate and devastating. A wave of anti-Semitism swept throughout Russia. Pogroms were initiated in 1903 and 1905, which resulted in the death of 2,500 Jews.[27] The Rothschilds, who were an integral part of the money cartel, were singled out for hatred, and their ties to the tsarist regime became greatly weakened. In the United States, Henry Ford was duped by agents of the Rockefellers into promulgating *The Protocols* within the United States.[28]

25   Geoffrey Jones, *Multinationals and Global Capitalism: From the Nineteenth to the Twenty-First Century* (New York: Oxford University Press, 2005), p. 48.

26   Josephson, *The "Federal" Reserve Conspiracy*, p. 72.

27   Robert Weinberg, *The Revolution in 1905 in Odessa: Blood on the Steps* (Bloomington, IN.: Indiana University Press, 1993), p. 164.

28   Josephson, *The "Federal" Reserve Conspiracy*, p. 92.

BANKROLLING BOLSHEVIKS

The Rockefellers continued to puppeteer developments in Russia by helping to bankroll the Russian Revolution. In *The Surrender of an Empire,* British historian Nesta Webster writes:

> Had the Bolsheviks been, as they are frequently represented, a mere gang of revolutionaries out to destroy property, first in Russia, and then in every other country, they would naturally have found themselves up against organized resistance by the owners of property all over the world, and the Moscow blaze would have been extinguished. It was only owing to the powerful influences behind them that a minority party was able to seize the reins of power and, having seized them, to retain their hold of them up to the present day.[29]

Similarly, Antony C. Sutton, a research fellow for the Hoover Institution for War, Revolution, and Peace, writes in his introduction to *Wall Street and the Bolshevik Revolution:*

> In brief, this is a story of the Bolshevik Revolution and its aftermath, but a story that departs from the usual conceptual straitjacket approach of capitalists versus Communists. Our story postulates a partnership between international monopoly capitalism and international revolutionary socialism for their mutual benefit. The final human cost of this alliance has fallen upon the shoulders of the individual Russian and the individual American. Entrepreneurship has been brought into disrepute and the world has been propelled toward inefficient socialist planning as a result of these monopoly maneuverings in the world of politics and internationalism.[30]

---

29 Nesta H. Webster, *The Surrender of an Empire* (London: Bowell Publishing, 1933), p. 74.

30 Antony C. Sutton, *Wall Street and the Bolshevik Revolution: A Remarkable True Story of the American Capitalists Who Financed the Russian Revolution* (London: Clairview, 2011), p. 19.

THE LURE OF COMMUNISM

After the Bolsheviks seized power, Standard Oil purchased the Russian oil fields, set up a refinery for the Soviets, and made arrangements to market the refined oil in Europe. The Rothschilds had been routed. Royal Dutch Shell lost their grip on the Russian oil fields. Chase Bank set up the American-Russian Chamber of Commerce, financed the raw material exports of the Soviets, and sold Russian bonds to American investors.[31] The tentacles of the Rockefeller oil empire now extended throughout Europe to Russia and China. The family had come to control most of the wealth of the world. No other family, including the Rothschilds of Europe and the Mitsuis of Japan, possessed half their riches.[32]

The Rockefellers continued to puppeteer developments in Russia by helping to bankroll the Russian Revolution. After the Bolsheviks seized power, Standard Oil purchased the Russian oil fields, set up a refinery for the Soviets, and made arrangements to market the refined oil in Europe. The Rothschilds had been routed.

---

31   Perloff, *The Shadows of Power*, p. 43.

32   Josephson, *The "Federal" Reserve Conspiracy*, p. 27.

The USSR proved to be a great place for the Rockefellers to conduct their business. They could control the country's oil production and withdraw their profits from Swiss bank accounts. There existed no way for a federal agency in the United States or elsewhere in the Western world to investigate their earnings. This arrangement allowed American money and technology to flow into the hands of Joseph Stalin, the Soviet premier, who used it to create "the big red war machine" that would represent the greatest existential threat to the United States.[33]

The Rockefellers became completely enamored with Communism. It represented a monopolist system of government, a government over which enterprising industrialists and bankers could gain control through loans to the government, the manipulation of the country's centralized banking system, and of course, bribes.[34] This realization eventually prompted the Rockefellers to provide support and funding to further the spread of socialism in the United States.

33 Allen, *The Rockefeller File*, p. 104.

34 Perloff, *The Shadows of Power*, p. 44.

13

THE THEFT

So unpopular was the [gold] confiscation order that no government official took credit for it. No congressman admitted to signing the bill into law. At the signing ceremony President Roosevelt stated that he was not the author of the bill, and even claimed that had not even read it. The secretary of the treasury said he had not read the bill either. Regardless, the secretary was quoted as saying, "It's what the experts wanted." Across the small towns of America, most people didn't trust the order. People were torn between keeping their hard-earned wealth, and obeying the government. Those that did turn in their gold were paid the official price for it, which was 20.66 USD per ounce. As of this writing, the price of one ounce of gold trades for 1,264.59 USD.

—STACK JONES, "THE BANKING SWINDLE," JANUARY 1, 2018

AT THE START OF THE GREAT DEPRESSION, the golden boy of the Rockefeller clan remained in the wings to assume his place within the Oval Office. Franklin Delano Roosevelt (FDR) had emerged from the bowels of the Council on Foreign Relations. His family had been involved in New York banking for decades and, thereby, developed a close relationship with the Rockefeller family. Franklin's uncle, Frederick Delano, had been the Vice Chairman of the original Federal Reserve board.[1]

---

1   "Frederic A. Delano," Federal Reserve History, n.d., https://www.federalreservehistory.org/people/frederic_a_delano, accessed February 13, 2019.

During the 1920s, FDR pursued a career on Wall Street, working as a bond writer and the organizer of a host of speculative ventures.[2] In 1928, John Raskob, vice president of both DuPont and General Motors, became the chairman of the Democratic National Committee and asked Roosevelt to accept the party's New York gubernatorial nomination. FDR declined, citing his debt of $250,000 for the polio resort that he had established at Warm Springs, Georgia. Raskob, on behalf of the Rockefellers and their associates, presented the reluctant candidate with a check to cancel out the debt, and FDR agreed to run, becoming, on January 1, 1929, New York's 44th governor.[3]

THE CARTEL GOES TO WASHINGTON

After the stock market crash, FDR rode an open road to the White House. Every twist and turn of the journey was maneuvered by Bernard Baruch. Baruch was not only a Wall Street broker but also a political broker, who had almost single-handedly brought Woodrow Wilson to the White House. During World War I, he had served as the head of the Wall Industries Board, a position that allowed him to make, along with the Rockefellers, $200 million

At the start of the Great Depression, the golden boy of the Rockefeller clan remained in the wings to assume his place within the Oval Office. Franklin Delano Roosevelt (FDR) had emerged from the bowels of the Council on Foreign Relations. "FDR-April-11-1945" by FDR Presidential Library & Museum is licensed under CC BY 2.0

---

2   James Perloff, *The Shadows of Power: The Council on Foreign Relations and the American Decline* (Appleton, WI: Western Islands, 2005), p 54.

3   Ibid.

from the war effort.[4] After the war, Baruch and the Rockefellers came up with the cash to establish the Council on Foreign Relations.[5] Regarding FDR's campaign, Hugh Johnson, one of Baruch's associates, said: "Every time a crisis came, B. M. [Bernard Baruch] either gave the necessary money or went out and got it."[6]

Once ensconced within the Oval Office, FDR surrounded himself with Rockefeller and CFR lackeys. Edward Stettinius, former board chairman of U.S. Steel, was named secretary of state, and Sumner Welles, a member of the Roosevelt family, became the deputy secretary of state. Norman Davis, president of the CFR, was selected as chairman of the Advisory Committee on Problems of Foreign Relations; and James Warburg, son of Paul Warburg, rose to prominence as a leading member of the president's brain trust.[7] And Nelson Rockefeller, newly graduated from Dartmouth College, became FDR's principal advisor.[8]

THE AGRICULTURAL ADJUSTMENT ACT

Under Rockefeller's insistence, Roosevelt pressured Congress to pass the Agricultural Adjustment Act (AAA), which wielded absolute control over the nation's farms. While millions of Americans faced starvation, the AAA decreed the destruction of crops to prevent overproduction and to stabilize falling prices. It also ordered the slaughter of six million pigs to prevent the cost of pork, lard, and soap from plummeting. In an effort to justify these actions, FDR took to the airwaves and said: "The ungoverned push for rugged individualism perhaps had an economic justification in the days when we had all the West to surge upon and

---

4   Ibid., p. 29.

5   Gary Allen, *None Dare Call It Conspiracy* (San Diego, CA: Dauphin Publications, 2013), pp. 83–84.

6   Hugh Johnson, *The Blue Eagle from Egg to Earth* (New York: Doubleday, 1935), p. 141.

7   Perloff, *The Shadows of Power*, p. 60.

8   Emanuel M. Josephson, *The "Federal" Reserve Conspiracy and Rockefellers: Their "Gold Corner"* (New York: Chedney Press, 1968), p. 95.

conquer; but this country has filled up now, and grown up. There are no more Indians to fight . . . . We must blaze new trails in the direction of a controlled economy, common sense, and social decency."[9]

The AAA now set a high price for crops, prompting farmers to expand their operations. Such expansion demanded that farmers obtain loans from commercial banks, many of which were now firmly united to the Rockefeller empire. They were also compelled to purchase seed, fertilizers, and other agrochemical goods from companies such as Monsanto, the Rockefeller-owned green giant that was gaining control of the America's agricultural industry. In addition, the expansion necessitated the purchase of new farm equipment from Rockefeller's International Harvester, the country's leading manufacturer of tractors, balers, cultivators, combines, crop dusters, manure spreaders, feed grinders, planters, plows, hay rakes, and milking machines. By liens and loans, farms throughout the country rapidly came under control of the Rockefellers, who now possessed the almighty power to raise or lower the price of produce.[10]

THE NATIONAL INDUSTRIAL RECOVERY ACT

On June 6, 1933, Congress ratified the National Industrial Recovery Act (NIRA), which represented the heart of the New Deal, and the ultimate attempt of the Rockefellers to exploit the Depression for their own purpose. The legislation had been written by Walter C. Teagle, president of Standard Oil of New Jersey, and Gerard Swope, president of Morgan-owned General Electric and a prominent member of the CFR.[11] The NIRA mandated the regulation of every aspect of American business in a manner that paralleled the formation of the fascist government in Italy. Every industry was to operate in collaboration with the

---

9   FDR's "Declaration of Interdependence," quoted in Stone and Kuznick, *The Concise Untold History of the United States*, p. 38.

10   Ibid., p. 107.

11   G. Vance Smith and Tom Gow, *Masters of Deception: The Rise of the Council on Foreign Relations* (Colorado Springs, CO: Freedom First Society, 2012), p. 49.

federal government in setting prices, wages, quantity of product, and working conditions. Under this system, the companies with the most employees had the most clout in determining policy. In the iron and steel industry, for example, Morgan's U.S. Steel possessed 511 votes, Allegheny Steel 17 votes, and Bethlehem Steel 16 votes. Giant corporations now possessed the ability to impose production, salary, and price standards that would drive their competition out of business. They could license producers, admit or bar newcomers from the industry, and even specify what equipment must be used in production.[12] In the iron and steel industry alone, there were more than 60 complaints against the oppressive new standards in the first months of 1933.[13] By the end of the year, the Compliance Division of the National Recovery Administration became swamped by a backlog of some 10,000 violation complaints.[14]

KILLING COMPETITION

Monopolies were now supported and sustained by federal mandate. Regulations ran amuck. The agency approved 557 basic and 189 supplemental industry codes in two years. Between 4,000 and 5,000 business practices were prohibited, some 3,000 administrative orders were promulgated in documents of over 10,000 pages, and tens of thousands of legal opinions were upheld and enforced by NRA officials.[15]

In his memoirs, Herbert Hoover maintained that Wall Street had attempted to pressure him into implementing the NIRA while he was still behind the desk in the Oval Office. He wrote:

---

12   Emanuel M. Josephson, *Rockefeller "Internationalist:" The Man Who Misrules the World* (New York: Chedney Press, 1952), p. 366.

13   Perloff, *The Shadows of Power*, p. 59.

14   Peter H. Irons, *The New Deal Lawyers* (Princeton, NJ: Princeton University Press, 1993), p. 36.

15   Gary Dean Best, *Pride, Prejudice, and Politics: Roosevelt Versus Recovery, 1933–1938* (New York: Praeger, 1991), p. 114.

Among the early Roosevelt fascist measures was the National Industrial Recovery Act (NIRA) of June 16, 1933. . . . These ideas were first suggested by Gerald Swope (of the General Electric Company) . . . [and] the United States Chamber of Commerce. During the campaign of 1932, Henry I. Harriman, president of that body, urged that I agree to support these proposals, informing me that Mr. Roosevelt had agreed to do so. I tried to show him that this stuff was pure fascism; that it was a remaking of Mussolini's "corporate state" and refused to agree to any of it. He informed me that in view of my attitude, the business world would support Roosevelt with money and influence. That for the most part proved true.[16]

CODE ENFORCEMENT

To enforce the regulations, the NIRA employed its own police force. In the garment district of New York, the code enforcers roamed through the area like storm troopers. They entered factories, lined up workers, and subjected them to interrogation. They expelled the factory owners from their own establishments to examine their books and records. Since night work was forbidden, the code enforcers battered down the doors of several factories with axes, looking for workers who were committing the crime of

In his memoirs, Herbert Hoover maintained that Wall Street had attempted to pressure him into implementing the NIRA while he was still behind the desk in the Oval Office.

16 Herbert Hoover, *Memoirs of Herbert Hoover, 1929–1941: The Great Depression* (New York: Macmillan, 1952), p. 420.

sewing a pair of pants after the mandated closing hour.[17]

The fascistic policy of the NIRA was crystallized in the case of Jack Magid, a New Jersey tailor. Magid pressed a suit for 35 cents, five cents less than the Tailor Code rate. For this offense, the tailor was arrested, convicted, fined $500, and sent to prison. The case created a public uproar. A judge hastily summoned Magid from his jail cell, remitted his sentence and fine, and offered to give the offender his own pants to press.[18]

ROOSEVELT'S REVENGE

On May 27, 1935, the Supreme Court ruled that the NIRA violated the borders of the U.S. Constitution. "Extraordinary conditions may call for extraordinary remedies," the court decreed, "but the argument necessarily stops short of an attempt to justify action which lies outside the sphere of constitutional authority. Extraordinary conditions do not create or enlarge constitutional power." The ruling may have stayed the transformation of America into a fascist state, but it failed to prevent Roosevelt and his Wall Street backers from creating an occult economy.

Roosevelt retaliated by sending a bill to Congress that would enable him to appoint as many as six additional Supreme Court justices. But eventually, this assault on the checks and balances of power proved to be too much for the president's friends on Capitol Hill to swallow, and the "court-packing plan" met with rejection. Former Chief Justice William Rehnquist later observed: "President Roosevelt lost this battle in Congress, but he eventually won the war to change the judicial philosophy of the Supreme Court. He won it the way our Constitution envisions such wars being won—by the gradual process of changing the

---

17   John Thomas Flynn, *The Roosevelt Myth* (Auburn, AL: Ludwig von Mises Institute, 2008), p. 46.

18   Ibid., p. 45.

federal judiciary through the appointment process."[19] But the damage had already been done. The holdings of the money cartel had been fortified, and hundreds of their competitors had been driven out of business.

THE GOLD BAN

On March 11, 1933, FDR issued an executive order forbidding gold payments by banks. Treasury Secretary Henry Morgenthau Jr., the son of a CFR founding member, said that the measure was aimed at those who horded quantities of gold and thereby hindered the Government's plans for a restoration of public confidence.[20] The order backfired. Thousands of Americans, fearful that their paper money was becoming worthless, withdrew their savings from banks to purchase gold from foreign and domestic markets. On April 5, 1933, Roosevelt responded to the mounting banking crisis by ordering all American citizens to surrender their gold to the government. No one in America was now allowed to own more than $100 in gold coins.[21] Roosevelt assured the country: "The order is limited to the period of the emergency." But the ban of owning gold remained on the books until 1974.

A FINGER ON THE GOLD

Nine months later, Executive Order 6102 became law: the Gold Reserve Act of 1934. The gold began to pour into the coffers of the Federal Reserve Bank in Washington, D.C. Guards, armed with machine guns, oversaw the transportation of gold bullion and coins from national and state banks throughout the country. "I am keeping my finger on the

---

19   David G. Savage, "Rehnquist Sees Threat to Judiciary," *Los Angeles Times*, January 1, 2005, http://articles.latimes.com/2005/jan/01/nation/na-scotus1, accessed February 13, 2019.

20   Gustav Cassell, *The Downfall of the Gold Standard* (New York: Augustus Kelly, 1966), pp. 118–19.

21   Barry J. Eichengreen, *Gold Fetters: The Gold Standard and the Great Depression* (New York: Oxford University Press, 1992), p. 321.

Nine months later, Executive Order 6102 became law: the Gold Reserve Act of 1934. The gold began to pour into the coffers of the Federal Reserve Bank in Washington, D.C. Guards, armed with machine guns, oversaw the transportation of gold bullion and coins from national and state banks throughout the country.

gold," Roosevelt announced to the press, and he did.[22] The gold that was confiscated and locked within the vaults of the Fed was never returned to the American people.

The legislators who voted for the Gold Reserve Act were told that the increased amount of the precious metal would permit the Federal Reserve to produce enough fiat money to end the Depression. They were hoodwinked into believing that the fractional reserve system mandated a new issuance of currency that must be backed by a "reserve" of 10 percent of its worth. And they were totally unaware that Roosevelt, upon the advice of his closest advisor, was planning to do away with the gold standard.

---

22   Eric Rauchway, "How Franklin Roosevelt Secretly Ended the Gold Standard," *Bloomberg*, March 21, 2013, https://www.bloomberg.com/view/articles/2013-03-21/how-franklin-roosevelt-secretly-ended-the-gold-standard, accessed February 13, 2019.

CITIZENS BECOME CRIMINALS

The federal mandate implied that government was the rightful owner of all the gold in the nation and that no American had a right to possess the precious metal. Roosevelt branded all those who did not turn over their gold as "hoarders." He defined *hoarding* as "the withdrawal and withholding of gold coin, gold bullion or gold certificates from the recognized and customary channels of trade."[23] Those who refused to comply with this order faced 10 years in prison and a fine of $10,000. Those who complied with the order received $20.66 per ounce for their gold.[24] Citizens had accepted a paper currency based on the government's pledge to redeem it in gold at $20.66 per ounce; then, when Roosevelt decided to default on that pledge, he also felt obliged to turn all citizens holding gold into criminals. Scores of Americans were now rounded up, fined, and sent to the slammer for having a fistful of gold dollars.[25]

FOREIGN GOLD

Foreigners also had gold confiscated and were forced to accept paper money as payment. The Uebersee Finanz-Korporation, a Swiss banking company, had $1,250,000 in gold coins for business use, which it entrusted to an American firm for safekeeping. In 1934, the Uebersee Finanz officials were shocked to find that their gold was confiscated by the U.S. government. They made appeals, but the appeals were denied. The officials were told that they were only entitled to paper money but not their gold coins. The Swiss company would have lost 40 percent of their gold's value if they tried to buy the same amount of gold with the

23   *The Public Papers and Addresses of Franklin Roosevelt* (New York: Random House, 1938), p. 112.

24   Stack Jones, "The Banking Swindle" from "An Essay on the History of Banking," January 1, 2018, https://criminalbankingmonopoly.wordpress.com/, accessed February 13, 2019.

25   "Bootleg Gold Ring Smashed in California," *Evening Independent,* April 13, 1939, https://news .google.com/newspapers?id=gupPAAAAIBAJ&sjid=klQDAAAAIBAJ&pg=5059,3562795&dq=13 +men+fall+into+trap+of+secret+service+agents+in+four+cities&hl=en, accessed February 13, 2019.

paper money that they received in exchange for their confiscated coins.[26]

Roosevelt stated that the ban on private ownership of the precious metal "was the first step also to that complete control of all monetary gold in the United States, which was essential in order to give the Government that element of freedom of action which was necessary as the very basis of its monetary goal and objective."[27] The Fed now began to churn out cash at an unprecedented level. The dollar lost 93 percent of its purchasing power, while the value of an ounce of gold rose to $35.[28]

A CONGRESSMAN'S OUTCRY

In 1933, Representative Louis T. McFadden of Pennsylvania took to the floor of Congress to denounce FDR's action as follows:

> Roosevelt seized the gold value of forty billions or more of bank deposits in the United States banks. Those deposits were deposits of gold values. By his action he has rendered them payable to the depositors in paper only, if payable at all, and the paper money he proposes to pay out to bank depositors and to the people generally in lieu of their hard earned gold values in itself, and being based on nothing into which the people can convert it the said paper money is of negligible value altogether. . . .
>
> The people of the U.S. are now using unredeemable paper slips for money. The Treasury cannot redeem that paper in gold or silver. The gold and silver of the Treasury has unlawfully been given to the corrupt and dishonest Fed. And the Administration has since had the effrontery to raid the country for more gold for the private interests by telling our patriotic citizens that their gold is needed to protect the currency.

---

26 "Ubersee Finanz Korporation, etc. v. Rosen," Circuit Court of Appeals, Second Circuit, April 6, 1936.

27 Franklin Roosevelt, quoted in Benjamin Anderson, *Economics and Public Welfare* (Indianapolis: Liberty Fund Press, 1949), p. 314.

28 James Bovard, "Money: The Great Gold Robbery," *Foundation for Economic Education*, June 1, 1999, https://fee.org/articles/money-the-great-gold-robbery/, accessed February 13, 2019.

It is not being used to protect the currency! It is being used to protect the corrupt and dishonest Fed. "The directors of these institutions have committed criminal offense against the United States Government, including the offense of making false entries on their books, and the still more serious offense of unlawfully abstracting funds from the United States Treasury!" Roosevelt's gold raid is intended to help them out of the pit they dug for themselves when they gambled away the wealth and savings of the American people.[29]

In the wake of making these remarks, McFadden experienced two attempts on his life. The first came in the form of two gunmen who fired at the congressman, after he alighted from a cab in front of a leading hotel in the nation's capital. The shots missed him. The second occurred when McFadden ingested food that had been poisoned at a Washington political gathering. His life was saved by a physician friend, who procured a stomach pump and administered emergency treatment.[30] The rescue, however, failed to save the country from its inevitable fate. In 1936, McFadden was voted out of office.

THE MYSTERY OF THE MISSING GOLD

The gold did not remain within the vaults of Fort Knox, a military facility constructed by FDR to house it. Tons of it were reportedly shipped to Basel, Switzerland, for the creation of the Bank for International Settlements (BIS). This monstrous facility was to serve as the central bank of all central banks as a Rockefeller-controlled entity that would oversee the economies of countries throughout the world. Additional tons were sold at rock-bottom prices to foreign bank and businesses of the money cartel.[31]

---

29 "Congressman McFadden on the Federal Reserve Corporation," Remarks in Congress, 1934, http://home.hiwaay.net/~becraft/mcfadden.html, accessed February 13, 2019.

30 Robert Edward Edmondson's account of the two assassination attempts in "Impeachment of the Federal Reserve," *Forbidden History*, October 27, 2015, http://batr.org/forbidden/102715.html, accessed February 13, 2019.

31 Ibid.

In 1974, when all the gold was gone from Fort Knox, President Richard Nixon repealed the Gold Act of 1934, making it possible for Americans to purchase gold again. As a result, gold prices soared to new heights, and the value of the bullion of the BIS and the money cartel became virtually incalculable. As soon as Nixon issued the repeal, Louise Boyer, the longtime personal secretary of Nelson Rockefeller, penned an article for the *National Tattler*, stating that the Rockefellers had instrumented the heist and had sold much of the gold to their foreign counterparts. Three days after the article appeared, Ms. Boyer mysteriously fell to her death from the 10th floor of her New York City apartment.[32]

The death of Boyer prompted Ed Durell, a wealthy Ohio industrialist, to launch a one-man campaign to solve the mystery of the missing gold. He sent thousands of letters to government officials, demanding to know how much gold remained at Fort Knox. In response to one of his letters, Edith Roosevelt the granddaughter of President Roosevelt wrote, "Allegations of missing gold from our Fort Knox vaults are being widely discussed in European financial circles. But what is puzzling is that the Administration is not hastening to demonstrate conclusively that there is no cause for concern over our gold treasure, if indeed it is in a position to do so." [33] Durell went to his death without fulfilling his mission. And, as of this writing, no audit of the gold supposedly stored at Fort Knox has ever been conducted.

A PRESIDENTIAL PUPPET

After confiscating the gold, the Roosevelt Administration appeared to set the price of the precious metal at random. Every morning at nine o'clock, Henry Morgenthau, the Secretary of the Treasury; Jesse Jones, the head of the Financial Reconstruction Corporation;[34] and George

---

32   Ibid.

33   Edith Roosevelt, quoted in ibid.

34   The RFC was a federal agency established in 1932 to provide financial support to state and local governments, and loans to banks, railroads, mortgage companies, anted other businesses.

Warren, the country's leading economic advisor, would meet with FDR over his breakfast of soft-boiled eggs to determine the gold price for that day. They began at $31.36 an ounce. The next morning, this rate was hiked to $31.54, then $31.76 and $31.82. It deemed as though they were acting at random. The morning exercise only served to push the price a little higher than the day before. On November 3, 1933, Roosevelt suggested that the cost of an ounce of gold should be raised 21 cents. When the others asked why, the president explained that it was a lucky number, three times seven.[35]

But the pricing was neither arbitrary not capricious. Roosevelt, throughout his years in the Oval Office, remained manipulated by the money trust. In *FDR: My Exploited Father-in-Law*, Curtis Dall, a syndicate manager for Lehman Brothers who married Anna Eleanor Roosevelt, wrote:

> For a long time I felt that FDR had developed many thoughts and ideas that were his own to benefit this country, the United States. But, he didn't. Most of his thoughts, his political ammunition, as it were, were carefully manufactured for him in advanced by the Council on Foreign Relations–One World Money group. Brilliantly, with great gusto, like a fine piece of artillery, he exploded that prepared "ammunition" in the middle of an unsuspecting target, the American people, and thus paid off and returned his internationalist political support.[36]

"Roosevelt," as Liaquat Ahamed confirmed in *Lords of Finance*, "did not even pretend to grasp the subtleties of international finance."[37] He

---

35 Liaquat Ahamed, *Lords of Finance: The Bankers Who Broke the World* (New York: Penguin Books, 2009), p. 472.

36 Curtis B. Dall, *FDR: My Exploited Father-in-Law* (Washington, D.C.: Action Associates, 1970), p. 67.

37 Ahamed, *Lords of Finance*, p. 458.

received direction, in part, from James Warburg, who served as FDR's chief financial advisor. The son of the founder of The Fed, Warburg would later tell a U.S. Senate subcommittee: "We shall have a one world government, whether we like it or not. The question is only whether world government will be achieved by consent or conquest."[38]

"THE END OF WESTERN CIVILIZATION"

Under the direction of Warburg, Acheson, Nelson Rockefeller, and other prominent members of the Council on Foreign Relations, Roosevelt secretly removed America from the gold standard on June 5, 1933. Informed of this decision, Lewis Douglas, the Director of the Bureau of the Budget, proclaimed "the end of Western Civilization."[39] The value of the dollar plummeted, the prices for everyday goods skyrocketed, and unemployed Americans wandered the streets. Whenever the panhandlers saw the wizened and wigged nonagenarian appearing from Rockefeller Center, they removed their caps to ask: "Brother, can you spare a dime?" The old man never refused them. He automatically fished one of the small coins from his pocket and said: "God bless you and God bless Standard Oil."[40]

38   James Warburg, Testimony, *Revision of the United Nations Charter: Hearings before a Senate Subcommittee on Foreign Relations* (Washington, DC: U.S. Government Printing Office, 1950), p. 494.

39   Rauchway, "How Franklin Roosevelt Secretly Ended the Gold Standard."

40   William Manchester, "The Founding Grandfather," *New York Times*, October 6, 1974, https://www.nytimes.com/1974/10/06/archives/the-founding-grandfather-he-saw-the-virtues-of-bigness-early-on-he.html, accessed February 13, 2019.

14

THE BEHEMOTH

It must not be felt that these heads of the world's chief central banks were themselves substantive powers in world finance. They were not. Rather, they were the technicians and agents of the dominant investment bankers of their own countries, who had raised them up and were perfectly capable of throwing them down. The substantive financial powers of the world were in the hands of these investment bankers (also called "international" or "merchant" bankers) who remained largely behind the scenes in their own unincorporated private banks. These formed a system of international cooperation and national dominance which was more private, more powerful, and more secret than that of their agents in the central banks. This dominance of investment bankers was based on their control over the flows of credit and investment funds in their own countries and throughout the world. They could dominate the financial and industrial systems of their own countries by their influence over the flow of current funds through bank loans, the discount rate, and the re-discounting of commercial debts; they could dominate governments by their control over current government loans and the play of the international exchanges. Almost all of this power was exercised by the personal influence and prestige of men who had demonstrated their ability in the past to bring off successful financial coups, to keep their word, to remain cool in a crisis, and to share their winning opportunities with their associates. In this system the Rothschilds had been preeminent during much of the nineteenth century, but, at the end of that century, they were being replaced by J. P. Morgan whose central office was in New York, although it was always operated as if it were in London (where it had, indeed, originated as George Peabody and Company in 1838).

—CARROLL QUIGLEY, *TRAGEDY & HOPE: A HISTORY OF THE WORLD IN OUR TIME*

ON MAY 17, 1930, the start of the Great Depression, the Bank for International Settlements (BIS), a financial institution, opened its headquarters in Basel, Switzerland. Like the Federal Reserve, it was a private financial institution that operated for the benefit of its shareholders. In 1930, the major shareholders were Europe's leading central banks: the Bank of England, the Bank of France, the National Bank of Belgium, Reichsbank, the Bank of Italy, the Bank of the Netherlands, and the Bank of Japan. Taking 14 percent of the new financial enterprise were three private firms: the First National Bank of New York, J. P. Morgan and Company, and the First National Bank of Chicago.[1]

The First National Bank of New York, now known as Citibank, became absorbed into the Rockefeller empire through strategic familial unions. Two sons of William Avery Rockefeller, John D.'s brother and business partner, were married to daughters of James Jewett Stillwell, First National Bank of New York's president and board chairman.[2] J. P. Morgan and Company and the First National Bank of Chicago, the other private owners of the BIS, would merge with Rockefeller's Chase Manhattan to become J. P. Morgan Chase, one of the world's largest financial institutions, with more than 5,100 branches.[3]

To settle this new crisis, the Young Conference, named in honor of Owen Young, its chairman, was held in Paris in 1929. Young was closely tied to the Rockefeller Empire and served as the president and chairman of the General Electric Company and RCA, two companies in which the Rockefellers were principal shareholders. A compromise had been reached at the Young Conference. The Germans would pay $500 million a year for the next 36 years to England and France, and

1   James C. Baker, *The Bank for International Settlements: Evolution and Evaluation* (Santa Clara, CA: Quorum, 2002), p. 20.

2   "Introduction: An Overview of the Rockefeller Empire," North American Congress on Latin America, September 25, 2007, https://nacla.org/article/introduction-overview-rockefeller-empire, accessed February 13, 2019.

3   "The History of JP Morgan Chase and Company," JP Morgan Chase Archives, n.d.

$375 million for the next 22 years after that to cover the Allies debt to the United States.[4]

The plan was approved at the First Hague Conference. Control of the German economy was returned to Berlin, and a new bank—the Bank for International Settlements—was established to administer the payments.[5] The BIS would serve to "commercialize" the payments, that is, to issue bonds against them, and would act as a lender to the Reichsbank, Germany's central bank, if the German currency weakened and the government found itself unable to make payments.[6]

THE MOTHER OF BANKS

Along with Owen Young, the founders of BIS were J. P. ("Jack") Morgan, Thomas W. Lamont, Seymour Parker Gilbert, Jackson Reynolds, and Gates W. McGarrah.[7] Lamont, an ambassador to the Paris Peace Conference of 1919, aided Rockefeller in the establishment of the Council on Foreign Relations.[8] Gilbert, a partner of J. P. Morgan, had served as the undersecretary of the Treasury for the Harding

---

4   Liaquat Ahamed, *Lords of Finance: The Bankers Who Broke the World* (New York: Penguin Books, 2009), p. 336.

5   Adam Lebor, *Tower of Basel: The Shadowy History of the Secret Bank that Runs the World* (New York: Public Affairs, 2013), p. 13.

6   Ahamed, *Lords of Finance*, p. 336.

7   Devon Douglas-Bowers, "History of the Bank for International Settlements," *Truthout*, October 17, 2015, http://www.truth-out.org/news/item/33234-history-of-the-bank-for-international-settlements, accessed February 13, 2019.

8   Nick Carbone and Ishaan Tharoor, "1929: Black Thursday and Thomas William Lamont," *Time*, November 11, 1929, http://newsfeed.time.com/2013/02/27/time-turns-90-all-you-need-to-know-about-modern-history-in-90-cover-stories/slide/1929-black-thursday-and-thomas-william-lamont/, accessed February 13, 2019. See also James Srodes, *On Dupont Circle: Franklin and Eleanor Roosevelt and the Progressives Who Shaped Our World* (Berkeley, CA: Counterpoint Press, 2012), pp. 151–153.

Administration.[9] Reynolds was a director of the Federal Reserve of New York and a Morgan economic advisor.[10] McGarrah, who became the first president of BIS, was an official at Chase Manhattan, owned by the House of Rockefeller, and the chairman of the Federal Reserve Bank of New York.[11]

Despite the fact that it was established as a result of the Young Conference, the BIS, in its statement of purpose, made no mention of the mandated reparations. It rather maintained that its objective was "to promote the cooperation of central banks and to provide additional facilities for international operations; and to act as trustees or agents in regard to international financial settlements entrusted to it under agreements with the parties concerned." Throughout its history, the BIS referred to itself not as an institution of settlements, but rather as "the central bankers' central bank," a place where bankers could meet in secret away from the prying eyes of the press and the nagging demands of the politicians.[12] The constitution of the BIS was written by Sir Walter Layton, editor of the *Economist.* Layton, in tandem with the Rothschild family, had created a consortium of British businessmen to promote a United Europe.[13]

The concept of a central bank had been advanced during the 1920s by British economist John Maynard Keynes, who called for the creation of a "supranational bank" that would take command of all national

---

9   Seymour Parker Gilbert, Register of Papers: Committee on the History of the Federal Reserve System, March 14, 1956, https://fraser.stlouisfed.org/files/docs/historical/brookings/16807_01_0030.pdf, accessed February 13, 2009.

10   Kevin Dowd and Richard Henry Timberlake, *Money and the Nation State: The Financial Revolution and the World Monetary Systems* (Oakland, CA: Independent Institute, 1998), p. 152.

11   Bowers, "History of the Bank for International Settlements."

12   Roger Auboin, "The Bank for International Settlements, 1930–1955," *Essays in International Finance*, Princeton University, May 1955, https://ies.princeton.edu/pdf/E22.pdf, accessed February 13, 2019.

13   Felix Klos, *Churchill on Europe: The Untold Story of Churchill's European Project* (London: I. B. Tauris, 2016), p. 82.

economies, set the exchange rate of all currencies, and manage the value of gold according to a standard commodity index.[14] Since the wealth of the world was being confined more and more to a small group of banking families, the formation of a bank to rule all banks appeared to be inevitable. In 1925, Montagu Norman, governor of the Bank of England, sent the following note to Benjamin Strong, governor of the Federal Reserve Bank of New York: "I rather hope that next summer we may be able to inaugurate a private and eclectic Central Banks 'Club,' small, at first, large in the future."[15]

A FORTRESS IMPREGNABLE

The headquarters of the BIS was a renovated hotel near the Basel central railroad station, where meetings were held under tight security and complete secrecy. No minutes, agenda, or attendance list was published in any form, and the building became "inviolate," meaning that the Swiss authorities possessed no authority over its premises. Correspondence to the bank was received by diplomatic couriers.[16] Such measures were necessary to safeguard the true purpose of the bank, which Carroll Quigley, one of America's leading economist, described as follows:

> The powers of financial capitalism had [a] far-reaching aim, nothing less than to create a world system of financial control in private hands able to dominate the political system of each country and the economy of the world as a whole. This system was to be controlled in a feudalist fashion by the central banks of the world acting in concert, by secret agreements arrived at in frequent private meetings and conferences. The apex of the system was to be the Bank for

---

14   David Felix, *Biography of an Idea: John Maynard Keynes and the General Theory of Employment, Interest, and Money* (Piscataway, NJ: Transaction Publishers, 1955), p. 77.

15   Montagu Norman, quoted in Lebor, *Tower of Basel*, p. 3.

16   Tyler Durden, "Meet the Secretive Group That Rules the World," *Zerohedge*, April 12, 2015, http://www.zerohedge.com/news/2015-04-11/meet-secretive-group-runs-world, accessed February 13, 2019.

International Settlements in Basel, Switzerland, a private bank owned and controlled by the world's central banks which were themselves private corporations.[17]

GAINING GOLD

As soon as it was established, the BIS abandoned its effort to settle the matter of Germany's delinquent payments for reparations and took up the task of stabilizing the world's economies. To accomplish this task, it was allocated control of the gold reserves that were held by its member banks. Gold now flowed out of Japan, Europe, and the United States into Basel.[18]

During the 1930s, Chiang Kai-shek, chairman of the National Government, was facing war on two fronts— from Mao Zedong's Communist insurgency and imperial Japan. As his government became increasingly unstable, Chiang began to transfer massive amounts of Chinese gold to the BIS and the Federal Reserve.

---

17   Carroll Quigley, *Tragedy and Hope: A History of the World in Our Time* (San Pedro, CA: GSG & Associates, 2004), p. 324.

18   Lebor, *Tower of Basel*, p. 13.

But the lion's share of precious metal came from China. During the 1930s, Chiang Kai-shek, chairman of the Nationalist government, was facing war on two fronts—from Mao Zedong's Communist insurgency and imperial Japan. As his government became increasingly unstable, Chiang began to transfer massive amounts of Chinese gold to the BIS and the Federal Reserve. A story concerning the transfer of 203.43 metric tons to Basel and New York was reported by the *New York Times* on February 19, 1937. In 1938, Chiang transported an additional 125,000 metric tons of gold for safekeeping.[19]

CONTROLLING COUNTRIES

Throught the power of this combined wealth, the BIS could save a country from economic disaster or drive it into a tailspin. And its transnational actions could take place without political or governmental interference. In the first six months of 1931, the BIS advanced $10 million to the Bank of Spain to stabilize the peseta; gave a credit of 100 million Austrian schillings to the Bank of Austria when the Credit-Anstalt bank went belly-up; and advanced five million dollars to the Hungarian National Bank, which was experiencing a revenue shortfall.[20]

AN ANOMALOUS FACILITY

The activities of the BIS superseded all political, moral, and religious ideologies. The sole concern was the control of capital by the flow of money. Capital represented the resources required to produce goods: coal, oil, iron ore, factories, machine tools, trucks, and roads. Money was the means of purchasing capital.[21] By manipulating the money supply and

---

19 Brandon Turbeville, "Secret 'Occult Economy' Coming out of the Shadows," *Blacklisted News*, March 15, 2012, http://blacklistednews.com/?news_id=18463&print=1, accessed February 13, 2019.

20 Larry Gelten, "The Great Bank Robbery," *New York Post*, May 12, 2013, https://nypost .com/2013/05/12/the-great-bank-robbery/

21 Jason Trennert, "Big Difference between Money and Capital," *Forbes*, August 26, 2011, https:// www.forbes.com/sites/greatspeculations/2011/08/26/big-difference-between-money-and-capital/#28a9b4933dc0, accessed February 13, 2019.

determining the value of all currencies, the directors of the BIS could hold absolute control over state and society. Personal principles were superfluous. Thus it came to pass that a group of international bankers, including members of the Reichsbank, met each month to manage international economies and to plan a one world order while war raged around them. And no one objected when Paul Hechler, a German deputy manager at the BIS, signed his correspondence, "Heil Hitler."[22]

Within the walls of the secure fortress in Basel, the American president of the bank transacted daily business through a French General Manager, who had a German Assistant General Manager, while the Secretary General was a subject of Italy. These men were in daily contact with one another as the bank continued to operate as the medium through which all central bankers could exchange finances, financial information, and the means of extracting profit from the international bloodbath.[23]

ACTS OF TREASON
Throughout World War II, Standard Oil provided the Third Reich with 48,000 tons of oil a month and 11,000 tons of tungsten, the metal necessary to make artillery shells and missiles. Without the ongoing flow of these supplies from the United States, Hitler's war machine would have come to a screeching halt.[24] These transactions took place under the cloak of secrecy at the BIS; the records remained concealed from the press and politicians; and the profits from the sale of these strategic supplies remained tax-exempt.

Not only did the Rockefellers supply the Third Reich with oil and tungsten, but they also were provided the Nazi scientists and engineers at IG Farben, Germany's leading chemical company, with hydrogenation

22   Lebor, *Tower of Basel*, p. 49.

23   Antony C. Sutton, *Wall Street and the Rise of Hitler*, chap. 1, "Wall Street Paves the Way for Hitler," HTML edition, 2000, https://www.bilderberg.org/bis.htm, accessed February 13, 2019.

24   Ibid.

Throughout World War II, Standard Oil provided the Third Reich with 48,000 tons of oil a month and 11,000 tons of tungsten, the metal necessary to make artillery shells and missiles. Without the ongoing flow of these supplies from the United States, Hitler's war machine would have come to a screeching halt. These transactions took place under the cloak of secrecy at the BIS.

patents and technology. These designs enabled Farben to produce synthetic oil, gasoline, and rubber (butyl) from coal.[25]

By 1939, Standard Oil was also producing tetraethyl-lead ("no-knock") aviation gasoline for the Luftwaffe. The financial arrangements for these transactions were conducted at the BIS, where Gates W. McGarrah, the Rockefeller lackey, remained in charge. The blatant treason of these acts became apparent when the Rockefellers refused to provide similar assistance to the U.S. War Department.[26]

In 1944, Standard Oil was indicted by Assistant Attorney General

25   Sutton, *Wall Street and the Rise of Hitler,* chap. 4, "Standard Oil Fuels World War II," HTML ed., http://www.reformation.org/wall-st-ch4.html, accessed February 13, 2019.

26   Ibid.

Thurman Arnold for deliberately blocking the production of synthetic rubber. The company pleaded guilty and agreed to release the patents and processes for use by the United States.[27] But the Rockefellers, who maintained ownership of Standard Oil, were never charged with aiding and abetting the enemy.

TOP SECRET LEAKS

The Rockefellers proved to be magnanimous with their fellow members of the cartel at the BIS. Since Nelson remained wired to the Roosevelt Administration and the Council on Foreign Relations retained control of the U.S. State Department, news from the Rockefeller Empire could be leaked about the projected American invasions of Europe. In the summer of 1942, news of the planned invasion of Algeria was sent to the governor of the French National Bank, who immediately contacted his German colleague in the BIS, SS Gruppenfüehrer Baron Kurt von Schröder, who represented the Stein Bank of Cologne. The Germans and their French subsidiaries used the information to make a killing of $175 million in a dollar-for franc-exchange scam.[28]

THE FUEHRER IS YOUR FRIEND

The Rockefellers used the Bank for International Settlements not only as a place to shield and store their ill-gotten gains from the Nazis but also as a facility to finance a public relations campaign for the Third Reich. Walter Teagle, chairman of Standard Oil of New Jersey, dispatched Ivy Lee, the New York publicity man for the Rockefellers, to work with Adolf Hitler and the Third Reich. Lee's task was to supply the Nazi government with intelligence on the American reaction to such matters as the German armament program, Germany's treatment of Christians, and the organization of the Gestapo. He was also to keep the American public

---

27 Emanuel M. Josephson, *Rockefeller "Internationalist"* (New York: Chedney Press, 1952), p. 395.

28 Alfred Mendez, "The World Central Bank: The Bank for International Settlements," Bilderberg .org, n.d., https://www.bilderberg.org/bis.htm, accessed February 13, 2019.

bamboozled by papering over the more evil aspects of Hitler's regime. For his services, Lee was paid first $3,000 then $4,000 annually through the Bank for International Settlements in the name of I. G. Chemie.[29]

The contract was, for obvious reasons, kept oral, and the money was transferred in cash. No entries were made in the BIS books of the employing companies or in those of Ivy Lee himself. After a short period of time, Lee's salary was increased to $25,000 per year, and he began circulating inflammatory Nazi propaganda in the United States, including virulent attacks on the Jews and the Versailles Treaty.[30] Few who read Lee's propaganda were aware that the Rockefellers were now in business with the firm that would produce the gas for the death camps.

The Rockefellers used the Bank for International Settlements not only as a place to shield and store their ill-gotten gains from the Nazis but also as a facility to finance a public relations campaign for the Third Reich.

29 Charles Higham, *Trading with the Enemy: An Expose of the Nazi-American Plot, 1933–1949* (New York: Delacorte Press, 1983), p. 33.

30 Ibid.

15

THE TRAITORS

Standard Oil can be considered an enemy national in view of its relationships with I.G. Farben after the United States and Germany had become active enemies.

—FEDERAL JUDGE CHARLES CLARK, SEPTEMBER 22, 1947

War is a racket. It always has been. It is possibly the oldest, easily the most profitable, surely the most vicious. It is the only one international in scope. It is the only one in which the profits are reckoned in dollars and the losses in lives. A racket is best described, I believe, as something that is not what it seems to the majority of the people. Only a small "inside" group knows what it is about. It is conducted for the benefit of the very few, at the expense of the very many. Out of war a few people make huge fortunes.

—MAJOR GENERAL SMEDLEY BUTLER, AUGUST 8, 1935

AT THE ONSET of World War II, the CFR established study groups to produce reports on specific foreign policy topics. The preparation of these reports did not represent idle academic exercises, but rather the means to advance the agenda of the CFR inner core. Admiral Chester Ward, another former council member, wrote: "Once the ruling members of the CFR have decided that the U.S. Government should adopt a particular policy, the very substantial research facilities of CFR are put to work to develop arguments, intellectual and emotional, to support the new policy, and to confound and discredit, intellectually and politically, any opposition."[1] Indeed, the studies generated by the council have resulted in the establishment of such international institutions as the United Nations, the World Bank, and the International Monetary Fund.

The study groups received funding from the Rockefeller, Carnegie, and Ford foundations, which shared many of the same trustees. John Foster Dulles served as the chairman of the Rockefeller and Carnegie foundations, while changing hats to assume his responsibilities as president Harry Truman's foreign policy advisor. CFR president John W. Davis served as a trustee for the Rockefeller and Carnegie Foundations, while running for president in a campaign heavily funded by Kuhn, Loeb & Company, the bank in which Paul Warburg, the founder of the Federal Reserve, was a partner. By 1960, many of the trustees of America's three leading foundations were executives from Bechtel Construction, Chase Manhattan, Kimberly-Clark, Monsanto Chemical, and other leading international business and banking firms.[2] Twelve of the 15 Rockefeller Foundation trustees, 10 of the 15 Ford Foundation trustees, and 10 of the 14 Carnegie Foundation trustees were members of the CFR.[3]

THE ESTABLISHED PATTERN

A pattern developed that would continue into the second decade of the 21st century. Corporate plans for expansion into new regions of the world were established by America's leading CEOs, many of whom served on the boards of major foundations. The foundations would fund CFR study groups that would inevitably uphold the soundness of the

---

1   Phyllis Schlafly and Chester Ward, *Kissinger on the Couch* (New Rochelle, NY: Arlington House, 1975), p. 151.

2   Daniel Estulin, *The True Story of the Bilderberg Group* (Waterville, OR: Trineday, 2009), p. 87.

3   Ibid.

expansion plans in reports that were passed on to the State Department for implementation. Thanks also to the reports of the study groups, the interests of America became synonymous with the interests of the Rockefellers and the money cartel.

Regarding the Rockefeller stranglehold on the U.S. State Department, columnist I. F. Stone writes: "The policy of the State Department is born in the offices of Standard Oil. From there it is transmitted to the Department of Defense, where the heads of the Army and Navy approve it. When this policy gets to the State Department, it becomes the policy of the government and is supposed to be confirmed by Congress quickly and without any changes whatever. When an order for laws designed to protect the interests of the oil kings comes from the Rockefeller dynasty itself, the entire Congress—from the small to the great—comes to 'attention' and does what the bosses order it to do."[4]

THE CHEMICAL COMPANY

Interessen-Gemeinschaft Farbenindustrie, the world's largest chemical company, had been created by a $30 million loan from Rockefellers' National City Bank. German bankers on the Farben Aufsichtsrat (the supervisory board of directors) included the Hamburg banker Max Warburg, whose brother Paul Warburg was a founder of the Federal Reserve System in the United States. Not coincidentally, in 1928, Paul Warburg became a director of American IG, Farben's industry wholly owned U.S. subsidiary, whose holdings came to include the Bayer Company, General Aniline Works, Agfa-Ansco, and Winthrop Chemical Company.[5]

4   I. F. Stone, quoted in Wayne Madsen, "The Rockefeller Family and the War in Syria," *The Revivers,* October 18, 2012, https://revivers.wordpress.com/2012/10/18/rockefeller-family-and-the-war-in-syria/, accessed February 13, 2019.

5   Antony Sutton, "The Empire of I. G. Farben," *Reformed Theology,* 2004, http://www.reformation. org/wall-st-ch2.html, accessed February 13, 2019.

Interessen-Gemeinschaft Farbenindustrie AG, the world's largest chemical company, had been created by a $30 million loan from Rockefellers' National City Bank. By 1933, the German chemical company had become so wealthy that it could fund the Nazi Party's rise to power. The ties to Hitler greatly increased the chemical company's worth. By 1943, IG Farben was the leading producer of Zyklon B gas, which was used in the concentration camps.

From the time of its creation, Farben entered into joint projects with Standard Oil, including the construction of experimental facilities in Bayway, New Jersey; Baytown, Texas; and Baton Rouge, Louisiana.[6] By 1933, the German chemical company had become so wealthy that it could fund the Nazi Party's rise to power. The ties to Hitler greatly increased the chemical company's worth. By 1943, IG Farben was the leading producer of Zyklon B gas, which was used in the concentration camps.[7]

---

6   Sutton, *Wall Street and the Rise of Hitler*, chap. 4, "Standard Oil Fuels World War II," HTML edition.

7   James Perloff, *The Shadows of Power: The Council on Foreign Relations and the American Decline* (Appleton, WI: Western Islands, 2005), p. 47.

A DELICATE SITUATION

Other Rockefeller firms came to aid the Third Reich, including the Paris office of the Chase Bank. An examination of the correspondence between Chase, New York, and Chase, France, from the date of the fall of France to May, 1942, discloses that the manager of the Paris office was "very vigorous in enforcing restrictions against Jewish property, even going so far as to refuse to release funds belonging to Jews in anticipation that a decree with retroactive provisions prohibiting such release might be published in the near future by the occupying authorities." The New York office manager, upon receiving this information, took no direct steps to initiate the dismissal of his Paris counterpart, since it "might react against our (Chase) interests as we are dealing, not with a theory but with a situation."[8]

NELSON GOES SOUTH

In 1941, Nelson, according to Emanuel Josephson, "dictated" to FDR his appointment as Coordinator of Inter-American Affairs, an agency created to promote Pan-Americanism. Nelson's first act was to obtain from Congress $6 billion to use at his discretion with no accounts rendered.[9] With cash in hand, he approached the leaders of various Latin American countries with a tidy offer. They could receive a portion of the money for "defense," if they were willing to come up with "deals of interest" to Standard Oil. The strategy was highly successful and, while the Second World War raged in Europe and the Pacific, Nelson managed to create for himself a "Latin American duchy" on the backs of U.S. taxpayers.[10]

By the war's end, the Rockefeller holdings south of the border included the International Petroleum Company of Peru, Colombia, and

---

8   Sutton, *Wall Street and the Rise of Hitler.*

9   Emanuel Josephson, *The "Federal" Reserve Conspiracy and Rockefellers: Their "Gold Corner"* (New York: Chedney Press, 1968), p. 134.

10   Ibid., p. 134.

Venezuela; the Panama Transport Company; Standard Oil Company of Brazil; Esso Productora de Petroleo of Argentina; Esso Refinadora de Petroleo of Argentina; Esso Sociedad Anonima Petrolera Argentina; Esso Standard Oil Company of Chile; Esso Standard Oil Company of Uruguay; Esso Standard Oil Company of Cuba; Esso Standard Oil of Puerto Rico; Esso Standard Oil of Lesser Antilles and the Guianas; Esso Standard Oil Company of Bermuda, the Bahamas, and Greater Antilles; Esso Standard Oil of Central America; and Standard Oil of the Canal Zone.[11]

In 1943, President Medina Angarita demanded an increase of the government's share of the oil extracted from Venezuela by Standard Oil.[12] He also charged the Rockefeller oil company with the theft of $20,000,000 by means of the false registry of the oil capacity of its tankers. A settlement reportedly was made in the amount of $9,000,000, and the indictment was quashed. But Angarita's political goose was cooked. He was immediately confronted with a "populist" revolution and driven from office.[13]

THE "OH-SO-SOCIAL SOCIETY"

In addition to serving as the Coordinator of Inter-American Affairs, Nelson also accepted a position as a director for the Office of Strategic Services (OSS), the wartime intelligence agency that had been established under the command of General William ("Wild Bill") Donovan. Staff positions within the OSS were reserved for members of wealthy American families, and the organization became known as the Oh-So-Social Society. In addition to Nelson, the directors came to include Henry Sturgis Morgan (son of J. P. Morgan Jr.), Nicholas Roosevelt, Paul Mellon (son of Andrew Mellon), David Bruce (Andrew Mellon's

---

11   Emanuel M. Josephson, *Rockefeller "Internationalist," The Man Who Misrules the World* (New York: Chedney Press, 1952), p. 22.

12   Barry Cannon, *Hugo Chavez and the Bolivian Revolution: Populism and Democracy in a Globalized Age* (Manchester, UK: Manchester University Press, 2010), p. 34.

13   Josephson, *Rockefeller "Internationalist,"* p. 45.

son-in-law), members of the Vanderbilt, Carnegie, du Pont, and Ryan families, and Allen Dulles. Dulles was a Princeton graduate and the senior partner at the Wall Street firm of Sullivan & Cromwell, which represented the Rockefeller empire and other mammoth trusts, corporations, and cartels. He was also a board member of the J. Henry Schroeder Bank, with offices in Wall Street, London, Zurich, and Hamburg and a principal of the Bank of New York. "Wild Bill" Donovan was an Ivy league lawyer who had married Ruth Ramsey, the heiress of one of the richest families in America.[14] Donovan justified the practice of recruiting the socially elite for the OSS by saying: "You can hire a second-story man and make him a better second-story man. But if you hire a lawyer or an investment banker or a professor, you have something else besides."[15]

THE BIRTH OF THE DRUG TRADE

Another principal player in the OSS was Paul E. Helliwell, who remains a forgotten figure despite the fact that few individuals have played a greater role in shaping the modern world. Helliwell was a well-heeled lawyer from Brooklyn. His father had been a prominent textile designer, and he was a good fit for the intelligence organization.[16]

While serving as the OSS Chief of Special Intelligence in the Yunnan province of China, Helliwell observed that General Chiang Kai-shek, leader of the Kuomintang (KMT), sold opium to Chinese addicts in order to raise funds for his army's planned war against the

14   Eustace Mullens, *The World Order* (New York: Modern History Project, 1983), p. 214.

15   Evan Thomas, *The Very Best Men: Four Men Who Dared* (New York: Touchstone, 1985), p. 9.

16   Paul Helliwell, Classified Information, Federal Bureau of Investigation, released under the Freedom of Information Act to Independent Research Associates, https://www.scribd.com/document/203142473/Paul-Helliwell, accessed February 13, 2019.

Communist forces of Mao Zedong.[17] Since his task was to provide covert assistance to the KMT, what better help could Helliwell provide than steady shipments of opiates for the good general? He received General Donovan's approval to set up a fleet of surplus planes, including C-47 Dakotas and C-46 Commandos, to provide a steady supply of refined opium to General Chiang.[18] The fleet, which became known as Civil Air Transport, transported weapons to a contingency force of the KMT in Burma. The "empty" planes were then loaded with drugs for their return trip to China.[19] The pilots who flew these bush-type aircraft were a motley group of men, who often served as agents or go-betweens with the Chinese National guerrillas and the opium buyers. Some were ex-Nazis, others part of the band of expatriates who emerge in countries following any war.[20] Helliwell and his compatriots had created a model for the trafficking in drugs that would result in the formation of Air America. Because of his efforts, Burma's Shan Plateau would emerge from a relatively minor poppy-cultivating area into the largest opium producing region of the world.[21]

THE WORLD COMMERCE CORPORATION

In 1945, Nelson participated with Donovan in the creation of the World Commerce Corporation (WCC).[22] The primary function of

---

17   Ibid.

18   Henrik Kruger, *The Great Heroin Coup: Drugs, Intelligence and International Finance* (Boston: South End Press, 1980), p. 68.

19   Joseph Trento, *Prelude to Terror: The Rogue CIA, the Legacy of America's Private Intelligence Network* (New York: Carroll and Graf, 2005), p. 48.

20   Peter Dale Scott, *American War Machine: Deep Politics, the CIA Global Drug Connection, and the Road to Afghanistan* (Washington, D.C.: Rowman and Littlefield, 2010), p. 58.

21   Alfred McCoy, testimony before the Special Seminar focusing on allegations linking CIA secret operations and drug trafficking, convened February 13, 1997, by Rep. John Conyers, dean of the Congressional Black Caucus.

22   Peter Dale Scott, *Drugs, Oil, and War: The United States in Afghanistan, Colombia, and Indochina* (Lanham, MD: Rowman and Littlefield, 2004), pp. 109–10.

the WCC was to buy and sell surplus U.S. weapons and munitions to foreign underworld groups, including the Kuomintang (KMT), the Nationalist Army under Chiang Kai-shek, and the Italian mafias. In exchange for the arms, the KMT provided the opium required to create the postwar intelligence agency.[23] Registered in Panama, the firm employed mob figure Sonny Fassoulis, a notorious drug dealer, to provide "services" to General Chiang.[24] John McCloy, another WCC director, was intricately tied to the Rockefeller family. McCloy was a director of the Rockefeller law firm Milbank, Tweed, Hadley, and McCloy, the Rockefeller bank Chase Manhattan, and the CFR.[25] Other members of prominent banking families served as WCC directors, including Charles Jocelyn Hambro of the Hambros Bank, Sydney Weinberg of Goldman Sachs, Richard Mellon of the Mellon Bank, and Lester Armour of City National Bank, a Chicago firm that later merged into J.P. Morgan Chase.[26] The WCC became instrumental in the CIA by providing the funds to Sicilian bandit Salvatore Giuliano to conduct the May Day Massacre in Portella della Ginestra, which killed 11 supporters of the Italian Communist Party and wounded 57.[27]

THE CREATION OF THE CIA

At the end of the good war, Wild Bill Donovan, along with members of the Council on Foreign Relations, drafted plans to create a postwar

---

23   Peter Dale Scott, "Operation Paper: The United States and Drugs in Thailand and Burma," *Asia-Pacific Journal* 8, no. 2 (November 1, 2010), http://japanfocus.org/-peter_dale-scott/3436, accessed February 13, 2019. See also Sterling and Peggy Seagrave, *Gold Warriors* (London: Bowstring, 2008), p. 324.

24   Bradley Ayers, "The War That Never Was" (New York: Bobbs Merrill, 1976), p. 78.

25   John Simkin, "John McCloy," *Spartacus Educational*, August 2014, http://spartacus-educational.com/USAmccloyJ.htm, accessed February 13, 2019.

26   Scott, *Drugs, Oil and War*, pp. 109–10.

27   Peter Dale Scott, "Deep Events and the CIA's Global Drug Connection." *Global Research*, September 8, 2008, http://www.globalresearch.ca/deep-events-and-the-cia-s-global-drug-connection/10095, accessed February 13, 2019.

central intelligence agency that would become known as the CIA. Aware of these plans, Helliwell came up with another brainstorm—a surefire means of gaining funding for covert operations.[28] The new agency, he realized, could obtain cold cash by adopting the same measures of General Chiang. It could supply smack to blacks in America's ghettos.

World War II had disrupted international shipping and imposed tight waterfront security that made smuggling of heroin into the United States almost impossible. Heroin supplies were small, and international crime syndicates fell into disarray. But opiates were becoming the rage of the jazz scene in Harlem, and the demand for China White was increasing day by day among black musicians in New York, where a hit could cost as much as $100. Helliwell, in dealing with Du Yuesheng and other drug lords in Burma, was keenly aware of this fact.

FOR BLACKS ONLY

The notion wasn't out of line with OSS protocol. Helliwell and his Army intelligence buddies in China were already involved in providing shipments of opium to General Chiang, and "three sticky brown bars" to Burmese addicts who could provide information concerning the military plans of Chairman Mao.[29] If similar bars could be made available to inner-city black dealers at rock-bottom rates, then the market could be cornered, and the demand could be caused to increase in an exponential manner. Helliwell knew that a drug epidemic might arise. But, he reasoned, the problem would remain confined to the lowest strata of society with little impact on the white middle-class America.

Helliwell's plan was adopted, and, working with Lucky Luciano, Joe Adonis, Santo Trafficante, and other members of the Italian Mafia, a shipment of heroin flowed into New York City during the summer of 1947.[30]

---

28   Declassified OSS documents show that Donovan's plans for the creation of a Special Intelligence Service to gather intelligence from countries throughout the world dates back to September 25, 1941. See "Memo Col. Donovan from Wallace B. Stevens," WIN #24299.

29   Penny Lernoux, *In Banks We Trust* (New York: Penguin Books, 1986), p. 79.

30   Peter Dale Scott, "Deep Events and the CIA's Global Drug Connection."

The 200 kilos of heroin for the test run would come from Schiaparelli, one of Italy's most respected pharmaceutical companies.[31] The product would be shipped by the Sicilian mob in crates of oranges. Half of the oranges in the crates would be made of wax and stuffed with 100 grams of pure heroin.[32] Additional heroin would be packed in cans of sardines, wheels of caciocavallo cheese, and barrels of olive oil.[33] Within Cuba, the heroin would be "cut" in laboratories under the control of the Trafficante clan. The drugs would be shipped to New York for distribution by Vito Genovese and his clan in the jazz clubs of Harlem.

The future of the CIA was no longer in jeopardy. Helliwell's analysis had been correct. The jazz clubs were the perfect spots to peddle the product. Soon some of the country's leading black musicians—Billie Holiday, Carl Drinkard (Count Basie's piano player), Theodore "Fats" Navarro, and Charlie Parker—became hopeless junkies who would die by overdose. Regarding this development, Harry Anslinger, then head of the Bureau of Narcotics, said: "Jazz entertainers are neither fish nor fowl. They do not get the million-dollar protection Hollywood and Broadway can afford for their stars who have become addicted, and there are many more than will ever be revealed. Perhaps this is because jazz, once considered a decadent kind of music, has only token respectability. Jazz grew up next door to crime, so to speak. Clubs of dubious reputation were, for a long time, the only places where it could be heard."[34]

---

31 Alfred W. McCoy, *The Politics of Heroin in Southeast Asia* (New York: Harper & Row, 1972), p. 24. See also Alexander Cockburn and Jeffrey St. Clair, *Whiteout: The CIA, Drugs and the Press* (New York: Verso, 1998), p. 130.

32 Claire Sterling, *Octopus: How the Long Reach of the Sicilian Mafia Controls the Global Narcotics Trade* (New York: Simon and Schuster, 1990), pp. 100–101.

33 Ibid.

34 John Bevilaqua, "Harry Anslinger: Head of the Bureau of Narcotics since 1930," *The Education Forum*, December 4, 2009, http://educationforum.ipbhost.com/index.php?showtopic=15084, accessed February, 13, 2019.

MOB CONNECTIONS

Nelson Rockefeller's role in forging an alliance between the Luciano crime family and the new intelligence agency should not be underestimated. In 1935, Nelson secured the services of the mob when he took over the construction of Rockefeller Center in the midst of downtown Manhattan. When the laborers began to rebel against the wages set by the National Recovery Administration at $15 for a 48-hour work week, Joe Adonis, a leader of Murder, Inc., was assigned the task of "convincing" the workers that they really didn't want a wage increase. Visits were made to the homes of the more vocal protestors. Knuckles were smashed and lives were threatened. The efforts of Adonis resulted in overwhelming success. A relationship had been made that would be of inestimable value to the Rockefeller family.[35]

A ROCKEFELLER LEGACY

Since heroin was a funding source for the CIA's covert operations throughout the postwar period, the Rockefellers remain deep involved in the drug trade. During the Vietnam era, the Nugan Hand Bank had been established by the Agency in Sydney, Australia, to purchase weapons for guerrilla forces in Indonesia, Thailand, Malaysia, Brazil, and the white Rhodesian government of Ian Smith and to import heroin into Australia from the Golden Triangle of Thailand, Laos, and Myanmar (Burma).[36]

The primary shareholder of the Nugan Hand Bank was Australian Pacific Holdings, a company that was owned and operated by the Rockefellers' Chase Manhattan Bank.[37] By 1974, the Australian bank

---

35   Emanuel M. Josephson, *The "Federal" Reserve Conspiracy,* (New York: Chedney Press, 1968) p. 95.

36   Penny Lernoux, *In Banks We Trust* (New York: Penguin Books, 1984), pp. 69–70.

37   Ken Thomas and David Hatcher Childress, *Inside the Gemstone File: Howard Hughes, Onassis, and JFK* (Kempton, IL: Adventures Unlimited Press, 1999), p. 93. See also Denise Pritchard, "Financial Takeover of Australia and New Zealand," *Opal File,* n. d., https://www.bibliotecapleyades.net/esp_sociopol_opalfile.htm, accessed February 13, 2019.

was doing billions in business. The heroin flowing into the United States at the Andrews Air Force bank and other military installations within the body bags of dead soldiers had produced a heroin epidemic that spread from the ghettoes to the staid neighborhoods of suburbia.

THE SAUDI OIL

While the good war was still raging, the Rockefellers began to develop the oil fields of Saudi Arabia for Standard Oil of California. For his good graces, the Rockefellers arranged for King Ibn Saud to receive $30 million from the U.S. Treasury.[38] The money was spent to provide support for the king, his 450 wives, and his 100 children. The king was granted other gifts from the American public, including multimillion-dollar airplanes and all-expense-paid tours of the United States for himself, his 45 sons, and his numerous retinues. In addition, the Rockefellers obtained for King Saud a "loan" of $25 million of taxpayers' money from the Export-Import bank to build a royal railroad from the Persian Gulf to his summer palace at Riyadh.[39] The venture was incredibly profitable. Aramco (the Arabian-American Oil Company), which Standard Oil established with the Saud dynasty, was soon shipping 850,000 barrels of oil a day to countries throughout the world. The value of these shipments amounted to $2 million a day (tax-free) for the Rockefeller Empire.[40]

PRICE GOUGING

Standard Oil sold the Saudi oil to the British Navy at 40 cents a barrel for fuel oil and 75 cents a barrel for diesel oil. The company more than doubled the price for the U.S. Navy, charging $1.05 a barrel for fuel

---

38   Ibid., p. 386.

39   Ibid., p. 387.

40   Ibid., pp. 388–89.

oil and $1.68 a barrel for diesel. After the war, a Senate Investigative Committee concluded that these prices amounted to an overcharge of $68 million. Moreover, it was also discovered that the oil provided to the U.S. Navy was of inferior quality.[41]

THE MARSHALL PLAN

Even after the war, the greed of the Rockefellers proved to be insatiable. In 1948, the Rockefellers and their associates within the Council on Foreign Relations were instrumental in the establishment and implementation of the Marshall Plan, a $12 billion ($100 billion in 2019) initiative to rebuild war-ravaged Western Europe. The Plan's directors included Dean Acheson (Nelson's close associate from the Roosevelt Administration), CFR president Allen Dulles, Winthrop Aldrich (son of Nelson Aldrich, one of the founders of the Fed), Alger Hiss (president of the Carnegie Endowment for International Peace that acted in league with the Rockefeller Foundation), Philip Reed (president of General Electric, in which the Rockefellers held principal interest), and Frank Altschul (an executive for Standard Oil).

On December 13, 1949, the *Chicago Tribune* published an editorial with the title "Rockefeller Profits from the Marshall Plan." The editorial noted the key role the Rockefellers played in obtaining Congressional approval of the Plan and went on to reveal the means by which they collected payment after payment for the same product within the first 45 days of the Plan's implementation. It read:

> Anglo-American Oil Company, Ltd., 100% owned British subsidiary of the Standard Oil Company of New Jersey, purchased from two other wholly owned subsidiaries of the same company, the Esso Export Corporation and the Standard Oil Export Corporation, $7,258,332 worth of products that were paid out of ECA funds. [ECA, the Economic Cooperation Administration, was set up to

---

41   Ibid., p. 388.

oversee the Marshall Plan] The transaction which was in effect merely a transfer of the products from one department to another of Standard Oil, netted it two profits at the expense of taxpayers.

Standard Francaise des Petroles, a French company 83%-owned by the Standard Oil Company of New Jersey, bought $4,020,210 worth of products from the Esso Export Corporation, a wholly owned subsidiary of Standard Oil, in the same type of deal.

Other subsidiaries of the Standard Oil Co. of New Jersey throughout the world engage in the same type of transactions with their mother companies at the expense of the American taxpayers.

Les Raffineries de la Vacuum Oil bought from Socony-Vacuum Oil Co., its parent company, $2,249,877 worth of products under the same conditions.[42]

War was such a lucrative racket that the Rockefellers saw fit to initiate one in Korea through their newly established global organization in New York that was created to fulfill the dream of Cecil John Rhodes.

---

42   "Rockefeller Profits from the Marshall Plan," quoted in ibid., p 418.

PART FOUR

THE GLOBAL NETWORK

16

MORDOR

I was early taught to work as well as play,
My life has been one long, happy holiday;
Full of work and full of play—
I dropped the worry on the way—
And God was good to me everyday.
—JOHN D. ROCKEFELLER, AGE 87

One Ring to rule them all, One Ring to find them,
One Ring to bring them all and in the darkness bind them
In the Land of Mordor where the Shadows lie.
—J. R. R. TOLKIEN, *THE FELLOWSHIP OF THE RING*

UNTIL THE TIME OF HIS DEATH IN 1938, John D. Rockefeller awoke in a cold sweat for fear that he would lose his vast fortune. He inculcated this fear in other members of his family. John D.'s daughter, Bessie Strong, ended her life, according to the family biographer,

William Manchester, "with the pitiful fear that she would die penniless."[1] Winifred Rockefeller Emeny, John D.'s grandniece, murdered her two children and committed suicide because of a fear of poverty. Another niece, Gladys, at age 21, was hospitalized for her mental condition. After each meal, she would save every crust of bread and every scrap of meat for fear that she could not afford another meal. She secreted the scraps of food under her pillow, refusing to trust them to the nurse. In an interview given the *Journal American* on November 19, 1961, Mary Clark Rockefeller, Nelson's first wife, said that her husband, despite his income of a million dollars a minute, was even more penny-pinching and penurious than his grandfather.[2] Mrs. Rockefeller further testified that Nelson spied on the domestic help to make sure that they did not eat too much food. Those whose appetites exceeded the limits of Nelson's stinginess were dismissed from the household.[3]

The fear of poverty, according to Emanuel M. Josephson, became the psychological basis for the Rockefeller family's support of Communism. They saw in the tenets of Karl Marx and Vladimir Lenin a means of concentrating the world's wealth into the hands of a ruling elite through the elimination of competition and the suppression of the masses. This belief, Josephson argues, was a leading factor in the family's support of the United Nations.[4]

CARNEGIE'S SIDEKICK

During World War II, John D. Rockefeller Jr. remained the head of the vast family empire. As a young man, Junior had developed a close relationship with Andrew Carnegie and spent several weeks every summer at

---

1   Emanuel M. Josephson, *The Truth about Rockefeller: "Public Enemy No. 1," Studies in Criminal Psychopathy* (New York: Chedney Press, 1962), pp. 91–92.

2   Ibid., pp. 21–22.

3   Ibid., p. 32.

4   Ibid., p. 30.

Skibo, the Carnegie estate in Scotland. Junior came to share Carnegie's internationalism and belief in the need of a global organization that would dissolve national sovereignty and impose global law over all the inhabitants of planet Earth.[5] Carnegie's last public appearance was at a gathering of Junior's Bible class at the Fifth Avenue Baptist Church in New York. The appearance was telling since Carnegie was instrumental in persuading Junior to shed his religious fundamentalism. Shortly after Carnegie addressed the Bible class, Junior announced to the group his belief that anyone who manifested "the moral spirit" of Jesus merited entrance into the Kingdom of Heaven, even if he or she refused to practice Christian rituals.[6]

Junior's internationalism was further enhanced by his friendship with Raymond B. Fosdick, who became his lawyer and closest adviser. Fosdick had been appointed to serve as undersecretary of the League of Nations by President Wilson.[7] In his fawning biography, *John D. Rockefeller, Jr.: A Portrait* (1956), Fosdick wrote: "More and more Mr. Rockefeller began to think in international terms. It is true that he had not favored the League of Nations when it was first proposed. Just as he had taken his church affiliations from his father, so his political loyalties were similarly inherited, and he had followed the Republican Party in its opposition to President Wilson. But his opinions were invariably marked by tolerance, and inflexibility was not part of his character."[8]

THE NEW ORGANIZATION

The United Nations, as conceived by the Council on Foreign Relations and funded by the House of Rockefeller, was never meant to be an

---

5   Peter Koss, *Carnegie* (New York: John Wiley and Sons, 2002), p. 474.

6   Ron Chernow, *Titan: The Life of John D. Rockefeller, Sr.* (New York: Vintage Books, 2004), pp. 639–40.

7   Ibid., p. 638.

8   Raymond E. Fosdick, *John D. Rockefeller, Jr.: A Portrait* (New York: Harper and Brothers, 1958), p. 216.

academic debating society. It was conceived to become an international regime that would control the world's weapons, wars, courts, tax collectors, and economy. The orders to create this new international organization came from the Rockefellers. The plans were drawn up in 1943 by a "secret steering committee" under Secretary of State Cordell Hull. The members of this committee—Leo Pasvolsky, Isaiah Bowman, Sumner Welles, Norman Davis, and Myron Taylor—were all prominent CFR members. The draft for the massive international agency, after passing Nelson Rockefeller's inspection, was presented on June 15, 1944, to President Roosevelt, who promptly gave it his approval.[9]

THE UN'S FOUNDING FATHERS

Delegates were now chosen by the U.S. State Department to meet with their foreign counterparts in San Francisco to devise a final plan. The following list of American delegates resembled a CFR roll call:

1. Theodore C. Achilles
2. James W. Angell
3. Hamilton Fish Armstrong
4. Charles E. Bohlen
5. Isaiah Bowman
6. Ralph Bunche
7. John M. Cabot
8. Mitchell B. Carroll
9. Andrew W. Cordier
10. John S. Dickey
11. John Foster Dulles
12. James Clement Dunn
13. Clyde Eagleton
14. Clark M. Eichelberger
15. Muir S. Fairchild
16. Thomas K. Finletter
17. Artemus Gates
18. Arthur J. Hepburn

9   James Perloff, *The Shadows of Power: The Council on Foreign Relations and the American Decline* (Appleton, WI: Western Islands, 2005), p. 71.

19. Julius C. Holmes	32. William L. Ransom
20. Philip C. Jessup	33. Nelson A. Rockefeller
21. Joseph E. Johnson	34. James T. Shotwell
22. R. Keith Kane	35. Harold E. Stassen
23. Foy D. Kohler	36. Edward R. Stettinius Jr.
24. John E. Lockwood	37. Adlai E. Stevenson
25. Archibald MacLeish	38. Robert Sweetser
26. John J. McCloy	39. James Swihart
27. Cord Meyer Jr.	40. Llewellyn E. Thompson
28. Edward G. Miller Jr.	41. Herman B. Wells
29. Hugh Moore	42. Francis Wilcox
30. Leo Pasvolsky	43. Charles W. Yost
31. Dewitt C. Poole	

The Secretary-General of the conference was U.S. State Department official Alger Hiss, a member of the CFR and a secret Soviet agent.[10] Nelson Rockefeller's pivotal part in drafting the final plan was memorialized by Drew Pearson, a Rockefeller journalistic lackey, in an article published on May 10, 1945.

10　William F. Jaspers, *Global Tyranny . . . Step-by-Step: The United Nations and the Emerging New World Order*, chap. 3, "The UN Founders," 1992, http://www.bibliotecapleyades.net/sociopolitica/global_tyranny/global_tyranny03.htm, accessed February 13, 2019.

THE PEARSON ARTICLE

SAN FRANCISCO.—*The play-by-play account of what went on behind the scenes after the Conference reluctantly voted to admit Argentina can now be revealed.*

After Stettinius forced a public vote on the issue despite Russian requests for delay, he found himself criticized by some of the press and public.

Upset, he hastily called a closed meeting of the U.S. delegation, charged with tension.

Young Rockefeller eulogized the way Stettinius had handled himself. "This country is fortunate to have its affairs in his hands," he praised.

Asst. Sec. Jimmy Dunn started to chime in, but was interrupted by shrewd Hamilton Fish Armstrong, key U.S. adviser:

"I am very disturbed by all this. I think we ought to call the press in and explain the American position. We are being called Fascists. Stettinius is being put in an unfair position."

Harold Stassen, of Minn., who had been cool to Argentina's admission, interrupted: "And what are you going to tell the press?"

John Foster Dulles said: "It's very important that the public does not view our delegation as reactionary."

Again Stassen interrupted: "Why must we be apologetic about something discussed fully here, then voted on and passed? The important thing is to work together. We can't avoid all differences between nations and people."

Stassen emphasized that there was justification for the American view, even if he didn't entirely endorse it himself. If there were no arguments, there was no use of a conference.

Stettinius thought Stassen's statement so good that he ought to broadcast it. Dunn protested the Russians were holding up the

Conference by refusing to permit Argentina to take up the chairman-
ship of a sub-committee. He launched upon an anti-Soviet tirade in
no uncertain terms.

Rockefeller endorsed Dunn's idea about giving Argentina a place on
a Conference committee, saying: "We must treat Argentina as well
as anyone else."

"I agree," chimed in Michigan's Sen. Vandenberg. "Now that we've
invited them, we must treat them right."

Stassen could not go along with them, saying: "It's bad enough we
let them in without giving them honors."

Vandenberg retorted, "Anything Rockefeller wants is o.k." [11]

THE LEAGUE REVIVED

The final draft was introduced to Congress on October 24, 1944, by
Senator Glen Taylor (D–ID) who called upon his fellow senators to go
on record favoring a world republic with an international police force. [12]
When it was presented for resolution, Senator Harold A. Burton (R–
OH) said: "We again have the chance to retrieve and establish, not a
League of Nations, but the present United Nations Charter, although
eighty percent of its provisions are, in substance, the same as those of
the League in Nations in 1919." [13]

This statement should have alerted the Senate that the charter represented no less than the League of Nations an abandonment of U.S.

11   Drew Pearson, quoted in Emanuel M. Josephson, *Rockefeller "Internationalist"* (New York: Chedney Press, 1952), pp. 401–2.

12   Joseph Preston Baratta, *The Politics of World Federation: United Nations, UN Reform, Atomic Control* (New York: Praeger, 2004), p. 155.

13   Harold Burton, quoted in Andrew Marshall, "Global Power and Global Government," *Global Research*, August 18, 2009, http://forum.prisonplanet.com/index.php?topic=129174.80;wap, accessed February 13, 2019.

sovereignty. It should have caused them to recall the rallying cry of Republicans in 1920 against such an organization: "The Republican Party stands for agreement among the nations to preserve the peace of the world . . . We believe that this can be done without depriving the people of the United States in advance of the right to determine for themselves what is just and fair, and without involving them as partici-pants and not as peacemakers in a multitude of quarrels, the merits of which they are unable to judge."[14]

RHODES RESURGENT

The most glaring problem with the resolution, which was signed into law by President Harry S. Truman on July 28, 1945, was that it represented a treaty between the United States and a world-governing organization. By law, a treaty can only be established between two sovereign nations, and the new organization was neither sovereign nor a state. Another problem was that the treaty called upon the United States to engage in military action at the discretion of foreign governments. This violated the Constitution, which mandated that Congress alone possessed the power to declare war. A third problem came with the stipulation that the President of the United States remain the supreme commander-in-chief of the military in times of peace, with the ability to engage at any time America's armed forces in military conflict.[15]

AN EXTRATERRITORIALITY

The Rockefellers played the central role not only in planning but also in funding the United Nations. The ideal site for the organiza-tion was Geneva, Switzerland, which had served as the headquarters for the League of Nations. But John D. Jr. objected to this neutral

---

14   Republican platform of 1920, quoted in G. Vance Smith and Tom Gow, *Masters of Deception: The Rise of the Council on Foreign Nations* (Colorado Springs, CO: Freedom First Society, 2012), pp. 36–37.

15   Marshall, "Global Power and Global Government."

location and shelled out $8 million for the construction of the UN in the midst of downtown New York City. The planners of the UN had said, "Anything that Rockefeller wants is okay." This proved true, even though the construction of the organization in Geneva would have saved American taxpayers billions of dollars and would have eliminated the necessity of creating an extraterritoriality in the midst of America's busiest city.[16]

The United Nations provided the Rockefellers with an "international front" to advance their business interests. By its charter, the United Nations is governed by three principal units: the Security Council, the General Assembly, and the Economic and Social Council. Under these units, hundreds of agencies and programs have been formed to impact every aspect of human activity from administering welfare programs to regulating the environment.

The United Nations, as conceived by the Council on Foreign Relations and funded by the House of Rockefeller, was never meant to be an academic debating society. It was conceived to become an international regime that would control the world's weapons, wars, courts, tax collectors, and economy. The orders to create this new international organization came from the Rockefellers.

Violators of these mandates are subjected to force, arrest, and trial in an international court of law.[17] Thus the brainstorm of Cecil Rhodes has crystallized into a political and economic reality.

The central source of power within the United Nations resides with the Security Council. This council consists of five permanent member-nations—the United States, the United Kingdom, France,

---

16   Josephson, *Rockefeller "Internationalist,"* p. 403.

17   Marten Zwanenburg, "United Nations and International Humanitarian Law," Oxford Public International Law, October 2015, http://opil.ouplaw.com/view/10.1093/law:epil/9780199231690/law-9780199231690-e1675, accessed February 13, 2019.

Russia, and China. Anyone of these member-nations possesses veto power over the final determinations. This relegation of power gives the organization a semblance of check and balance. But semblance is not reality, and the real control resides with the money cartel, who can force member-nations, even Russia, to comply with its interest since it possesses control over their economies. This control became evident on June 27, 1950, when the Security Council adopted Resolution 83, which determined that the attack on the Republic of Korea by Communist forces from North Korea constituted a "breach of peace" that warranted an immediate show of force.[18]

POLICE ACTION

In accordance with the Potsdam Conference, Korea, a protectorate of Japan, was divided in half along the 38th parallel. The northern half was occupied by the Soviet Union and the southern half by the United States. Stalin named Kim Il-Sung, one of his protégés, to serve as the premier of North Korea; he provided his military officials to train a North Korean army of 150,000 recruits, and he supplied the Communist army with tanks and fighter planes. On June 25, 1950, a force of 75,000 North Koreans poured over the 38th parallel in an invasion that was designed to reunite the country.[19]

Truman responded to the invasion by turning to the United Nations for a deployment of its Peacekeeping Forces. It was a bit of a ruse since American soldiers comprised 85 percent of this force. The ruse was compounded when the Security Council voted to approve the deployment, even though the war could have been prevented if the Soviets had exercised their veto. But the Soviets were not present at the critical meeting. Instead, they had staged a walkout in protest of the UN's refusal to provide a seat in its general assembly for Red China.[20]

18   Yong-jin Kim, *Major Powers and Korea* (Silver Spring, MD: Research Institute on Korean Affairs, 1973), p. 46.

19   Ibid.

20   Perloff, *The Shadows of Power*, p. 91.

Stalin named Kim Il-sung, one of his protégés, to serve as the premier of North Korea; he provided his military officials to train a North Korean army of 150,000 recruits, and he supplied the Communist army with tanks and fighter planes. On June 25, 1950, a force of 75,000 North Koreans poured over the 38th parallel in an invasion that was designed to reunite the country. "Kim Il-sung" by yeowatzup is licensed under CC BY 2.0

THE SOVIET MYSTERY

Why would the Soviets opt to pass up an opportunity to protect their surrogate operation in North Korea? Was a blunder of this magnitude really intentional? These questions have dogged historians for decades. The answers may be discovered by following the money.

By 1927, Rockefeller-owned Standard Oil of New York and its subsidiary, the Vacuum Oil Company, had purchased the Russian oil fields and constructed a massive refinery in Batumi on the coast of the Black Sea.[21] In accordance with the deal, the Rockefellers gained

---

21   Alexander Igolkin, "Early Lessons of Mutually Beneficial Cooperation," *Oil of Russia* mgazine, no. 3, 2004, http://www.oilru.com/or/17/230/, accessed February 13, 2019.

the right to market Soviet oil in Europe, while the Bolsheviks received a loan of $75 million.[22] During this same time, Rockefeller-owned Chase National Bank had established the American-Russian Chamber of Commerce, which financed Soviet raw material exports and sold Soviet bonds in the United States.[23]

In 1935, Stalin expropriated many foreign investments in Russia, but the holdings of the House of Rockefeller were not touched.[24] Other Rockefeller investments were made in the Soviet Union, including the construction of a truck factory that created tanks and rocket launchers.[25] The total holdings of Chase National, Standard Oil, the Guaranty Trust Company, and other firms controlled or owned by the Rockefellers remained concealed from public scrutiny. The profits from these enterprises flowed into numbered accounts at Swiss banks so that they could never be audited by American legislators or U.S. Treasury officials.[26] It was all a matter of high finance. The creation of another superpower by the House of Rockefeller proved to be an incredibly profitable venture. The Soviet Union began producing T-34/85 tanks and MiG-15 fighter jets for the North Korean army with financing from the House of Rockefeller.

THE WAR BOOM

The Korean War also produced a windfall for the American holdings of the money cartel, including the Rockefeller family. It necessitated, as John Whiteclay Chambers writes in *The Oxford Companion to American Military History*, "a permanent military-industrial establishment in

22   Gary Allen, *The Rockefeller File* (Seal Beach, CA: '76 Press, 1976), p. 107.

23   Mark M. Rich, *The Hidden Evil: The Financial Elite's Covert War against the Civilian Population* (Raleigh, NC: Lulu Press, 2009), p. 58.

24   Ibid.

25   Ibid.

26   Allen, *The Rockefeller File,* p. 107.

peacetime as well as wartime or, at least, in cold as well as hot war."[27] Since the war mandated a quadrupling in military spending, the fortunes of the Rockefellers and the other global banking families increased exponentially. The Rockefellers had heavily invested in Boeing, McDonnell Aircraft, and other leading firms that received lucrative contracts with the Department of Defense. In addition to its oil companies (Exxon, Mobil, Texaco, Atlantic-Richfield, Standard Oil of California, Standard Oil of Indiana, and Marathon), the family had acquired majority control in steel companies (Inland Steel, Wheeling-Pittsburgh Steel, and National Steel) and chemical companies (Merck, Pfizer, and Wyeth), all of which reaped enormous profits from the so-called police action.[28] International Harvester, the Rockefeller-owned agricultural equipment company, emerged as one of the country's leading defense contractors by producing aerial torpedoes, military bulldozers, M7 tanks, 37mm cannon shells, 57mm anti-tank guns, aircraft cannons, and other munitions. An extra bonus to these earnings was the remilitarization of Japan, which not only forced the Rockefeller-owned firms to go into overdrive but also gave rise to the Rockefeller-dominated Nippon Oil and Energy.[29]

Throughout the conflict, Standard Oil of California in conjunction with the Texas Company, through their Caltex joint subsidiary, provided the North Koreans and Chinese Communists with the oil that they required to fly the planes and drive the tanks that slaughtered the GIs fighting with the South Koreans. The oil was paid for at the expense of American taxpayers, including the American soldiers who

27 John Whiteclay Chambers, *The Oxford Companion to American Military History* (New York: Oxford University Press, 2000), p. 439.

28 Allen, *The Rockefeller File*, pp. 31–33.

29 Staff Report, "Japan: The Politics of Oil," *Executive Intelligence Review*, March 29, 1977, https://larouchepub.com/eiw/public/1977/eirv04n13-19770329/eirv04n13-19770329_066-japan___the_politics_of_oil.pdf, accessed February 13, 2019.

were slaughtered and maimed, through the Marshall Plan.[30]

The war was particularly ugly. The UN strategy involved the "mass killing of civilians" through extensive bombings. On August 12, the U.S. Air Force dropped 626 tons of bombs on North Korea; two weeks later, the daily tonnage increased to 800 tons. The carpet bombings resulted in the destruction of 78 cities and thousands of villages. By the time an armistice was signed on July 27, 1953, a third of the population of North Korea—over three million people—had been wiped out.[31] The official U.S. casualty list showed that 36,914 American soldiers had died in the conflict, and 7,800 remained unaccounted for.[32] The struggle resulted neither in territorial gain or loss. The objective of the war had been containment, not liberation or victory. The terms of the armistice called for the creation of a demilitarized zone (DMZ) between North and South Korea. Each side was to be 2,200 yards from the center. The DMZ was to be patrolled by both sides at all times.[33] And so it had come to this: America's wars were to be waged with limited rules of engagement and indefinite outcomes to advance the purpose of the global bankers, who had brought the United Nations into being.

Despite the military failure of the Korean War, the CFR continued its campaign for more and more power to be granted to the United Nations, including the institution of a permanent force to police the planet. In *Freedom from War: The United States Program for General and Complete Disarmament in a Peaceful World,* a publication from the U.S. State Department, Dean Rusk and other CFR members called for the transference of all tactical and strategic military weapons to the United States. Draftees of this document argued universal peace could only be

30   Josephson, *The Truth about Rockefeller,* p. 142.

31   Michel Chossudovsky, *The Globalization of War: America's 'Long War' against Humanity* (Montreal, Quebec: *Global Research* Publishers, 2015), pp. 26–30.

32   CNN Library, "Korean War Fast Facts," *CNN News,* June 21, 2016, http://www.cnn.com/2013/06/28/world/asia/korean-war-fast-facts/, accessed February 13, 2019.

33   Ibid.

achieved by this means.[34] They overlooked the fact that the majority of the UN member nations were dictatorships with a deep-seated repugnance for constitutional republics and that the gatherings of the General Assembly were characterized by rabid anti-American rants.

LUCIFER'S REEMERGENCE

The planners of the New World Order, including Rhodes and Nathan Rothschild, were intensely interested in the occult—an interest that gave rise to the Society of Psychic Research and the Theosophist Movement. Their obsession was shared by their disciples, including the founders of the United Nations. The Lucis Trust became an official consultative agency of the UN and its publishing arm. Founded in 1922 as the Lucifer Publishing Company by Alice Bailey, a disciple of Helena Petrova Blavatsky, the chartered purpose of the Trust was as follows: "To encourage the study of comparative religion, philosophy, science and art; to encourage every line of thought tending to the broadening of human sympathies and interests, and the expansion of ethical religious and educational literature; to assist or to engage in activities for the relief of suffering and for human betterment; and, in general, to further worthy efforts for humanitarian and educational ends."[35] The leading sponsors of Lucis Trust included Henry Clausen, Supreme Grand Commander of the Supreme Council, 33rd Degree, Southern District Scottish Rite; John D. Rockefeller IV; the Rockefeller Foundation; the Marshall Field family; World Bank president Robert McNamara; U.S. Ambassador to Moscow and IBM president Thomas Watson; Undersecretary of State Alexis Johnson, and the United Theosophists of New York City.[36]

Bailey's ultimate objective in establishing Lucis Trust was to be about

---

34   Smith and Gow, *Masters of Deception*, pp. 68–71.

35   Lucis Trust Charter, cited in Curtis A. Chamberlain, *The Judas Epidemic: Exposing the Betrayal of the Christian Faith in Church and Government* (Bloomington, IN: WestBow Press, 2011), p. 111.

36   Lyndon La Rouche, "Real History of Satanism," La Rouche Publications, January 17, 2015, http://www.rense.com/general61/satanism.htm, accessed February 13, 2019.

a one-world religion under the guiding light of Lucifer. She wrote: "The day is dawning when all religions will be regarded as emanating from one spiritual source; all will be seen as unitedly providing the one root out of which the universal religion will inevitably emerge."[37] In keeping with this objective, the Trust established World Goodwill, an agency within the UN that seeks to harness the "spiritual qualities of human beings" in order to issue forth a new era of enlightenment. Signatories to the World Goodwill document included: Helmut Schmidt, former chancellor of West Germany; Malcolm Fraser, former Australian prime minister; Oscar Arias Sanchez, former prime minister of Costa Rica; Israeli president Shimon Peres; Robert McNamara; Federal Reserve Chairman Paul Volcker; and Jimmy Carter.[38] Aside from Lucis Trust and World Goodwill, the scent of sulfur could also be discerned in the creation of the UN's two evil sisters: the International Monetary Fund and the World Bank.

---

37   Alice A. Bailey, *Ponder on This: A Compilation* (Washington, D.C.: Lucis Publishing, 2003), p. 294.

38   Terry Melanson, "Lucis Trust, Alice Bailey, World Goodwill, and the False Light of the World," *Conspiracy Archive*, May 8, 2005, http://www.conspiracyarchive.com/NewAge/Lucis_Trust.htm, accessed February 13, 2019.

17

TWINS OF EVIL

Just between you and me, shouldn't the World Bank be encouraging more migration of the dirty industries to the LDCs [less-developed countries]?... I think the economic logic behind dumping a load of toxic waste in the lowest wage country is impeccable and we should face up to that...I've always thought that under-populated countries in Africa are vastly under-polluted, their air quality is probably vastly inefficiently low compared to Los Angeles or Mexico City... The concern over an agent that causes a one in a million change in the odds of prostrate cancer is obviously going to be much higher in a country where people survive to get prostrate cancer than in a country where under 5 mortality is 200 per thousand...The problem with the arguments against all of these proposals for more pollution in LDCs (intrinsic rights to certain goods, moral reasons, social concerns, lack of adequate markets, etc.) could be turned around and used more or less effectively against every Bank proposal for liberalization.

—LAWRENCE H. SUMMERS, CHIEF ECONOMIST OF THE WORLD BANK, IN AN INTERNAL MEMO DATED DECEMBER 12, 1991. SUMMERS WENT ON TO BECOME THE U.S. TREASURY SECRETARY IN THE CLINTON ADMINISTRATION AND PRESIDENT OF HARVARD UNIVERSITY.

IN ADDITION TO the United Nations, the Council on Foreign Relations (CFR), through its War and Peace Studies Project, also spawned the International Monetary Fund (IMF) and the World Bank. The Articles of Agreement for these organizations were drawn up at an international conference of 44 allied countries at the Mount Washington Hotel and

Resort in Bretton Woods, New Hampshire. The War and Peace Studies Project was funded entirely by the Rockefeller Foundation, and the control of the CFR fell into the hands of David Rockefeller, the youngest of John D. Jr.'s sons, who had joined the organization in 1941.[1]

Outwardly, the IMF was supposed to be a philanthropic endeavor to address the problem of poverty and starvation throughout the world by controlling international exchange rates and stabilizing currencies.[2] Clandestinely, the new world financial institution represented a grandiose scheme so that the nations of the world would relinquish their sovereignty to the money cartel.[3] As A. K. Chesterton wrote: "The World Bank and the IMF were not incubated by hard pressed governments engaged in waging war, but by a supra-national Money Power, which could afford to look ahead to the shaping of a post-war world that would serve its interests."[4]

TRANSFERENCE OF WEALTH

The funding for the IMF, which established its headquarters in Washington, D.C., was based on a quota system with the most industrialized countries providing the greatest share of revenue. But the lion's share (over 30 percent) came from the United States taxpayers, since the currencies of other countries were not transferable into gold. FDR had confiscated the gold of the American citizenry and removed the nation from the gold standard. But everybody else in the world could still exchange their paper dollars for gold at the fixed price of $35 per

---

1   Peter Grose, *Continuing the Inquiry: The Council on Foreign Relations from 1921 to 1966*, Council on Foreign Relations Press, November 1982, https://www.cfr.org/book/continuing-inquiry, accessed February 13, 2019.

2   Emanuel M. Josephson, *The "Federal" Reserve Conspiracy and Rockefellers* (New York: Chedney Press, 1968), p. 159.

3   Ibid.

4   A. K. Chesterton, quoted in Jack Kenney, "The Federal Reserve: Bankers for the New World Order," *New American*, January 2014, https://www.thenewamerican.com/economy/item/17312-the-federal-reserve-bankers-for-the-new-world-order, accessed February 13, 2019.

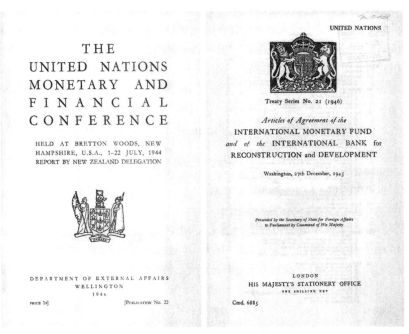

The funding for the IMF, which established its headquarters in Washington, D.C., was based on a quota system with the most industrialized countries providing the greatest share of revenue. "International Monetary Fund formed 1945" by Archives New Zealand is licensed under CC BY-SA 2.0

ounce.[5] The result of this arrangement was the ongoing transference of America's wealth to overseas banks, and the recognition of the dollar as the basis of the global economy.

Each nation was required to maintain the value of its currency within 10 percent of the value of the dollar. This demand forced countries to bolster their paper money with shipments of gold to the IMF. This stipulation came with the recognition of the right to establish the price of gold at any value they might fancy.[6] This right eventually enabled members of the money cartel to multiply their wealth almost beyond measure.

---

5   G. Edward Griffin, *The Creature from Jekyll Island,* 5th Edition (Westlake Village, CA: The Reality Zone, 2017), p. 90.

6   Josephson, *The "Federal" Reserve Conspiracy and Rockefellers,* p. 161.

A GOAL BEYOND GOLD

As long as the dollar remained redeemable in gold, the amount of currency that could be created by the money cartel in charge of the IMF remained limited. John Maynard Keyes, the leading British economist at the Bretton Woods Conference, recognized this problem as soon as the IMF was established. He wrote: "I felt that the leading central bank would never voluntarily relinquish the then existing forms of the gold standard, and I did not desire a catastrophe sufficiently violent to shake them off involuntarily. The only practical hope lay in a gradual evolution in the forms of a managed world currency, taking the existing gold standard as a starting point."[7]

The ultimate goal of the group who gathered at Bretton Woods was the creation of a world currency called the *bancor*. At the conference, Mariner Eccles, a governor of the Federal Reserve Board, noted: "An international currency is synonymous with international government."[8] But this act proved to be even too radical for acceptance by the American dignitaries in attendance who, strange to say, retained a modicum of patriotism.

THE NEW MONEY

The plan to wean the world from gold came to fruition on August 15, 1971, when President Richard Nixon signed an executive order declaring that the United States no longer would redeem its paper dollars for gold.[9] Nixon was acting on the advice of Secretary of State Henry Kissinger, a lifelong appendage of the Rockefeller interests, and budget

---

7   John Maynard Keynes, *The Collected Writings of John Maynard Keyes* (New York: Macmillan, 1971), 5: xx.

8   Mariner Eccles, quoted in G. Vance Smith and Tom Gow, *Masters of Deception: The Rise of the Council on Foreign Relations* (Colorado Springs: Freedom First Society, 2012), p. 60.

9   Griffin, *The Creature from Jekyll Island*, p. 91.

adviser George Shultz, later secretary of state and chairman of the vast Bechtel construction giant.[10]

After Nixon's executive order, the IMF now could function as the world's central bank by providing an unlimited issue of its own fiat currency to member nations. This new money, based solely on the money cartel's statement of its worth, was called Special Drawing Rights (SDR). The member nations of the IMF were now compelled to make their currencies fully exchangeable for SDR. This meant that the new IMF currency was legal tender in every industrialized country, including the United States.[11]

A DOUBLE-EDGED SWORD

The SDRs became tantalizing to every Third World country that sought to enter the modern age. The new currency was backed by gold; convertible into any form of cash; and available in large amounts to all takers, provided they had the means (including natural resources) to secure the loans. Eventually, as economist Dennis Turner explains, the following pattern was set: "SDRs are turned into loans to Third-World nations by the creation of checking accounts in the commercial or central banks of the members in the name of debtor governments. These bank accounts are created out of thin air. The IMF creates dollars, francs, pounds, or other hard currencies and gives them to a Third World dictator, with inflation resulting in the country where the currency originated. . . . Inflation is caused in the industrialized nations while wealth is transferred from the general public to the debtor nation. And the debtor nation doesn't repay."[12]

But the sword is two-edged. Nations borrow SDRs primarily to pay

---

10   F. William Engdahl, *Gods of Money: Wall Street and the Death of the American Century* (Wiesbaden, DEU: Edition Engdahl, 2010), p. 163.

11   Stack Jones, "An Essay on the History of Banking," *The Banking Swindle*, January 1, 2018, https://criminalbankingmonopoly.wordpress.com/, accessed February 13, 2019.

12   Dennis Turner, quoted in Griffin, *The Creature from Jekyll Island*, p. 90.

interest on their mounting debts. This would be fine and dandy, save for the fact that the IMF charges interest on every SDR that it produces from its computer system. And so, the loans, for the most part, do not serve to bolster failing economies. They simply create a steady flow of wealth from borrowing nations to the money changers who control the IMF and are not subjected to any international supervision.

THE DOLLAR'S DEMISE

The dollar, severed from the gold standard, ceased to serve as the official IMF currency and was compelled to compete with other currencies—primarily the mark and the yen—on its relative value to the countries. Over the decades, the dollar became increasingly discounted. Still and all, it remained a favored medium of exchange since America, as a country, remained wide open to foreign investors, who could buy American real estate, American factories and industrial plants, American mining companies and shopping centers without the restrictions placed on such purchases by other nations. For this reason, the Federal Reserve continued to churn out massive amounts of fiat paper money, since the demand for such dollars seemed to be endless.[13]

This situation permitted Americans to finance its enormous trade deficits with more and more money made out of nothing and allowed them to purchase cars, cell phones, computers, clothing, generic drugs, and 70-inch high-definition television sets at cut-rate prices, while the foreign manufacturers got the greenbacks. By the 21st century, this flood of dollars, which continued to be discounted, caused inflation to raise its hoary head until America was rapidly approaching the time, when foreign manufacturers no longer will accept dollars for their goods and the Federal Reserve no longer will be able to finance its enormous trade deficit by churning out paper money.[14]

---

13   Ibid., pp. 93–94.

14   Ibid.

THE NEW FEUDALISM

Since the IMF possessed the power to regulate currencies and to establish exchange rates, the new international bank ruled in 1988 that world bankers must raise their reserve capital to eight percent by 1992. This demand placed a ceiling on fractional reserve lending practices. Countries throughout the world began to scramble for capital—treasury bonds from other countries, foreign currencies, gold and other liquidable assets. To acquire this capital, countries were forced to sell stock in their public utilities and nationalized companies. Japan, which had one of the lowest capital reserves, was hit so hard by this new requirement that its economy collapsed almost immediately. Within a matter of days, 50 percent of the value of Japan's stock market was swept away, along with 60 percent of the value of the country's commercial real estate. In an effort to prop up the collapsing economy, the Bank of Japan lowered the interest rate to one-half of one percent—practically giving away money to anyone willing to spend it. The effort was fruitless, and the depression continued to worsen.[15] In 2009, Japan signed a $100 billion borrowing agreement with the IMF. This amount was equivalent to 31 percent of the IMF's total funds.[16] Japan, in effect, had become a vassal of the new international bank.

Mexico was also hard hit by the regulation to fortify its reserve capital to eight percent. The country received a $20 billion bailout from the United States. But even that amount could not ward off financial disaster. Mexico's debt continued to escalate, and new loans from the IMF were created to cover the interest on old loans. Mexico, too, was forced to sell off its assets, which were gobbled up by the money cartel.[17]

As the financial disaster continued to spread, the IMF continued

---

15 Jones, "An Essay on the History of Banking."

16 "IMF Survey: IMF Signs $100 Billion Borrowing Agreement with Japan," International Monetary Fund, February 13, 2009, https://www.imf.org/en/News/Articles/2015/09/28/04/53/sonew021309a, accessed February 13, 2019.

17 Jones, "An Essay on the History of Banking."

to churn out more and more SDRs by the mere stroke of a pen on one of its ledgers. Eventually, the new world bank attained absolute economic power over the people of the world, as it alone could decide what countries would receive further loans, and what countries would not.[18]

THE SECOND SISTER

While the IMF purportedly provides loans to stabilize economies, the World Bank shelled out loans to war-ravaged and underdeveloped nations.[19] Through the years, the majority of the presidents of the World Bank have come from the stables of the Council on Foreign Relations. Eugene Meyer, the first president of the World Bank (1945), was a CRF official and the former chairman of the Federal Reserve. He was succeeded by John J. McCloy (1947–1949), who also served as the

While the IMF purportedly provides loans to stabilize economies, the World Bank shelled out loans to war-ravaged and underdeveloped nations. Through the years, the majority of the presidents of the World Bank have come from the stables of the Council on Foreign Relations. "World Bank building" by AgnosticPreachersKid is licensed under CC BY-SA 3.0

CFR chairman.[20] All of these men had strong ties to Wall Street. McCloy was a partner of the Wall Street corporate law firm of Milbank, Tweed, Hope, Hadley & McCloy, which had long served the Rockefeller family and the Chase Bank as legal counsel. From there, he moved to become chairman of the board of the Chase Manhattan Bank, a director of the Rockefeller Foundation and of Rockefeller Center.[21]

---

18   Ibid.

19   Ron Chernow, *The House of Morgan: An American Banking Dynasty and the Rise of Modern Finance* (New York: Grove Press, 1990), p. 518.

20   Smith and Gow, *Masters of Deception*, p. 60.

21   Murray N. Rothbard, "Rockefeller, Morgan, and War," Mises Institute, April 30, 2017, https://mises.org/library/rockefeller-morgan-and-war, accessed February 13, 2019.

The World Bank established its headquarters in Washington, D.C. in 1945. Its membership consisted of the same 44 nations that belonged to the IMF. Like its sister agency, it was controlled by "one dollar, one vote" rather than the "one country, one vote" UN system. Since the United States provided nearly 20 percent of the money required to fund the World Bank, the New York bankers (Morgan, Rockefeller, and Kuhn-Loeb) gained a permanent place among the Bank's executive directors and the exclusive right to appoint the Bank president.[22]

This latest Rockefeller creation was supposed to serve as the savior of mankind by enabling foreign governments to provide care for those most in need. The loans were provided on generous terms, usually at rates below market, and for durations as long as 50 years.[23] The lion's share of the cash, which amounted to $30 billion, came from the U.S. taxpayers.[24]

TERMS AND CONDITIONS

But there is a snare to the World Bank's every transaction. The money, like IMF loans, is provided with very exacting conditions, known as structural adjustment programs (SAPs).[25] One SAP is the immediate reimbursement to the country's creditors, such as Morgan Stanley, Chase Manhattan, and Citibank. Another is the country's agreement to sell off its key assets, including their water supply, their pipelines, and their power systems to buyers provided by the World Bank/IMF. A third condition is the country's commitment to take remedial steps, including a restructuring of its government and the resettlement of

---

22 Asad Ismi, "Impoverishing a Continent: The World Bank and the IMF in Africa," Halifax Initiative Coalition, July 2004, http://www.halifaxinitiative.org/updir/ImpoverishingAContinent.pdf, accessed February 13, 2019.

23 Ibid., p. 95.

24 Ibid.

25 Ibid.

populations, dictated by World Bank/IMF officials.[26]

The SAPs have caused devastating results for countries who accept the loans. The World Bank/IMF forced Argentina and Ecuador to liquidate its public holdings in order to comply with the repayment demands. In this way, Rockefeller-affiliated Citibank seized control of 50 percent of Argentina's banks; Rockefeller-owned British Petroleum assumed ownership of Ecuador's pipelines; and Enron, a shell company tied to the House of Rothschild, obtained the Great Lakes, which provide water to Buenos Aires.[27]

KILLING THE THIRD WORLD

Other SAPs include the lowering of existing wages, the raising of the interest rate, the downsizing of all state facilities, the phasing out of statutory minimal wages, and the termination of "surplus" teachers and health-care workers.[28] In extreme circumstances, even the resettlement of existing populations is required.[29] Such a program got underway in Tanzania, which has received more aid per capita from the World Bank than any other country. Thousands of Tanzanians were driven from their villages, which were set ablaze, and loaded like cattle into trucks for relocation in government villages.[30]

On average, Third World countries face as many as 67 conditions

---

26   Peter Palms, "Building the New World Order with the IMF and the World Bank and Taypayers Pay the Bill," *Thom Hartmann Program*, October 9, 2015, https://www.thomhartmann.com/users/dr-peterpalms/blog/2015/10/building-new-world-order-imf-and-world-bank-and-taxpayers-pay-bill, accessed February 13, 2019.

27   Greg Palast, "World Bank Secret Documents Consume Argentina," *Greg Palast.com*, March 4, 2002, http://www.gregpalast.com/world-bank-secret-documents-consumes-argentinaalex-jones-interviews-reporter-greg-palast/, accessed February 13, 2009.

28   Michel Chossudovsky, *The Globalization of War: America's "Long War" against Humanity* (Montreal: Global Research 2015), pp. 125–31.

29   Ibid.

30   G. Edward Griffin, *The Creature from Jekyll Island*, p. 98.

for every World Bank loan. Some countries are hit with a far higher number of demands. Uganda, for example, where 23 percent of the children under five are malnourished, faced a staggering 197 conditions attached to its World Bank development finance grant in 2005. Anxious to uphold the conditions, Ugandan security forces engaged in mass detentions, torture, and the killing of hundreds of prisoners.[31]

THE AFRICAN NIGHTMARE

Zimbabwe, formerly known as Rhodesia in honor of Cecil Rhodes, serves as a prime example of the effects of SAPs on a Third World economy. In accordance with stipulations from the IMF/World Bank, the leftist government confiscated and nationalized many of the farms that were owned by white settlers. The most desirable properties became occupied by leading government officials, while the least desirable farms were transformed into state-run collectives. The collectives were such miserable failures that the natives who worked the farms were forced to beg for food.[32]

By 1992, one year after Zimbabwe became subjected to the IMF/World Bank, the economy went into a deep recession, with the GDP falling by nearly eight percent. Twenty-five percent of the public workers were laid off, and unemployment began to soar, reaching 50 percent in 1997. By 1999, 68 percent of the population was living on less than two dollars a day.[33] The per capita budget for health care fell from $22 in 1990 to $11 in 1996, causing a 30 percent decline in the quality of medical services. Twice as many women were dying of childbirth in Harare hospitals in 1993 than in 1990. By 1995, the number of cases of tuberculosis had quadrupled. At the dawn of the 21st century,

---

31 Ibid.

32 Ibid, pp. 98–99.

33 Ismi, "Impoverishing a Continent."

one-fourth of Zimbabwe's population was infected with HIV/AIDS.[34]

According to a three-year study released in 2002 by the Structural Adjustment Participatory Review International Network (SAPRIN) in collaboration with the World Bank, SAPs have been "expanding poverty, inequality, and insecurity around the world. They have torn at the heart of economies and the social fabric. . . increasing tensions among different social strata, fueling extremist movements and delegitimizing democratic political systems. Their effects, particularly on the poor, are so profound and pervasive that no amount of targeted social investments can begin to address the social crises that they have engendered." [35]

ANTI-AMERICAN ANIMUS

Since the World Bank and the IMF are located in Washington, D.C., and controlled the Houses of Morgan and Rockefeller, the people who have been subjected to SAPs manifest a strong anti-American animus. They assume that the twin banks are part of a corrupt capitalistic government that seeks to deprive them of life's basic necessities. Within 40 years of the creation of these sister organizations, violent riots directed against Americans and caused by the austerity programs erupted in Argentina, Bolivia, Brazil, Ecuador, Egypt, Haiti, Liberia, Peru, and the Sudan.[36]

Concerning these occurrences, Luis Ignacio Silva, a prominent Brazilian politician, said: "Without being radical or overly bold, I will tell you that the Third World War has already started—a silent war, not for that reason any the less sinister. This war is tearing down Brazil, Latin America, and practically all the Third World. Instead of soldiers dying, there are children; instead of millions of wounded, there are millions of unemployed; instead of destruction of bridges, there is the tearing down of factories, schools, hospitals, and entire economies. It

---

34   Ibid.

35   SAPRIN, "The Policy Roots of Economic Crisis and Poverty: A Multi-Country Participatory Assessment of Structural Adjustment," April 2002.

36   "IMF Hands Out Prescriptions for Sour Economic Medicine," *Insight*, February 9, 1987.

is a war by the United States against the Latin American continent and the Third World. It is a war over the foreign debt, one which has as its main weapon interest, a weapon more deadly than the atom bomb, more shattering than a laser beam."[37]

---

37 Luis Ignatio Silva, quoted in Susan George, *A Fate Worse Than Debt: The World Financial Crisis and the Poor* (New York: Grove Press, 1990), p. 238.

18

UNHOLY GHOST

The period extending from the Korean war (1950–53) to the present is marked by a succession of U.S. sponsored theater wars (Korea, Vietnam, Cambodia, Afghanistan, Iraq, and Yugoslavia), various forms of military intervention, including low intensity conflicts, "civil wars" (The Congo, Angola, Somalia, Ethiopia, Rwanda, Sudan), military coups, U.S. sponsored death squadrons and massacres (Chile, Guatemala, Honduras, Argentina, Indonesia, Thailand, Philippines), covert wars in support of al Qaeda "freedom fighters" (Soviet-Afghan war), U.S.-NATO covert wars using al Qaeda as foot soldiers (Syria), U.S.-NATO sponsored humanitarian military interventions: Libya in 2011 (aerial bombings combined with support to al Qaeda rebels). The objective has not been to win in these wars but in essence to destabilize these countries as nation states as well as impose a proxy government which acts on behalf of Western interests. Accounting for these various operations, the United States has attacked, directly or indirectly, some 44 countries in different regions of the developing world since 1945, a number of them many times.

MICHEL CHOSSUDOVSKY, *THE GLOBALIZATION OF WAR*, 2015

IN 1946, General Hoyt S. Vandenberg, as director of Central Intelligence (DCI), recruited Allen Dulles, a lawyer for the House of Morgan and the president of the CFR, "to draft proposals for the shape and organization of what was to become the Central Intelligence Agency in 1947." The meeting took place within offices within Rockefeller Center.

By the time the CIA was officially established by President Truman in 1947, David Rockefeller assumed control of the inner core of the CFR and the Rockefeller and Carnegie Foundations allocated $34 million for the new Agency to engage in covert activities.[1] Dulles promptly formed an advisory group of Wall Street investment bankers or lawyers, who were prominent CFR officials. In 1948, Truman appointed Dulles to chair a committee to review the CIA's performance, and Dulles again appointed two New York lawyers from the CFR to assist him.[2]

As soon as Dulles took charge of the CIA, the Rockefellers became the private bankers for the new intelligence empire, and David became an important source for off-the-books cash to the spy agency.[3] Thomas Braden, who served as the head of the CIA's International Organizations Division, said: "I often briefed David semi-officially and with Allen's permission. [David] was of the same mind as us, and very approving of everything we were doing . . . Sometimes David would give me money to do things which weren't in the budget. He gave me a lot

In 1946, General Hoyt S. Vandenberg, as director of Central Intelligence (DCI), recruited Allen Dulles, a lawyer for the House of Morgan and the president of the CFR, "to draft proposals for the shape and organization of what was to become the Central Intelligence Agency in 1947."

---

1   Eric Dubay, *The Atlantean Conspiracy* (Durham, NC: Lulu, 2009), p. 74.

2   Ibid.

3   Ibid.

of money for causes in France."[4] A troika had been formed that would advance the interests of the Rockefeller family and other members of the money cartel throughout the world.

THE MILITARY-INDUSTRIAL ESTABLISHMENT

Under David Rockefeller's rule, the CFR would come to include not only the leading military-industrial firms but also almost every major business and bank in the country, including Bank of America, Merrill Lynch, Chevron, Exxon Mobil, J.P. Morgan Chase, Morgan Stanley, Goldman Sachs, Shell Oil, American Express, Barclays, Lockheed Martin, Lazard, Soros Fund Management, Prudential Financial, IBM, General Electric, Facebook, FedEx, Rothschild North America, Northrop Grumman, Microsoft, Raytheon, Merck and Company, Standard and Poor's, Sony Corporation of America, Time Warner, and Walmart.[5] A small sampling of the prominent names on the 2015 membership roster is as follows: Elliot Abrams, Madeleine Albright, Bruce Babbit, James Baker, Warren Beatty, Michael Bloomberg, Sidney Blumenthal, John Bolton, Zbigniew Brzezinski, Warren Buffett, Paul Bremer, Jimmy Carter, Dick Cheney, Warren Christopher, Henry Cisneros, Wesley Clark, Bill Clinton, Chelsea Clinton, George Clooney, Katie Couric, Scott Cuomo, Christopher Dodd, Alfonse D'Amato, Diane Feinstein, Timothy Geithner, Ruth Bader Ginsburg, Alan Greenspan, Chuck Hagel, Teresa Kerry Heinz, Vernon Jordan, Joseph Kennedy III, Edward Kennedy Jr., Henry Kissinger, Charles Krauthammer, John Kerry, Bernard Lewis, Joe Lieberman, John McCain, George Mitchell, Janet Negroponte, Alice Rivlin, Grover Norquist, Sam Nunn, Janet Napolitano, Colin Powell, Condoleezza Rice, John Roberts, John D. Rockefeller IV, David Rockefeller, David Rockefeller Jr., Nicholas Rockefeller, Steven Rockefeller, Donna Shalala, Susan Rice, Douglas

---

4   Thomas Braden, quoted in Ibid.

5   Council on Foreign Relations, brochure, 2017, http://i.cfr.org/content/about/About_CFR_2016.pdf, accessed February 13, 2019.

Schoen, Joe Scarborough, William Roper, George Soros, Jonathan Soros, Lesley Stahl, Diane Sawyer, Laura Tyson, Cyrus Vance, Barbara Walters, Paul Wolfowitz, and Janet Yellen.[6]

PROJECT MK-ULTRA

Throughout the 1950s, the Rockefeller Foundation provided funding for Project MK-Ultra, code name given to a program of experiments intended to identify and develop drugs and procedures to be used in interrogations in order to weaken the individual and force confessions through mind control. The operation was officially sanctioned in 1953 and officially halted in 1973. MK-Ultra used numerous methods to manipulate people's mental states and alter brain functions, including the surreptitious administration of drugs (especially LSD) and other chemicals, hypnosis, sensory deprivation, isolation, and

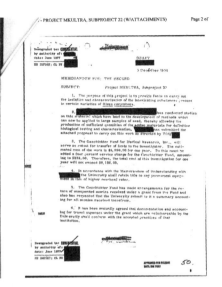

Throughout the 1950s, The Rockefeller Foundation provided funding for Project MK-Ultra, a mind-control program. With such, experiments were conducted to identify and develop drugs and procedures to be used in interrogations in order to weaken the individual and force confessions through mind control. "Subproject22" is licensed under CC BY-SA 3.0

other forms of psychological torture. The ultimate goal of the project was to produce Manchurian Candidates who could eliminate such pesky characters as Fidel Castro.[7] But it also included studies in means

---

6   Council on Foreign Relations, membership roster, http://www.cfr.org/about/membership/roster.html, accessed February 13, 2019.

7   Jeffrey St. Clair and Alexander Cockburn, "House of Horrors: The CIA, Dr. Gottlieb and MK-Ultra," Sott.net, November 19, 2017, https://www.sott.net/article/368300-House-of-horrors-The-CIA-Dr-Gottlieb-and-MK-Ultra, accessed February 13, 2019.

of controlling the thoughts of the American people by public relations, advertising, hypnosis, and other forms of suggestion.[8]

OIL AND BANANAS

David Rockefeller also began initiating CIA covert activities to feather the family nest, including a coup in Iran to oust the democratically elected government of Prime Minister Mohammad Mossadegh. In 1928, the Rockefeller's Standard Oil, the Royal Dutch-Shell, and the Anglo-Iranian Oil Company had formed a powerful oil cartel. But Mossadegh nationalized Iran's oil production, breaking the oil cartel and causing the Rockefeller family to lose control of the vast oil reserves at the basin of the Caspian Sea. In 1953, Dulles began to transfer millions in black funds to Iranian General Fazlollah Zahedi. The funds were to be used "in any way that would bring about the fall of Mossadegh."[9] The coup leaders under General Zahedi planted anti-Mossadegh propaganda in the Iranian press, mounted demonstrations against the government, and bribed public officials to ensure the prime minister's ouster. Next, they staged terror attacks that could be blamed on Mossadegh. They machine-gunned civilians, bombed mosques, and distributed pamphlets that read: "Up with Mossadegh, up with Communism, down with Allah." Following the coup, Mossadegh was tossed into prison, the Shah Reza Pahlavi was restored to power, and the Rockefellers gained control of half of Iran's oil production.[10]

THE BANISHMENT OF ARBENZ

One year later, the CIA, under Allen Dulles's direction, would launch another coup of a democratically elected government for the sake of the Rockefeller family. Jacob Arbenz, who became president of Guatemala

8   Steve Kangas, "A Timeline of CIA Atrocities," *Global Research,* June 9, 1997, http://www.globalresearch.ca/a-timeline-of-cia-atrocities/5348804, accessed February 13, 2019.

9   Dubay, *The Atlantean Conspiracy,* p. 76.

10   Ibid.

in 1950, had been a progressive leader who introduced the minimum wage and a policy of universal suffrage. But in 1952, he initiated a land reform program aimed at the redistribution of the country's farm's acreage. The program entailed the expropriation of the vast holdings of the United Fruit Company, which owned 42 percent of the entire country and never shelled out a cent in taxes.[11] The company, which operated as a state within the state, also owned the country's telephone and telegraph systems as well as almost all of the railroad tracks. United Fruit's legal council had been John Foster Dulles and the Dulles brothers were principal shareholders in the firm.[12]

To remove Arbenz from office, the CIA employed the talents of Tommy "the Cork" Corcoran, who had assisted Helliwell in the creation of Cargo Air Transport and Sea Supply.[13] A smear campaign was launched in which Arbenz was depicted as an agent of the Soviet Union, a tyrant who had conducted a bloody purge of his opponents, and as a thief who had raided the treasury of the impoverished country.[14] Corcoran created a rebel force of mercenaries that launched a series of violent attacks against the Arbenz government. The attacks included an invasion of Guatemala City that was supported by a CIA bombing campaign. On June 27, 1954, Arbenz was expelled from office. The CIA replaced him with a series of right-wing dictators whose bloodthirsty policies would kill over 100,000 Guatemalans in the next 40 years.[15]

---

11   David McAdam, "United Fruit Company," *Oligarch Kings: Power, Politics and America's Noble Families,* May 21, 2010.

12   Ibid.

13   Henrik Kruger, *The Great Heroin Coup: Drugs, Intelligence and International Finance* (Boston: South End, 1980), p. 68.

14   Talbot, *The Devil's Chessboard,* p. 253.

15   Ibid.

Over the course of the latter half of the 20th century, the relationship between the CIA and the Rockefellers became so close that highly classified documents were stored within a vault in a carriage house of Nelson Rockefeller's residence in Pocantico, New York.

A PATTERN OF OPERATION

Other covert activities were undertaken by the CIA to protect Rockefeller interests, including the overthrowing of Joao Goulart in Brazil and Salvador Allende in Chile followed the same pattern. First, the Rockefeller holdings were threatened by a popular or democratically elected official who attempted to nationalize the foreign-owned industries, to protect the interests of the peons, or to redistribute the wealth. Then, the CIA cultivated home-grown opposition groups with offers of cash and power. Next, the popular government was overthrown by propaganda, rigged elections, death squads, economic sabotage, and assassinations. Finally, the government was topped, and the rebels were hailed as patriotic liberators.[16]

Over the course of the latter half of the 20th century, the relationship between the CIA and the Rockefellers became so close that highly classified documents were stored within a vault in a carriage house of Nelson Rockefeller's residence in Pocantico, New York.

---

16   Dubay, *The Atlantean Conspiracy,* p. 77.

19

LUCIFER'S LAIR

The chief geopolitical prize is Eurasia . . . Now a non-Eurasian power is preeminent in Eurasia—and America's global primacy is directly dependent on how long and how effectively its preponderance on the Eurasian continent is sustained . . . To put it in a terminology that harkens back to the more brutal age of ancient empires, the three great imperatives of imperial geo-strategy are to prevent collusion and maintain security dependence among the vassals, to keep tributaries pliant and protected, and to keep the barbarians from coming together.

—ZBIGNIEW BRZEZINSKI, *THE GRAND CHESSBOARD*, 1997

DAVID ROCKEFELLER PLAYED A KEY ROLE in the creation of the Bilderberg Group at the Hotel De Bilderberg in Oosterbeek in 1954. The group brings together the most powerful bankers, businessmen, top academic and university leaders, and government officials from Europe and North America. From the beginning, the gatherings were extremely exclusive affairs in which utmost secrecy was demanded from its original 73 participants. Ten "rapporteurs" were selected to introduce the talking points on the agenda and to lead the group discussions, including David Rockefeller.[1] The organization was set up to serve

---

1   Dubay, *The Atlantean Conspiracy*, 77.

David Rockefeller played a key role in the creation of the Bilderberg Group at the Hotel De Bilderberg in Oosterbeek in 1954. The group brings together the most powerful bankers, businessmen, top academic and university leaders, and government officials from Europe and North America. "Bilderberg—Oosterbeek" by Michiel1972 is licensed under CC BY-SA 4.0

as a clandestine "global think tank" with the intent of linking "governments and economies in Europe and North America amid the Cold War."[2] Over the years, the "Bilderbergers" have come to include the world's most influential figures. A list of some attendees is as follows:

FROM THE UNITED STATES

Dean Acheson (Secretary of State under Truman), Allen Dulles (CIA director), Owen Lattimore (CFR, former Director of Planning and Coordination for the State Department), Christian Herter (Secretary of State under Eisenhower), Gabriel Hauge (Assistant to President Eisenhower, later Chairman of Manufacturers Hanover Trust Co.), George F. Kennan (former U.S. Ambassador to the Soviet Union), Dean Rusk (Kennedy's Secretary of State, former President of the Rockefeller Foundation), Robert S. McNamara (Kennedy's Secretary of Defense and former President of the World Bank), C. Douglas Dillon (Secretary of Treasury in the Kennedy and Johnson Administrations, from Dillon, Read and Co.), George Ball (CFR, Johnson's undersecretary of State, foreign policy consultant to Nixon), Henry A. Kissinger (Secretary of State under Nixon; Chairman, Kissinger Associates), Donald H. Rumsfeld (President Ford's and George W. Bush's Secretary of Defense), Zbigniew Brzezinski (Carter's National Security

Advisor), Cyrus Vance (Secretary of State under Carter), Philip Jessup (representative to the International Court), Winston Lord (CFR, Clinton's Assistant Secretary of State), Alan Greenspan (Chairman, Federal Reserve System), former President Gerald Ford, Sen. Walter Mondale (later Vice President under Carter), Sen. William J. Fulbright (from Arkansas, a Rhodes Scholar), Sen. Henry M. Jackson, Sen. Jacob J. Javits (NY), Sen. Adlai Stevenson III, Sen. Charles Mathias (MD), Sen. Lloyd Bentsen (Chairman of the Senate Finance Committee, Secretary of the Treasury under Bill Clinton), Rep. Thomas S. Foley (former Speaker of the House), Rep. Donald F. Frase, Rep. Henry S. Reuss, Rep. Donald W. Riegle, Gen. Walter Bedell Smith, Gen. Andrew J. Goodpaster (former Supreme Allied Commander in Europe, and later superintendent of the West Point Academy), Gen. Alexander Haig (NATO Commander, former assistant to Kissinger, later became Secretary of State under Reagan), Lt. Gen. John W. Vogt (former Director of the Joint Chiefs of Staff), David Rockefeller, Nelson Rockefeller, Laurance Rockefeller, James Rockefeller (Chairman, First National City Bank), John D. Rockefeller IV (Governor of West Virginia, now U.S. Senator), Henry J. Heinz II (Chairman of the H. J. Heinz Co.), Robert O. Anderson (Chairman of Atlantic-Richfield Co. and head of the Aspen Institute for Humanisitic Studies), Henry Ford III (head of the Ford Motor Co.), Thomas L. Hughes (President of the Carnegie Endowment for International Peace), Joseph Johnson (President of the Carnegie Endowment for International Peace), William P. Bundy (former President of the Ford Foundation, and editor of the CFR's *Foreign Affairs* magazine), Shepard Stone (Director of International Affairs for the Ford Foundation), Paul G. Hoffman (of the Ford Foundation, U.S. Chief of Foreign Aid, and head of the U.N. Special Fund), John J. McCloy (former President of the Chase Manhattan Bank), Eugene Black (former President of the World Bank), Bill Moyers (journalist),

William F. Buckley (editor of *National Review*), Paul B. Finney (editor of *Fortune* magazine), Gardner Cowles (Editor-in-Chief and Publisher of *Look* magazine), Arthur Taylor (former Chairman of CBS-TV), Father Theodore M. Hesburgh (former President of Notre Dame University), David J. McDonald (President of the United Steelworkers Union), former President George H. W. Bush, former President William Clinton, former President George W. Bush, and former President Barack Obama.

FROM GREAT BRITAIN AND CANADA:
Prince Phillip (of Great Britain, husband of Queen Elizabeth II), Lord Louis Mountbatten, Denis Healy (former British Defense Minister), Edward Heath (former Prime Minister of England), Harold Wilson (former Prime Minister of England), Margaret Thatcher (former Prime Minister of England), Lester Pearson (former Prime Minister of Canada), Donald S. MacDonald (Canadian Minister of National Defense), Tony Blair (former Prime Minister of England), and David Cameron (former Prime Minister of England).

FROM EUROPE:
Baron Edmond de Rothschild, Manlio Brosio (Secretary-General of NATO), Dirk U. Stikker (Secretary-General of NATO), Valery Giscard d'Estang (President of France), Helmut Schmidt (former Chancellor of West Germany), Prince Claus (of the Netherlands), Paul van Zeeland (Prime Minister of Belgium), Giovanni Agnelli (Chairman of Fiat in Italy), Otto Wolff (German industrialist), Wilfred S. Baumgartner (Bank of France), Guido Carli (Bank of Italy), Marcus Wallenberg (Chairman of Stockholm's Enskiida Bank), Pierce Paul Schweitzer (Managing Director of the International Monetary Fund), and Imbriani Longo (Director-General of the Banco Nationale del Lavoro in Italy), Angela Merkel (Chancellor of Germany), and Emmanuel Macron (President of France).[3]

---

3   David Allen Rivera, "Final Warning: A History of the New World Order," 1994, http://modernhistoryproject.org/mhp?Article=FinalWarning&C=8.3, accessed February 13, 2019.

THE REGULAR ATTENDEES

Every Bilderberg meeting includes the presidents and chairmen of the Bank for International Settlements, the International Monetary Fund, the World Bank, and the Federal Reserve, along with the directors of the FBI and the CIA, the CEOs of the world's most powerful corporations, the secretaries eneral of NATO, American senators, members of the U.S. House of Representatives, European prime ministers, and leaders of opposition parties.[4] Since the time of its establishment, every American president has appeared at the annual event, with the sole exception of Donald Trump. However, in 2017, President Trump sent several of his top officials, including National Security Advisor H. R. Nelson and Secretary of Commerce Wilbur Ross, to take part in the proceedings.[5]

Despite the fact that the richest and most powerful individuals in the world gather every year in a luxury hotel to conduct meetings that the press is forbidden to attend and no public statements are ever issued, the mainstream press has decided that the meetings, which are conducted in total secrecy, are not newsworthy.[6] The hotels are closed to all outside guests. Those who attend the meetings are granted military protection. Every delivery vehicle that arrives at the hotel is searched from top to bottom and then escorted, by armed guard, to the tradesmen's entrance. For the sake of added security, the Bilderbergers bring their own chefs, cooks, waiters, secretaries, busboys, cleaning staff, and bodyguards.[7]

THE FOUNDING FATHERS

The European founders of the group included Joseph Retinger and

---

4   Daniel Estulin, *The True Story of the Bilderberg Group*, 2nd ed., (Walterville, OR: TrineDay, 2009), p. xxiv.

5   Alex Newman, "Top Trump Officials Attend Bilderberg Summit. Why?" *New American*, June 2, 2017, https://www.thenewamerican.com/world-news/north-america/item/26162-top-trump-officials-attend-globalist-bilderberg-summit-why, accessed February 13, 2019.

6   Estulin, *The True Story of the Bilderberg Group*, p. xxv.

7   Ibid., p. 25.

Prince Bernhard of the Netherlands. Prince Bernhard had been a member of the Nazi Party until 1934, three years prior to his marrying the Dutch Queen Juliana, and had worked for the German industrial giant, IG Farben, who was linked to Standard Oil. Retinger was the founder of the European Movement (EM), a organization dedicated to creating a federal Europe. The EM was funded by the Council on Foreign Relations and the Rockefeller Foundation.[8] He was also a top official in Royal Dutch Shell, the Dutch-British conglomerate, which was controlled by the Rothschilds.[9]

Along with David Rockefeller, the most prominent Americans involved with the formation of the Bilderberg Group were Dean Rusk (a top official with the Council on Foreign Relations who was then the head of the Rockefeller Foundation), Joseph Johnson (another Council leader who was head of the Carnegie Endowment), and John J. McCloy (a top Council leader who became chairman of Chase Manhattan Bank in 1953 and was also chairman of the board of the Ford Foundation). Everyone involved in setting up the new think tank was closely related to the Rockefeller Empire.

THE BILDERBERG OBJECTIVES

By empowering international agencies, including the United Nations, the International Monetary Fund, the World Bank, and the World Trade Organization, the Bilderbergers, under the direction of the Rockefellers, intend to destroy national identities and to establish one government with one set of values. Within this global government, there will be no middle class, only rulers and workers. Their plan calls for zero growth societies, the centralized control of all education, the empowerment of the United Nations to levy a direct tax on all world citizens, the expansion of NATO into Eastern Europe and Asia so that

---

8   Holly Sklar, ed., *Trilateralism: The Trilateral Commission and Elite Planning for World Management.* (Boston: South End Press: 1980), 161–62.

9   Estulin, *The True Story of the Bilderberg Group*, p. 20.

This blueprint for this New World Order was set forth by Zbigniew Brzezinski (left), one of David Rockefeller's closest associates, in his 1970 book *Between Two Ages: America's Role in the Technetronic Era.*

it can serve as the UN's world army, the right of the International Court of Justice at The Hague to impose laws that are binding on all peoples of all nations, and the imposition of a universal socialist welfare system to ensure economic equality and the end of predatory capitalism.[10] This blueprint for this New World Order was set forth by Zbigniew Brzezinski, one of David Rockefeller's closest associates, in his 1970 book *Between Two Ages: America's Role in the Technetronic Era.*[11] A PhD from Harvard, Brzezinski became a founding father, along with David Rockefeller, of the Trilateral Commission. He later served as National Security Advisor of Presidents Jimmy Carter and Barack Obama and

---

10   Ibid., pp. 41–43.

11   Zbigniew Brzezinski, *Between Two Ages: America's Role in the Technetronic Era* (New York: Viking, 1970), https://archive.org/stream/pdfy-z5FBdAnrFME2m1U4/Zbigniew%20Brzezinski%20-%20 Between%20Two%20Ages_djvu.txt, accessed February 13, 2019.

as a member of President George H. W. Bush's National Security Task Force and the Foreign Intelligence Advisory Board.[12]

THE BILDERBERG ACCOMPLISHMENTS

The Bilderberg Group discussions have resulted in the 1973 oil crisis, the economic demise of the Soviet Union, the removal of Margaret Thatcher from her position as Britain's prime minister, the fall of Kosovo, the timetable for the 2003 invasion of Iraq, and many of the CIA's covert operations, including the creation of a pan-Islamic movement to destabilize the Middle East, Central Asia, and Christian Europe.[13]

The group also created the European Union (EU) and the *euro* as a new international currency. The initial plans for the EU were drafted by the Action Committee for a United States of Europe (ACUE), an organization chaired by William "Wild Bill" Donovan and Allen Dulles, two of the Rockefellers' closest allies. The EU was established to become a European superstate that would assume Britain's place on the United Nations Security Council. This superstate would have its own president and parliament, its own judicial system that would establish laws binding to all the residents of Europe, and its own Department of Defense with its own armed forces.[14] It represented a vital step toward the Rockefeller goal of creating Eurasia, the union of the world's largest continent into one vast political and economic entity that would be ripe for plunder.

THE DREAM OF EURASIA

Eurasia, as envisioned by the Bilderbergers, would stretch from France to China and from India to Russia. Free trade would flow from principality to principality, and the various peoples would live under common

---

12   Patrick Briley, "Zbigniew Brzezinski," Euro-Med, September 16, 2008, https://www. bibliotecapleyades.net/sociopolitica/sociopol_brzezinski06.htm, accessed February 13, 2019.

13   Estulin, *The True Story of the Bilderberg Group*, pp. 35–48.

14   Marshall, "Bilderberg 2011: The Rockefeller World Order and the 'High Priests of Globalization.'"

rule and common law. After establishing the Bank for International Settlements, the International Monetary Fund, the World Bank, the United Nations, and a United Europe, the establishment of Eurasia was an achievable goal. Through the Council on Foreign Relations, the Rockefellers had gained control of the U.S. State Department and had placed the perfect individual in the cabinet of President Richard Nixon to undertake this task. His name was Henry Kissinger.

DR. STRANGELOVE

Kissinger had graduated from Harvard in 1950 as a Rockefeller Foundation Fellow in political science. In 1956, he was invited by the Rockefellers to join the Council on Foreign Relations, where he became a major force in shaping international policy.[15] Explaining Kissinger's rise in the CFR, J. Robert Moskin, author of *The U.S. Marine Corps Story*, writes: "It was principally because of his long association with the Rockefellers that Henry Kissinger became a force in the Council. The *New York Times* called him 'the Council's most influential member,' and

In 1956, Henry Kissinger was invited by the Rockefellers to join the Council on Foreign Relations, where he became a major force in shaping international policy.

a Council insider says that 'his influence is direct and enormous—much of it through the Rockefeller connection.'"[16]

15   G. Vance Smith and Tom Gow, *Masters of Deception: The Rise of the Council on Foreign Relations* (Colorado Springs, CO: Freedom First Society, 2012), p. 166.

16   Robert Moskin, quoted in Ibid.

During the 1960s, Kissinger served as Nelson Rockefeller's chief foreign affairs advisor and the mastermind behind Nelson's campaign for the presidency. The relationship between the two men was so close that Kissinger dedicated his memoir, *The White House Years*, to Nelson, describing him as "the single most influential person in my life."[17]

WAKING "THE SLEEPING GIANT"

When Richard Nixon became president, he appointed Kissinger as secretary of state in accordance with advice of the Rockefeller family.[18] In this position, Kissinger tirelessly advanced the agenda of the Rockefellers and the Bilderbergers, including the promulgation of free trade between all nations. This agenda prompted him in July 1971 to visit China, where he negotiated a trade agreement by which the Communist country would receive "most favored nation status" with the United States, a status that would permit Chinese goods to flow into America free of charge. Kissinger was accompanied by Winston Lord, a member of the National Security Council staff, who later became president of the CFR. By the time Nixon visited China the following year, the terms of the deal had been set in stone. The treaty, which was ratified by Congress, caused David Rockefeller to gloat: "The Chinese are not only purposeful and intelligent, [but] they also have a large pool of cheap labor. So they should be able to find ways to get trading capital."[19] Of course, the Chinese found ways of getting trading capital. However, the funds did not come from their own resources, but rather from the IMF/World Bank, which proceeded to supply the communist country with billions of tax-free loans.[20]

---

17   James Perloff, *The Shadows of Power: The Council on Foreign Relations and the American Decline* (Appleton, WI: Western Islands, 2005), p. 145.

18   Ibid., pp. 145–146.

19   David Rockefeller, quoted in Gary Allen, *The Rockefeller File* (Seal Beach, CA: '76 Press, 1976), p. 121.

20   G. Edward Griffin, *The Creature from Jekyll Island: A Second Look at the Federal Reserve* (Westlake Village, CA: American Media, 2017), p. 122.

GOODBYE "MADE IN AMERICA"

Manufacturing plants sprouted up throughout China. The products and goods were produced in these plants by workers making less per month than union workers in America were making per hour. Women working in the Timberland Shoe Company in Guangdong Province, labored 14 hours a day at 22 cents per hour. At a factory making Kathie Lee [Gifford] handbags for WalMart, the highest wages were seven dollars a week.[21]

Compounding the problem for American manufacturers was China's manipulation of its currency. By 2010, China had devalued the yuan by 45 percent, cutting in half the cheap labor for companies moving to China and doubling the price of U.S. goods entering the communist country. The trade deficit stood at $266 billion.[22]

Throughout America, factories began to relocate to Southeast Asia, and an ever-increasing number of American workers found themselves on the unemployment line. The following list[23] is of the companies that moved their manufacturing facilities to China:

AT&T	AIG Financial
Abbott Laboratories	Agrilink Foods, Inc. (ProFac)
Abercrombe & Fitch	Allergan Laboratories
Acer Electronics	American Eagle Outfitters
Ademco Security	American Standard
Adidas	American Tourister
ADI Security	Ames Tools
AGI–American Gem Institute	Amphenol Corporation

---

21 Jon E. Dougherty, "Free Trade v. Slave Trade: Brutal Chinese Working Conditions Benefit WalMart, Others," *WorldNetDaily*, May 24, 2000, http://www.hartford-hwp.com/archives/55/312.html, accessed February 13, 2019.

22 Pat Buchanan, *Suicide of a Superpower* (New York: Thomas Dunne Books, 2011), p. 13.

23 Jie's World Staff, "American and International Companies in China."

Amway Corporation
Analog Devices, Inc.
Apple Computer
Armani
Armour Meats
Ashland Chemical
Ashley Furniture
Associated Grocers
Audi Motors
AudioVox
AutoZone, Inc.
Avon

Banana Republic
Bausch & Lomb, Inc.
Baxter International
Bed, Bath & Beyond
Belkin Electronics
Best Buy
Best Foods
Big 5 Sporting Goods
Black & Decker
Body Shop
Borden Foods
Briggs & Stratton

Calrad Electric
Campbell's Soup
Canon Electronics
Carole Cable
Casio Instrument
Caterpillar, Inc.
CBC America

CCTV Outlet
Checker Auto
CitiCorp
Cisco Systems
Chiquita Brands International
Claire's Boutique
Cobra Electronics
Coby Electronics
Coca-Cola Foods
Colgate-Palmolive
Colorado Spectrum
ConAgra Foods
Cooper Tire
Corning, Inc.
Coleman Sporting Goods
Compaq
Crabtree & Evelyn
Cracker Barrel Stores
Craftsman Tools (Sears)
Cummins, Inc.

Dannon Foods
Dell Computer
Del Monte Foods
Dewalt Tools
DHL
Dial Corporation
Diebold, Inc.
Dillard's, Inc.
Dodge-Phelps
Dole Foods
Dollar Tree Stores, Inc.
Dow-Corning

Eastman Kodak
EchoStar
Eclipse CCTV
Edge Electronics Group
Electric Vehicles USA, Inc.
Eli Lilly Company
Emerson Electric
Enfamil
Estee Lauder
Eveready

Family Dollar Stores
FedEx
Fisher Scientific
Ford Motors
Fossil
Frito-Lay
Furniture Brands International

GAP Stores
Gateway Computer
General Electric
General Foods International
General Mills
General Motors
Gentek
Gerber Foods
Gillette Company
Goodrich Company
Goodyear Tire
Google
Gucci
Guess?

Haagen-Dazs
Harley Davidson
Hasbro Company
Heinz Foods
Hershey Foods
Hitachi
Hoffman-LaRoche
Holt's Automotive Products
Home Depot
Honda
Honeywell
Hoover Vacuum
Hormel Foods
HP Computer
Hubbell Inc.
Huggies
Hunts-Wesson Foods

IBM
ICON Office Solutions
Ikea
Intel Corporation

J.C. Penney
J. M. Smucker Company
JVC Electronics
John Deere
Johnson Control
Johnson & Johnson
Johnstone Supply

KB Home
Keebler Foods

Kenwood Audio
KFC, Kentucky Fried Chicken
Kimberly-Clark
Knorr Foods
K-Mart
Kohler
Kohl's Corporation
Kraft Foods
Kragen Auto

Land's End
Lee Kum Kee Foods
Lexmark
LG Electronics
Lipton Foods
L.L. Bean, Inc.
Logitech
Libby's Foods
Linens 'n Things
Lipo Chemicals, Inc.
Lowe's Hardware
Lucent Technologies
Lufkin

Mars Candy
Martha Stewart Products
Mattel
McCormick Foods
McDonald's
McKesson Corporation
Megellan GPS
Memorex
Merck & Company

Michael's Stores
Mitsubishi Electronics
Mitsubishi Motors
Mobile Oil
Molex
Motorola
Motts Applesauce
Multifoods Corporation

Nabisco Foods
National Semiconductor
Nescafe
Nestlé Foods
Nextar
Nike
Nikon
Nivea Cosmetics
Nokia Electronics
Northrop Grumman
NuSkin International
Nutrilite (Amway)
Nvidia Corporation (G-Force)

Office Depot
Old Navy
Olin Corporation
Olympus Electronics
Orion-Knight Electronics

Pacific Sunwear, Inc.
Pampers
Panasonic
Pan Pacific Electronics

Panvise

Papa Johns

Payless Shoesource

Pelco

Pentax Optics

Pep Boy's

Pepsico International

PetsMart

Petco

Pfizer, Inc.

Philips Electronics

Phillip Morris Companies

Pier 1 Imports

Pierre Cardin

Pillsbury Company

Pioneer Electronics

Pitney Bowes, Inc.

Pizza Hut

Plantronics

PlaySchool Toys

Polaris Industries

Polaroid

Polo (Ralph Lauren)

Post Cereals

Price-Pfister

Pringles

Praxair

Proctor & Gamble

PSS World Medical

Pyle Audio

Qualcomm

Quest One

Radio Shack

Ralph Lauren

RCA

Reebok International

Reynolds Aluminum

Revlon

Rohm & Hass Company

Samsonite

Samsung

Sanyo

Shell Oil

Schwinn Bike

Sears-Craftsman

Seven-Eleven (7-11)

Sharp Electronics

Sherwin-Williams

Shure Electronics

Sony

Speco Technologies/Pro Video

Shopko Stores

Skechers Footwear

SmartHome

Smucker's (J. M. Smucker's)

Solar Power, Inc.

Spencer Gifts

Stanley Tools

Staples

Starbucks Corporation

Steelcase, Inc.

STP Oil

Subway Sandwiches

Sunglass Hut

Sunkist Growers
SunMaid Raisins
Switchcraft Electronics
SYSCO Foods
Sylvania Electric

3-M
Tai Pan Trading Company
Tamron Optics
Target
TDK
Tektronix, Inc
Texas Instruments
Timex
Timken Bearing
TNT
Tommy Hilfiger
Toro
Toshiba
Tower Automotive
Toyota
Toys "R" Us, Inc.
Trader Joe's
Tripp-lite
True Value Hardware
Tupper Ware
Tyson Foods

Uniden Electronics
UPS

Valspar Corporation
Victoria's Secret
Vizio Electronics
Volkswagen
VTech

Walgreen Company
Walt Disney Company
Walmart
WD-40 Corporation
Weller Electric Company
Western Digital
Westinghouse Electric
Weyerhaeuser Company
Whirlpool Corporation
Wilson Sporting Goods
Wrigley
WW Grainger, Inc.
Wyeth Laboratories

X-10
Xelite
Xerox

Yahoo
Yamaha
Yoplait Foods
Yum Brands

Zale Corporation

PROTECTIONISM FORSAKEN

The economic situation in America worsened as more countries, including India and Pakistan, received most favored status. By 2010, 50,000 manufacturing plants in America had shut down. Almost everything that Americans purchased came from overseas manufacturers: shoes, clothes, cars, furniture, TVs, appliances, bicycles, toys, cameras, and computers.[24] The goods flowed into the country free of charge, violating the principles of America's founding fathers. Alexander Hamilton had written:

> The superiority antecedently enjoyed by nations who have preoccupied and perfected a branch of industry, constitutes a more formidable obstacle than either of those which have been mentioned, to the introduction of the same branch into a country in which it did not before exist. To maintain, between the recent establishments of one country, and the long-matured establishments of another country, a competition upon equal terms, both as to quality and price, is, in most cases, impracticable. The disparity, in the one, or in the other, or in both, must necessarily be so considerable, as to forbid a successful rivalship, without the extraordinary aid and protection of government.[25]

Cheap foreign labor and tax-free imports also impacted the defense industry. In 2010, Senator Fritz Hollings wrote: "Today, the United States has less manufacturing jobs than in April 1941. Long before the recession, South Carolina had lost its textile industry, North Carolina its furniture industry, Michigan its automobile industry. The defense industry has been off-shored. We had to wait months to get flat panel displays from Japan before we launched Desert Storm. Boeing can't build a fighter plane except for the parts from India. Sikorsky can't

---

24   Ibid, p. 12.

25   Alexander Hamilton, quoted in Ian Fletcher and Jeff Ferry, "America Was Founded as a Protectionist Nation," *Huffington Post*, September 12, 2010, http://www.huffingtonpost.com/ian-fletcher/america-was-founded-as-a_b_713521.html, accessed February 13, 2019.

build a helicopter except for the tail motor from Turkey. Under law, the Secretary of Commerce lists those items vital to our national security but Congress fails to make sure we can produce these items for our defense. Today, we can't go to war except for the favor of a foreign country."[26]

THE WORLD TRADE ORGANIZATION

On January 1, 1995, the World Trade Organization (WTO) came into being with headquarters in Geneva, Switzerland. It was set up to integrate nations into a world order without tariffs or other economic barriers. The principal beneficiaries were the 80,000 transnational corporations that account for two-thirds of the world trade. A 2014 *New Science* study showed that 1,318 core transnational corporations, through interlocking boards of directors, owned 80 percent of global revenues, and 147 of them formed a "super entity" that controlled 40 percent of the wealth of the entire network.[27] Not surprisingly, this "super entity" was dominated by the business interests of the House of Rockefeller.

The WTO represented one of the final steps in the creation of a New World Order. It was empowered under international law to police the economic and social policies of its 164 member states, thereby derogating the sovereign rights of national governments. "Under WTO rules," noted economist Michel Chossudovsky writes, "the banks and multinational corporations (MNCs) can legitimately manipulate market forces to their advantage leading to the outright re-colonization of national economies."[28]

---

26   Fritz Hollings, "Fifth Column: The Enemy within the Trade War," *Huffington Post*, March 18, 2010, http://www.huffingtonpost.com/sen-ernest-frederick-hollings/fifth-column-the-enemy-wi_b_323833.html, accessed February 13, 2019.

27   Takis Fotopoulos, "The Transnational Elite and the New World Order (NWO)," *Global Research*, October 28, 2014, http://www.globalresearch.ca/%CF%84he-transnational-elite-and-the-nwo-as-conspiracies/5410468, accessed February 13, 2019.

28   Michel Chossudovsky, *The Globalization of Poverty and the New World Order* (Montreal, Quebec: Global Research, 2003), p. 26.

FOR THE SAKE OF THE DREAM

To advance the creation of Eurasia, the Bilderbergers, under David Rockefeller's instruction, issued invitations to power planners from Japan and China to attend the annual gatherings. The attendees came to include Nobuo Tanaka, Japan's Executive Director of International Energy; Fu Ying, China's Vice Minister of Foreign Affairs; and Huang Yiping, professor of economics at Peking University (China's Harvard).[29]

In keeping with its global ambitions, the Bilderberg Group has been attempting to create a new global currency to replace the U.S. dollar. The new money will be the International Monetary Fund's Special Drawing Rights (discussed in the previous chapter). This development, according to the *Washington Post*, will transform the IMF "into a veritable United Nations for the world economy."[30]

THE HIGH PRIESTS

By the second decade of the 21st century, the Bilderberg Group represented the high priests of the New World Order, while David Rockefeller emerged as the pope. Regarding his role in reshaping the world, David Rockefeller wrote in his *Memoirs* (2002): "For more than a century ideological extremists at either end of the political spectrum have seized upon well-publicized incidents such as my encounter with Castro to attack the Rockefeller family for the inordinate influence they claim we wield over American political and economic institutions. Some even believe we are part of a secret cabal working against the best interests of the United States, characterizing my family and me as 'internationalists' and of conspiring with others around the world to build a more integrated global political and economic structure–one world,

---

29   Marshall, "Bilderberg 2011: The Rockefeller World Order and the 'High Priests of Globalization.'"

30   Anthony Faiola, "A Bigger, Bolder Role Is Imagined for the IMF," *Washington Post*, April 20, 2009: http://www.washingtonpost.com/wp-yn/content/article/2009/04/19/AR2009041902242. html?hpid=topnews, accessed February 13, 2019.

if you will. If that's the charge, I stand guilty, and I am proud of it."[31]

And if this admission wasn't sufficient, David Rockefeller at the conclusion of the Bilderberg Conference in 1991 said: "We are grateful to the *Washington Post*, the *New York Times*, *Time* magazine, and other great publications whose directors have attended our meetings and respected their promises of discretion for almost 40 years. It would have been impossible for us to develop our plan for the world if we had been subjected to the lights of publicity during those years. But the world is more sophisticated and prepared to march towards a world government. The supranational sovereignty of an intellectual elite and world bankers is surely preferable to the national auto-determination practiced in past centuries."[32]

31   David Rockefeller, *Memoirs* (New York: Random House, 2002), pp. 404–5.

32   David Rockefeller, quoted in Gordon Laxer, "Radical Transformative Nationalisms Confront the US Empire," *Current Sociology*, 51, no. 2 (March 2003).

PART FIVE

THE DOGS OF WAR

20

JUDICIAL TYRANNY

At the establishment of our Constitutions, the judiciary bodies were supposed to be the most helpless and harmless members of the government. Experience, however, soon showed in what way they were to become the most dangerous; that the insufficiency of the means provided for their removal gave them a freehold and irresponsibility in office; that their decisions, seeming to concern individual suitors only, pass silent and unheeded by the public at large; that these decisions, nevertheless, become law by precedent, sapping, by little and little, the foundations of the constitution, and working its change by construction, before any one has perceived that that invisible and helpless worm has been busily employed in consuming its substance. In truth, man is not made to be trusted for life if secured against all liability to account.

—THOMAS JEFFERSON, *LETTER TO ADAMANTIOS CORAY*, OCTOBER 31, 1823

IN COLONIAL AMERICA, lawyers learned their trade by serving as apprentices under practicing attorneys. An ordinary citizen could practice law even without an apprenticeship. Such a citizen also could serve as a district attorney, an attorney general, or a judge in any court of law.[1]

---

1   David Dodge, "The Missing 13th Amendment: No Lawyers Allowed in Public Office," *Millennium Report*, October 24, 2015, http://themillenniumreport.com/2015/10/the-missing-13th-amendment-no-lawyers-allowed-in-public-office/, accessed February 13, 2019.

Moreover, those accused of a crime could choose anyone to represent him, even a common cobbler or the village blacksmith.[2] No one practicing law in the time before the Revolutionary War possessed a title of nobility. Judges were not addressed as "Your Honor," and lawyers did not attach the rank of "Esquire" to their signatures. There were no national bar associations. The only organization that certified lawyers was the International Bar Association (IBA) in London. The IBA was closely associated with the Bank of England and was chartered by the king.[3]

After the Revolutionary War, the delegates to the Constitutional Congress sought to sever all ties between the new Republic and Great Britain. For this reason, they drafted Article 7, Section 9, which declares: "No Title of Nobility shall be granted by the United States: And no Person holding any Office of Profit or Trust under them, shall, without the Consent of the Congress, accept of any present, Emolument, Office, or Title, of any kind whatever, from any King, Prince or foreign State."[4] The Framers believed that this clause would prevent the country from falling into the clutches of the International Bar Association.[5]

THE 13TH AMENDMENT

But the Framers failed to attach a penalty for adopting a foreign title to the clause, and the prohibition against titles became largely ignored; and the British Crown succeeded in gaining power and influence over American legislations, including the lawyers who served in the House of Representatives and the Senate. This influence was so great that in 1794, the U.S. Congress approved the Jay Treaty by which the New Republic became compelled to pay 600 pounds sterling to King George

---

2   Ibid.

3   Ibid.

4   "The Constitution of the United States of America: Analysis and Interpretation," Centennial Edition, *Analysis of Cases Decided by the Supreme Court of the United States to June 26, 2013* (Washington, D.C.: U.S. Government Printing Office, 2013.)

5   Ibid.

III as reparation for the American Revolution.[6]

This outrageous payment of "reparation" for the country that instigated and lost the Revolutionary War prompted the members of Congress to draft a 13ᵗʰ Amendment to the Constitution, which would punish all lawyers and judges who maintained foreign titles with loss of citizenship. This Amendment, which was approved by Congress in January 1810, upheld the following: "If any citizen of the United States shall accept, claim, receive or retain any title of nobility or honor, or shall, without the consent of Congress accept and retain any present, pension, office or emolument of any kind whatever, from any emperor, king, prince or foreign power, such person shall cease to be a citizen of the United States and shall be incapable of holding any office of trust or profit under them, or either of them."[7]

THE RATIFICATION PROCESS

In order for this amendment to become the law of the land, it had to be ratified by 13 of the 19 existing states. The amendment became ratified by the states below on the following dates:

Maryland, Dec. 25, 1810

Kentucky, Jan. 31, 1811

Ohio, Jan. 31, 1811

Delaware, Feb. 2, 1811

Pennsylvania, Feb. 6, 1811

New Jersey, Feb. 13, 1811

Vermont, Oct. 24, 1811

---

6   "The Jay Treaty," Acts of the Third Congress of the United States, March 3, 1794, https://www.loc.gov/law/help/statutes-at-large/3rd-congress/c3.pdf, accessed February 13, 2019.

7   Jerry Adler, "The Move to 'Restore' the 13ᵗʰ Amendment," *Newsweek*, July 26, 2010, https://www.newsweek.com/move-restore-13th-amendment-74391, accessed February 13, 2019.

Tennessee, Nov. 21, 1811

Georgia, Dec. 13, 1811

North Carolina, Dec. 23, 1811

Massachusetts, Feb. 27, 1812

New Hampshire, Dec. 10, 1812

Before a thirteenth state could ratify, the War of 1812 broke out, and the British invaded America. By the time the war ended in 1814, the British had set a torch to the Capitol and the Library of Congress. The momentum to ratify the proposed amendment was lost in the tumult of war.[8]

On December 31, 1817, four years after the end of the war, Congress asked President James Monroe to establish the status of the Amendment. Three months later, President Monroe reported that Secretary of State John Quincy Adams had obtained confirmation that 12 states had ratified the Amendment and three (New York, Rhode Island, and South Carolina) had rejected it.[9] The fate of the new legislation rested with Virginia.

THE GREAT MYSTERY

What happened next remains one of the great mysteries of American history. On March 10, 1819, the Maryland legislature passed Act 280, which contained the following directive: "Be it enacted by the General Assembly, that there shall be published an edition of the Laws of this Commonwealth in which shall be contained the following matters, that is to say: the Constitution of the United States and the amendments

---

8   Dodge, "The Missing 13th Amendment: No Lawyers Allowed in Public Office."

9   Ibid.

thereto."[10] This act represented the official instructions on the official laws to be included in the republication of the Virginia Civil Code. The list included the 13th Amendment to the U.S. Constitution, which stripped citizenship from all judges and lawyers who assumed foreign titles.

Members of the Virginia legislature apparently were aware that the ratification by their state was necessary so that the 13th Amendment would become the law of the land. For this reason, they tripled the printing order to 40,000 and sent copies to President Monroe as well as former Presidents James Madison and Thomas Jefferson.[11] Several historians argue that there was a failure of the Virginia lawmakers to dispatch a communiqué to Congress of their state's decision regarding the passage of the 13th Amendment. But legal scholars contend that the printing of the document by the state's legislature represents prima facie evidence of its ratification.[12]

NATIONWIDE RECOGNITION
States throughout the country, upon receiving copies of the new Virginia Civil Code, assumed that the 13th Amendment had been codified. Rhode Island and Kentucky placed it among their laws in 1822. The Ohio legislature ordered the first printing of the New Amendment in 1824 for distribution throughout the state. Maine ordered 10,000 copies of the Constitution with the 13th Amendment for use in the schools in 1825, and again in 1831 for their Census Edition. The amendment appeared in the Indiana Revised Laws of 1831, and it was published by the Northwestern Territories in 1833. Ohio recirculated the document in 1831 and 1833. And it was upheld as the law of the

10   TONA Research Committee, "Legislative Extracts Relative to Amendments of the Constitution of the United States of America," compiled by Suzanne Nevling, "Commonwealth of Virginia: 1810 to 1819," posted May 2000, http://www.amendment-13.org/legextracts.html, accessed February 13, 2019.

11   Dodge, "The Missing 13th Amendment: No Lawyers Allowed in Public Office."

12   Ibid.

nation by the Wisconsin Territory in 1839; Iowa Territory in 1843; Ohio again in 1848; Kansas Statutes in 1855; and Nebraska Territory six times in a row from 1855 to 1860.[13]

THE AMENDMENT DISAPPEARS

In 1849, when Virginia decided to revise the 1819 Civil Code of Virginia, which had contained the 13th Amendment for 30 years, members of the legislature contacted J. M. Clayton, secretary of state under President Zachary Taylor, asking if this amendment had been ratified or had been published by mistake in the previous compilation of the state's laws. Clayton, relying on the information gathered by John Quincy Adams in 1818, replied that the amendment had not been ratified by a sufficient number of states. Even today, the Congressional Research Service tells anyone who asks about this 13th Amendment the same story: only 12 states, not the requisite 13, had ratified.[14] The action by the Virginia legislature in 1819 had been either forgotten or cast in the trash heap of history by the lawyers who presided over the Halls of Congress.

LINCOLN'S 13TH AMENDMENT

Another version of the 13th Amendment, known as the Corwin Amendment, was proposed in December 1860 by William Seward, a senator from New York who would later become Abraham Lincoln's secretary of state. It read as follows: "No amendment shall be made to the Constitution which will authorize or give to Congress power to abolish or interfere, within any State, with the domestic institutions thereof, including that of persons held to labor or service by the laws of said State."[15]

---

13 Ibid.

14 Ibid.

15 "The 'Ghost Amendment' That Haunts Lincoln's Legacy," *Cognoscenti*, WBUR (Boston's Public Radio Station), February 18, 2013, https://www.wbur.org/cognoscenti/2013/02/18/the-other-13th-richard-albert, accessed February 13, 2019.

This amendment represented an effort to placate the South and to contain secessionist sentiment. It proposed to protect slavery by giving each state the power to regulate the "domestic institutions" within its borders, to dispossess Congress of the power to "abolish or interfere" with slavery, and to make itself un-amendable by the proviso that "no amendment shall be made to the Constitution" that would undo it.[16]

After Seward proposed the Corwin Amendment, newly elected President Lincoln defended the states' rights to adopt it. In his first inaugural address, Lincoln declared that he had "no objection" to the Corwin Amendment, nor that it be made "un-amendable." In early 1861, the Corwin Amendment won two-thirds support in both the House and the Senate. Ohio was the first state to ratify. Maryland and Illinois followed suit, but the onset of the Civil War interrupted the ratification process. Had it been ratified, the 13th Amendment would forever protect slavery instead of abolishing it.[17]

THE THIRD 13TH AMENDMENT

On January 31, 1865, another 13th Amendment (which prohibited slavery in Section 1 and ended states' rights in Section 2) was proposed. On April 9th, the Civil War ended with General Lee's surrender. On April 14th, President Lincoln was assassinated. On December 6th, the "new" 13th Amendment was ratified, thereby replacing and effectively erasing the original 13th Amendment that had prohibited "titles of nobility" and "honors."[18]

THE AMERICAN BAR ASSOCIATION

After the dissolution of the original 13th Amendment, American bar organizations and agencies began to appear and exercise political power.

---

16   Ibid.

17   Ibid.

18   Dodge, "The Missing 13th Amendment: No Lawyers Allowed in Public Office."

The union between the Rockefellers and American Bar Association was established when Elihu Root, a member of the Pilgrim Society and founding father of the CFR, became the president of the ABA in 1915. Under Root's leadership and with Rockefeller funding, the ABA emerged as the organization that provided accreditation to law schools throughout America. "American Bar Association Washington DC" by Tony Webster is licensed under CC BY-SA 4.0

The most powerful of these was the American Bar Association (ABA), which came into being in 1870. It was established by the House of Rothschild and, thereby, eventually linked to the Rockefellers and the money cartel.[19] Judges and lawyers throughout the country became a breed apart with foreign titles and dictatorial control in a court of law.

The union between the Rockefellers and American Bar Association was established when Elihu Root, a member of the Pilgrim Society and founding father of the CFR, became the president of the ABA in 1915.[20] Under Root's leadership and with Rockefeller funding, the ABA emerged as the organization that provided accreditation to law schools throughout America. This power was formidable since graduation from an ABA-accredited law school became a prerequisite for state bar examinations.[21] The very first laws passed by states, upon joining the ABA, was the prohibition of private citizens from practicing law. These unconstitutional rulings ensured that the APA would gain sole control of the interpretation and administration of the law.

The ABA also set forth legal positions that become federal law by

19　Susan Norgren, *When the Golden Egg Cracks* (Carlsbad, California: Balboa Press, 2012), p. 28.

20　"ABA Timeline," American Bar Association, 2018, https://www.americanbar.org/about_the_aba/timeline/, accessed February 13, 2019.

21　"ABA-Approved Law Schools by Year," American Bar Association, 2017, https://www.americanbar.org/groups/legal_education/resources/aba_approved_law_schools/by_year_approved/, accessed February 13, 2019.

pronouncement of the Supreme Court. It drafted the legislation for abortion rights, discrimination against LGBT people, same-sex marriage, and mandatory sentencing standards. It oversaw the federal judicial nomination process by vetting nominees and giving them a rating, ranging from "not qualified" to "well qualified." And, in keeping with the directives of John D. Rockefeller, the ABA advanced "the rule of law" throughout the world.[22]

THE AMERICAN LAW INSTITUTE

The American Law Institute was created in 1923 by the Laura Spellman Rockefeller Memorial Fund to restate "United States common law" to meet the needs of "societal changes." Common law represented the system of laws that was brought to America by English settlers. It involved the wide spectrum of

The American Law Institute was created in 1923 by the Laura Spellman Rockefeller Memorial Fund to restate "United States common law" to meet the needs of "societal changes." "ALI.headquarters" by SPDuffy527 is licensed under CC BY-SA 3.0

activity: marriage, the right of private property, the nature of money, criminal justice (including the punishment for murder, rape, and theft), and the regulations of human sexuality, including the laws against sodomy.

The common law in America was based on the presumption that the power of government resided with the common people and not with an elite group of power brokers.[23] It stood in sharp opposition to the British Equity, Maritime or Admiralty Laws (laws of contract), which placed legal power in the hands of an elite class of aristocrats. Common law

---

22   "Where We Work," American Bar Association, 2018, https://www.americanbar.org/advocacy/rule_of_law/where_we_work/, accessed February 13, 2019.

23   Howard Fisher and Dale Pond, "Our American Common Law," Delta Spectrum Research, 2010, https://www.svpvril.com/OACL.html, accessed February 13, 2019.

formed the basis for the Declaration of Independence, the Constitution, and the Bill of Rights.[24]

NO LAW OF GOD

The power, invested in the ALI, became virtually limitless since it allowed the directors of the Institute to rewrite the laws of the land in accordance with the dictates of their funding agency. In 1938, 15 years after the creation of the AFI, Supreme Court Justice Louis Brandeis in *Erie Railroad v. Tompkins* proclaimed it was a "fallacy" to assume there is any "transcendental body of law" by which federal or state courts could judge common cases. Instead, only the laws of state legislatures or opinions of state supreme courts could stand as binding.[25]

Out of this legal stance emerged the Supreme Court decrees regarding prayer in school, abortion, and gay rights. These rulings were made in strict compliance with the position of the Rockefeller Foundation, which endorsed religious indifferentism, Planned Parenthood, and the proliferation of abortion clinics and same-sex marriage.[26]

THE SCALIA STATEMENT

On February 25, 2015, Supreme Court Justice Antonin Scalia decried the restatement of common law by the AFI in his dissenting opinion on *Kansas v. Nebraska* on February 25, 2015. Scalia wrote:

> I write separately to note that modern Restatements—such as the Restatement (Third) of Restitution and Unjust Enrichment (2010), which both opinions address in their discussions of the disgorgement remedy—are of questionable value, and must be used with caution.

---

24 Ibid.

25 Herb Titus, *The Common Law* (Chapel Hill, NC: Professional Press, 1998), p. 6.

26 Gary Allen, *The Rockefeller File* (Seal Beach, CA: '76 Press, 1976), p. 136. Scott Roberts, "West Virginia US Senator Jay Rockefeller Announces Same-Sex Marriage Support," *Pink News,* March 26, 2013, https://www.pinknews.co.uk/2013/03/26/west-virginia-us-senator-jay-rockefeller-announces-same-sex-marriage-support/, accessed February 13, 2019.

The object of the original Restatements was "to present an orderly statement of the general common law." Restatement of Conflict of Laws, Introduction, p. viii (1934). Over time, the Restatements' authors have abandoned the mission of describing the law, and have chosen instead to set forth their aspirations for what the law ought to be . . . Restatement sections such as that should be given no weight whatever as to the current state of the law, and no more weight regarding what the law ought to be than the recommendations of any respected lawyer or scholar.[27]

Less than a year later, Scalia's body was found under mysterious circumstances at a ranch in Shafter, Texas.[28]

FDR'S JUDGES

The Rockefellers' control of the judiciary was facilitated by Nelson Rockefeller's position as chief advisor and confidant to Franklin Delano Roosevelt.[29] On May 27, 1935, the Supreme Court ruled that the FDR's National Industrial Recovery Act violated the borders of the U.S. Constitution. "Extraordinary conditions may call for extraordinary remedies," the court decreed, "but the argument necessarily stops short of an attempt to justify action which lies outside the sphere of constitutional authority. Extraordinary conditions do not create or enlarge constitutional power." Roosevelt, under Nelson Rockefeller's direction, retaliated by sending a bill to Congress that would enable him to appoint as many as six additional Supreme Court justices.

Eventually, this assault on the checks and balances of power proved

---

27 Glen G. Lammi, "Will the American Law Institute 'Restate' or Try to Rewrite U.S. Copyright Law?" *Forbes*, April 28, 2015, https://www.forbes.com/sites/wlf/2015/04/28/will-the-american-law-institute-restate-or-try-to-rewrite-u-s-copyright-law/#27ac8fa379d1, accessed February 13, 2019.

28 Judy Melina, "Justice Scalia's Unexplained Death Points to a Problem," *CNN*, February 20, 2016, https://www.cnn.com/2016/02/18/opinions/justice-scalia-no-autopsy-melinek/index.html, accessed February 13, 2019.

29 Emanuel M. Josephson, *Rockefeller "Internationalist"* (New York: Cheney Press, 1952), pp. 43–46.

to be too much for the president's friends on Capitol Hill to swallow, and the "court-packing plan" met with rejection. Former Chief Justice William Rehnquist later observed: "President Roosevelt lost the Court-packing battle, but he won the war for control of the Supreme Court— not by any novel legislation, but by serving in office for more than twelve years, and appointing eight of the nine Justices of the Court."[30]

The justices, who were appointed by FDR, had strong ties to the money cartel. Felix Frankfurter, whose career was sponsored by Jacob Schiff, became the founding father of the American Civil Liberties Union (ACLU). William O. Douglas, who vacationed with Nelson at FDR's Shangri-La retreat, ruled that trees must be granted "legal personhood" under federal law.[31] Harlan F. Stone, who served as the Chief Justice, was a partner in the law firm of Sullivan & Cromwell, which represented the Rockefeller family.[32] He changed federal law and the course of American history by his misinterpretation of the Constitution's Commerce Clause.

THE WARREN COURT

When Nelson Rockefeller joined the cabinet of Dwight D. Eisenhower as assistant secretary of health, education, and welfare, he, once again, obtained the appointments of his legal lackeys to the Supreme Court. Earl Warren, who became the chief justice, had been an employee of Associated Oil, a subsidiary of Standard Oil.[33] John Marshall Harlan was a Rhodes Scholar and Rockefeller lawyer.[34] Potter Stewart, a

---

30   David G. Savage, "Rehnquist Sees Threat to Judiciary," *Los Angeles Times,* January 1, 2005, http://articles.latimes.com/2005/jan/01/nation/na-scotus1, accessed February 13, 2019.

31   Richard Norton Smith, *Nelson Rockefeller: On His Own Terms* (New York: Random House, 2014), p. 2.

32   Melvin I. Brodsky, *Division and Discord: The Supreme Court under Stone and Vinson, 1941–1953* (Columbia: University of South Carolina Press, 1997), p. 10.

33   "Earl Warren" Rational Wiki, June 29, 2018, https://rationalwiki.org/wiki/Earl_Warren, accessed February 13, 2019.

34   David E. Rosenbaum, "Man in the News," *New York Times,* September 24, 1971, https://www.nytimes.com/1971/09/24/archives/a-lawyers-judge-john-marshall-harlan.html, accessed February 13, 2019.

prominent member of Yale's Skull and Bones Society, was an associate of Dinsmore and Shohl, a Cincinnati law firm that represented the Rockefellers' interests.[35]

THE NEW NATIONAL SOCIALISM

By orchestrating the proceedings of the Supreme Court, the Rockefellers instituted their own form of National Socialism, which would strip the states of their sovereign powers and place the American citizenry under the tyrannical rule of a centralized government that would control every aspect of their lives. By court order, Americans were compelled to bus their children to schools within inner-city ghettos where the educational system had been dumbed down for the sake of racial equality. They were obliged to pay taxes that went to support the abortion mills that had been set up by the Rockefeller foundations. They were commanded to remove all traces of the Christian religion from the public parks, schools, and buildings. They were ordered to transform their privately owned all-male academies into coed institutions. They were forced to allow the flood of pornography to pour into their cities, towns, and villages.

At the end of the second decade of the 21st century, Americans lived and died under a system ruled by the gavel of the Supreme Court. Noted American journalist Chris Hedges describes this development as follows:

> The supposed clash between liberal and conservative judges is largely a fiction. The judiciary, despite the Federalist Society's high-blown rhetoric about the sanctity of individual freedom, is a naked tool of corporate oppression. The most basic constitutional rights—privacy, fair trials and elections, habeas corpus, probable-cause requirements, due process and freedom from exploitation—have been erased for many, especially the 2.3 million people in our prisons, most having been put there without ever going to trial. Constitutionally protected

---

35 "Dinsmore," *Dinsmore History*, n. d., https://www.dinsmore.com/history/, accessed February 13, 2019.

statements, beliefs, and associations are criminalized. Our judicial system, as Ralph Nader has pointed out, has legalized secret law, secret courts, secret evidence, secret budgets, and secret prisons in the name of national security.

Our constitutional rights have steadily been stripped from us by judicial fiat. The Fourth Amendment reads: "The right of the people to be secure in their persons, houses, papers, and effects, against unreasonable searches and seizures, shall not be violated, and no Warrants shall issue, but upon probable cause, supported by Oath or affirmation, and particularly describing the place to be searched, and the persons or things to be seized." Yet our telephone calls and texts, emails and financial, judicial and medical records, along with every website we visit and our physical travels, can be and commonly are tracked, recorded, photographed and stored in government computer banks.

The executive branch can order the assassination of U.S. citizens without trial. It can deploy the military into the streets to quell civil unrest under Section 1021 of the National Defense Authorization Act (NDAA) and seize citizens—seizures that are in essence acts of extraordinary rendition—and hold them indefinitely in military detention centers while denying them due process.

Corporate campaign contributions, which largely determine who gets elected, are viewed by the courts as protected forms of free speech under the First Amendment. Corporate lobbying, which determines most of our legislation, is interpreted as the people's right to petition the government. Corporations are legally treated as persons except when they carry out fraud and other crimes; the heads of corporations routinely avoid being charged and going to prison by paying fines, usually symbolic and pulled from corporate accounts, while not being forced to admit wrongdoing. And corporations have rewritten the law to orchestrate a massive tax boycott.[36]

---

36   Chris Hedges, "The Corruption of the Law," *Common Dreams,* August 21, 2017, https://www.commondreams.org/views/2017/08/21/corruption-law, accessed February 13, 2019.

THE CONSTITUTION'S COMMERCE CLAUSE

These developments took place as a result of two judicial measures. The first was the Supreme Court's misinterpretation of the Commerce Clause of the Constitution (Article 1, Section 8), which granted Congress the power "to regulate Commerce with foreign Nations, and among the several States, and with the Indian Tribes." [37] The original intent of the Framers of the Constitution in adopting this clause was to prevent the creation of trade barriers between the states and, at the same time, to reserve for the U.S. legislature (the House of Representatives and the Senate) the right to restrict and regulate trade with foreign countries. In 1942, Harlan Stone opted to ignore the Framers' intent and set forth a broad interpretation of the clause as follows: "The Commerce power extends to those intrastate activities which in a substantial way interfere with or obstruct the granted power."[38] This interpretation of a clause regarding trade barriers allowed the federal court to regulate business activities within every state in the Union, including matters concerning sexual and racial discrimination in hotels, restaurants, theaters, and housing developments.

AN "EVOLVING" DOCUMENT

How could the Commerce Clause concerning trade between the states and foreign governments be used by nine judges to strip cities, towns, and villages of the United States of their right to uphold the Judeo-Christian principles that were upheld by the vast majority of American citizens? The answer resides in a statement made by Supreme Court Justice William J. Brennan, one of the architects of the judicial revolution. In an op-ed piece for the *New York Times* in 1997, Brennan admitted that the original intent of the Framers of the U.S. Constitution was no longer a factor in determining the meaning of the articles and amendments that had been

---

37   U.S. Constitution, Article 1—The Legislative Branch, Section 8—The Powers of Congress, https://www.usconstitution.net/xconst_A1Sec8.html, accessed February 13, 2019.

38   Harlan Fiske Stone, quoted in Samuel Francis, "Judicial Tyranny," *New American*, April 14, 1997, https://www.thenewamerican.com/usnews/constitution/item/15053-judicial-tyranny, accessed February 13, 2019.

set to paper. He wrote: "I approached my responsibility of interpreting it [the Constitution] as a 20th-century American, for the genius of the Constitution rests not in any static meaning it may have had in a world dead and gone but in its evolving character."[39]

According to Brennan, the Constitution did not stand for anything that could not be altered. No law within the country remained fixed or binding. No right existed that could not be abrogated. The Constitution was no longer a document that anchored the freedom and liberties of the American people. It was rather an *evolving* document whose meaning could be undermined or subverted to comply with the "progressivism" of nine justices in black robes. And this progressivism had been instilled within them by the policy papers of the ABA and the legal training they had received in ABA-accredited schools.

THE "INCORPORATION" DOCTRINE

The second means by which judicial tyranny was imposed upon the American people came with the so-called "Incorporation Doctrine," which represented a broad interpretation of Section 1 of the 14th Amendment, which held: "No state shall make or enforce any law which shall abridge the privileges or immunities of citizens of the United States; nor shall any state deprive any person of life, liberty, or property, without due process of law; nor deny to any person within its jurisdiction the equal protection of the laws."[40] The original intent of the Framers of this amendment, which was ratified on July 9, 1868, was to uphold the Civil Rights Act of 1866. This act had been drafted to protect the rights of recently emancipated slaves in the South and had been explicitly defined as the right "to make and enforce contracts; to sue, be parties; to give evidence; to inherit, purchase, lease, sell, hold, and convey real and personal property; and to full and equal benefit of

---

39   William J. Brennan, quoted in ibid.

40   14th Amendment, U.S. Constitution, July 9, 1868, *Legal Information Institute,* Cornell Law School, https://www.law.cornell.edu/constitution/amendmentxiv, accessed February 13, 2019.

all laws and proceedings for the security of person and property, and shall be subject to like punishment."[41] Such rights were deemed essential for the emancipated slaves, who were now citizens, to possess in order to function in society and to safeguard their freedom.[42]

"THE LINCHPIN OF JUDICIAL ACTIVISM"

In 1947, Justice Hugo Black in the case of *Adamson v. California* ruled that Section 1 of the 14th Amendment "incorporates" the Bill of Rights into the Constitution and makes the Bill of Rights applicable to all states. This notion of "incorporation" provided the basis for the constitutional revolution over which Earl Warren and his court presided during the 1950s and the 1960s. It transformed the original intent of the Bill of Rights as a means to prevent federal tyranny into a means by which the federal government, through the Supreme Court, could limit the sovereignty of every state in the union. "Upon this rock," legal scholar Douglas Bradford writes in *This World*, "rests the authority of the federal judiciary to oversee busing, quotas, school district boundaries, abortion, Miranda warnings, probable cause for arrest, prison and asylum standards, libel, pornography, subversive speech, and the separation of church and state. Incorporation has emerged as the linchpin of judicial activism in the twentieth century."[43]

A FORGOTTEN CASE

Before the ratification of the 14th Amendment, the Supreme Court held in the 1833 case of *Barron v. Baltimore* that the first eight amendments of the Constitution, known as the Bill of Rights, possessed no power over state governments but remained strictly limited to the federal

---

41 Ibid.

42 Francis, "Judicial Tyranny."

43 Douglas Bradford, quoted in ibid.

government. The case involved a wharf owner, John Barron, who sued the city of Baltimore for damages caused when the city, engaged in street construction, dumped tons of soil and sand in the waters near his wharf, making the harbor too shallow for most vessels.

The Supreme Court decided that the Bill of Rights, including the Fifth Amendment, applied only to the federal government and not independent states, such as Maryland. In the ruling, Supreme Court Justice John Marshall wrote:

> The Constitution was ordained and established by the people of the United States for themselves, for their own government, and not for the government of the individual states. Each state established a constitution for itself, and in that constitution, provided such limitations and restrictions on the powers of its particular government, as its judgment dictated. The people of the United States framed such a government for the United States as they supposed best adapted to their situation and best calculated to promote their interests. The powers they conferred on this government were to be exercised by itself; and the limitations on power, if expressed in general terms, are naturally, and, we think, necessarily, applicable to the government created by the instrument. They are limitations of power granted in the instrument itself; not of distinct governments, framed by different persons and for different purposes.
>
> If these propositions be correct, the Fifth Amendment must be understood as restraining the power of the general government, not as applicable to the states. In their several constitutions, they have imposed such restrictions on their respective governments, as their own wisdom suggested; such as they deemed most proper for themselves. It is a subject on which they judge exclusively, and with which others interfere no further than they are supposed to have a common interest. . . .
>
> Had the Framers of these Amendments intended them to be limitations on the powers of the state governments, they would have imitated the framers of the original Constitution, and have expressed

that intention. Had congress engaged in the extraordinary occupation of improving the constitutions of the several states, by affording the people additional protection from the exercise of power by their own governments, in matters which concerned themselves alone, they would have declared this purpose in plain and intelligible language.

But it is universally understood, it is a part of the history of the day, that the great revolution which established the constitution of the United States, was not effected without immense opposition. Serious fears were extensively entertained, that those powers which the patriot statesmen, who then watched over the interests of our country, deemed essential to union, and to the attainment of those invaluable objects for which union was sought, might be exercised in a manner dangerous to liberty. In almost every convention by which the Constitution was adopted, amendments to guard against the abuse of power were recommended. These Amendments demanded security against the apprehended encroachments of the general government-not against those of the local governments. In compliance with a sentiment thus generally expressed, to quiet fears thus extensively entertained, amendments were proposed by the required majority in Congress, and adopted by the states. These Amendments contain no expression indicating an intention to apply them to the state governments. This court cannot so apply them.[44]

This monumental decision was tossed to the wind by Justices Hugo Black and later William O. Brennan with their insistence that every state government must operate in complete compliance not only with the Bill of Rights but also with "penumbras" by which other rights are implied but not specified in the Constitution.[45]

---

44   "Barron v. City of Baltimore," United States Supreme Court, January Term, 1833, *Find Law*, https://web.archive.org/web/20080516101253/http://laws.findlaw.com/us/32/243.html, accessed February 13, 2019.

45   Francis, "Judicial Tyranny."

DEMOCRACY BE DAMNED

Because of the abandonment of *Barron v. Baltimore*, judicial tyranny gained a stranglehold on United States citizens during the latter half of the 20th century. The will of the people was ignored, and compliance with the iron-fisted demands of the nine justices, who were appointed for life to their positions, was enforced by federal officials. Democracy became an illusion. In 1994, California voters passed by a substantial margin a ballot measure known as Proposition 187, which denied most public benefits, such as welfare, to illegal aliens. Within a year, a federal judge ruled the law unconstitutional, and waves of undocumented migrants began to flood America's southern border. In 1996, the voters of California passed Proposition 209, a ballot measure that abolished affirmative action programs and racial discrimination by the state government. Within three weeks, a federal judge ruled the new law unconstitutional. In 1992, voters in Colorado passed an amendment to the state constitution that prohibited local jurisdictions from adopting laws that forbade discrimination on the basis of sexual orientation. This measure, known as Amendment 2, sought to deny special legal protection and privileges to homosexuals and to protect the rights of those who refused to do business with them, including landlords. Federal courts, including the U.S. Supreme Court in its 1996 decision *Romer v. Evans*, declared that Amendment 2 was unconstitutional.[46] A complete list of such rulings, including those that order state and county prisons to release convicted criminals and prohibit public displays of religious symbols, would fill another volume. And they were all made under the direction of the American Law Institute by members of the American Bar Association.

A GLUT OF LAWYERS

Judicial tyranny extended over the legislative branch of the U.S. government, since the House of Representatives and the Senate became filled

---

46   Ibid.

with ABA lawyers. Within the 115th Congress, there were 168 representatives and 50 senators who were licensed lawyers and members of the American Bar Association.[47] Most had been groomed for public service by the political action committees (PACs) of companies and organizations under Rockefeller control, including ExxonMobil PAC, J.P. Morgan Chase PAC, American Bank Association PAC, Boeing Company PAC, Honeywell International PAC, New York Life Insurance Company PAC, Monsanto Company Citizenship Fund, Pfizer PAC, General Electric PAC, the Sierra Club Political Committee, Merck PAC, MetLife PAC, Union Pacific Fund for Better Government, Human Rights Campaign, and the Planned Parenthood Action Fund.[48]

ORBIS NON SUFFICIT

The onset of judicial tyranny throughout the United States remained rooted in the Rockefeller family's pathological fear of poverty that had been passed on from generation to generation. Throughout his life, John D. confessed that he often awoke at night in a cold sweat for fear that he had lost his great wealth. Regarding this phobia, Emanuel M. Josephson, a Rockefeller biographer, writes:

> Fear of poverty was imposed by John D. on those about him, especially on his family, to such an extent that it became the mainspring of the character of the Rockefeller enterprises. This fear could be allayed only by such complete domination of the community and of the world that no one could ever rise to offer competition or to threaten to impoverish him. This mental condition gave rise to a super-Napoleonic complex, a driving urge to rule the U.S. and the world.[49]

---

47 Jennifer E. Manning, "Membership of the 115th Congress: A Profile," *Congressional Research Service*, October 1, 2018, https://fas.org/sgp/crs/misc/R44762.pdf, accessed February 13, 2019.

48 Allen, *The Rockefeller File*, pp. 31–35.

49 Emanuel M. Josephson, *Rockefeller "Internationalist"* (New York: Cheney Press, 1952), p. 17.

Through their funding of America's educational system, they controlled what people learned and how people thought. Through their investments in the media (including their alleged purchase of the *New York Times*[50]), they controlled the information that people received and the positions on political issues that people should adopt. Through their grants to the country's Christian seminaries, they controlled what people believed and what deity people should worship. Through their involvement with the Federal Reserve System, the Bank for International Settlements, the International Monetary Fund, and the World Bank, they controlled the global economy and the manner in which people labored to earn their daily bread. Through their establishment of the Council on Foreign Relations, they controlled the U.S. State Department, and the policies that people must support and the manner by which people are governed. Through their "philanthropies," they controlled population growth and engaged in the advancement of eugenics. Through the CIA, they controlled ongoing covert operations and the rise and fall of nations. Through their support of the American Bar Association and the American Law Institute, they controlled the laws that people were obliged to obey and the rights people were allotted. But even this power was insufficient to put the Rockefellers' fear to rest.

---

50   Ibid., p. 20.

21

THE END OF LIBERTY

He [King George III] has obstructed the Administration of Justice, by refusing his Assent to Laws for establishing Judiciary powers.

He has made Judges dependent on his Will alone, for the tenure of their offices, and the amount and payment of their salaries.

He has erected a multitude of New Offices, and sent hither swarms of Officers to harass our people, and eat out their substance.

He has kept among us, in times of peace, Standing Armies without the Consent of our legislatures.

He has affected to render the Military independent of and superior to the Civil power.

He has combined with others to subject us to a jurisdiction foreign to our constitution, and unacknowledged by our laws; giving his Assent to their Acts of pretended Legislation:

. . . For protecting them, by a mock Trial, from punishment for any Murders which they should commit on the Inhabitants of these States:

For imposing Taxes on us without our Consent:

For depriving us in many cases, of the benefits of Trial by Jury:

For taking away our Charters, abolishing our most valuable Laws, and altering fundamentally the Forms of our Governments:

For suspending our own Legislatures, and declaring themselves invested with power to legislate for us in all cases whatsoever.

—THOMAS JEFFERSON, DECLARATION OF INDEPENDENCE, JULY 4, 1776

THE VIEW OF THE CONSTITUTION as an "evolving document" caused Americans to fall prey to a legal system in which they possessed neither a right nor a power to oppose the demands of an oppressive government ruled by a money cartel. They can be summoned to appear before a grand jury at a federal court hundreds of miles from their homes, held for days in rooms without furniture, including chairs, and subjected to hours of questioning without legal representation by prosecuting attorneys. If they refuse to answer questions or offer "unsuitable" answers, they can be hauled off to jail for an indefinite stay. No judges are present to question or curb the questioning by the prosecuting attorneys, and no measures are in play to protect innocent individuals who are summoned to testify. Court stenographers transcribe the proceedings, but their records remain sealed to reporters and concerned citizens.[1]

These developments occur in sharp contradiction to the purpose of grand juries, which had been set forth in *Branzburg v. Hayes* (1971) as follows: "The Grand Jury has the dual function of determining if there is probable cause to believe that a crime has been committed and of protecting citizens against unfounded criminal prosecutions."[2] This purpose was tossed to the wind in 1976, when the Supreme Court ruled in *Imbler v. Pachtman* that prosecutors cannot face civil lawsuit for prosecutorial abuses, not even the knowing or reckless presentation of false testimony.[3]

A HAM SANDWICH

The ability of grand juries to act in complete secrecy and without

1   Martin Armstrong, "Mueller's Tyrannical Indictment = The Very Reason We Had a Revolution," *Armstrong Economics*, February 19, 2018, https://www.armstrongeconomics.com/international-news/rule-of-law/muellers-questionable-indictment/, accessed March 7, 2019.

2   "Branzburg v. Hayes," Legal Information Institute, June 29, 1972, https://www.law.cornell.edu/supremecourt/text/408/665, accessed March 7, 2019.

3   "Imbler v. Pachtman," Justia Supreme Court Center, March 2, 1976, https://www.oyez.org/cases/1975/74-5435, accessed March 7, 2019.

supervision by reporters or objective observers was unanimously upheld by the Supreme Court in the *Douglas Oil Company v. Petrol Stops Northeast* (1979). The rationale behind the decision was that "if pre-indictment proceedings were made public, many prospective witnesses would be hesitant to come forward voluntarily."[4]

The grand jury system has become so despotic that it was decried by Circuit Court Judges Evans, Posner, and Easterbrook who in their decision regarding *U.S. v. Ross* wrote: "Realistically, federal grand juries today provide little protection for criminal suspects whom a U.S. Attorney wishes to indict. Nevertheless, that is not a realism to which judges are permitted to yield."[5]

The grand jury rooms were not like regular courtrooms. They were set up like small amphitheaters. The members of the grand jury peered down at the table and chair where the witnesses were seated. Off to one side was the stenographer's table. If a witness was perplexed or petrified, he could request permission to leave the room in order to confer with his lawyer in the hallway. Such an act was almost always unwise since it gave the jury the perception that the witness had something to hide. The prosecutors ran the show from start to finish, and the jury inevitably abided by their wishes. As Sol Wachtler, chief judge of the New York Court of Appeals, once quipped: "A grand jury would indict a ham sandwich if that's what the prosecutor wanted."[6]

THE 100-MILE ZONE

Most Americans assume that border-related policies only impact people living in border towns, like El Paso or San Diego. The reality is that

---

4   "Douglas Oil Co. v. Petrol Stops Northeast," *Justia*, Supreme Court, April 18, 1979, https://supreme.justia.com/cases/federal/us/441/211/, accessed March 7, 2019.

5   "U.S. v. Ross," No. 04-2124, *Leagle*, June 20, 2005, https://www.leagle.com/decision/200511834 12f3d77111103, accessed March 7, 2019.

6   Sol Wachtler, quoted in Tom Wolfe, *The Bonfire of the Vanities* (New York: Farrar, Straus, Giroux, 1987), p. 603.

interior enforcement operations by Border Patrol agents encroach deep into and across the United States, affecting the majority of Americans. In 1953, the U.S. Department of Justice established a 100-mile border zone in which American citizens no longer possess their rights under the 4th Amendment. Within this zone, federal agents have the right to conduct property searches without warrants and conduct dragnets by which motorists can be stopped, searched, and interrogated even when there is no "probable cause" of wrongdoing.[7]

Roughly, two-thirds of the United States' population lives within the 100-mile zone—that is, within 100 miles of a U.S. land or coastal border. That's about 200 million people. Connecticut, Delaware, Florida, Hawaii, Maine, Massachusetts, New Hampshire, New Jersey, New York, Rhode Island, and Vermont reside entirely or almost entirely within this zone, which means the cities in which Americans no longer retain their Constitutional rights, include New York City, Los Angeles, Chicago, Houston, Philadelphia, Phoenix, San Antonio, San Diego, and San Jose.[8]

THE CONSTITUTIONALITY OF WAR

Article 1, Section 8 of the U.S. Constitution maintains that Congress alone has the power to declare war. Opposition to executive wars were voiced by many Framers, including John Jay, who wrote in the *Federalist*: "It is too true, however disgraceful it may be to human nature, that nations in general will make war whenever they have a prospect of getting any thing by it; nay, absolute monarchs will often make war when their nations are to get nothing by it, but for purposes and objects merely personal, such as a thirst for military glory, revenge for personal

7   Chris Rickerd, "Customs and Border Protection's (CBP'S) 100-Mile Rule," American Civil Liberties Union, n. d., https://www.aclu.org/other/aclu-factsheet-customs-and-border-protections-100-mile-zone?redirect=immigrants-rights/aclu-fact-sheet-customs-and-border-protections-100-mile-zone, accessed March 7, 2019.

8   Ibid.

affronts, ambition, or private compacts to aggrandize or support their particular families or partisans."[9]

At the Constitutional Convention, Pierce Butler argued "for vesting the power in the president, who will have all the requisite qualities, and will not make war but when the nation will support it." Butler's motion did not receive so much as a second.[10] James Wilson, in praise of reserving for Congress the right to declare war, said, "This system will not hurry us into war; it is calculated to guard against it. It will not be in the power of a single man, or a single body of men, to involve us in such distress; for the important power of declaring war is vested in the legislature at large: this declaration must be made with the concurrence of the House of Representatives: from this circumstance we may draw a certain conclusion that nothing but our interest can draw us into war."[11]

On April 2, 1798, James Madison wrote to Thomas Jefferson: "The constitution supposes, what the History of all Governments demonstrates, that the Executive is the branch of power most interested in war, and most prone to it. It has accordingly with studied care vested the question of war in the Legislature."[12]

THE *UNITED STATES V. SMITH*

Throughout the colonial period, Congress retained authority to both declare and make war (i.e., initiate war). This was clearly expressed in court rulings. In *United States v. Smith* (1806), a circuit court rejected

---

9   John Jay, *Federalist* no. 4, Yale Law School, Avalon Project, http://avalon.law.yale.edu/18th_century/fed04.asp, accessed March 7, 2019.

10   Pierce Butler, quoted in Thomas Woods, "The Constitution Is Clear on Presidential War Power," Tenth Amendment Center, December 30, 2009, https://tenthamendmentcenter.com/2009/12/30/the-constitution-is-clear-on-presidential-war-powers/, accessed March 7, 2019.

11   James Wilson, quoted in ibid.

12   James Madison, Letter to Thomas Jefferson, April 2, 1798, *The Framers' Constitution*, University of Chicago, http://press-pubs.uchicago.edu/founders/documents/a1_8_11s8.html, accessed March 7, 2019.

the idea that a president or his assistants could unilaterally authorize military adventures against foreign governments. The court put the matter bluntly: "Does [the President] possess the power of making war? That power is exclusively vested in Congress." If a nation invaded the United States, the president would have an obligation to resist with force. But there was a "manifest distinction" between going to war with a nation at peace and responding to an actual invasion. The court ruled: "In the former case, it is the exclusive province of Congress to change a state of peace into a state of war."[13]

THE LINCOLN LETTER

This position was upheld throughout the 19th century. In a letter to his law partner in 1848, Abraham Lincoln wrote:

> *Allow the President to invade a neighboring nation, whenever* he *shall deem it necessary to repel an invasion, and you allow him to do so,* whenever he may choose to say *he deems it necessary for such purpose—and you allow him to make war at pleasure. Study to see if you can fix* any limit *to his power in this respect, after you have given him so much as you propose. If, to-day, he should choose to say he thinks it necessary to invade Canada, to prevent the British from invading us, how could you stop him? You may say to him, "I see no probability of the British invading us"* but he will say to you *"be silent; I see it, if you don't."*
>
> The provision of the Constitution giving the war-making power to Congress, was dictated, as I understand it, by the following reasons. Kings had always been involving and impoverishing their people in wars, pretending generally, if not always, that the good of the people was the object. This, our Convention understood to be the most oppressive of all Kingly oppressions; and they resolved to so frame the Constitution that no one man should hold the power of bringing

---

13 "United States v. Smith," Circuit Court, District of New York, July 15, 1806, Law Resources, https://law.resource.org/pub/us/case/reporter/F.Cas/0027.f.cas/0027.f.cas.1192.pdf, accessed March 7, 2019.

this oppression upon us. But your view destroys the whole matter, and places our President where kings have always stood.[14]

HARRY GIVES 'EM HELL

With the United Nations in place, President Harry Truman threw this stipulation to the wind and decided that under the new global government an Act of Congress was no longer necessary for deploying American troops to armed combat in foreign lands. When questioned about his unconstitutional action at a news conference, Truman said: "We are not at war." Asked whether it would be more correct to call the conflict "a police action under the United Nations," he replied: "That is exactly what it amounts to."[15]

In the wake of Truman's unprecedented action, Congress acquiesced its authority, inaugurating a new age of endless war. The Constitutional Forum addresses the monumental importance of Truman's decision as follows:

> Truman denied that he need congressional authorization before deploying the troops in Europe, and his decision triggered the so-called "great debate" on the constitutionality of his action. Several senators, among them Paul Douglas and Thomas Connelly, argued that the president has the power under the Constitution to move troops overseas, both in pursuance of treaty obligations and by virtue of his constitutional powers as commander in chief of the armed forces. In contrast, Taft and John Bricker criticized the president's action as grossly unconstitutional. The outcome of the debate was a substantial victory for the president. The Senate adopted a weak resolution expressing its "approval" of the president's action, but declaring it to be "the sense

---

14 Abraham Lincoln, quoted in Conor Friedersdorf, "Abraham Lincoln's Warning about the Presidents and War," *Atlantic,* July 13, 2012, https://www.theatlantic.com/politics/archive/2012/07/abraham-lincolns-warning-about-presidents-and-war/259767/, accessed March 7, 2019.

15 Harry Truman quoted in Louis Fisher, "Unconstitutional Wars from Truman Forward," *Humanitas* 30, 2017, http://www.nhinet.org/fisher30-1.pdf, accessed March 7, 2019.

of the Senate" that in the future the president ought to obtain the approval of Congress prior to the assignment of troops abroad, "in the interests of sound constitutional processes and of national unity." The acquiescence of Congress in the fact of Truman's usurpation of power inaugurated a new theme in matters of war and peace.[16]

On August 12, 1950, the U.S. Air Force dropped 626 tons of bombs on North Korea; two weeks later the daily tonnage increased to 800 tons. The carpet bombings resulted in the destruction of 78 cities and thousands of villages. By the time an armistice was signed on July 27, 1953, a third of the population of North Korea—more than three million people—had been wiped out.[17] The official U.S. casualty list showed that 36,914 American soldiers had died in the conflict, and 7,800 remained unaccounted for.[18] The struggle resulted neither in territorial gain or loss. The objective of the war had been containment, not liberation or victory. The terms of the armistice called for the creation of a demilitarized zone (DMZ) between North and South Korea. Each side was to be 2,200 yards from the center. The DMZ was to be patrolled by both sides at all times.[19] America's wars were to be waged with limited rules of engagement and indefinite outcomes to advance the purpose of the global bankers, who had brought the United Nations into being.

A FALSE FLAG

On August 4, 1964, all nationally televised programs were interrupted for this urgent message from U.S. President Lyndon B. Johnson:

---

16 "The Constitution: The Continuing War Powers Controversy," *New American Nation,* n.d., https://www.americanforeignrelations.com/A-D/The-Constitution-The-continuing-war-powers-controversy.html, accessed March 7, 2019.

17 Michel Chossudovsky, *The Globalization of War: America's 'Long War' against Humanity* (Montreal, Quebec: *Global Research* Publishers, 2015), pp. 26–30.

18 CNN Library, "Korean War Fast Facts," *CNN News,* April 30, 2018, http://www.cnn.com/2013/06/28/world/asia/korean-war-fast-facts/, accessed March 7, 2019.

19 Ibid.

My fellow Americans: As President and Commander in Chief, it is my duty to the American people to report that renewed hostile actions against United States ships on the high seas in the Gulf of Tonkin have today required me to order the military forces of the United States to take action in reply.

The initial attack on the destroyer Maddox, on August 2nd, was repeated today by a number of hostile vessels attacking two U.S. destroyers with torpedoes. The destroyers and supporting aircraft acted at once on the orders I gave after the initial act of aggression. We believe at least two of the attacking boats were sunk. There were no U.S. losses.

The performance of commanders and crews in this engagement is in the highest tradition of the United States Navy. But repeated acts of violence against the Armed Forces of the United States must be met not only with alert defense, but with positive reply. That reply is being given as I speak to you tonight. Air action is now in execution against gunboats and certain supporting facilities in North Viet-Nam which have been used in these hostile operations.

In the larger sense this new act of aggression, aimed directly at our own forces, again brings home to all of us in the United States the importance of the struggle for peace and security in southeast Asia. Aggression by terror against the peaceful villagers of South Viet-Nam has now been joined by open aggression on the high seas against the United States of America.

The determination of all Americans to carry out our full commitment to the people and to the government of South Viet-Nam will be redoubled by this outrage.[20]

The next morning, Johnson appeared before Congress to gain the approval for direct military involvement in the Vietnam Civil War. The

---

20   Lyndon B. Johnson, "Gulf of Tonkin Address," August 4, 1964, https://usa.usembassy.de/etexts/ speeches/rhetoric/lbjgulf.htm, accessed March 7, 2019.

resolution was passed by a vote of 416 to 0 in the House and 88 to 2 in the Senate. The resolution read: "Congress approves and supports the determination of the President, as Commander in Chief, to take all necessary measures to repel any armed attack against the forces of the United States and to prevent further aggression." How any congressman could approve the resolution without realizing that it was a declaration of war remains one of the great mysteries of the 20th century. After the vote, Johnson said to his undersecretary of state: "Hell, those stupid sailors were just shooting at flying fish."[21]

President Lyndon B. Johnson appeared before Congress to gain the approval for direct military involvement in the Vietnam War. The resolution was passed by a vote of 416 to 0 in the House and 88 to 2 in the Senate.

DEATH AND DECEPTION

The country was now involved in another unconstitutional war that would lead to over 50,000 deaths and millions of Vietnamese casualties. The official story of the cause remained the same throughout the course of the war. North Vietnamese torpedo boats launched an "unprovoked attack" against a U.S. destroyer on "routine patrol" in the Tonkin Gulf on August 2nd, and, two days later, North Vietnamese PT boats launched a torpedo attack on two U.S. destroyers in another act of unwarranted aggression. But there was a problem. It was all a hoax. The sailors really were shooting at flying fish. The second attack never happened. In a 2005 *New York Times* article, Scott Shane wrote: "President Lyndon B. Johnson cited the supposed attack to persuade Congress to authorize broad military action in Vietnam, but most

---

21   Scott Shane, "Vietnam Study, Casting Doubts, Remains Secret," *New York Times*, October 31, 2005, http://www.nytimes.com/2005/10/31/politics/vietnam-study-castingdoubts-remains-secret.html?_r=0, accessed March 7, 2019.

historians have concluded in recent years that there was no second attack. The N.S.A. historian, Robert J. Hanyok, found a pattern of translation mistakes that went uncorrected, altered intercept times and selective citation of intelligence that persuaded him that mid level agency officers had deliberately skewed the evidence."[22]

What's more, the first attack was not unprovoked, as the president intimated. The destroyer *Maddox* was not engaged in routine patrol. It was rather engaged in maneuvers to coordinate attacks on North Vietnam by the South Vietnamese navy and the Laotian air force.[23]

KILLING FOR "CONTAINMENT"

By April 1965, Johnson had deployed 75,000 combat troops to Vietnam; that number rose to half a million by the end of 1967. The U.S. dropped three times as many bombs on the tiny country of Vietnam as it did in all of World War II. The bombs included chemical weapons of mass destruction, including napalm and white phosphorous that burned all skin from the bone.[24]

The overall policy of the Vietnam War, as developed by George Keenan, Dean Acheson, and other CFR officials, was "containment," the attempt to confine the Communist countries to their existing borders.[25] It was the same policy that failed in Korea. Containment implied limited warfare. Victory was not an objection but rather a liability. James E. King, in a piece published by *Foreign Affairs* in 1957, explained this new concept of limited warfare as follows:

22   Ibid.

23   Lt. Commander Pat Peterson, "The Truth about Tonkin," *Naval History* magazine, February 2008, https://www.usni.org/magazines/navalhistory/2008-02/truth-about-tonkin, accessed March 7, 2019.

24   Oliver Stone and Peter Kuznick, *The Concise Untold History of the United States* (New York: Gallery Books, 2014), p. 198.

25   Michael O'Malley, "The Vietnam War and the Tragedy of Containment," History 122, George Mason University, n. d., https://chnm.gmu.edu/courses/122/vietnam/lecture.html, accessed March 7, 2019.

By April 1965, Johnson had deployed 75,000 combat troops to Vietnam; that number rose to half a million by the end of 1967.

We must be prepared to fight limited actions ourselves. Otherwise we shall have made no advance beyond 'massive retaliation,' which tied our hands in conflicts involving less than our survival. And we must be prepared to lose limited actions. No limitation could survive our disposition to elevate every conflict in which our interests are affected to the level of total conflict with survival at stake. Armed conflict can be limited only if aimed at limited objectives and fought with limited means. If we or our enemy relax the limits on either objectives or means, survival will be at stake, whether the issue is worth it or not.[26]

It was a concept that was easily sold to President Johnson, who had appointed a CFR member to virtually every strategic position in his administration.[27]

---

26   James E, King, "Nuclear Plenty and Limited War," *Foreign Affairs*, January 1957.

27   Allen, *The Rockefeller File*, p. 110.

THE TRADE DEAL

Of course, the U.S. Defense Department, the Pentagon, and the Johnson Administration were well aware that over 85 percent of the war materiel for the Viet Cong came from factories within the Soviet Union. But as soon as Congress approved the resolution for direct American involvement in the Vietnam War, David Rockefeller met with Soviet premier Nikita Khrushchev in Moscow to draft a trade agreement that would extend most-favored nation status within the Soviet Communist bloc. The treaty was approved by President Johnson and went into effect on October 13, 1966. Regarding this development, the *New York Times* published the following report:

> The United States put into effect today one of President Johnson's proposals for stimulating East-West trade by removing restrictions on the export of more than four hundred commodities to the Soviet Union and Eastern Europe. . . Among the categories from which items have been selected for export relaxation are vegetables, cereals, fodder, hides, crude and manufactured rubber, pulp and waste paper, textile and textile fibers, crude fertilizers, metal ores and scrap, petroleum gas and derivatives, chemical compounds and products, dyes, medicines, fireworks, detergents, plastic materials, metal products and machinery, and scientific and professional instruments.[28]

Virtually all of the "non-strategic" items on the list could be used as instruments of war. A machine gun, for example, was deemed strategic and not part of the agreement, but the tools and parts to manufacture machine guns and the chemicals necessary to propel the machine gun bullets were considered "non-strategic."[29]

The Rockefellers became the principal benefactors of this bloody arrangement. They set up with the House of Rothschild the International

28   *New York Times*, quoted in ibid.

29   Ibid.

Basic Economy Corporation to build rubber goods plants and aluminum-producing factories for the Vietnam People's Air Force, which was bombing American forces.[30]

THE HIDDEN AGENDA

But more was at stake in Southeast Asia than the ideology of containment, and the immediate opportunity to reap financial benefits from the conflict. The region produced the poppy crops that were becoming one of the world's most valuable commodities. Without the flow of heroin from the Golden Triangle of Burma, Laos, and Thailand, the funding for the CIA's covert operations, which opened new markets for the money cartel, would come to an abrupt halt. And many of these operations, as noted in chapter 19, were undertaken at the behest and for the benefit of the Rockefellers.

By 1958, the opium trade in Southeast Asia became so brisk that a second drug supply line was established by the CIA. This route ran from dirt airstrips within the Annamite Mountains of Laos to Saigon's international airport for transshipment to Europe and the United States.[31] Saigon had become a city of strategic importance to the heroin industry.

HIGH ON HEROIN

The heroin business was booming. By 1971, there were more than 500,000 heroin addicts in the U.S., producing a cash flow of $12 billion. Three million, fifty-four thousand Americans admitted on a government survey to using heroin at least once. Down at the morgue, where people don't lie, the numbers told a different story: 41 percent of the drug-related deaths were now linked to heroin.[32]

30   Ibid., p. 111.

31   Alfred W. McCoy, *The Politics of Heroin: CIA Complicity in the Global Drug Trade* (Chicago: Lawrence Hill Books, 2003), p. 153.

32   Robert Young Pelton, *The World's Most Dangerous Places* (New York: Harper Resource, 2003), p. 158.

Southeast Asia remained the main source of opium. From Laos alone, over a ton a month arrived in Saigon on C-47 military transport planes that had been provided by the CIA to the Royal Lao Army.[33] So much opium was flowing into Saigon that 30 percent of the U.S. servicemen in Vietnam became heroin addicts.[34] Some of this same heroin was smuggled into the United States in body bags containing dead soldiers. When DEA agent Michael Levine attempted to bust this operation, he was warned off by his superiors since such action could result in the exposure of the supply line from Long Tieng.[35]

New money laundries for the heroin trade were required, and the House of Rockefeller was more than willing to offer its service.

33 Alexander Cockburn and Jeffrey St. Clair, *Whiteout: The CIA, Drugs and the Press* (New York: Verso, 1998), p. 246.

34 Ibid., p. 249.

35 Ibid.

22

THE ROAD TO PERDITION

As the twenty-first century gets underway, the imbalance of wealth and democracy in the United States is unsustainable, at least by traditional yardsticks. Market theology and unelected leadership have been displacing politics and elections. Either democracy must be renewed, with politics brought back to life, or wealth is likely to cement a new and less democratic regime-plutocracy by some other name. Over the coming decades, American exceptionalism may face its greatest test simply in convincing the American people to continue to believe in its comfort and reassurance.

—KEVIN PHILLIPS, *WEALTH AND DEMOCRACY*, 2002

SINCE HEROIN REMAINED the principal source of the CIA's covert operations, the Rockefeller family became deeply involved in the drug trade. The Nugan Hand Bank had been established by the Agency in Sydney, Australia, to purchase weapons for guerrilla forces in Indonesia, Thailand, Malaysia, Brazil, and the white Rhodesian government of Ian Smith and to import heroin into Australia from the Golden Triangle of Thailand, Laos, and Myanmar (Burma).[1]

The primary shareholder of the Nugan Hand Bank was Australian,

---

1   Penny Lernoux, *In Banks We Trust* (New York: Penguin Books, 1984), pp. 69–70.

and Pacific Holdings, a company that was owned and operated by the Rockefellers' Chase Manhattan Bank.[2] By 1974, the Australian bank was doing billions in business. The heroin flowing into the United States at the Andrews Air Force bank and other military installations within the body bags of dead soldiers had produced a heroin epidemic that spread from the ghettoes to the college campuses, where students mounted massive protests against the war.

THE NEW NETWORK

With the fall of Saigon, the drought in Southeast Asia, and the eradication of the poppy fields in Burma and Thailand, the CIA set its sights on the Golden Crescent, where the highlands of Afghanistan, Pakistan, and Iran all converge, for a new source of drug revenue. Since the seventeenth century, opium poppies had been grown in this region by local tribesmen, and the market remained regional. By the 1950s, very little opium was produced in Afghanistan and Pakistan, with about 2,500 acres in both countries under cultivation.[3] At the close of the Vietnam War, the fertile growing fields of Afghanistan's Helmand Valley were covered with vineyards, wheat, and cotton.[4]

The major problem for the CIA was the Afghan government of Noor Mohammed Taraki, who sought to eradicate poppy production in the border regions of the country that remained occupied by radical Islamic fundamentalists. This attempt at eradication sprang from Taraki's desire

---

2   Ken Thomas and David Hatcher Childress, *Inside the Gemstone File: Howard Hughes, Onassis, and JFK* (Kempton, IL: Adventures Unlimited Press, 1999), p. 93. See also Denise Pritchard, "Financial Takeover of Australia and New Zealand," *The Opal File*, n.d., https://www.bibliotecapleyades.net/esp_sociopol_opalfile.htm, accessed March 7, 2019.

3   Alexander Cockburn and Jeffrey St. Clair, *Whiteout: The CIA, Drugs and the Press* (New York: Verso, 1998), p. 261.

4   Ibid.

The major problem for the CIA was the Afghan government of Noor Mohammed Taraki, who sought to eradicate poppy production in the border regions of the country that remained occupied by radical Islamic fundamentalists.

to unite all the Pashtun tribes under Kabul rule.[5] The fundamentalists spurned such efforts not only because of their desire to keep the cash crops but also because they viewed the Taraki government as *shirk* (blasphemy). The modernist regime advocated female education and prohibited arranged marriages and the bride price. By 1975, the tension between government and the fundamentalists erupted into violence when Pashtun tribesmen mounted a revolt in the Panjshir valley north of Kabul.[6] The tribesmen were led by Gulbuddin Hekmatyar, who became the new darling of the CIA.

5   Alfred W. McCoy, *The Politics of Heroin: CIA Complicity in the Global Drug Trade* (Chicago: Lawrence Hill Books, 2003), p. 476.

6   Ibid.

THE MUSLIM MADMAN

Hekmatyar made his public debut in 1972 at the University of Kabul by killing a leftist student. He fled to Pakistan, where he became an agent of Inter-Services Intelligence (ISI), and the leader of Hezb-e-Islami, an organization dedicated to the formation of a "pure" Islamic state, ruled by the most intransigent interpretation of Sunni law.[7] Hekmatyar urged his followers to throw acid in the faces of women not wearing a veil, kidnapped rival Islamic chieftains, and in 1977, began to build up an arsenal, courtesy of the CIA.[8] The Agency also began to funnel millions to ISI, which became transformed into its surrogate on the Afghan border.[9]

The CIA believed that Hekmatyar, despite the fact that he was clearly unhinged, would be of inestimable value not only in undermining the Taraki government but also in gaining control of the poppy fields in the Helmand Valley. Its faith was not misplaced. Throughout 1978, a year before the Soviet invasion, Hekmatyar and his *mujahideen* ("holy warriors") burned universities and girls' schools throughout Afghanistan and gained feudal control over many of the poppy farmers. The pro-Taraki militants, aware of the destabilization plot, assassinated Adolph "Spike" Dubbs, the U.S. Ambassador to Kabul, on February 14, 1979.[10]

Hekmatyar's actions caused heroin production to rise from 400 tons in 1971 to 1,200 tons in 1978. After the assassination of Dubbs and the flow of millions to Hekmatyar's guerrilla army, the production soared to 1,800 tons, and a network of laboratories was set up by the

---

7   Robert Pelton, *The World's Most Dangerous Places* (New York: Harper Resource, 2003), p. 342.

8   Cockburn and St. Clair, *Whiteout*, p. 264.

9   McCoy, *The Politics of Heroin*, p. 474.

10 Jeffrey Lord, "Jimmy Carter's Dead Ambassador," *American Spectator*, October 23, 2012, https://spectator.org/jimmy-carters-dead-ambassador/, accessed March 7, 2019.

Throughout 1978, a year before the Soviet invasion, Hekmatyar and his *mujahideen* ("holy warriors") burned universities and girls' schools throughout Afghanistan and gained feudal control over many of the poppy farmers.

mujahideen along the Afghan-Pakistan border.[11] The morphine base was transported by caravans of trucks from the Helmand Valley through northern Iran to the Anatolian plains of Turkey.

THE HOLY WAR

In the summer of 1979, six months before the Soviet invasion, the U.S. State Department issued a memorandum making clear its stake in the mujahideen: "The United States' larger interest . . . would be served by the demise of the Taraki regime, despite whatever setbacks this might mean for future social and economic reform in Afghanistan. . . . The overthrow of the DRA [Democratic Republic of Afghanistan] would show the rest of the world, particularly the Third World, that the Soviet's view of the socialist course of history as being inevitable is

---

11   Ibid.

not accurate."[12]

In September 1979, Taraki was killed in a coup organized by Afghan military officers. Hafizullah Amin became installed as the country's new president. Amin had impeccable Western credentials. He had been educated at Columbia University and the University of Wisconsin. He had served as the president of the Afghan Students Association, which had been funded by the Asia Foundation, a CIA front.[13] After the coup, he met regularly with U.S. Embassy officials, while the CIA continued to fund Hekmatyar's rebels in Pakistan. Fearing a fundamentalist, U.S.-backed regime at its border, the Soviets invaded Afghanistan on December 27, 1979.[14]

The CIA got what it wanted. The holy war had begun. For the next decade, black aid—amounting to more than $3 billion—would be poured into Afghanistan to support the holy warriors, making it the most expensive covert operation in U.S. history.[15] Such vast expenditures demanded an exponential increase in poppy production, which Hekmatyar and his fellow jihadists were pleased to provide.

THE BCCI AND ROCKEFELLER
The CIA established the Bank of Credit and Commerce International (BCCI) in Karachi to serve as a laundry for the drug money generated within the Golden Crescent of Afghanistan, Pakistan, and Iran. The BCCI mushroomed into a vast criminal enterprise with 400 branches in 78 countries, including First American Bank in Washington, D.C., the National Bank of Georgia, and the Independence Bank of Encino,

---

12 U.S. State Department memorandum, reproduced in Cockburn and St. Clair, *Whiteout*, pp. 262–263.

13 Ibid., p. 263.

14 Ibid.,

15 Ibid., p. 259.

California.[16] Virtually free from scrutiny, it engaged not only in money laundering the heroin proceeds but also arms trafficking on a grand scale, including the sale of French-made jet fighters to Chile and Chinese silkworm missiles to Saudi Arabia. By 1985, it became the seventh largest financial institution in the world, handling the money for Iraqi dictator Saddam Hussein, Panamanian strongman Manuel Noreiga, Palestinian terrorist Abur Nidal, al Qaeda chieftain Osama bin Laden, Liberian president Samuel Doe, and leading members of the Medellin Cartel.[17]

The enormity of the bank's operations was evidenced by its transfer of $4 billion in covert aid to Iraq from 1985 to 1989. For the Iraqi transfer, the BCCI made use of the Atlanta branch of Banca Nazionale del Lavoro (BNL), an Italian bank with ties to the IOR. Henry Kissinger sat on BNL's international advisory board, along with Brent Scowcroft, who became President George H. W. Bush's national security advisor, and David Rockefeller.[18]

A NEW HIGH

Heroin production in Afghanistan rose from 400 tons in 1971 to 1,800 tons in 1979 with the help of the CIA, and a network of laboratories was set up by the mujahideen along the Afghan-Pakistan border.[19] The morphine base was transported by caravans of trucks from the Helmand Valley through northern Iran to the Anatolian plains of Turkey. Business was booming. In 1979, the "flood" of heroin from Afghanistan

16 Jonathan Beaty and S. C. Gwynne, "BCCI: The Dirtiest Bank of All," *Biblioteca Pleiades*, July 29, 1991, http://www.bibliotecapleyades.net/sociopolitica/sociopol_globalbanking118.htm, accessed March 7, 2019.

17 David Sirota and Jonathan Baskin, "Follow the Money: How John Kerry Busted the Terrorists' Favorite Bank," *Washington Monthly*, August 2004, http://www.washingtonmonthly.com/features/2004/0409.sirota.html, accessed March 7, 2019.

18 Lucy Komisar, "The Case That Kerry Cracked," *Alter Net*, October 22, 2004, http://www.alternet.org/story/20268/the_case_that_kerry_cracked, accessed March 7, 2019.

19 Ibid.

inundated the United States, capturing over 60 percent of the market. In New York City alone, the mob sold two tons of smack, which registered a "dramatic increase in purity."[20] Heroin addiction in the states climbed back to 450,000. Within a year, street sales increased by 22 percent and the addiction rate reached 500,000.[21] It was an enormous development for the Rockefeller family. The cash from the drug trade flowed into CIA-controlled banks, including the Bank of Credit and Commerce, to America's most prestigious financial institutions, including Citibank in which the Rockefeller family held controlling interest.[22]

The rise in heroin usage had enormous ramifications on the CIA. Michel Chossudovsky, the noted Canadian economist, explains:

> The excessive accumulation of money wealth from the proceeds of the drug trade has transformed the CIA into a powerful financial entity. The latter cooperates through a web of corporate shells, banks, and financial institutions wielding tremendous power and influence. These CIA-sponsored "corporations" have, over time, been meshed into the mainstay of the business and corporate establishment, not only in weapons production and the oil business, but also in banking and financial services, real estate, etc. In turn, billions of narco dollars are channeled—with the support of the CIA—into spheres of "legitimate" banking, where they are used to finance bona fide investments in a variety of economic activities.[23]

20 McCoy, *The Politics of Heroin*, p. 463.

21 Ibid., pp. 464–465.

22 Peter Dale Scott, "Opium and the CIA: Can the U.S. Triumph in the Drug-Addicted War in Afghanistan?" *Global Research*, April 5, 2010, http://www.globalresearch.ca/opium-and-the-cia-can-the-us-triumph-in-the-drug-addicted-war-in-afghanistan/18522, accessed March 7, 2019.

23 Michel Chossudovsky, *America's "War on Terrorism"* (Montreal, Quebec: *Global Research*, 2005), p. 118.

THE TROUBLE WITH THE TALIBAN

But all this came to a screeching halt on January 27, 2000, when Mullah Omar and the leaders of the Taliban announced their plans to ban poppy production within the Islamic Emirate of Afghanistan.[24] As a result, the opium poppy harvest fell from 4,600 tons in 1999 to 81 tons in 2001.[25] The situation had to be addressed by the military-industrial complex in a forceful way.

While heroin was one cause of the war on terrorism, oil was another. The situation in Afghanistan had become worrisome to the House of Rockefeller, which had been instrumental in bringing the Taliban to power in 1996. Through the Union Oil Company of California (Unocal), the Rockefellers had arranged to provide the group with weapons and military instructors. This aid had enabled the Taliban to capture Kabul and to oust Afghan president Burhanuddin Rabbani from office.[26]

The Unocal gifts of arms and advisors were given with the belief that the Taliban would provide assistance in the creation of a massive oil pipeline that would run from the oil wells of Turkmenistan through the mountains of Afghanistan to the port city of Karachi, Pakistan, on the Arabian Sea. It was a project that could not take place without a dominant central regime in place to suppress the country's tribal warlords.[27] The 1,040-mile-long pipeline would have a shipping capacity of one million barrels of oil per day and would resolve the vexing problem of seizing control of the vast wealth of oil and natural gas that surrounded the land-locked Caspian Sea.[28]

24 McCoy, *The Politics of Heroin*, p. 505.

25 Ibid, p. 518.

26 Richard James DeSocio, *Rockefellerocracy: Assassinations, Watergate, and Monopoly of "Philanthropic" Foundations* (Bloomington, IN: Author's House, 2013), pp. 97–98. Also Richard Labeviere, *Dollars for Terror* (New York: Algora Press, 2000), p. 272.

27 Simon Reeve, *The New Jackals: Ramzi Yousez, Osama bin Laden, and the Future of Terrorism* (Boston: Northeastern University Press, 1999), p. 190.

28 Chossudovsky, *America's "War on Terrorism*, p. 82.

"THE GRAND CHESSBOARD"

Unocal also planned, through its subsidiary Centgas, to build another pipeline—this one for natural gas that would follow the same route through Afghanistan.[29] In the great game of geo-economics, the two pipelines represented the integral parts of the plan to gain control of the republics of Central Asia, as Zbigniew Brzezinski had set forth as follows in *The Grand Chessboard*:

> The world's energy consumption is bound to vastly increase over the next two or three decades. Estimates by the U.S. Department of Energy anticipate that world demand will rise by more than 50 percent between 1993 and 2015, with the most significant increase in consumption occurring in the Far East. The momentum of Asia's economic development is already generating massive pressures for the exploration and exploitation of new sources of energy and the Central Asian region and the Caspian Sea basin are known to contain reserves of natural gas and oil that dwarf those of Kuwait, the Gulf of Mexico, or the North Sea.[30]

RAISING THE STAKES

The Soviet Union had discovered the vast Caspian Sea oil fields in the late 1970s and attempted to take control of Afghanistan to build a massive north-south pipeline system to allow the Soviets to send their oil directly through Afghanistan and Pakistan to the Indian Ocean seaport. The result was the decades-long Soviet-Afghan war. The Russians then attempted to control the flow of oil and gas through its monopoly on the pipelines in the former Soviet republics that surrounded the Caspian Sea: Turkmenistan, Kazakhstan, and Azerbaijan. The leaders of these countries saw through this Russian monopolistic ploy and began to consult with Western oil executives, including Condoleezza Rice of Chevron (the predecessor of Rockefeller-owned Standard Oil

---

29   Ibid., p. 80.

30   Zbigniew Brzezinski, *The Grand Chessboard: American Primacy and Its Geostrategic Imperatives* (New York: Basic Books, 1998), p. 125.

of California).[31] Ms. Rice, a prominent CFR member, later became President George W. Bush's national security advisor.

The black operations of the CIA, under the direction of Standard Oil and the House of Rockefeller, began to thrust further along the 40th parallel from the Balkans through these Southern Asian Republics of the former Soviet Union. The U.S. military has already set up a permanent operations base in Uzbekistan. This so-called "anti-terrorist strategy" was designed to consolidate control over Middle Eastern and South Asian oil, and contain and neutralize the former Soviet Union.[32]

Realizing its weaker position vis-à-vis the United States, Russia joined the Shanghai Cooperation Organization (SCO), which included China, Kazakhstan, Kyrgyzstan, Tajikistan, and Uzbekistan. Its membership in the SCO represented Russia's attempt to maintain its traditional hegemony in Central Asia.[33] Thus the stakes in the chess game became sky-high since the winner gained global economic hegemony.

THE TALIBAN IN TEXAS

Once they conquered Kabul, the leaders of the Taliban were whisked off in a U.S. military transport to Houston, Texas, where they were wined and dined by Unocal officials, who had hired Henry Kissinger and Richard Armitage (who would become George W. Bush's deputy secretary of state) as consultants. Concerning the gatherings, LA reporter Jim Crogan wrote:

> [UNOCAL's top executive Barry] Lane says he wasn't involved in the Texas meetings and doesn't know whether then-Governor George W. Bush, an ex–oil man, ever had any involvement. Unocal's Texas spokesperson for Central Asia operations, Teresa Covington, said the consortium delivered three basic messages to the Afghan groups. "We

---

31   Ibid, p. 82.

32   Norman D. Livergood, "The New U.S.-British Oil Imperialism," April, 17, 2005, http://blog.lege.net/content/oil/, accessed March 7, 2019.

33   Ibid.

gave them the details on the proposed pipelines. We also talked to them about the projects' benefits, such as the transit fees that would be paid," she says. "And we reinforced our position the project could not move forward until they stabilized their country and obtained political recognition from the U.S. and the international community." Covington says the Taliban were not surprised by that demand. . . .

In December 1997, UNOCAL arranged a high-level meeting in Washington, D.C. for the Taliban with Clinton's undersecretary of state for South Asia, Karl Inderforth. The Taliban delegation included Acting Minister for Mines and Industry Ahmad Jan, Acting Minister for Culture and Information Amir Muttaqi, Acting Minister for Planning Din Muhammad and Abdul Hakeem Mujahid, their permanent U.N. delegate.

Two months later UNOCAL vice president for international relations John Maresca testified before a House Committee on International Relations about the need for multiple pipeline routes in Central Asia. Maresca briefed the members about the proposed Afghan pipeline projects, praising their economic benefits and asking for U.S. support in negotiating an Afghan settlement.[34]

Despite such power players, a final agreement was not reached because the Taliban was being pursued by other oil interests, including representatives from SCO. Meanwhile, the tentative U.S. ties to the Taliban were offset by Moscow's support for the Northern Alliance, the group of Islamic militants who ruled northern Afghanistan.[35] Pressure was applied to Mullah Omar, the leader of the Taliban, to come to a decision regarding the Unocal offer. But no commitment from the chieftain was forthcoming. And the situation was becoming increasingly untenable.

---

34   Jim Crogan, "The Oil War," *LA Weekly*, November 28, 2001, http://www.laweekly.com/news/the-oil-war-2134105, accessed March 7, 2019.

35   Staff Report, "Russia Bolsters Northern Alliance," *BBC News,* October 22, 2001, http://news.bbc.co.uk/2/hi/south_asia/1612898.stm, accessed March 7, 2019.

THE EMBASSY BOMBINGS

By 1998, the American power elite realized they had to set up a more cooperative government in Kabul. Plans were made to launch a terror attack against America that could be blamed on bin Laden and the host of Islamic militants that inhabited Afghanistan, including the Taliban. On August 7, the U.S. embassies in Kenya and Tanzania were bombed. The attack killed 234 people, twelve of them American, and wounded 5,000 more.[36] The event sent shock waves throughout the U.S. On August 20, President Bill Clinton responded by launching a cruise missile attack on al Qaeda's alleged residential and military complexes in Khost, Afghanistan, and the bombing of the al-Shifa Pharmaceutical Plant near Khartoum in the Sudan, where bin Laden once lived. The CIA had informed Clinton that these attacks would catch the al Qaeda leaders unaware, since no member of the mujahideen would believe that the United States was capable of such decisive action. The Agency further affirmed that the al-Shifa plant was producing deadly VX nerve gas.[37]

"OUR MISSION WAS CLEAR"

Following the attack, Clinton addressed his fellow countrymen from the Oval Office by saying:

> Our mission was clear: to strike at the network of radical groups affiliated with and funded by Osama bin Laden, perhaps the pre-eminent organizer and financier of international terrorism in the world today ... Earlier today, the United States carried out simultaneous strikes against terrorist facilities and infrastructures in Afghanistan. It contained key elements of bin Laden's network and infrastructure and has served as the training camp for literally thousands of terrorists around the globe. We have reason to believe that a gathering of key-terrorist

36 Michael Grunwald, "CIA Halted Plot to Bomb U.S. Embassy in Uganda," *Washington Post*, September 25, 1998, https://www.washingtonpost.com/archive/politics/1998/09/25/cia-halted-plot-to-bomb-us-embassy-in-uganda/8c8fd38b-1c6f-4570-ba14-126601660bf6/?utm_term=.5af04628e933, accessed March 7, 2019.

37 Rohan Gunaratna, *Inside al Qaeda: Global Network of Terror* (New York: Berkeley Books, 2002), p. 63.

leaders was to take place there today, thus underscoring the urgency of our actions. Our forces also attacked a factory in Sudan associated with the bin Laden network. The factory was involved in the production of materials for chemical weapons.[38]

The Clinton announcement was of vital importance to the shadow government. It identified Osama bin Laden as mankind's greatest enemy and the Taliban as a group that served him. The announcement also informed the American public that new attacks were in the works, and that weapons of mass destruction were in production to be used against them. The problem was that none of it was true. Bin Laden and his Muslim pals were not in the Khost camp. They were, as the CIA was well aware, safe and sound within a *madrassah* in Pakistan. Although the missiles struck the camps, the only casualties were local farmers and some low-level militants.[39] And the Sudan pharmaceutical plant was not involved in making nerve gas or any other chemical weapon. It produced common over-the-counter drugs, including ibuprofen.[40]

A FALSE FLAG OPERATION

What's more, information surfaced that the attack on the embassies was not conducted by al Qaeda, but rather a false flag operation that could be blamed on bin Laden. A key indicator of this contention was the involvement of Ali A. Mohamed, also known as Ali "the American" in the bombing. Following the attack, he was labeled as the "point man" who had masterminded the operation. Two years after the blasts, Mohamed was arrested by the American authorities and pleaded guilty to conspiracy to murder. It then came to light that the alleged al Qaeda bomber had an impeccable U.S. military service record. He had been trained at Fort Bragg, North Carolina, and worked as an instructor in explosives at the

38   Bill Clinton, quoted in Peter L. Bergen, *Holy War, Inc.: Inside the Secret World of Osama bin Laden* (New York: Simon and Schuster, 2002), p. 125.

39   Ibid.

40   Ibid.

John F. Kennedy Special Warfare Center and School until 1989.[41]

The official government narrative claimed that Mohamed, who was married to an American citizen and who had lived in California, was all the while working as a double agent for al Qaeda and that he had become a blood-thirsty jihadi by the time of the embassy attacks in 1998. This narrative was circulated by the American media. One story in the *San Francisco Chronicle*, in 2001, conveyed the sense of treachery as follows: "Bin Laden's man in Silicon Valley—'Mohamed the American'—orchestrated terrorist acts while living a quiet suburban life in Santa Clara." In reality, throughout the 1990s, Mohamed was working for the American secret services in East Africa, including Kenya.[42]

"VANISHED INTO THIN AIR"

"There is no way that U.S. intelligence handlers did not know of every move made by Mohamed," Ralph Schoenman, a reporter who has spent decades investigating the 1998 bombings maintains. "This guy was recruited by the CIA in Cairo, where he was a major in the Egyptian army. He was then a handpicked graduate of Fort Bragg for American Special Forces, and he went on to instruct green berets in PSYOPS and explosives at the JFK School of Warfare. We are talking about the strictest security clearance in the U.S. military. And yet the official account expects the public to believe that somehow Mohamed's connections with bin Laden's al Qaeda slipped their attention and that he carried out the U.S. embassy bombings in a rogue fashion for the supposed enemy."[43]

Supporting Schoenman's contention is the fact that, despite pleading guilty in a New York court in 2000 to conspiracy to murder American citizens, Mohamed has never been sentenced to confinement. There

---

41   Finian Cunningham, "Kenyan False Flag Bomb Plot Aimed at Tightening Sanctions Noose on Iran," *Global Research*, July 6, 2012, http://www.globalresearch.ca/kenyan-false-flag-bomb-plot-aimed-at-tightening-sanctions-noose-on-iran/31795, accessed March 7, 2019.

42   Ibid.

43   Ralph Schoenman, quoted in ibid.

are no records of subsequent court proceedings, and his whereabouts, to this day, remain unknown. His Californian wife, Linda Sanchez, was quoted in 2006 as saying of her husband: "He can't talk to anybody. Nobody can get to him. They have Ali pretty secret. It's like he just kinda vanished into thin air."[44]

DREAM FULFILLED

In August 1998, the merger of Amoco and BP produced the world's largest oil company.[45] The House of Rockefeller was now united with the House of Rothschild, and the two nations became inextricably bound both economically and politically. Billions of dollars now flowed into joint military industrial interest and such defense contractors as Lockheed Martin, Northrop Grumman, General Dynamics, Boeing, and Raytheon.[46] Britain's new Labor government under Prime Minister Tony Blair now became America's unconditional ally.[47]

After the merger of the oil giants, the primary concern of the new power elite was the need to build the trans-Afghan pipeline and the threat to the world economy posed by the Taliban's ban on poppy production. They realized during their clandestine meetings that these problems could only be resolved by the invasion and occupation of Afghanistan and the removal of the Taliban from power.

THREE STEPS TOWARD ENDLESS WAR

The first step toward meeting these objectives had been the bombing of the two African embassies, which resulted in making the Taliban synonymous with al Qaeda even though the two groups were sharply at odds. In 1998, Mullah Omar rejected bin Laden's repeated calls for violence

---

44   Linda Sanchez, quoted in ibid.

45   Chossudovsky, *America's "War on Terrorism,"* pp. 84–85.

46   Ibid., p. 15.

47   Ibid., p. 86.

against Americans and rejected the al Qaeda chieftain's religious rulings as "null and void."[48] Moreover, the scruffy Taliban leader resented the arrogance of the Arab mujahideen, whose aristocratic attitude toward Pashtun customs and beliefs had become intolerable. Tensions between the two Islamic militant groups became so tense that gunfire broke out between the Taliban soldiers and bin Laden's bodyguards.[49] In June 1998, the Taliban struck a deal with Saudi officials to send bin Laden to a Saudi prison in exchange for Saudi support and U.S. recognition of its legitimacy in ruling the country.[50] Prince Turki bin Faisal, head of the Saudi General Intelligence Agency, confided to the Clinton Administration that the exchange was "a done deal."[51]

But after the missile attacks, Prince Faisal retuned to Afghanistan to find the one-eyed Taliban mullah a changed man. "Mullah Omar became very heated," the prince said. "In a loud voice he denounced all our efforts and praised bin Laden as a worthy and legitimate scholar of Islam."[52]

On September 11, 2001, Islamic terrorists hijacked four American airliners; two crashed into New York's World Trade Center, one into the Pentagon in Arlington County, Virginia, and the fourth in a field near a reclaimed coal strip mine near Shanksville, Pennsylvania. "WTC smoking on 9-11" by Michael Foran is licensed under CC BY 2.0

48 Bergen, *Holy War Inc: Inside the Secret World of Osama bin Laden*, p. 166.

49 Tim Weiner, "Terror Suspect Said to Anger Afghan Hosts," *New York Times,* March 4, 1999, http://www.nytimes.com/1999/03/04/world/terror-suspect-said-to-anger-afghan-hosts.html, accessed March 7, 2019.

50 William C. Rempel, "Saudi Tells of Deal to Arrest Terror Suspect: Afghans Backpedaled on Hand-Over of bin Laden after U.S. Embassy Blasts, Riyadh official says.," *Los Angeles Times,* August 8, 1999, http://articles.latimes.com/1999/aug/08/news/mn-63689, accessed March 7, 2019.

51 Ibid.

52 Prince Turki bin Faisal, quoted in Jane Corbin, *al Qaeda: In Search of the Terrorist Network That Threatens the World* (New York: Thunder Mouth Press, 2003), pp. 69–70.

The second step toward legitimizing an invasion of Afghanistan was the appointment of Hamid Karzai as the head of the interim government in Kabul. Before this appointment, Karzai had acted as a consultant and lobbyist for Unocal in its negotiations with the Taliban and as a CIA covert operator who had funneled U.S. aid to Mullah Omar and his band of radical Muslim students.[53]

The third and final step was the creation of an incident of enormous proportion that would warrant the planned invasion. That incident came on September 11, 2001, when Islamic terrorists hijacked four American airliners; two crashed into New York's World Trade Center, one into the Pentagon in Arlington County, Virginia, and the fourth in a field near a reclaimed coal strip mine near Shanksville, Pennsylvania. It resulted in the deaths of 2,292 Americans, public and private property destruction in excess of $21 billion, and the loss of more than 200,000 jobs.[54]

The war without end had started.

---

53   Chossudovsky, *America's "War on Terrorism,"* p. 88.

54   Tom Templeton and Tom Lumley, "9/11 in Numbers," *Guardian*, August 17, 2002.

23

FALSE FLAGS UNFURLED

Recently declassified documents show yet more American false flag plotting, this time against the Soviet Union. A three-page memo written by members of the National Security Council, suggested that the US government should acquire Soviet aircraft which would be used to stage attacks and provide the pretext for war. Such aircraft, the memo said, "could be used in a deception operation designed to confuse enemy planes in the air, to launch a surprise attack against enemy installations or in a provocation operation in which Soviet aircraft would appear to attack US or friendly installations to provide an excuse for US intervention." The government even considered producing the soviet planes domestically in a massive covert operation. They went so far as to acquire estimates from the Air Force on the cost and length of time such an operation would take.
—DANIELLE RYAN, "FALSE FLAGS ARE REAL," APRIL 16, 2018

U.S. intelligence officers are reporting that some of the insurgents in Iraq are using recent-model Beretta 92 pistols, but the pistols seem to have had their serial numbers erased. The numbers do not appear to have been physically removed; the pistols seem to have come off a production line without any serial numbers. Analysts suggest the lack of serial numbers indicates that the weapons were intended for intelligence operations or terrorist cells with substantial government backing. Analysts speculate that these guns are probably from either Mossad or the CIA. Analysts speculate that agent provocateurs may be using the untraceable weapons even as U.S. authorities use insurgent attacks against civilians as evidence of the illegitimacy of the resistance.
—"UPI HEARS," UNITED PRESS INTERNATIONAL, JUNE 3, 2005

ON AUGUST 2, 1990, Saddam Hussein ordered a half million Iraqi troops to invade and occupy Kuwait. The reason for the invasion was reasonable. Kuwait, while Iraq was locked up in a deadly war with Iran, had pilfered $2.4 billion in oil from the Rumdia oil field—an Iraqi oil field—and still Kuwaiti emir Amir Jabir al-Almad refused to absolve even the interest on Iraqi's debt to his country.[1]

This development posed no threat to U.S. national security, but it jeopardized the interests of the House of Rockefeller and the House of Rothschild, who feared that Hussein would invade Saudi Arabia and absorb the oil fields in the Persian Gulf.[2] These two banking families controlled the world's largest oil companies, including Exxon and BP. They had created Saudi Aramco in the 1930s and remained the largest purchasers of Mideastern oil. This position enabled them to establish oil prices—a position that became threatened when Saddam Hussein's invading army appeared at the Saudi border.[3]

The Reagan Administration, under the guidance of George Schultz and other CFR members, had sided with Iraq during the decade-long Iran-Iraq War. It had shelled out billions in agricultural credits and hundreds of millions of dollars in advanced weaponry to Saddam. The weapons were transported to Iraq by a circuitous route through Egypt and Saudi Arabia since the House of Saud was also intent upon ending the reign of the Ayatollah Khomeini in Iran.[4] The U.S., under Reagan, further equipped the Iraqi army with satellite intelligence supplemented

---

1   William L. Cleveland, *A History of the Modern Middle East,* 3rd ed. (Boulder, CO: Perseus Books, 2004), p. 479.

2   Paul Johnson, *Modern Times: The World from the Twenties to the Nineties,* rev. ed. (New York: Harper Collins, 1992), p. 769.

3   Noam Chomsky, "Gulf War Pullout," *Z Magazine,* February 1991, https://chomsky.info/199102__/, accessed March 7, 2019.

4   Mark Danner, "Taking Stock of the Forever War," *New York Times,* September 11, 2005, http://www.nytimes.com/2005/09/11/magazine/taking-stock-of-the-forever-war.html, accessed March 7, 2019.

by AWACS (Airborne Warning and Control Systems) reconnaissance that could be used to direct weapons against Iranian suicide brigades.[5]

SADDAM AS BABY KILLER

But when Saddam Hussein ventured into Kuwait, President George H. W. Bush, a prominent CFR member, became intent upon launching a war against America's old ally. Bush's ties to big oil interests, including Standard Oil, were extensive.[6] Early in his career, he made millions with the drilling of the first offshore oil well in Kuwait. He also became associated with the Carlyle Group, a leading defense contractor, which numbered the Saudi royal family and the government of Kuwait among its customers.[7] In this way, Bush Sr. was wired to the Rockefellers, the Saudis, and the military-industrial complex. Members of his cabinet were similarly wired. Secretary of Defense Dick Cheney, a CFR director, became the chief executive officer of Halliburton.[8] And Secretary of State James Baker, another

On August 2, 1990, Saddam Hussein ordered a half million Iraqi troops to invade and occupy Kuwait. This development posed no threat to U.S. national security, but it jeopardized the interests of the House of Rockefeller and the House of Rothschild, who feared that Hussein would invade Saudi Arabia and absorb the oil fields in the Persian Gulf.

---

5   Ibid.

6   Kevin Phillips, *American Dynasty: Aristocracy, Fortune, and the Politics of Deceit in the House of Bush* (New York: Viking, 2004), p. 343.

7   Naomi Klein, "James Baker's Double Life," *Nation*, October 12, 2004, https://www.thenation.com/article/james-bakers-double-life/, accessed March 7, 2019.

8   Jarrett Murphy, "Cheney's Halliburton Ties Remain," *CBS News*, September 26, 2003, http://www.cbsnews.com/news/cheneys-halliburton-ties-remain/, accessed March 7, 2019.

CFR member, became senior counselor of the Carlyle Group.[9]

The problem for Bush was how to justify U.S. military involvement against Iraq. Amir Jabir al-Ahmad al-Jabir al-Sabah, the emir of Kuwait, was certainly not a sympathetic character. Stories were widely circulated about his profligate lifestyle. The emir, according to unsubstantiated accounts, was syphilitic, kept seventy wives, and married a virgin every Thursday.[10]

The answer to the problem came with the raising of a false flag. Bush and his cabinet began to circulate stories that Hussein had ordered his soldiers to enter Kuwaiti hospitals in order to remove babies from incubators and to cast them on the floor to die.[11] Repeating this concocted tale five times over the national airwaves, Bush said: "I don't think that Adolf Hitler ever participated in anything of that nature."[12]

THE PERSIAN GULF WAR

On January 14, 1991, Bush Sr. launched the Persian Gulf War, which, as it turned out, wasn't much of a war. But it did allow the military-industrial complex, thanks to 24-hour television coverage on CNN, to showcase their latest technology in warfare: stealth bombers, cruise missiles, "smart" bombs, and laser guidance systems that pinpointed targets and minimized civilian casualties. Within a matter of days, the Iraqi air force was obliterated, along with airfields, missile sites, and communication centers.[13] Throughout Iraq, most means of modern life were destroyed. All electrically operated installations ceased to

---

9   Klein, "James Baker's Double Life."

10   Daniel Pipes, "Heroes and Knaves of the Kuwait Crisis," in *A Restless Mind: Essays in Honor of Amos Perimutter,* ed. Benjamin Frankel (London: F. Cass, 1996), p. 96.

11   Craig Unger, *House of Bush, House of Saud* (New York: Scribner's, 2004), p. 137.

12   George H. W. Bush, quoted in ibid.

13   Robert Young Pelton, *The World's Most Dangerous Places,* 4th ed. (New York: HarperCollins, 2000), p. 574.

function. Food could not be preserved. Water could not be puri-
fied. Sewage could not be pumped away. Nine thousand homes were
destroyed or damaged beyond repair.[14]

SUGAR BABIES

Following the war, economic sanctions were placed on Iraq, which
resulted in a shortage of medical supplies and food. Malnutrition and
disease increased at an alarming rate. By 1998, nearly one million Iraqis,
mostly young children and the elderly, had died because of the embargo.
Diseases that had been nearly eradicated reappeared, including polio,
cholera, and typhoid. Cancer rates soared due to a proliferation of the
uranium used in the smart bombs.[15] In 1993, physicians discovered a
new disease. Iraqi mothers, too malnourished to breastfeed and unable
to buy powdered milk, began feeding their babies sugared water or tea.
Almost all the babies died. The doctors called them "sugar babies."[16]

Shortly after the Persian
Gulf War began, Middle East
Watch, a New York–based
human rights organization, sent
investigators to Iraq to verify
the stories about Iraqi soldiers
entering hospitals and removing
infants from incubators. They
were unable to locate any
doctor, nurse, medical worker,

On January 14, 1991, Bush Sr. launched the Persian
Gulf War, which, as it turned out, wasn't much of
a war.

---

14   Arti Ahtisaari, UN undersecretary for administration and management, *Report to the Security
      Council,* March 20, 1991, http://www.un.org/Depts/oip/background/reports/s22366.pdf, accessed
      March 7, 2019.

15   Felicity Arbuthnot, "Cradle to Grave: The Impact of the UN Embargo," *New Internationalist*
      magazine, January-February 2005, https://newint.org/features/2005/01/01/business/, accessed
      March 7, 2019.

16   Ibid.

or mother of a newly born child who could support the accounts that had caused the conflict.[17]

THE KOSOVO MASSACRES

Bush was not alone is raising a false flag to initiate a war in order to protect the interests of the CIA, the defense contractors, and the money cartel. In 1999, President Bill Clinton ordered the U.S. Air Force, under the auspices of NATO, to conduct a bombing campaign that reduced Kosovo to a mound of rubble. Between March 24 and June 10, 37,465 missions were flown, destroying every stronghold of the Christian Serbs. The bombing was justified, Clinton and his administration argued, because the Serbs were committing genocide by murdering thousands of Muslim Albanians for the sake of ethnic cleansing. Since Kosovo was part of Yugoslavia, Clinton blamed Slobodan Milosevic for the alleged atrocities and compared the Yugoslavian president (much in the same manner that George H. W. Bush spoke of Saddam Hussein) to Adolf Hitler. "Though his ethnic cleansing is not the same as the ethnic extermination of the Holocaust, the two are related; both vicious, pre-meditated, systematic oppression fueled by religious and ethnic hatred," Clinton told a group of 200 Veterans of Foreign Wars members at the National Defense University at Fort McNair.[18]

Stories surfaced in the *New York Times* and the *Washington Post* about a massacre in the small village of Racak, where the bodies of Muslim Albanians were left to rot in the street. Investigative reporters from *Le Figaro* and *Le Monde* were dispatched to verify these accounts. They discovered that the bodies had been placed in unnatural positions, that the site of the "massacre" was completely devoid of cartridges, and

---

17 Unger, *House of Bush, House of Saud*, p. 137.

18 Staff Report, "Clinton: NATO Must Stop Milosevic's Atrocities against Kosovo," *CNN News*, May 13, 1999, http://www.cnn.com/ALLPOLITICS/stories/1999/05/13/clinton.kosovo/, accessed March 7, 2019.

that the villagers were unable to identify the victims.[19]

Another widely circulated story used to justify U.S. intervention concerned a mine in Trepca, where thousands of bodies of Muslim Albanians were allegedly dumped. In the wake of the war, a French gendarmerie spelunking team descended half a mile into the mine to the bottom in search of bodies. They found none. Some villagers said that the bodies were burned in a nearby furnace. A second French team inspected the ashes. They found no teeth, no bones, and no trace of human remains.[20]

SIDING WITH THE ENEMY

For aid in their struggle for independence, the Muslim Albanians turned to bin Laden and the mujahideen. By 1995 more than six thousand holy warriors from Chechnya, Egypt, and Saudi Arabia had made their way to the Balkans in preparation for the struggle against the Christian Serbs.[21]

Bin Laden visited the area three times between 1994 and 1996 to establish al Qaeda training camps throughout the Balkans.[22] He also shelled out $700 million to establish the Kosovo Liberation Army (KLA). The purpose of this organization was to drive the Christian Serbs from Kosovo, to topple the government of Slobodan Milosevic, and to unite the Muslims of Kosovo, Macedonia, and Albania into the Islamic Republic of Greater Albania.[23]

---

19   Johnson, *Modern Times*, p. 715.

20   Daniel Pearl and Robert Block, "Despite Tales, the War in Kosovo Was Savage, But Wasn't Genocide," *Wall Street Journal,* December 31, 1999, https://www.wsj.com/articles/SB946593838546941319, accessed March 7, 2019.

21   Staff Report, "Ibrahim Rugova: Pacifist at the Crossroads," *BBC News*, May 5, 1999, http://news.bbc.co.uk/1/hi/special_report/1998/kosovo/110821.stm, accessed March 7, 2019.

22   Marcia Christoff Kurop, "Al Qaeda's Balkan Links," *Wall Street Journal*, November 1, 2001, https://www.wsj.com/articles/SB1004563569751363760, accessed March 7, 2019.

23   Paul Wolf, "The Assassination of Ahmad Shah Massoud," *Global Research*, September 14, 2003, http://www.globalresearch.ca/articles/WOL309A.html, accessed March 7, 2019.

THE END OF THE CHRISTIAN SERBS

President Clinton, along with Secretary of State Madeleine Albright, Secretary of Defense William Cohen, and CIA director George Tenet (all CFR members), praised the KLA as "freedom fighters." In no time at all, millions of U.S. dollars were flowing to the Muslim rebels in the form of military training and field advice.[24] The United States was now in league with the terrorist group that was purportedly intent upon its destruction. History doesn't get any crazier than this.

In the wake of the war, more than 200 Christian churches and monasteries in Kosovo were put to the torch. Accounts surfaced of the mass execution of Serbian farmers, the murders of scores of priests, and "granny killings" (the drowning of elderly women in bathtubs.)[25] Of the 200,000 Serbs who lived in Kosovo before the war, only 400 were left when the conflict came to an end.[26]

HIDDEN REASONS FOR THE WAR

After the Christians had been purged from Kosovo, the Pentagon established Camp Bondsteel on the border of Kosovo and Macedonia. This massive military base came to house over 6,000 U.S. troops. The purpose of the camp was to protect the Balkan route whereby heroin flowed from Afghanistan via Turkey to Western Europe.[27] Another purpose of the 1,000-acre military installation was to provide protection for the Trans-Balkan pipeline, which was to channel Caspian Sea

24 Tom Walker and Aiden Laverty, "CIA Aided Kosovo Guerrilla Army All Along," *Sunday Times* (London), March 12, 2000, https://www.globalpolicy.org/component/content/article/192/38782.html, accessed March 7, 2019.

25 "Kosovo Fact-Finding Mission," A White Paper of the Religious Freedom Coalition, August 2004, http://www.documentshare.org/culture-and-the-arts/kosovo-fact-finding-mission-a%C2%80%C2%93-august-2004/, accessed March 7, 2019.

26 Ibid.

27 Michel Chossudovsky, *The Globalization of War* (Montreal, Quebec: *Global Research*, 2015), p. 111.

oil from the Bulgarian Black Sea port of Burgas to the Adriatic. The feasibility study for the pipeline had been drafted by the engineering division of Halliburton.[28]

And so the pattern persisted. False flag after false flag was unfurled to bring the United States into military conflict, while the American people, sapped of their strength and spirit, remained incapable of responding with cries of indignation, let alone outrage. America had become a corporation, and its citizens were not shareholders.

IRAQ'S WEAPONS OF MASS DESTRUCTION

In 2003, President George W. Bush and his CFR cabinet proclaimed that Saddam Hussein was now in league with al Qaeda and planning an attack on American soil that would eclipse the events of 9/11. Hussein, they maintained, had developed weapons of mass destruction that would soon be unleashed upon the hapless inhabitants of major U.S. cities.

This false news was repeated over and over again on 532 separate occasions by Bush, Vice President Cheney, National Security Advisor Condoleezza Rice, Defense Secretary Donald Rumsfeld, Secretary of State Colin Powell, and Deputy Defense Secretary Paul Wolfowitz.[29]

BLOOD FOR OIL AND NATURAL GAS

None of it was true. No weapons of mass destruction had been found. No plans to develop nuclear bombs had been made. No biological laboratories were fabricating sinister germ warfare. The laboratories that Bush declared the U.S. invading forces had found turned out to be innocuous facilities that were manufacturing hydrogen for weather balloons.[30] Despite the fact that Saddam Hussein was dragged from a hole, placed on trial before a kangaroo court, and lynched, no ties between

---

28 Ibid., p. 118

29 Charles Lewis, *935 Lies: The Future of Truth and the Decline of America's Moral Integrity* (New York: Public Affairs, 2014), p. 253.

30 Ibid., p. 256.

the Iraqi ruler and al Qaeda were ever substantiated.

The war was launched to create a strategy of tension within Iraq. This allowed Anglo-American big oil companies under control of the money cartel to seize Iraqi oil fields and to further their control over the world's supply of energy.[31] Immediately after Bush announced "mission accomplished," Exxon Mobil, Chevron, Shell, and BP set up shop in Iraqi along with a slew of oil service companies, including Halliburton.[32]

Another purpose was to further the plans for the construction of a natural gas pipeline that would run from the North Pars, an Iranian port city on the Persian Gulf, to Damascus in Syria via Iraq. Most European countries remained dependent upon Russia for its supply of natural gas. Therefore, the pipeline would serve to cripple Russia economically while furthering the interests of the House of Rockefeller and the House of Rothschild.[33]

Plans for the conquest and occupation of Iraq had been in the works for several years. In *Winning Modern Wars*, General Wesley Clark writes of meeting Pentagon officials shortly after 9/11 who said that the military campaign included the invasion of seven countries, beginning with Iraq, then Syria, Libya, Iran, Somalia, and Sudan.[34]

GADDAFI AS A MASS MURDERER

In 2011, when Islamic extremists took up arms against the government of Muammar Gaddafi in Libya, the U.S. national news outlets, in tandem with the CFR Administration of President Barack Obama, announced that the Libyan ruler was planning the mass murder of men, women, and

---

31   F. William Engdahl, "The Secret Stupid Saudi-US Deal on Syria: Oil Pipeline War," *Global Research*, October 14, 2014, http://www.globalresearch.ca/the-secret-stupid-saudi-us-deal-on-syria/5410130, accessed March 7, 2019.

32   Antonia Juhasz, "Why the War in Iraq Was Fought for Big Oil," *CNN*, April 15, 2013, http://www.cnn.com/2013/03/19/opinion/iraq-war-oil-juhasz/index.html, accessed March 7, 2019.

33   Ibid.

34   Wesley Clark, *Winning Modern Wars* (New York: Public Affairs, 2003), p. 130.

children in Benghazi to cower the populace into submission. Therefore, Libya had to be bombed to smithereens for the sake of humanity.[35]

Justifying the bombing, Secretary of State Hillary Clinton said: "We had a murderous dictator . . . threatening to massacre large numbers of the Libyan people. We had our closest allies in Europe burning up the phone lines begging us to help them try to prevent what they saw as a mass genocide, in their words. And we had the Arabs standing by our side saying, 'We want you to help us deal with Gaddafi.'"[36]

UNMASKING MENDACITIES

Of course, it wasn't true. On March 17, 2011, Gaddafi announced to the rebels in Benghazi, "Throw away your weapons, exactly like your brothers in Ajdabiya and other places did. They laid down their arms and they are safe. We never pursued them at all." Subsequent investigation revealed that when Gaddafi regime forces retook Ajdabiya in February 2011, they did not attack or kill any innocent civilians. The Libyan ruler also attempted to appease protesters in Benghazi with an offer of development aid before finally deploying troops in an attempt to end the rebellion.[37]

What's more, an Amnesty International investigation in June 2011 could not corroborate any allegation of mass human rights violations by Gaddafi regime troops. It rather uncovered evidence that rebels in Benghazi made false claims and manufactured evidence. The investigation concluded: "Western media coverage has from the outset presented a very one-sided view of the logic of events, portraying the

35   Kevin Sullivan, "A Tough Call on Libya That Still Haunts," *Washington Post*, February 3, 2016, http://www.washingtonpost.com/sf/national/2016/02/03/a-tough-call-on-libya-that-still-haunts/?utm_term=.917df391c0b8, accessed March 7, 2019.

36   Hillary Clinton, quoted in ibid.

37   Washington Blog Staff, "Libya War Was Based on Lies, Bogus Intelligence, NATO Supported and Armed the Rebels. British Parliamentary Report," September 25, 2016, http://www.globalresearch.ca/libya-war-was-based-on-lies-bogus-intelligence-nato-supported-and-armed-the-rebels-british-parliamentary-report/5547356, accessed March 7, 2019.

protest movement as entirely peaceful and repeatedly suggesting that the regime's security forces were unaccountably massacring unarmed demonstrators who presented no security challenge."[38]

SIDING WITH THE ENEMY—PART II

The Libyan Islamic Fighting Group, the organization of the rebels who opposed Gaddafi, was closely associated with al Qaeda. Secretary of State Clinton and President Obama were well aware of this fact before they deployed bombers and troops to topple the Gaddafi government. A U.S. intelligence report issued months before the bombings contained this finding: "There is a close link between al Qaeda, jihadi organizations, and the opposition in Libya."[39]

Oil-rich Libya was the most prosperous country in Africa. Education, medical treatment, and electricity were free, and gas sold for forty-two cents a gallon. Women who gave birth were supported with cash grants and couples with cash gifts from the government on their wedding day. Libya's state bank provided loans without interest and provided free startup capital to farmers.[40]

GADDAFI'S CRIME AGAINST THE MONEY CARTEL

Gaddafi's independence from big oil and the money cartel was the cause of his demise. Earlier in life Gaddafi's goal was to organize Arabs as a bloc that could withstand Western demands and depredations. He turned to Pan-Africanism and refused to join the U.S. Africa Command. Gaddafi also attempted to introduce a gold-based African currency that would free Africans from American financial hegemony.[41]

---

38   Ibid.

39   Ibid.

40   Paul Craig Roberts, "Hillary's War Crime: The Murder of Muammar Gaddafi. 'We Came, We Saw, He Died," *Global Research,* October 21, 2016, http://www.globalresearch.ca/hillarys-war-crime-the-murder-of-muammar-gaddafi-we-came-we-saw-he-died/5552094, accessed March 7, 2019.

41   Ibid.

Gaddafi used Chinese energy companies to develop Libya's energy resources, thereby bypassing the interests of the Anglo-American big oil and banking establishments. The power elite, already upset with Russian presence in the Mediterranean, became faced with Chinese presence as well. Gaddafi was playing ball with the wrong people, and he had to go.[42]

On October 20, 2011, during the Battle of Sirte, Gaddafi was found hiding in a culvert by the rebel forces. He was beaten with rifle butts, sodomized with bayonets, and shot several times in the head.[43] Upon receiving word of Gaddafi's demise, a gleeful Hillary Clinton said: "We came. We saw. He died."[44]

AN UNANSWERED QUESTION

Is ISIS (the Islamic State of Iraq and Syria) a creation of the Obama Administration, the CIA and the U.S. State Department under Hillary Clinton? This question, which was raised by Donald Trump during his campaign for the White House, was dismissed as absurd by the national media.[45] But evidence points to an affirmative answer. Gordon Duff, senior editor of *Veterans Today*, confirmed that the ISIS terrorists were trained in Jordan and Syria by U.S. Major General (retired) Paul E. Vallely and other senior military consultants.[46] Vallely is a Fox News military analyst and the founder of the U.S. Army Psychological Warfare

---

42   Ibid.

43   Martin Chulov, "Gaddafi's Last Moments: 'I Saw the Hand Holding the Gun, and I Saw It Fire,'" *Guardian*, October 20, 2012, https://www.theguardian.com/world/2012/oct/20/muammar-gaddafi-killing-witnesses, accessed March 7, 2019.

44   Hillary Clinton, quoted in Roberts, "Hillary's War Crime: The Murder of Muammar Gaddafi."

45   Tom LoBianco and Elizabeth Landers, "Trump: Clinton, Obama 'Created Isis,'" *CNN*, January 3, 2016, http://www.cnn.com/2016/01/02/politics/donald-trump-barack-obama-hillary-clinton-created-isis/index.html, accessed March 7, 2019.

46   Chip Tatum, "ISIS Commander Confirmed by Veterans Today," Wiki Army, 2013, http://www.wikiarmy.com/index.php/15-breaking-news/97-isis-commander-confirmed-by-veteranstoday.

School.[47] To establish his case, Duff has provided videos of Vallely and other American military officials with ISIS commandos.[48]

Support for this startling assertion was provided by Aaron Klein of *WorldNetDaily*, who unearthed evidence that the ISIS forces were and are trained at a secret U.S. military base in the Jordanian town of Safawi.[49] This report has been corroborated by *Der Spiegel*, Germany's leading newsmagazine. Additional support came from Edward Snowden, the NSA (National Security Agency) whistle-blower, who produced classified government documents that show that Abu Bakr al-Baghdadi, the leader of ISIS, is a CIA operative.[50]

MUSLIM CONFIRMATION

Leaders from the Muslim world confirm these findings. Nabil Na'eem, the founder of the Islamic Democratic Party, who appeared on the pan-Arab TV station al-Maydeen to say that all current al-Qaeda affiliates, including ISIS, work for the CIA. Mr. Na'eem could be imparting false information, but his claim is upheld by Bahaa al-Araji, Iraq's deputy prime minister, and other leading Iraqi officials. Mr. Araqi is a devout Shia and Mr. Na'eem is a militant Sunni. The two men share little in common and have completely different political and religious agendas.[51]

---

47   Ibid.

48   Ibid.

49   Aaron Klein, "Blowback! U.S. Trained Islamists Who Joined ISIS," *WorldNetDaily*, June 17, 2014, http://www.wnd.com/2014/06/officials-u-s-trained-isis-at-secret-base-in-jordan/, accessed March 7, 2019.

50   Staff, "ISIS Leader a Confirmed CIA Puppet," *Hang the Bankers*, July 21, 2014, http://www.hangthebankers.com/isis-leader-a-confirmed-cia-puppet/, accessed March 7, 2019.

51   David D. Kirkpatrick, "Suspicions Run Deep in Iraq That C.I.A. and the Islamic State Are United," *New York Times*, September 20, 2014, https://www.nytimes.com/2014/09/21/world/middleeast/suspicions-run-deep-in-iraq-that-cia-and-the-islamic-state-are-united.html?_r=0, accessed March 7, 2019.

THE COVERT PURPOSE OF ISIS

According to several news analysts, the purpose of ISIS is to create a state of "endless war" that will serve to exhaust Saudi and Iranian military resources; to bring about the dissolution of Syria and Iraq; and to collapse the Arab countries into small states that can be manipulated by the U.S.-dominated money cartel, which seeks control of their natural resources.[52] This thesis is supported by classified CIA documents that affirm that arms for ISIS came, compliments of the U.S., from the arsenal of Muammar Qaddafi. The shipment of these weapons to ISIS in Syria was supervised in 2012 by David Petraeus, the CIA director who would soon resign when it was alleged that he was having an affair with his biographer.[53]

THE PATRIOT ACT

As a result of the endless wars without borders, the citizens of the United States became stripped of the liberties, once viewed as God-given, by the Patriot Act of 2001. No longer did they possess freedom of association. The government now could monitor religious and political institutions without suspecting criminal activity to assist terror investigation. No longer were they granted freedom of information. The government closed once-public immigration hearings, secretly detained hundreds of people without charges, and encouraged bureaucrats to resist requests for the disclosure of public records. No longer did they possess freedom of speech. The government could prosecute librarians or keepers of any other records if they told anyone that the government was seeking information related to a terror investigation. No longer did they retain a right to legal representation. The government could monitor federal

52 Kurt Nimmo, "Former Al-Qaeda Commander: ISIS Works for CIA," *Infowars*, July 12, 2014, https://www.infowars.com/former-al-qaeda-commander-isis-works-for-the-cia/, accessed March 7, 2019.

53 David E. Sanger, "Rebel Arms Flow Is Said to Benefit Jihadis in Syria," *New York Times*, October 14, 2012, http://www.nytimes.com/2012/10/15/world/middleeast/jihadists-receiving-most-arms-sent-to-syrian-rebels.html, accessed March 7, 2019.

prison jailhouse conversations between attorneys and clients, and deny lawyers to Americans accused of crimes. No longer were they free from unreasonable searches. Government could search and seize their belongings, including their personal papers, without probable cause for the sake of a terror investigation. And no longer were they granted the right to a speedy and public trial. The government now could jail anyone, including its citizens, without a trial on charges of terrorism.

In the past, these rights characterized the citizens of the United States, who deemed them so precious that they were willing to die to sustain and uphold them. But at the dawn of the 21st century, they had surrendered them without a whimper. They were no longer Americans. They had become citizens of the world.

24

KILLING HIPPOCRATES

Soon after the medical monopoly was formed, it began to push its agenda of destroying all competition. A well-organized and well-funded nationwide purge of all non-MDs was undertaken. Over the course of the first half of the 20th century this medical monopoly managed to shut down over 40 medical schools. Their idea was to keep the number of doctors low in order to keep fees up. After WW II the medical monopoly started rigidly controlling how many of each medical specialty it would allow to be trained. The medical monopoly also managed to outlaw or marginalize over 70 healthcare professions. Protection of the healthcare consumer was, as always, the rationale for this power grab. Whether the object of destruction by the medical monopoly be homeopaths, midwives, chiropractors, or internet prescribers, the purge is conducted in the same manner. No scientific proof or research data is offered to discredit these practitioners. The entire approach is one of character assassination.

—DR. HENRY JONES, MISES INSTITUTE, FEBRUARY 25, 2005

IN 1907, Bakelite became the first plastic made from oil and scientists began to develop "petrochemicals" for the medical industry.[1] This represented a splendid opportunity for John D., who realized that the desperately ill would liquidate their life's savings to recover their

---

1   Chris Kanthan, "How Rockefeller Founded Modern Medicine and Killed Natural Cures," *World Affairs,* October 20, 2015, https://worldaffairs.blog/2015/10/20/how-rockefeller-founded-modern-medicine-and-killed-natural-cures/, accessed March 8, 2019.

health.[2] The major problem was the popularity of natural/herbal medicine. Almost half the doctors and medical colleges in the U.S. practiced holistic medicine, using knowledge from Europe and Native Americans. The holistic drugs were developed from natural plants, herbs, and vegetables. They were readily available and incredibly inexpensive. By replacing holistic drugs with petrochemicals, a fortune beyond the scope of human imagination could be amassed. The fact that many of the new chemical concoctions would be poisonous remained a minor concern.[3]

In 1901, John D. salaried a group of physicians to chart his conquest of the medical industry. The group included Dr. L. Emmet Holt, Christian A. Herter, T. Mitchell Pruden, Herman M. Biggs, William H. Welch, Theobald Smith, and Simon Flexner. These men became the founding fathers of the Rockefeller Institute for Medical Research. They received a salary of $20,000 for the first ten years, which increased to $1,000,000 in the eleventh.

Once the Institute was established, John D. used his money and influence to place the American Medical Association (AMA) under the control of George H. Simmons, one of his henchmen.[4] Simmons was a "quack abortionist," who had received his medical degree from a diploma mill operated by the Rush Medical School that later evolved into the medical department of the University of Chicago—established by the Rockefeller Foundation.[5] Prior to the Rockefeller takeover, the AMA was a union of physicians.

THE BIRTH OF BIG PHARMA

By 1910, Rockefeller had gained controlling shares of I. G.

---

2   Emanuel M. Josephson, *Rockefeller "Internationalist"* (New York: Chedney Press, 1952), p. 102.

3   Ibid.

4   Ibid., pp. 104–105.

5   Ibid.

Farbenindustrie (IGF), the massive German pharmaceutical company, which became the base of his medical monopoly.[6] During World War II, IGF assisted Hitler by producing chemicals and poisons, including Zyklon B gas for Hitler's death camps. Inmates at the camps also became the human guinea pigs for the tests of medicines and vaccines that resulted in thousands of deaths.[7]

At the 1947 Nuremberg Trials, twenty-four IGK executives were accused of crimes against humanity, mass murder, slavery, and other crimes.[8] Telford Taylor, the leading prosecutor at the trials, said: "Not 'the Nazi lunatics' but these accused are responsible for this war. And, if they are not punished for their crimes, the harm they will do to future generations, is much greater than Hitler could ever have done if he were alive."[9] After the trials, IGF was dismantled and split into Hoechst, BASF, and the Bayer Company, all of which remained under the control of the Rockefellers. With the assistance of Nelson Rockefeller, who was assistant secretary of state for American Republic Affairs under Harry S. Truman, all convicted IGF executives were released from prison to resume their positions in the drug industry. The prediction of Telford Taylor came true.[10]

In addition to Hoechst, BASF, and the Bayer Company, the Rockefeller Drug Trust came to include Merck and Company; American Home Products and its subsidiaries Winthrop Chemical and Sterling Products; Lederle Laboratories; and American Cyanamid, which gave rise to Pfizer, Procter and Gamble, and Davis and Geck.[11]

---

6 Ty Bollinger, "The History of the AMA," *Cancer Truth*, February 11, 2012, https://www.cancertruth.net/ama-history/#, accessed March 8, 2019.

7 Ibid.

8 Charl du Randt, *Demonized Doctoring* (Cape Town, South Africa: Rapture Publications, 1999), p. 226.

9 Telford Taylor, quoted in ibid., pp. 226–227.

10 Ibid., p. 227.

11 Josephson, *Rockefeller "Internationalist,"* p. 28.

THE FLEXNER REPORT

With funds from the Carnegie and Rockefeller Foundations, Abraham Flexner, Simon's brother, traveled throughout the country to write a report on the status of medical colleges and hospitals. The *Flexner Report*, which was endorsed by the AMA, called for the closing of all medical schools that endorsed homeopathic medicine, the licensing of all practicing physicians by the AMA, and the promotion of drugs derived from oil and concocted in approved laboratories. Congress endorsed this support and granted the AMA by law complete control of the medical industry. As a result, half of the 165 medical schools in the United States were forced to close, and thousands of physicians lost their right to practice medicine.[12]

OSLER'S OUTCRY

The issuance of the Flexner Report was met with considerable opposition. William Osler, whose text book *Principles and Practice of Media* was the standard in every American medical school, maintained that implementation of the Flexner Report would limit the focus of physicians so that they would focus on the disease and not the patient. He believed that a generation of clinical prigs would be created, individuals who were removed from the realities and messy details of their patients' lives. Osler believed that the Flexnerians had their priorities wrong in situating the advancement of knowledge as the overriding aspiration of the academic physician. He placed the welfare of patients and the education of students as the most important priorities.

Osler's mentee, Harvey Cushing, voiced the same sentiments, basing his reservations on his background of several generations of practicing physicians. Their voices were hushed by the irresistible seduction of large sums of money tied to implementation of the full-time system.[13]

---

12   Ibid., p. 106

13   Thomas P. Duffy, "The Flexner Report—100 Years Later," *Journal of Biology and Medicine*, September 2011, https://www.ncbi.nlm.nih.gov/pmc/articles/PMC3178858/, accessed March 8, 2019.

THE TAKEOVER

Rockefeller now provided over $100 million to colleges and hospitals to take over the medical industry. Within a short period of time, the curricula of America's medical schools was streamlined and homogenized. All medical students were learning the same thing, and medicine was all about using patented drugs that had been concocted from petrochemicals. Scientists received grants to study how plants cured diseases, but the goal of such research was to identify the effective chemicals in the plants so that they could be synthetically re-created and patented.[14]

Regarding the Rockefeller takeover of the medical industry, G. Edward Griffin, in a *Corbett Report* interview, said:

> The takeover of the medical industry was accomplished by the takeover of the medical schools . . . Rockefeller and Carnegie came into the picture and said: "We will put up the money." They offered tremendous amounts of money to the schools that would agree to cooperate with them. The donors said to the schools: "We're giving you all this money, now would it be too much to ask if we could put some of our people on your Board of Directors to see if our money is spent wisely?" Almost overnight all of the major universities received large grants from these sources and also accepted one, two, or three of these people that I mentioned on their Board of Directors and the schools literally were taken over by the financial interests that put up the money.
>
> Now what happened as a result of that is the schools did receive an infusion of money; they were able to build new buildings; they were able to add expensive equipment to their laboratories; they were able to hire top-notch teachers; but, at the same time as doing that, they eschewed the whole thing in the direction of pharmaceutical drugs. That was the efficiency of philanthropy.
>
> The doctors from that point forward in history would be taught

---

14   Kanthan, "How Rockefeller Founded Modern Medicine and Killed Natural Cures."

pharmaceutical drugs. All of the great teaching institutions in America were captured by the pharmaceutical interests in this fashion, and it's amazing how little money it really took to do it.[15]

"GOOD MEDICAL PRACTICES"

"Good medical practice" no longer meant what was good for the patient. One such example was the widespread use of radium in the treatment of cancer despite the fact that radiation caused untold misery and the spread of cancer throughout the body.[16] Few observers took note that much of the medical radium came from Bayer and company and other medical firms in which the Rockefellers held controlling interest.

Another example of "good medical practice" was the writing of prescriptions for testosterone, a male hormone synthesized with the Rockefeller laboratories. Produced for a few pennies, it was sold in the 1950s at the retail rate of a million dollars a pound for the restoration of sexual vigor. Thousands of American men flocked to their physicians to obtain a prescription. The drug caused so much cancer among its users that a warning against its use was eventually issued by the U.S. Department of Health.[17]

SOME SIDE EFFECTS

In 1940, a new drug called sulfathiazole was created by Winthrop Drug Company, a part of the Rockefeller Drug Trust, and approved by J. J. Durrett, a Rockefeller appointee to the Food and Drug Administration. Sulfathiazole became widely used for the treatment of gonorrhea, pneumonia, tonsillitis, and dysentery.[18] The Rockefeller "authorities"

---

15   G. Edward Griffin, quoted in James Corbett, "How & Why Big Oil Conquered the World," *The Corbett Report*, October 6, 2017, https://www.corbettreport.com/bigoil/, accessed March 8, 2019.

16   Josephson, *Rockefeller "Internationalist,"* p. 106.

17   Ibid.

18   Tigger Montague, "Down the Rabbit Hole: The Rise of Western Medicine ," BioStar, September 24, 2016, https://www.biostarus.com/blogs/formulators-corner/down-the-rabbit-hole-the-rise-of -western-medicine-in-the-us.

dictated the use of this new sulfa drug in such large doses that the pills poisoned the patients and in three hundred cases, killed them. When it was brought to light that sulfathiazole destroys niacin, an essential human nutrient, and causes a deadly disease known as pellagra, the news was barred from medical journals, which obtained their revenue from Winthrop and other Rockefeller-owned drug companies.[19]

Following sulfathiazole came the synthetically produced ACTH (adrenocorticotropic hormone) for spasms and seizures. When administered to young children, the drug distorted the shape of the head and face since it interfered with natural growth and development. The accounts of the moon-faced children were hushed up by the Rockefeller medical establishment, including their lackeys in the AMA.[20] This repression of the effects of such dangerous drugs as synthetic testosterone, sulfathiazole, and ACTH allowed the Rockefeller cartel to bull the sale of stock in their drug companies to astronomical levels.

MUSTARD GAS

Cancer became the disease that produced the greatest amount of revenue for the Rockefeller drug cartel, which concocted such treatments as radiation and chemotherapy. The latter was manufactured by Louis Goodman and Alfred Gilman, two pathologists funded by the Rockefeller Institute, from a deadly poison known as mustard gas. This gas had been deployed by the German army against British and Canadian forces near Ypres, Belgium, in 1917.[21]

After experimenting on animals, Goodman and Gilman located a human subject, known only by his initials J.D., who had advanced lymphoma and such a massive tumor on his jaw that he could neither

---

19   Josephson, *Rockefeller "Internationalist,"* p. 113.

20   Ibid., p. 114.

21   Simon Persson, "Don't Fall For Big Pharma's Scam—Learn How They Have Hidden the Cure for Cancer," *Cancer Wisdom,* July 15, 2017, https://www.cancerwisdom.net/why-there-is-no-cure-for-cancer/#, accessed March 8, 2019.

swallow nor sleep. After receiving several injections of nitrogen mustard, the tumor shrank and J.D. was able to eat again. The treatment was proclaimed a success, and chemotherapy gained the approval of the FDA. Little mention was made of the fact that J.D. died several weeks after receiving the injections.[22]

With the development of chemotherapy and radiation, cancer became a multibillion-dollar business that swelled the fortune of the Rockefeller family. Cancer patients in the United States were shelling out $65,000 a month for treatments.

A STANDARD TREATMENT

Chemotherapy now became the standard treatment for anyone with an advanced stage of cancer. Little attention was paid to the fact that the new miracle drug destroyed healthy as well as cancerous cells; that it did not remove or dissolve the cause of cancer; that the tumors usually grew back within a short period of time; and that the five-year survival rate for those undergoing such treatment was 2.1 percent. Nor was attention focused on the horrendous side effects, which included diarrhea, fatigue, organ damage, vomiting, numbness, water retention, bleeding, acute abdominal pain, low platelet counts, kidney malfunction, and hair loss.[23]

With the development of chemotherapy and radiation, cancer became a multibillion-dollar business that swelled the fortune of the Rockefeller family. Cancer patients in the United States were shelling out $65,000 a month for treatments. The pharmaceutical industry's 20 top-selling cancer drugs generated sales of $53 billion in 2013.[24]

22 Ibid.

23 Simon Persson, "The Horrible Side Effects of Chemotherapy That Kills," *Cancer Wisdom*, July 14, 2016, https://www.cancerwisdom.net/side-effects-of-chemotherapy/#, accessed March 8, 2019.

24 Ibid.

Roche's Rituxan, Avastin, and Herceptin led the pack, with $21 billion in sales for these three drugs alone, and Roche was an integral part of the Rockefeller Drug Cartel.[25]

Naturally, the Rockefellers wanted to safeguard the flow of such revenue into their coffers by suppressing the mountains of evidence concerning the environmental causes of cancer and the development of possible cures. In his book *The Politics of Cancer Revisited*, Dr. Samuel Epstein writes: "The cancer establishment has also failed to provide the public, particularly African American and underprivileged ethnic groups, with their disproportionately higher cancer incidence rates, with information on avoidable carcinogenic exposures, thus depriving them of their right-to-know and effectively preventing them from taking action to protect themselves a flagrant denial of environmental justice."[26]

HERBAL TEA

In 1922, Rene Caisse, a Canadian nurse, began to treat cancer patients with an herbal tea, which she had developed from a formula used by the Ojibwe tribe of Native Americans. She called the tea Essiac—her name spelled backwards. Hearing of the miraculous cures produced by the tea, Dr. Charles Brusch of Toronto sought Caisse's help in treating his patients. The formula was further refined and tested under laboratory conditions. Brusch and Caisse now began to promote Essiac as a cheap and effective cure for cancer.[27]

The news of the purported new cure caught the attention of the medical industry, and stories appeared in medical journals about health risks associated with herbal tea consumption. In response, the FDA

25   "Rockefeller Foundation," *Source Watch,* https://www.sourcewatch.org/index.php/Rockefeller_ Foundation, accessed March 8, 2019.

26   Samuel Epstein, quoted in Bollinger, "The History of the AMA."

27   David Jockers, "Why Essiac Tea Should Be Part of Your Cancer Fighting Program," *The Truth about Cancer,* October 12, 2015, https://thetruthaboutcancer.com/essiac-tea-cancer-fighting/, accessed March 8, 2019.

outlawed the drug and engineered the arrest of Caisse for practicing medicine without a license. Throughout the remaining years of her long life, Caisse was subjected to arrest after arrest, despite the testimony of thousands of patients who claimed that the tea had cured their cancer. In 1978, Caisse died at the age of ninety, and her original formula remained banned from public consumption.[28]

THE BANNED STUDY

The Rockefellers' stranglehold on the medical industry ensured that not only treatments but also studies concerning cancer were banned. In 1970, Dr. Ryke Geerd Hamer, chief of internal medicine at the University of Munich, began to research the link between cancer and unresolved emotional conflict. His study was prompted by the fact that he had developed testicular cancer after the murder of his son, Dirk. Hamer had been in good health throughout his life and came to believe that the cancer was a result of Dirk's death.[29]

After years of interviewing cancer patients, Hamer believed that he had discovered the link and offered his findings to the medical staff at the University of Tübingen so that they could be tested by the medical students. The staff not only rejected his offer but also presented him with an ultimatum: He could either deny his findings or face expulsion from his position at the University of Munich.[30] Hamer stood his ground, accepted his dismissal, and continued with his research. In 1986, a German court withdrew Hamer's right to practice medicine. By this time, he had analyzed over 10,000 cases and developed his Five Biological Laws of disease. In 1997, Hamer was extradited to France, where he was sentenced to three years in prison for the illegal practice of medicine without the possibility of parole.[31] His career had come to an inglorious end.

---

28   Persson, "The Horrible Side Effects of Chemotherapy That Kills."

29   Ibid.

30   Ibid.

31   Ibid.

THE SUPPRESSED DISCOVERY

During World War II, physicians discovered that small doses of magnesium, a common mineral, produced salubrious results for patients suffering from myasthenia gravis, a disease that can be fatal. The discovery gained no mention in medical journals and was excluded for use in medical institutions. The reason for the suppression resided in the fact that the Rockefeller drug cartel owned Hoffman-La Roche, a pharmaceutical company that produced prostigmine, a costly drug that provides temporary relief for victims in the early stages of the disease but hastens their death in the later stages.[32]

HOXSEY'S WAR

In 1922, Harry Hoxsey, the son of a veterinarian, developed a remedy for cancer from a formula that his father used on animals. He opened a clinic in Taylorsville, Illinois, which produced such profound results that Hoxsey was summoned to meet with Dr. Morris Fishbein, the head of the American Medical Association. Under Fishbein's supervision, Hoxsey administered his formula to a Chicago police officer, whose cancer prognosis was terminal. The cop was cured, and Fishbein, on behalf of the Rockefeller Institute, offered to procure the rights to the formula. But

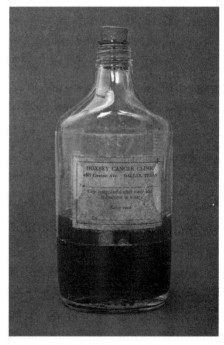

In 1922, Harry Hoxsey, the son of a veterinarian, developed a remedy for cancer from a formula that his father used on animals.

---

32 Josephson, *Rockefeller "Internationalist,"* pp. 108–109.

Hoxsey turned down the offer, since it contained no assurance that the formula would be made readily available to cancer patients throughout the country. Thus began Hoxsey's war with the AMA. Every time, he opened a clinic, the AMA ordered the FDA to close it. Hoxsey was arrested more than 100 times in two years. Eventually, he was forced to flee to Tijuana, Mexico.[33]

THE SECRET EXPERIMENT

From 1947 to 1948, the Rockefeller Foundation in conjunction with the Johns Hopkins University of Medicine, the Johns Hopkins Bloomberg School of Public Health, and the John Hopkins Health System Corporation sponsored venereal disease experiments on the inhabitants of Guatemala.[34] The Central American country was an ideal place to conduct such tests since prostitution had been legalized, and the sex workers were obliged to show up twice a week at a clinic for health inspection. At the clinic, the prostitutes were injected with syphilis and gonorrhea and were forced to have sex with psychiatric hospital patients, prison inmates, and military conscripts. A total of 1,308 subjects were involved, including 10-year-old orphans. One case study reads:

> Berta was a female patient in the Psychiatric Hospital . . . In February 1948, Berta was injected in her left arm with syphilis. A month later, she developed scabies (an itchy skin infection cause by a mite). Several weeks later, Dr. Cutler noted that she also developed red bumps where he had injected her arm, lesions on her arms and legs, and her skin was beginning to waste away from her body. Berta was not treated for syphilis until three months after her injection. Soon after, on August 23, Dr. Cutler wrote that Berta appeared as if she was going to die, but he did not specify why. That same day he put gonorrheal pus

---

33   Persson, "The Horrible Side Effects of Chemotherapy That Kills."

34   Sushma Subramanian, "Worse than Tuskegee," *Slate* magazine, February 26, 2017, http://www. slate.com/articles/health_and_science/cover_story/2017/02/guatemala_syphilis_experiments_ worse_than_tuskegee.html, accessed March 8, 2019.

from another male subject into both of Berta's eyes, as well as in her urethra and rectum. He also re-infected her with syphilis. Several days later, Berta's eyes were filled with pus from the gonorrhea, and she was bleeding from her urethra. Three days later, on August 27, Berta died.[35]

At the conclusion of the experiments, hundreds were blind, hundreds more mentally and physically incapacitated, and 83 had undergone an agonizing death.

GOT MILK?

By 1940, the Rockefellers had acquired America's largest milk-producing plants, including the Bordon Company and National Dairy Products, and the Cherry-Barrel Corporation, which possessed a monopoly on the milk pasteurization process.[36] The family now formed a Milk Trust and initiated a campaign to convince the gullible public that all good health required the consumption of three glasses of milk a day. The campaign was endorsed by the American Medical Association, and milk was distributed in school cafeterias throughout the country. Few realized that milk was not a source of strength and vitality but rather a licensed spreader of disease and death. Milk transmitted more diseases than any other food or beverage. It was a leading cause of tuberculosis, scarlet fever, streptococcus infections,

The Rockefellers initiated a campaign to convince the gullible public that all good health required the consumption of three glasses of milk a day. "MNSF MilkBooth" by BenFranske is licensed under CC BY-SA 3.0

---

35   Staff Report, "U.S. Medical Tests in Guatemala 'Crime against Humanity,'" *BBC News*, October 2, 2010, https://web.archive.org/web/20160102060840/http://www.bbc.co.uk/news/world-us-canada-11457552, accessed March 8, 2019.

36   Raymond W. Bernard, *The Revolt against Chemicals* (Whitefish, MT: Kessinger Publishing, 2012), p. 75.

kidney and heart disease, undulant fever, and infantile paralysis. Excessive consumption of milk was linked to childhood illnesses, hardening of the arteries, premature senility, and cancer.[37] But such facts were suppressed, and the milk campaign persisted.

HOLISTIC HOLOCAUST

From June 19, 2015, to June 22, 2018, over 90 practitioners of holistic medicine went to their graves under mysterious circumstances, proving that it is not safe to practice medicine that is not sanctioned by the Rockefeller drug cartel. A partial listing of the doctors who met an untimely end is as follows:

JUNE 19, 2015—Dr. Jeff Bradstreet, who practiced holistic medicine in Georgia, was found dead in a river with a gunshot wound to his chest.

JUNE 21, 2015—Dr. Baron Holt, 33, died of a drug overdose by a street drug, "Molly."

JUNE 21, 2015—Dr. Bruce Hedendal was found dead, and no cause of death has been listed. Hedendal treated countless patients with late-stage cancer, and his treatments put the cancer into remission.

JUNE 29, 2015—Holistic MD Theresa Sievers was found murdered in her home. Known as the "Mother Teresa of South Florida," her husband and children were attending a family reunion in Connecticut when she was murdered. The authorities said that she was targeted and that her murder wasn't random.

JUNE 29, 2015—Jeffrey Whiteside, MD, a pulmonologist, disappeared while vacationing with family. Numerous reports called it "mysterious," saying that he was on foot and vanished without a trace. Police searched for three weeks. Colleagues joined in the

---

37   Josephson, *Rockefeller "Internationalist,"* p. 122.

search along with bloodhounds, but not a shred of evidence surfaced. Whiteside's death was later ruled a suicide, but the local press called the investigation "a mess."

JULY 3, 2015—Patrick Fitzpatrick, MD, was reported missing while traveling from North Dakota to neighboring Montana. His truck and trailer were found on the side of the road. Authorities said that he seemed to have vanished into thin air.

JULY 21, 2015—Dr. Nicholas Gonzalez, a holistic MD, died suddenly of some mysterious cause. The church at Dr. Gonzalez's funeral in New York was packed with the patients he'd put in remission (some with stage IV pancreatic cancer) and who are still in remission decades later. Dr. Gonzalez also said in several interviews, including the last one before his death, that Big Pharma was intent upon his demise.

AUGUST 12, 2015—Osteopath Dr. Mary Bovier was found slain in her home in Pennsylvania. Her significant other, another osteopath, was questioned and released. There were no other suspects.

SEPTEMBER 7, 2015—Twenty-nine holistic doctors in Germany were poisoned by an overdose of a hallucinogenic drug.

SEPTEMBER 16, 2015—Best-selling author and holistic MD Mitch Gaynor was found dead outside his country home an hour from Manhattan, where he practiced. He had been on RT, decrying the pharmaceutical industry, not long before he died.

OCTOBER 11, 2015—Dr. Marie Paas was found dead of an alleged suicide.

OCTOBER 29, 2015—Jerome E. Block, holistic MD, allegedly jumped to his death from his Central Park West residence.

NOVEMBER 2015—A dozen doctors, mostly holistic, met an untimely end because of freak accidents and occurrences. The list includes the following: Dick Versendaal, MD; Janelle Bottorff,

MD; William Snow, MD; Wade Shipman, MD; Chris Coffman, MD; Christopher Spradley, MD; Robert Grossman, MD; David Knotts, MD; Anthony Keene, MD; Kenneth Rich, MD; and Jamie Zimmerman, MD.

JANUARY 23, 2016—A top MD, John Marshall, 49, 4th generation former Marine, who'd served in Afghanistan and had survival training, was found dead in the Spokane River.

JANUARY 23, 2016—Dr. Nabil El Sanadi, president and CEO of Broward Health, was found dead in a public restroom of an alleged suicide. Dr. Sanadi was brought in to assist Broward Health in December 2014, after they had been under federal investigation for corruption.

FEBRUARY 14—HIV and cancer researcher in Seattle, Cheryl DeBoer was found dead in a culvert with a plastic bag over her head. Investigators quickly state that there's no evidence of homicide, but her mother and other relatives publicly said that there's no way she crawled 1.5 miles through brambles, water, and mud to commit suicide in a culvert.

MARCH 23, 2016—Prominent holistic doctor Henry Han was found murdered on his seven-acre Santa Barbara estate, along with his wife and five-year-old daughter. All were shot and wrapped in plastic.

MARCH 24, 2016—Dr. Elbert Goodier III was murdered in his office while treating a patient.

APRIL 6, 2016—Dr. John Harsch, a self-described holistic medicine MD, was killed while riding his bicycle with a group of friends. He was the only one hit by the car.

FEBRUARY 12, 2016—Dr. Rose Polge apparently walked off her job, where she worked at Torbay Hospital in Devon (UK), and went missing for almost two months. She'd allegedly written a letter to the Health Secretary concerning a political situation involving doctors at the hospital. Police later recovered her body from the sea, more than 50 miles away from where a hoodie, believed to have belonged to her, was found. The inquest into her death proved inconclusive.

MAY 6, 2016—Dr. Vibeke Rasmussen was found dead in the Boston area. She taught natural health, nutrition, and biology at a local university and had been stabbed to death in her home.

MAY 6, 2016—Dr. Jyrki Suutari, an outspoken holistic doctor in the Los Angeles area, with a loving family and a newborn child, allegedly took his life in the garage of his home on Mother's Day.

MAY 15, 2016—Thomas Bruff, MD, died in a private plane crash in the mountains of Southern California.

JUNE 13, 2016—Tim Shelton, DC, died in a freak accident when a tractor rolled over on him.

JULY 7, 2016—In July, holistic doctor and acupuncturist Dr. Jenny Shi, 65, was found dead in her upscale Creekside Drive home in Palo Alto, California. The Santa Clara County Coroner's Office found the cause of death to be multiple stab wounds. Shi owned several acupuncture clinics in the Bay Area.

MAY 7, 2017—Dr. John Greg Hoffmann, who at one point lost his medical license but got it back for his alternative practices as an MD, died from injuries sustained when his car went off a cliff. Investigators found the accident suspicious since there were no tire marks.

MAY 29, 2017—Dr. Christopher King, a famous holistic MD, was shot to death on Memorial Day, while eating at a popular organic restaurant in Boulder, Colorado.

JULY 28, 2017—Dr. Glen Scarpelli and his wife both allegedly jumped out of a window from their holistic clinic (located on Madison Avenue in Manhattan), leaving behind neatly typed and packaged suicide notes in plastic baggies.

NOVEMBER 26, 2017—Dr. Miguel Crespo, stem cell and cancer researcher, was found dead in the bathroom on the 8th floor at the famous Weill Cornell Medical Center Hospital on the Upper East Side of Manhattan. Authorities said they were investigating a possible overdose even though no drugs were found at the scene.

DECEMBER 3, 2017—Dr. James Winer, the outspoken and controversial holistic doctor (and radio show host in several states), was found dead on a sidewalk in Pittsburgh. No autopsy was conducted.

DECEMBER 10, 2017—Dean Lorich, MD, was found dead in his Park Avenue home bathroom by his 11-year-old daughter. Police immediately called it a suicide. Dr Lorich was one of America's most gifted surgeons, who had operated on celebrities, including Bono of U2. Despite his renowned surgical precision, authorities said he missed his heart with the knife and instead stabbed himself in the torso.

JANUARY 11, 2018—Dr. Clive Bridgham, of East Providence, Rhode Island, was found dead in his home. Police believed he had been murdered. Bridgham had been selected by the Rio Olympic Sports Medicine Committee to assist the health services team during the 2016 Summer Games.

FEBRUARY 23, 2018—Holistic Dr. Mark Flanagan of Seguin died after allegedly hanging himself. He was described by his family and friends as fit, healthy, and fun-loving.

APRIL 2, 2018—The incinerated body of holistic Dr. Norman Valdes Cotten Jr. was found in Pontiac, Missouri. Authorities used dental records to confirm his identity.

APRIL 19, 2018—World-famous traditional healer and elder Olivia Arévalo Lomas of the Shipibo-Konibo indigenous people of Peru was assassinated at her home near the town of Yarinacocha. She was shot five times in the heart. The murder took place in the presence of her children.

APRIL 29, 2018—Biohacker and CEO of Ascendance Biomedical, Aaron Traywick was found dead in a spa in Washington, D.C., face-down, doing flotation therapy in very shallow water.

JUNE 16, 2018—Dr. Chris Cheung of Walnut Creek, California, died after his outrigger canoe overturned in the Berkeley Marina. Cheung was reportedly paddling alone. His body was found floating in the water while his vest was in the boat. The manner of death remains undetermined.

JUNE 22, 2018—Dr. Tristan Beaudette, 35, of Irvine, California, was bleeding from a chest wound when deputies found him in a tent at a Malibu Creek State Park campsite. He had been camping with his girls when someone gunned him down in front of his daughters. Beaudette was the associate director of Allergan Pharmaceuticals and oversaw the development of some of their late-stage clinical trials, including sustained release combination products and intraocular implants for the company. There were no suspects.

THE NEW SNAKE OIL

The wheel of fortune remained round.

The Rockefeller story had begun with snake oil. "Devil Bill" Rockefeller, John D.'s father, had traveled to towns and villages, ped-dling his concoction of crude oil as a remedy for cancer. Throughout the early years of the 20th century, John D. repackaged his father's formula and sold it as a laxative called Nujol.[38] And John D.'s cancer cures, including radiation and chemotherapy, became the new family snake oil that was administered day after day to desperate patients throughout the country.

The apple hadn't fallen far from the tree.

---

38   Eustace Mullins, *The Rockefeller Syndicate*, chap. 10, excerpted from *Murder by Injection* (Cork, IE: Omnia Veritas, 2012), http://www.eustacemullins.us/wp-content/works/Books/Extracts/ Eustace%20Mullins%20-%20Extract%20from%3B%20Murder%20by%20Injection%20-%20 The%20Rockefeller%20Syndicate.pdf, accessed March 8, 2019.

25

KILLING TRUTH

We're in a lot of trouble! Because you people, and 62 million other Americans are listening to me right now. Because less than 3 percent of you people read books. Because less than 15 percent of you read newspapers. Because the only truth you know is what you get over this tube. Right now, there is a whole and entire generation that never knew anything that didn't come out of this tube! This tube is the Gospel. The ultimate revelation. This tube can make or break presidents, popes, prime ministers. This tube is the most awesome goddamn force in the whole godless world and woe is us if it ever falls into the hands of the wrong people!

And when the largest company in the world controls the most awesome, goddamn propaganda force in the whole godless world who knows what shit will be peddled for truth on this network! So you listen to me. Listen to me! Television is not the truth. Television's a goddamned amusement park! Television is a circus, a carnival, a traveling troupe of acrobats, storytellers, dancers, singers, jugglers, sideshow freaks, lion tamers and football players. We're in the boredom-killing business.

But you people sit there, day after day, night after night, all ages, colors, creeds. We're all you know. You're beginning to believe the illusions we're spinning here. You're beginning to think that the tube is reality and that your own lives are unreal. You do whatever the tube tells you! You dress like the tube, you eat like the tube, you raise your children like the tube, you even think like the tube. This is mass madness, you maniacs! In God's name, you people are the real thing! We are the illusion!

—PADDY CHAYEFSKY (SCRIPTWRITER), *NETWORK*, 1976

BY 1976, the Rockefellers controlled every leading news outlet in the United States.[1] They could dictate what news should be conveyed to the public and what news should be withheld. Americans remained unaware that they had been dragged into World War II, the Korean Conflict, the Vietnam War, and the war on "terror" by the money cartel; that the Depression had occurred by design; that their gold had been shipped to Basel, Switzerland, to create an occult economy; that their educational, religious, judicial, and political systems were ruled by the Rockefellers; that their constitutional rights and national sovereignty had vanished; that the CIA had become an agency that served almost solely to advance Rockefeller interest; and that the U.S. State Department remained in the hands of the Council on Foreign Relations (CFR), who alone possessed the power to draft and dictate national and international policy.

THE STORY SOURCE

As soon as the CFR was established in 1921, the editors and publishers of America's leading newspapers were obliged to join the CFR in order to obtain news of national and international developments and of the adoption of new political and economic strategies. Every leading mover and shaker in the country, including the industrial giants, the global bankers, and the political and military leaders, met each week in secret at the Pratt House in New York. Those who were excluded from

Every leading mover and shaker in the country, including the industrial giants, the global bankers, and the political and military leaders, met each week in secret at the Pratt House in New York. Those who were excluded from these meetings were deprived of any insight into the inner workings of the nation and the world. "Harold Pratt House" by Gryffindor is licensed under CC BY-SA 3.0

---

1   Gary Allen, *The Rockefeller File* (Seal Beach, California: '76 Press, 1976), pp. 65–76.

these meetings were deprived of any insight into the inner workings of the nation and the world.

In 1937, Arthur Hay Sulzberger, chairman of the board of the *New York Times*, became a prominent CFR member, and stories circulated that the Rockefellers had purchased the nation's most prestigious newspaper for $17.5 million. The stories gained credibility when Sulzberger, that same year, became a trustee of the Rockefeller Foundation.[2] Following these developments, a flock of top *Times* executives and reporters were granted CFR membership, including Sulzberger's son-in-law Orvil E. Dryfoos and his grandson Arthur Ochs "Punch" Sulzberger, both of whom would ascend to the position of publisher of the nation's most prestigious newspaper. Other *Times* staffers who became part of the CFR rank and file were Harding Bancroft, James Reston, A. M. Rosenthal, Seymour Topping, Max Vrankel, Harrison Salisbury, C. l. Sulzberger, and David Halberstam.[3]

FIT FOR PROFIT

The emergence of the Council on Foreign Relations as a main source of inside information for the *New York Times* provided the Rockefellers and their ilk with the opportunity of manufacturing stories in order to produce political and economic results. "All the news that is fit to print became, in many instances, all the news that the Rockefellers deem fit for profit—even accounts that are completely untrue and outlandish. To protect their oil interests in the Caspian Sea, the Rockefellers arranged for stories to appear in the *Times* by Walter Duranty that depicted the Soviet Union under Stalin as a "socialist paradise."[4] Such portrayals of Communist Russia caused the American public to express no qualms about becoming Stalin's ally during World War II, even though the Soviet dictator (unbeknownst to the readers of the *New York Times*) had

---

2   Emanuel M. Josephson, *Rockefeller "Internationalist"* (New York: Chedney Press, 1952), p. 19.

3   Allen, *The Rockefeller File*, p. 67.

4   S. J. Taylor, *Stalin's Apologist: Walter Duranty, the "New York Times" Man in Moscow* (New York: Oxford University Press, 1990), p. 6.

engaged in pogroms that would put Adolf Hitler to shame. The *Times* was the perfect outlet for the tales of the "socialist paradise." Speaking of the power of the premier New York newspaper to influence public opinion, James Reston wrote: "A significance of the *Times* is its multiplier effect. What appears in the *Times* automatically appears later in other places."[5]

Representatives of every major newspaper and magazine in the country flocked to seek entrance at the Pratt House. The membership list of the CFR came to include editors, publishers, and correspondents from the Associated Press, Reuters, the *New York Post*, the *Washington Post*, the *Washington Times*, the *Los Angeles Times*, and the *Wall Street Journal*, along with the *Arkansas Gazette*, the *Des Moines Register*, the *Des Moines Tribune*, the Guy Gannett Company, the *Houston Post*, the *Minneapolis Star*, the *Minneapolis Tribune*, the *Denver Post*, and the *Louisville Courier*.[6] They all joined in the perpetuation of bogus news and false reporting.

INTELLECTUAL PROSTITUTES

This development was neither unnoticed nor unacknowledged. In 1953, John Swinton, former chief of staff at the *New York Times*, stated the following at the New York Press Club: "There is no such thing in America as an independent press. You know it and I know it. . . . The business of the journalist is to destroy truth; to lie outright; to pervert; to vilify; to fawn at the feet of mammon, and to sell his county and his race for his daily bread. You know it, and I know it and what folly is this toasting an independent press? We are the tools and vassals for rich men behind the scenes. We are the jumping jacks, they pull the strings and we dance. Our talents, our possibilities, and our lives are all the property of other men. We are intellectual prostitutes."[7]

---

5   James Reston, quoted in Allen, *The Rockefeller File*, p. 66.

6   Ibid., pp. 67–68.

7   John Swinton, "On the Independence of the Press (1953)," *Constitution Society*, January 28, 1999, https://www.constitution.org/pub/swinton_press.htm, accessed March 8, 2019.

Despite this outcry, the "intellectual prostitutes" continued to gather at the Pratt House to spin their latest stories. In 1968, Admiral Chester Ward, a former member of the CFR, wrote: "Out of its 1,551 members, 60 were listed in official CFR reports as engaged in 'journalism.' An additional 61 were listed in 'communications management,' a highly descriptive title, because CFR members do indeed 'manage' mass communications media, especially the influential segments. They control or own major newspapers, magazines, radio, and television networks."[8]

OPERATION MOCKINGBIRD

The Rockefellers' control over the CIA tightened their stranglehold over the media during the postwar era. In 1953, Allen Dulles, the CIA director and Rockefeller lackey, initiated Operation Mockingbird. This undertaking consisted of the recruitment of leading journalists and editors to fabricate stories and to create smoke screens in order to cast the Agency's agenda in a positive light. Among the news executives who took part in this undertaking were William Paley of the Columbia Broadcasting System, Henry Luce of Time Inc., Arthur Hays Sulzberger of the *New York Times*, Barry Bingham Sr. of the Louisville *Courier-Journal*, and James Copley of the Copley News Service. Entire news organizations eventually became part of Mockingbird, including the American Broadcasting Company, the National Broadcasting Company, the Associated Press, United Press International, Reuters, Hearst Newspapers, Scripps-Howard, *Newsweek*, the Mutual Broadcasting System, the *Miami Herald*, the *Saturday Evening Post*, and the *New York Herald-Tribune*. With over 400 journalists now on the take along with mainstream news outlets, the Agency could operate to expand the Rockefeller interests in Europe, the Middle East, and South America, without fear of exposure.[9] Americans would remain uninformed of the CIA's involvement in the heroin trade. They would be kept in the dark about the Agency's participation in overthrowing democratically elected governments in Iran, Guatemala,

---

8   Ibid., p. 66.

9   Carl Bernstein, "The CIA and the Media," *Rolling Stone*, October 20, 1977.

Turkey, Greece, Brazil, Argentina, Chile, and Bolivia. They would not be aware that the CIA's covert operations on behalf of the Rockefellers would bring them into a series of endless wars.

Operation Mockingbird would persist into the 21st century, and CIA files regarding such monumental undertakings as Operation Gladio and Operation Condor would remain classified as confidential and unavailable for inspection. The refusal to disclose any information about these undertakings was in keeping with the compliance of the media. Katharine Graham, publisher of the *Washington Post* and a Mockingbird operative, said: "There are some things the general public does not need to know, and shouldn't. I believe democracy flourishes when the government can take legitimate steps to keep its secrets and when the press can decide whether to print what it knows."[10]

THE POWER OF ADVERTISING

The Rockefellers' stranglehold remained virtually unbreakable since they also controlled the big businesses that provided the advertising revenue for the media. At the snap of their fingers, the family could cause the cessation of ads from the country's leading drug companies, automobile manufacturers, banks, airlines, insurance firms, retail outlets, food distributers, and oil companies. Such action would cause most media outlets to fold. Newspapers, in particular, derive over three-fourths of their revenue from advertising. In 1968, Ike McAnally, a columnist for the *New York Daily News*, wrote: "The most persistent influence upon the editorial policies of metropolitan newspapers today is the large advertiser. In many instances these advertisers . . . make open and contemptuous demands upon the front offices of newspapers to support the left wing. . . . Newspapers have surrendered unconditionally to left wing front office pressures, real and imaginary."[11]

---

10   Katharine Graham, quoted in Alexander Cockburn and Jeffrey St. Clair, *Whiteout: The CIA, Drugs and the Press* (New York: Verso, 1998), p. 31.

11   Ike McAnally, quoted in Allan, *The Rockefeller File*, pp. 74–75.

NETWORK CONTROL

By 1952, when television succeeded the newspaper as the primary creator of public opinion, the Rockefellers had seized control of the tube. William S. Paley, chairman of the board of CBS, became a CFR member and a trustee of the Ford Foundation. Along with Paley, other CBS executives were sucked into the CFR's vortex, including Frank Stanton, who served as CBS's president and a trustee of the Rockefeller Foundation and the Carnegie Institute; Arthur Taylor, who succeeded Stanton as president; Michael O'Neill of CBS publications; CBS directors Roswell Gilpatrick, Courtney Brown, Henry Schact, and William Burden; and CBS newsmen Charles Collingwood, Richard C, Hottelet, Marvin Kalb, Larry LeSueur, Daniel Schorr, and Walter Cronkite.[12]

It was a small wonder that CBS aired a two-hour special on Friday, December 28, entitled "The Rockefellers." The program, which was narrated by Cronkite, was (in the words of Gary Allen) "so sugary it must have sent thousands of diabetics scrambling for their insulin."[13]At the conclusion of the program, Cronkite stared into the camera and said that if any family had to possess so much wealth and power, it was fortunate for everyone that it was the Rockefellers.[14] Walter failed to mention that the family whom he praised possessed controlling interest in his network.[15]

Along with CBS, the Rockefellers extended their tentacles to NBC and ABC. David Sarnoff, the head of NBC, became a fixture at the Pratt House, along with NBC directors Thornton Bradshaw and John Petty and the network's leading newsmen John Chancellor and Irving R. Levine. The principal interest of this network, too, remained in the hands of the

---

12   Ibid., pp. 68–69.

13   Ibid.

14   Ibid.

15   Ibid.

Rockefellers.[16] The same was true of ABC, America's third network, which had fallen under the control of the Chase Manhattan Bank.[17]

THE ONE-EYED TUBE

The one-eyed tube in the living room of homes throughout the country became the central point of American interest and fixation. Television viewing was encouraged by parents, often as a means of controlling the children, who would stare at the screen for hours on end. The content of the first children's programs was banal and mentally destructive; even more destructive was the replacement of real family interaction by television viewing, as the dinner table was replaced by the "TV dinner" in front of the tube. Not surprisingly, the children became increasingly covetous of the items advertised by the media, demanding that they be given such things, lest they not be like their friends.[18]

In 1975, Eric Trist and Fred Emery of London's Tavistock Institute published their findings of the impact of 20 years of television on American society in a work entitled *Futures We're In*. They reported that the average daily viewing time had risen steadily over the two decades since the introduction of the medium to become a daily activity that ranked only behind sleep and work. The average American now stood glued to the tube for six hours a day. Television, the researchers concluded, had become an addictive drug that served to "shut down the central nervous system of man." Strange to say, Trist and Emery found nothing wrong with this development, even though their findings indicated that television was producing a brain-dead generation.[19]

---

16   Ibid.

17   Ibid.

18   "Who Controls the Media?" *The Global Movement*, January 2012, http://www.theglobalmovement. info/wp/areas-of-focus/global-financial-war/who-controls-the-media, accessed March 8, 2019.

19   Ibid.

Television, the Tavistock researchers discovered, could control how people thought and what they thought. It could cause them to abandon their long-held beliefs and convictions; it could transform their morality. Knowing this, the Rockefeller Foundation began funding research in mind control.

THE FUTURE IS FEAR

Television, the Tavistock researchers discovered, could control how people thought and what they thought. It could cause them to abandon their long-held beliefs and convictions; it could transform their morality. Knowing this, the Rockefeller Foundation began funding research in mind control. An early study performed by Carl Hovland of Yale University showed that fear was a primary factor in manipulating human behavior. Fear, Hovland found, did not have to be imminent but could concern matters of the future.[20]

This finding prompted the Rockefeller Foundation to fund experiments in mind control under the auspices of the CIA—an undertaking that became known as MK-Ultra. The ideal subjects for these experiments were the children who had been placed in the Catholic orphanages of Quebec. The overriding purpose of this venture was to identify the means by which human beings could be transformed into dutiful citizens of the New World Order.

THE DUPLESSIS ORPHANS

In post–World War II Montreal, thousands of children who had been placed in Catholic orphanages were suddenly proclaimed as mentally retarded and handed over to Catholic asylums for the insane. The motive for the reclassification was money. Subsidies for orphans, under

---

20   Punam Anand Keller and Lauren Goldberg Block, "Increasing the Persuasiveness of Fear Appeals: The Effect of Arousal and Elaboration," *Journal of Consumer Affairs* 22, No. 4, March 1966, https://www.jstor.org/stable/2489793?seq=1#page_scan_tab_contents, accessed March 8, 2019.

the government of Prime Minister Maurice Duplessis, were $1.25 per day for orphans and $2.75 per day for mental patients. Moreover, the church could receive substantial financial assistance for building new psychiatric hospitals. Mr. Duplessis was much praised by the press for his commitment to the mental health of the people of Quebec.[21]

FORCED LABOR, SEXUAL ABUSE, AND PHYSICAL TORTURE
Over 20,000 children, most from unwed mothers, ended up in the Catholic asylums.[22] The asylums were run by such religious orders as the Sisters of Providence, the Sisters of Mercy, the Gray Nuns of Montreal, the Sisters of Charity of Quebec, the Little Franciscans of Mary, the Brothers of Notre Dame-de-la-Misericorde, and the Brothers of Charity.[23] Children were subjected to forced labor and physical torture. "They would plunge our heads into ice-cold water if we did something wrong," Clarina Duguay, a surviving Duplessis orphan, said. Duguay also testified to being chained to a bed and forced to scrub the floors of the asylum from morning to night.[24]

Martin Lecuyer, another survivor, said that the children received no schooling but were sent to work on nearby farms. "The farmers would pay the religious community for the work we did," he said. "This was

---

21 Clyde H. Farnsworth, "Orphans of the 1950's, Telling of Abuse, Sue Quebec," *New York Times*, May 21, 1993, http://www.nytimes.com/1993/05/21/world/orphans-of-the-1950-s-telling-of-abuse-sue-quebec.html?pagewanted=all, accessed March 8, 2019.

22 News Staff, "Duplessis Orphans Want Montreal Burial Site Dug Up," CTV News—Montreal, Canada, June 18, 2004, https://web.archive.org/web/20111022154328/http://www.ctv.ca/CTVNews/Canada/20040619/duplessis_orphans_040618/, accessed March 8, 2019.

23 Clyde H. Farnsworth, "Orphans of the 1950's."

24 Christine Hahn, "The Worst of Times: How Psychiatry Used Quebec's Orphans as Guinea Pigs," *Freedom*, May 22, 2003, http://www.freedommag.org/english/canada/reports/page01.htm, accessed March 8, 2019.

slavery, that's the word for it."[25] At night, Lecuyer claimed that he was regularly sexually assaulted by a religious brother from the time he was 11. When he complained to a superior about the abuse, he was beaten with a leather strap.[26]

CHEMICAL EXPERIMENTATION

But the sexual abuse, forced labor, and torture paled in comparison with the drug experimentation that was conducted with Rockefeller funding under the cloak of MK-Ultra. The children served as guinea pigs for Chlorpromazine, a drug known as a "chemical bully club" because of its mental and physical consequences. A chief side effect of the drug is tardive dyskinesia, a central nervous system disorder that results in grotesque facial conditions and involuntary body movements. The use of Chlorpromazine on the orphans was part of the MK-Ultra mind control program of the CIA.[27] Dr. Ewen Cameron, the psychiatrist who conducted appalling tests on human subjects at McGill University, spearheaded much of the experimentation with, of course, Rockefeller funding.[28]

In addition to Chlorpromazine, the children were also subjected to electric shock, lobotomies, mental conditioning by ongoing television and radio broadcasts, and doses of additional drugs, many hallucinogenic. Clarina Duguay said that she began receiving Chlorpromazine two weeks after she arrived at St. Julien Hospital. The nuns had told her the drug would help her sleep. It did more than that. "It made me a zombie," she maintained. "I had no energy. I was always feeling sleepy,

---

25   Peter Rakobowchuk, "Duplessis Orphan Can't Forget Sexual Abuse Almost 60 Years Ago," *Brooks Bulletin*, December 21, 2006, http://www.bishop-accountability.org/news2006/11_12/2006_12_21_Rakobowchuk_DuplessisOrphan.htm, accessed March 8, 2019.

26   Ibid.

27   Hahn, "The Worst of Times."

28   Ibid.

had a hard time getting up. I was getting the drug every night."[29]

Paul St. Aubain, another Duplessis orphan, said he was lobotomized at St. Michel Archange, a Catholic asylum in Joliette, when he was 18. "I wasn't ill," Mr. St. Aubain said. "They did it without my consent, without my permission. They were experimenting on me. I was their prisoner." He said he was also subjected to electroshock therapy and daily doses of psychiatric drugs.[30]

PIG STY

Many of the children, like Mr. St. Aubain, suffered permanent brain damage. Some died. Their bodies were buried on an 800-acre plot of ground on the outskirts of Montreal that was next to a pig sty. The land was owned by the Archdiocese of Montreal, which was governed by Cardinal Paul-Emile Leger, a leader of the progressive party at Vatican II. Albert Sylvio, a Duplessis orphan who had been placed at St. Jean de Dieu, recalled transporting more than 60 bodies of fellow orphans to a mass grave site during the 1950s. "We put them in cardboard boxes," he said. "There was never any ceremony. Some had died on the operating table. Some had been sick and some committed suicide."[31]

Death had its reward for the religious sisters and brothers in charge of the orphans. The bodies of many of the children were sold to local medical schools for dissection. A Quebec law passed in 1942 allowed the members of religious orders to sell unclaimed remains for $10.[32]

THE SUCCESSFUL RESULTS

The results of the experimentation were highly beneficial for the Rockefellers. They now knew, based upon the research conducted with

29   Ibid.

30   William Marsden, "Duplessis Orphans Call for Exhumations," *National Post*, June 19, 2004, http://canadiangenocide.nativeweb.org/duplessis_orphans.html, accessed March 8, 2019.

31   Ibid.

32   Ibid.

drugs and hypnosis, that the key factor, as the Tavistock researchers had discovered, remained fear. By 1960, the Rockefellers employed their control of the media to proclaim the message that the world was grossly overpopulated, that the earth's natural resources were being depleted, and that the climate was undergoing a disastrous change. They became convinced that this new message would cause the peoples of the world to band together in a new alliance to save the planet. The news of the impending doom would cause international law to be imposed upon all nations. Sharp sanctions would be in effect for all violators by global watchdogs. Life on planet Earth was coming to an end.

This was the new snake oil.

And the public swallowed it.

26

KILLING UNDESIRABLES

The Rockefellers' support for eugenics began early in the twentieth century, and included support for the Eugenics Record Office. In 1913 John D. Rockefeller, Jr. ("Junior") incorporated a group, which became a major force in supporting birth control clinics and played a pioneering role in the modern field of population studies. As early as 1922, The Rockefeller Foundation sent money to fund German eugenics. Of Germany's 20-plus Kaiser Wilhelm Institute science centers, Rockefeller money built or supported three which "made their mark for medical murder" under the Nazis. One institute was for brain research. During part of Hitler's rule, it employed Hermann J. Muller, a Rockefeller-funded American socialist and geneticist. It later received "brains in batches of 150–250" derived from Holocaust victims. Another center, the Eugenics Institute, listed its 1935 activities as follows: "the training of SS doctors; racial hygiene training; expert testimony for the Reich Ministry of the Interior on cases of dubious heritage; collecting and classifying skulls from Africa; studies in race crossing; and experimental genetic pathology." Junior began funding Margaret Sanger in 1924. Surely he knew of her 1922 book, The Pivot of Civilization. *In it Sanger said, "Birth control . . . is really the greatest and most truly eugenic program."*

—REBECCA R. MESSALL, "EUGENICS, ROCKEFELLER, AND *ROE V. WADE*," 2005

The superior species the eugenics movement sought was populated not merely by tall, strong, talented people. Eugenicists craved blond, blue-eyed Nordic types. This group alone, they believed, was fit to inherit the earth. In the process, the movement intended to subtract emancipated Negroes, immigrant Asian laborers, Indians, Hispanics, East Europeans, Jews, dark-haired hill folk, poor people, the infirm and really anyone classified outside the gentrified genetic lines drawn up by American raceologists. How? By identifying so-called "defective" family trees and subjecting them to lifelong segregation and sterilization programs to kill their bloodlines. The grand plan was to literally wipe away the reproductive capability of those deemed weak and inferior—the so-called "unfit." The eugenicists hoped to neutralize the viability of 10 percent of the population at a sweep, until none were left except themselves.

—EDWIN BLACK, "THE HORRIFYING AMERICAN ROOTS OF NAZI EUGENICS"

Malthus, a British political economist, argued that increases in population would eventually diminish the ability of the world to produce enough food. He based this conclusion on the thesis that populations expand in such a way as to overtake the development of sufficient land for crops. "Thomas Robert Malthus" by John Linnell is licensed under CC BY 4.0

IN 1893, John D. Rockefeller Jr. enrolled at Brown University, where he fell under the influence of professors who were enamored by Thomas Malthus. Malthus, a British political economist, had argued that increases in population would eventually diminish the ability of the world to produce enough food. He based this conclusion on the thesis that populations expand in such a way as to overtake the development of sufficient land for crops.[1] The leading exponent of the Malthus theory at Brown was Elisha Benjamin Andrews, a one-eyed, larger-than-life Civil War veteran. Andrews influenced

---

1   "Thomas Malthus (1766–1834)," *BBC*, 2014, http://www.bbc.co.uk/history/historic_figures/malthus_thomas.shtml, accessed April 8, 2019.

Junior directly in the courses he taught and eventually became the young man's mentor. Andrews considered rapid population growth, through both natural increase and immigration, the greatest threat to mankind and exhorted his students, as Christians, to promote birth control and sterilization. Junior took these lessons to heart. In 1894, Junior wrote "The Dangers to America Arising from Unrestricted Immigration," his sophomore essay in which he denounced immigrants as "the scum of foreign cities; the vagabond, the tramp, the pauper, the indolent, the ignorant are hardly better than beasts."[2]

DEFECTIVE GERM PLASMS

At Brown, Junior was also exposed to the work of Sir Francis Galton, a prominent and prolific Victorian scientist. After reading Charles Darwin's *Origin of the Species*, Galton became convinced that humanity could be improved through selective breeding. He launched a new field of research that he called *eugenics*, which means "well born." He encouraged healthy, capable people of above-average intelligence to bear more children with the idea of building an "improved" human race. Some followers of Galton combined his emphasis

After reading Charles Darwin's *Origin of the Species*, Sir Francis Galton became convinced that humanity could be improved through selective breeding. He launched a new field of research that he called *eugenics*, which means "well-born."

---

2   John D. Rockefeller Jr.'s "The Dangers to America Arising from Unrestricted Immigration" in John Ensor Harr and Peter J. Johnson. *The Rockefeller Century: Three Generations of America's Greatest Family* (New York: Scribner's, 1988), pp. 452–453.

on ancestral traits with Gregor Mendel's research on patterns of inheritance in an attempt to explain the generational transmission of genetic traits, including stupidity and criminality in human beings. These traits, Galton and his disciples maintained, were transmitted from generation to generation by "defective germ plasms."[3] Moreover, if Mendel's concepts could be used to determine the color and size of a pea, the same concepts could be used to determine the social and intellectual characteristics of a human being.

At a time when the working poor were reproducing at a greater rate than successful middle- and upper-class members of society in Western Europe and the United States, these ideas garnered considerable interest. One of the most famous proponents of eugenics was Theodore Roosevelt, who warned that the failure of Anglo-Saxon couples to produce large families would lead to "race suicide."[4]

THE PROMOTION OF EUGENICS
After graduating from Brown, Junior and his father set up trusts, including the Rockefeller Institute for Medical Research (1901), the General Education Board (1903), the Rockefeller Sanitary Commission (1909), the Rockefeller Foundation (1913), and the Bureau of Social Hygiene (1913). The primary purpose of these philanthropies was the problem of overpopulation, especially among the lowest classes of society, and the promotion of eugenics.[5]

As soon as it was established, the Rockefeller Foundation funded the creation of a Eugenics Record Office (ERO) to register the genetic

3   "Origins of Eugenics: From Sir Francis Galton to Virginia's Racial Integrity Act of 1924," Claude Moore Health Sciences Library, 2004, http://exhibits.hsl.virginia.edu/eugenics/2-origins/, accessed April 8, 2019.

4   Ibid.

5   Rebecca Messall, "The Long Road of Eugenics: From Rockefeller to *Roe v. Wade*," *Human Life Review*, October 11, 2005, http://www.orthodoxytoday.org/articles5/MessallEugenics.php, accessed April 8, 2019.

background of every man, woman, and child in America (and, eventually, the world), so that every person could be categorized by his or her family line and assigned a genetic rating. Once completed, steps could be taken to eliminate those with the lowest eugenic value from the gene pool.[6] In addition, Junior funded the ERO's plan to institutionalize "mentally deficient" female convicts in order to study their germ plasms and to stop them from having children.[7]

Employing the "science" of cephalometry, which concentrates on the variations in size, shape, and proportion of human skulls, the ERO researchers concluded that larger skulls held larger brains, which resulted in increased intelligence. The races with the highest average "cephalic index" were Nordics. Hence individuals from northwestern Europe and the Scandinavian countries were smarter than individuals from other parts of the world.[8]

TWO FOSDICKS

In setting up the trusts, Junior developed close ties to the Fosdick brothers: Reverend Harry E. Fosdick, who served as his spiritual consultant, and Raymond E. Fosdick, who became his lawyer. The three men shared a passion for population control and social reform. In one of his sermons, Reverend Fosdick stressed the importance of eugenics by saying: "Few matters are more pressingly important than the application to our social problems of such well-established information in the realm of eugenics as we actually possess. The failure to do this is almost certainly going to put us in the position of endeavoring to cure symptoms while basic causes of social degeneration and disorder go

---

6   James Corbett, "How & Why Big Oil Conquered the World," *The Corbett Report*, October 6, 2017, https://www.corbettreport.com/bigoil/, accessed April 8, 2019.

7   Ibid.

8   "American Eugenics Research—Racism Masquerading as 'Science,'" Alliance for Human Research Protection, n.d., http://ahrp.org/1913-u-s-eugenics-research-association/, accessed April 8, 2019.

untouched."[9] While the Reverend was spreading the gospel of eugenics from his pulpit at the Riverside Church in New York, Raymond was setting up the American Birth Control League with Margaret Sanger.[10]

THE CALL FOR DEATH PANELS

Fueled by the support of the Rockefellers, the field of eugenics transformed from the speculative discussions of a few mad scientists into the social cause of an entire generation. By the end of World War I, economists, politicians, authors, political activists, and mainline ministers were extolling the need to eradicate the germ plasms of the lower stock of humanity. Marie Stopes, who founded Britain's first birth control clinic, railed against "hordes of defectives," calling for the compulsory sterilization of all women who were "unfit for parenthood." Alexander Graham Bell, the inventor of the telephone, campaigned for the "eradication of the deaf race" by governments intervening to stop deaf people from marrying. Nobel Prize–winning playwright and author George Bernard Shaw called for the creation of a government panel that would require everyone to come before it in order to justify their existence. Those who failed to provide ample justification, Shaw maintained, should be killed by the state.[11] Paul Popenoe, the U.S. Army's venereal disease specialist, wrote the widely used textbook *Applied Eugenics,* in which he argued: "From an historical point of view, the first method which presents itself is execution. Its value in keeping up the standard of the race should not be underestimated."[12]

It wasn't just playwrights, such as Shaw, and pseudoscientists, such as Popenoe, who advocated the establishment of death panels. In 1915,

9   Harry E. Fosdick, quoted in Christine Rosen, *Preaching Eugenics* (New York: Oxford University Press, 2004), p. 116.

10   Messall, "The Long Road of Eugenics."

11   Corbett, "How & Why Big Oil Conquered the World."

12   Edwin Black, "The Horrifying American Roots of Nazi Eugenics," *History News Network*, September 2003, http://historynewsnetwork.org/article/1796, accessed April 8, 2019.

Madison Grant, the director of the Rockefeller-sponsored American Eugenics Society, stated the following: "Mistaken regard for what are believed to be divine laws and a sentimental belief in the sanctity of human life tend to prevent both the elimination of defective infants and the sterilization of such adults as are themselves of no value to the community. The laws of nature require the obliteration of the unfit and human life is valuable only when it is of use to the community or race."[13]

"THREE GENERATIONS OF IMBECILES ARE ENOUGH"

Such words produced action. In 1907, Indiana became the first state to enact a eugenics sterilization law, and within five years, a dozen other states followed suit by ruling that all individuals deemed unfit by a medical panel were to be sterilized against their will. By 1930, 32 states passed eugenic sterilization laws. So many poor Southerners underwent the procedure that it became known as a "Mississippi appendectomy."[14] Between 60,000 and 70,000 Americans were herded up and sent to sterilization mills.[15] In its first 25 years of eugenic legislation, California sterilized 9,782 individuals. Most of the victims were women who had been classified as "bad girls" and diagnosed as "passionate," "oversexed" or "sexually wayward." Some women were sterilized because of what was deemed an abnormally large clitoris or labia.[16]

The legalization for enforced sterilization was upheld by the U.S. Supreme Court. In 1927, Chief Justice Oliver Wendell Holmes issued the following ruling: "It is better for all the world, if instead of waiting to execute degenerate offspring for crime, or to let them starve for their

---

13   Madison Grant, quoted in Corbett, "How & Why Big Oil Conquered the World."

14   Andrea DenHoed, "The Forgotten Lessons of the American Eugenics Movement," *New Yorker*, April 27, 2016, https://www.newyorker.com/books/page-turner/the-forgotten-lessons-of-the-american-eugenics-movement, accessed April 8, 2019.

15   Black, "The Horrifying American Roots of Nazi Eugenics."

16   Ibid.

imbecility, society can prevent those who are manifestly unfit from continuing their kind. . . . Three generations of imbeciles are enough."[17]

But this ruling was not sufficient for many eugenicists, who demanded the legalization of euthanasia. John Randolph Hayes, a California physician, called for the medical murder of the mentally ill by saying: "There are thousands of hopelessly insane in California, the condition of those minds is such that death would be a merciful release. How long will it be before society will see the criminality of using its efforts to keep alive these idiots, hopelessly insane, and murderous degenerates. . . . Of course the passing of these people should be painless and without warning. They should go to sleep at night without any intimation of what was coming and never awake."[18]

THE HITLER CONNECTION
In Germany, Adolf Hitler paid close attention to the developments in America. In his jailhouse journal, *Mein Kampf,* he wrote: "There is today one state in which at least weak beginnings toward a better conception [of immigration] are noticeable. Of course, it is not our model German Republic, but the United States."[19]

As soon as Hitler became the chancellor of Germany in 1933, he reached out to American eugenicists for assistance, which the Rockefellers were pleased to provide. Money from the Rockefeller Foundation flowed into Germany's eugenics research centers, including the Kaiser Wilhelm Institute, which used the cash to construct a major building that was dedicated to German race biology.[20] Ernst Rudin became the head of research for the Kaiser Wilhelm Institute and a key

---

17 Oliver Wendell Holmes, quoted in ibid.

18 John Randolph Haues, quoted in "American Eugenics Research—Racism Masquerading as 'Science.'"

19 Adolf Hitler, quoted in Black, "The Horrifying American Roots of Nazi Eugenics."

20 Ibid.

architect of Hitler's eugenics program. Rudin coedited the official rules and commentary on the Law for the Prevention of Defective Progeny, which was passed on July 14, 1933. The law was modeled after the legislation that had been passed in the United States and upheld by the U.S. Supreme Court. The Law for the Prevention of Defective Progeny formed "Genetic Health Courts," which could order the sterilization of "defectives" in eight different categories: the feeble-minded, schizophrenics, manic depressives, sufferers of Huntington's chorea, epileptics, those with hereditary deformities, the blind, and the deaf. Alcoholics, a ninth category, were to be optionally added to the list, with a caution against inclusion of ordinary barflies. By the end of the year, 62,400 Germans were found unfit to breed and sterilized against their will.[21]

Beginning in 1940, at Rudin's instructions, thousands of Germans taken from old age homes, mental institutions, and other custodial facilities were systematically gassed. Between 50,000 and 100,000 were eventually killed.[22] Leon Whitney, executive secretary of the Rockefeller-funded American Eugenics Society, declared of Nazism: "While we were pussy-footing around . . . the Germans were calling a spade a spade."[23]

THE "TOTAL SOLUTION"

Due to Rockefeller largesse, Otmar Freiherr von Verschuer and Josef Mengele were able to set up the Institute for Hereditary Biology and Racial Research at Frankfort University, where they initiated a research program on twins. Verschuer wrote in *Der Erbarzt*, a eugenics journal, that the work of his facility coupled with the German war would yield a "total solution to the Jewish problem.[24]

After the war, eugenics was declared a crime against humanity, and the experimentations that lead to the deaths of six million Jews came to an

---

21   Corbett, "How & Why Big Oil Conquered the World."

22   Black, "The Horrifying American Roots of Nazi Eugenics."

23   Leon Whitney, quoted in ibid.

24   Ibid.

end. The German scientists, who were placed on trial at Nuremberg, cited the California statutes and the ruling of Oliver Wendell Holmes in their defense—to no avail. They were found guilty and sent to the gallows.[25]

THE NEGRO PROBLEM

In 1944, before eugenics became rebranded as molecular biology to separate it from the death camps of Adolf Hitler, Gunther Myrdal, a Rockefeller fellow, wrote *An American Dilemma: The Negro Problem and Modern Democracy* in which he explained how the only way "to get rid of the Negroes" was by means of controlling their fertility. He maintained that this process would have to be accomplished surreptitiously: "But as we shall find, even birth control for Negroes as well as for whites will, in practice, have to be considered primarily as a means to other ends than that of decreasing the Negro problem. If there were no caste differences, there would be no more need for birth control among Negroes than among whites. But until reforms are carried out, and as long as the burden of caste is laid upon American Negroes, even an extreme birth control program is warranted by reasons of individual and social welfare."[26] Myrdal continued as follows: "A serious difficulty is that of educating Southern Negroes to the advantages of birth control. Negroes, on the whole, have all the prejudices against it that other poor, ignorant, superstitious people have. More serious is . . . that even when they do accept it, they are not very efficient in obeying instructions. An intensive educational campaign is needed, giving special recognition to the prejudices and ignorance of the people. . . . The use of Negro doctors and nurses is essential."[27]

---

25   Ibid.

26   Gunther Mytdal, quoted in Messall, "The Long Road of Eugenics."

27   Ibid.

MEET MARGARET SANGER

Junior also championed eugenics through birth control by funding the work of Margaret Sanger and the American Birth Control League, where Raymond Fosdick served as Sanger's general counsel. In a memo to Junior, Fosdick wrote: "Personally, I believe that the problem of population constitutes one of the great perils of the future and if something is not done along the lines that these people are suggesting, we shall hand down to our children a world in which the scramble for food and the means of subsistence will be far more bitter than anything we have at present."[28]

John D. Rockefeller Jr. also championed eugenics through birth control by funding the work of Margaret Sanger and the American Birth Control League, where Raymond Fosdick served as Sanger's general counsel.

Sanger shared Junior's concerns regarding the birth rates of the poor, the mentally deficient, the indolent, and the physically deformed. In *The Pivot of Civilization*, Sanger advanced the need for coerced sterilization by writing: "Possibly drastic and Spartan methods may be forced upon American society if it continues complacently to encourage the chance and chaotic breeding that has resulted from our stupid, cruel sentimentalism." She added: "Birth control, which has been criticized as negative and destructive, is really the greatest and most truly eugenic program." In a chapter entitled "The Fertility of the Feeble-Minded," she wrote: "Modern conditions of civilization, as we are continually being reminded, furnish the most favorable breeding-ground for the

---

28   Harr and Johnson, *The Rockefeller Century*, p. 191.

mental defective, the moron, the imbecile. . . . We protect the members of a weak strain . . . up to the period of reproduction, and then let them free upon the community, and encourage them to leave a large progeny of 'feebleminded': which in turn, protected from mortality and carefully nurtured up to the reproductive period, are again set free to reproduce, and so the stupid work goes on of preserving and increasing our socially unfit strains."[29]

THE MEDICAL MANUAL

Junior arranged for Sanger's pronouncements to receive the imprimatur of the American Medical Association. In June 1928, Dr. Robert L. Dickinson, Sanger's business partner, hosted an exhibit on the surgery of sterilization at the American Medical Association. After the exhibit, universities and hospitals throughout the country engaged in research to further the cause of enforced sterilization, by various means, including vaccines.[30]

In 1934, the National Committee on Maternal Health, an agency funded by Rockefeller's Bureau of Social Hygiene, published *The Control of Contraception*, an illustrated manual by Dr. Dickinson, in which the esteemed eugenicist wrote: "All feeble minded women under fifty of whatever level of mentality, should be sterilized . . . The safe procedure is to sterilize any feeble minded girl as close as possible to puberty." As to sterilizing males, "any feeble minded male of whatever grade who is not confined in an institution had best be sterilized, as sudden violent outbreaks are likely to occur in which he will rape any available female, of whatever age."[31]

---

29   Margaret Sanger, *The Pivot of Civilization* (New York: Bretano's, 1922), pp. 64–65.

30   Messall, "The Long Road of Eugenics."

31   Robert Latou Dickinon and Louise Stevens Bryant, *Control of Conception: An Illustrated Medical Manual* (Baltimore: The Williams & Wilkins Company, 1938), p. viii.

MR. POPULATION

John D. Rockefeller III (1906–1978), would facilitate the continuation
of the eugenics movement after World War II to such an extent that he
became known in some circles as "Mr. Population."[32] He had four brothers,
Nelson (1908–1979), Laurance (1910–2004), Winthrop (1912–1973),
and David (1915–2018), with their own spheres of power over the U.S.
State Department, the United Nations, the Federal Reserve System, the
Central Intelligence Agency, the World Bank, the International Monetary
Fund, the national educational system, the American judiciary and
medical establishment, the oil industry, Latin America, the governor-
ships of New York and Arkansas, the airline industry, the pharmaceutical
industry, the conservation movement, the military-industrial complex, the
Metropolitan Museum of Art, the Museum of Modern Art, the Museum
of Natural History, the national media, the Chase National Bank, the
World Trade Organization, and by the creation of the National Council
of Churches, mainline Protestantism.

THE POPULATION COUNCIL

In 1952, JDR III established the Population Council "to stimulate,
encourage, promote, conduct and support significant activities in the
broad field of population." Like its founder, the Population Council's
other members were concerned about population issues, and like
other population organizations, including Planned Parenthood, high-
ranking Population Council leaders were well connected to the eugenics
movement. Frederic Osborn, one of the four original trustees of the
Population Council along with JDR III, was the founding father of the
American Eugenics Society and a charter member of Margaret Sanger's
Citizens Committee for Planned Parenthood.[33]

Frank W. Notestein, another founding trustee, was a member of

---

32   Messall, "The Long Road of Eugenics."

33   Ibid.

the American Eugenics Society and the Medical Advisory Board for Margaret Sanger's Birth Control Federation. In 1947, Notestein became the first executive director of the Population Division of the United Nations. Under Notestein's leadership, the Population Council produced a film entitled "Family Planning," which starred Walt Disney's iconic cartoon character Donald Duck. It was released to indoctrinate families on the use of birth control.[34]

General Thomas Parran Jr., the fourth trustee, was America's sixth Surgeon General. He was instrumental in the establishment of the World Health Organization, and his name even appeared on the public health building of the University of Pittsburgh as "one of the giants of 20th-century medicine."[35] Parran's legacy was tainted in 2010 when the U.S. government apologized to Guatemala for the syphilis experiments that exposed 1,308 men, women, and children to syphilis without consent from 1946 to 1948. Parran, as a Rockefeller lackey, had approved of the experiments.[36]

In the Population Council's 1964 annual report, JDR III is listed as chairman of the board, Notestein as president, and Osborn as chairman of the Executive Committee. The list of trustees now included representatives of the World Health Organization, the Rockefeller Institute, Harvard, the Carnegie Institute of Washington, the *New York Times*, AT&T, and the University of Chicago. The Population Council's finance committee was made up of representatives from AT&T, Continental Can Company, General Electric, and Chase Manhattan Bank.[37] Few organizations had amassed such power and wealth so quickly.

---

34 Carole Novielli, "The Population Council Has a Shocking 65-Year History, and It's Nothing to Celebrate," *Live Action*, November 14, 2017, https://www.liveaction.org/news/population-council-founded-eugenicists-promoting-abortion-turns-65/, accessed April 8, 2019.

35 Ibid.

36 Ibid.

37 Messall, "The Long Road of Eugenics."

THE MODEL PENAL CODE

Against the background of the rise of the Population Council, the Rockefellers made use of the American Law Institute to create the Model Penal Code text designed to stimulate and assist U.S. state legislatures to update and standardize their penal laws through which abortion laws were loosened, state by state, on the basis of sex studies by the Kinsey Institute. In *Kinsey: Crimes and Consequences,* Judith Reisman documented the criminal conduct and outright fraud perpetrated by the Kinsey Institute in its sex studies. The Rockefeller Foundation had also funded the Kinsey Institute.[38]

The Model Penal Code allowed for eugenic abortion to kill disabled babies. It also allowed the killing of healthy babies if they were conceived from incest or rape. The country was now well on its way to killing its children.

---

38   Ibid.

27

KILLING INNOCENCE

To the Rockefellers, socialism is not a system for redistributing wealth—especially not for redistributing their wealth—but a system to control people and competitors. Socialism puts power in the hands of the government. And since the Rockefellers control the government, government control means Rockefeller control. You may not know this, but you can be sure they do! When the Rockefellers join the UN's World Population Conference in calling for the promotion "of a new economic order by eradicating the cause of world poverty, by ensuring the equitable distribution of the world resources, by eliminating the injustices of existing world trade systems and exploitation perpetuated by capitalistic corporations," something smells as fishy as an unwashed tuna boat. Curbing population growth is just part of the Rockefeller war on the American family. According to John H. Knowles, president of the Rockefeller Foundation and one of America's foremost promoters of the slaughter of the unborn, the goal of the foundation is to achieve the capacity in America for 1.8 million abortions every year.

—GARY ALLEN, *THE ROCKEFELLER FILE*, 1976

THE POPULATION COUNCIL would produce developments that would transform the course of human history. It would give rise to the U.S. government's endorsement of Zero Population Growth (ZPG), the legalization of abortion, the so-called Green Revolution, the creation of genetically modified organisms (GMOs), and the pseudoscience of climate change. It would initiate international summits that would call for the imposition of international laws regarding the environment. It would extend the control of the World Bank and the International Monetary Fund so that the planet's natural resources could be plundered by the money cartel. It would persuade the great mass of mankind that life on planet Earth was coming to an end, and in this way, it would set the stage for Armageddon.

In 1957, JDR III's Population Council, Laurance Rockefeller's Conservation Foundation and Margaret Sanger's Planned Parenthood set up an ad hoc committee at the United Nations to study the "population crisis." The committee mapped out a full population control program in a study entitled "Population: An International Dilemma." The study maintained that population growth, in rich nations as well as poor, posed a dire threat to political and economic stability and could only be resolved by a policy of Zero Population Growth.[1] Individuals would no longer be subjected to enforced sterilization in the age of eugenics. Rather, they would be conditioned to sterilize themselves.

One year later, the American Law Institute, a Rockefeller creation, placed the mother's well-being ahead of the fetus when it proposed that abortion be made legal for reasons including the mental or physical health of the mother, pregnancy due to rape and incest, and fetal deformity.[2]

THE DRAPER REPORT

In 1959, JDR III was appointed to the Committee on Foreign Assistance by President Dwight D. Eisenhower. The membership of this Committee included William Draper, who had been a partner in Dillon,

---

1   Steve Weissman, "Why the Population Bomb Is a Rockefeller Baby," *Ramparts, Eco-Catastrophe*, 1970, https://pulsemedia.org/2009/10/03/why-the-population-bomb-is-a-rockefeller-baby/, accessed March 13, 2019.

2   "Abortion History Timeline," National Right to Life, https://nrlc.org/archive/abortion/facts/abortiontimeline.html, accessed March 13, 2019.

Read & Company, a firm that underwrote foreign bonds and arranged funding for the Rockefeller oil industry; Hugh Moore, who had worked with Sanger to create the International Planned Parenthood Federation; and John J. McCloy, the chairman of Chase Manhattan Bank.[3] The first breakthrough toward making population control official government policy was the Committee's issuance of The Draper Report.

This report maintained that population growth was cancelling economic gains in less developed countries, thereby necessitating the union of financial foreign aid with family planning, fertility control research, and the formation of national population plans. The report was met by such a storm of protest from the National Catholic Welfare Conference that President Eisenhower made an abrupt about-face and refrained from endorsing it. Speaking to a *Newsweek* correspondent, Eisenhower said: "I can't imagine anything more emphatically a subject that is not a proper political or government activity or function or responsibility. . . . This government will not, as long as I am here, have a positive policy doctrine in its program that has to do with this problem of birth control. That's not our business."[4]

Nevertheless, the report represented the first government document to take a stance on the birth control, and it received the ringing endorsement of liberal Protestant groups, including the Unitarian Fellowship, and such influential U.S. senators as Hubert Humphrey (D–MN), Stuart Symington (D–MO), and Adlai Stevenson (D–IL).[5]

---

3   International Press Service, "How Rockefeller Nurtured and Controlled the ZPG Plan for Depopulation," *Executive Intelligence Review*, July 22, 1974, https://larouchepub.com/eiw/public/1974/eirv01n12-19740722/eirv01n12-19740722.pdf, accessed March 13, 2019.

4   Dwight David Eisenhower, quoted in Donald T. Critchlow, *Intended Consequences: Birth Control, Abortion, and the Federal Government in Modern America* (New York: Oxford University Press, 2001), p. 44.

5   Ibid.

"THE MOST DANGEROUS BOMB OF ALL"

The Draper Report became the rallying cry for the population movement. Millions were raised for Planned Parenthood's World Population Emergency Campaign and the Victor Fund Drive.[6] Full-page ads now appeared in leading newspapers throughout the country, touting the idea of Zero Population Growth. In October, 1959, Arthur Krock published a column entitled "The Most Dangerous Bomb of All" in the *New York Times*. He wrote: "In the rush of the great nations to produce nuclear weapons capable of agonizing mass destruction, and now to find means to turn them into the utilities of peace, their Governments have paid small attention to the limitation of a more dangerous instrument for the destruction of civilization that is swiftly being assembled. The social scientists have called this weapon 'the population bomb.'" Krock concluded his column by warning of the emergence of a world inhabited "by billions of half-alive, starving peasants, condemned to short, miserable lives of hatred and hunger."[7]

GRISWOLD V. CONNECTICUT

The great leap forward for the U.S. official endorsement of birth control came with the 1965 Supreme Court ruling in the case of *Griswold v. Connecticut*. Estelle Griswold, the executive director of the Planned Parenthood League of Connecticut, and Dr. Charles Lee Buxton, a physician at the New Haven Planned

The great leap forward for the U.S. official endorsement of birth control came with the 1965 Supreme Court ruling in the case of *Griswold v. Connecticut*.

---

6   Michael Barker, "The Original Population Bomb," *Swans Commentary*, November 7, 2011, http://www.swans.com/library/art17/barker92.html, accessed March 13, 2019.

7   Arthur Krock, quoted in Michelle Goldberg, *The Means of Reproduction: Sex, Power, and the Future of the World* (New York; Penguin, 2009), p. 49.

Parenthood clinic, had been arrested for giving birth control information to married couples. This violated the Comstock Act of 1873, which defined contraceptives as obscene and illicit and made it a federal offense to disseminate birth control through the mail or across state lines.[8] The case against Griswold and Buxton was compounded by a state law in Connecticut that made it possible for married couples to be arrested for using condoms in the privacy of their own bedrooms.[9]

The Supreme Court ruled that married couples possessed the right to use birth control, and that the Connecticut law violated the "right to marital privacy." Although the Bill of Rights does not explicitly mention "privacy," Justice William O. Douglas wrote that for the majority, the right was to be found in the "penumbras" and "emanations" of other constitutional protections, such as the self-incrimination clause of the Fifth Amendment. Douglas wrote, "Would we allow the police to search the sacred precincts of marital bedrooms for telltale signs of the use of contraceptives? The very idea is repulsive to the notions of privacy surrounding the marriage relationship."[10] Justice Arthur Goldberg issued a concurring opinion in which he used the Ninth Amendment in support of the ruling.[11]

LBJ'S "NEW LOOK"
The decision emboldened the proponents of Zero Population Growth. Two weeks after the Supreme Court ruling, President Lyndon Baines Johnson (LBJ), at the 20th-anniversary celebration of the United Nations in San Francisco (June 25, 1965), said: "Let us in all our lands— including this land—face forthrightly the multiplying problems of our

---

8   "Anthony Comstock's 'Chastity Laws,'" *American Experience,* PBS, n.d, https://www.pbs.org/wgbh/americanexperience/features/pill-anthony-comstocks-chastity-laws/, accessed March 13, 2019.

9   Ibid.

10   James Petersen, *The Century of Sex* (New York: Grove Press, 1999), p. 298.

11   Ibid.

multiplying populations and seek the answers to this most profound challenge to the future of all the world. Let us act on the fact that less than five dollars invested in population control is worth a hundred dollars invested in economic growth."[12]

THE OFFICIAL ENDORSEMENT

In November 1965, the official endorsement of birth control by the U.S. government was made when President Johnson convoked the White House Conference on International Cooperation. Chaired by JDR III and William Draper, the Conference concluded that the matter of overpopulation had become so great that the specter of starvation now loomed over planet Earth.[13] The members urged LBJ to extend birth control assistance throughout the world as an addendum to foreign aid.[14] Impressed by the "public support" for the recommendations of the Conference, Johnson persuaded Congress to support his "New Look" in international affairs, which permitted him to judge a nation's "self-help" in population planning as a criterion for giving Food for Peace aid. The "New Look" combined population control with agricultural development, international education, encouragement of private overseas investment, and multilateral institution building. Separate legislation allowed the U.S. Department of Health, Education, and Welfare to initiate a birth control program for domestic consumption.[15] The stage was set for the Rockefellers to control the world's population.

---

12 Lyndon Baines Johnson, quoted in Roger C. Avery, "Lowering the Boom," *Humanist* 26, no. 1 (January 1966), https://search.proquest.com/openview/e8aea55eab2a592a92504804f95694ad/1?pq-origsite=gscholar&cbl=1817324, accessed March 13, 2019.

13 International Press Service, "How Rockefeller Nurtured and Controlled the ZPG for Depopulation."

14 Steve Weissman, "Why the Population Bomb Is a Rockefeller Baby," *Rampart*, 1970, *Eco-Catastrophe*, 1970, https://pulsemedia.org/2009/10/03/why-the-population-bomb-is-a-rockefeller-baby, accessed March 13, 2019.

15 Ibid.

In 1966, Lawrence Lader's book *Abortion,* which would be cited by Justice Harry Blackmun in *Roe v. Wade,* was published by Bobbs-Merrill. In the book, Lader said: "The frightening mathematics of population growth overwhelms piecemeal solutions and timidity. No government, particularly of an underdeveloped nation, can solve a population crisis without combining legalized abortion with a permanent, intensive contraception campaign." He maintained that legalized abortion was the only solution. "The ultimate reality," Lader wrote, "[is] that only legalized abortion can cut to the core of the problem . . . . We have reached the point where warnings are no substitute for a decisive population policy . . . As a result of the baby boom after World War II, and a sharp increase in the number of women of procreative age, the U.S. population should double in the next forty or fifty years."[16] Lader had served on the board of directors of the New York–based Association for the Study of Abortion (ASA), which was funded by members of the Rockefeller family.[17]

THE SENATE SUBCOMMITTEE

From 1965 to 1968, the Senate Government Operations Subcommittee on Foreign Aid Expenditures held 41 days of hearings on legislation to reorganize the Department of State and the Department of Health, Education, and Welfare. The transcripts, in 18 bound volumes titled "Population Crisis," contained the testimony of 120 witnesses who spoke in favor of population control, and one or two witnesses who spoke against it. Almost all of the witnesses who advocated population control were employed by or affiliated with Rockefeller-funded universities or organizations, including the Rockefeller Institute, the

---

16   Lawrence Lader, *Abortion* (Indianapolis: Bobbs-Merrill, 1966), pp. 142–43.

17   Rebecca Messall, "The Long Road of Eugenics: From Rockefeller to *Roe v. Wade,*" *Human Life Review,* October 11, 2005, http://www.orthodoxytoday.org/articles5/MessallEugenics.php, accessed March 13, 2019.

Brookings Institution, the National Council of Churches, and the Population Council. At the hearings, future president George Herbert Walker Bush, then a congressman from Texas, said: "I think there is some feeling among some of the more militant civil rights people that any effort in Planned Parenthood is going to try to breed the Negro out of existence, which is absolutely ridiculous." JDR III, in his testimony, said: "If this simple device [IUD] continues to justify expectations, it will represent a major breakthrough in population control, and might even change the history of the world."

REAGAN ENDORSES ABORTION

On April 25, 1967, Colorado governor John A. Love signed the first American Law Institute model abortion law in the United States, allowing abortion in cases of permanent mental or physical disability of either the child or mother or in cases of rape or incest. Love said: "The new law does several things. First it extends beyond the possible death of the woman or her serious physical injury to include mental impairment of a serious and permanent nature when verified by a psychiatrist. It also extends to cases in which it is likely that the child would

Ronald Reagan signed the California Therapeutic Abortion Act, one of the most liberal abortion laws in the country, in 1967, legalizing abortion for women whose mental or physical health would be impaired by pregnancy, or whose pregnancies were the result of rape or incest.

have a grave and permanent physical deformity or mental retardation. Finally it extends to certain cases of rape and incest. . . . The bill itself is completely permissive, not requiring any hospital, doctor, nurse, potential mother or any other person to act in any way to terminate a pregnancy at any time."[18]

Ronald Reagan signed the California Therapeutic Abortion Act, one of the most liberal abortion laws in the country, in 1967, legalizing abortion for women whose mental or physical health would be impaired by pregnancy or whose pregnancies were the result of rape or incest. The same year, the Republican strongholds of North Carolina and Colorado made it easier for women to obtain abortions. In 1970, New York, under Governor Nelson Rockefeller, eliminated all restrictions on women seeking to terminate pregnancies up to 24 weeks' gestation.[19]

NIXON'S COMMISSION

On March 16, 1970, President Richard M. Nixon appointed JDR III as the chairman of the newly created Commission on Population Growth and the American Future. In accepting the appointment, Rockefeller said: "The average citizen doesn't appreciate the social and economic implications of population growth and what it does to the quality of all our lives. Rather than think of population control as a negative thing, we should see that it can be enriching."[20]

Within months, the Commission recommended that "present state laws restricting abortion be liberalized along the lines of the New York State Statute, such abortions to be performed on request by duly licensed physicians under conditions of medical safety."[21] The

---

18 John Love, quoted in "Colorado Gov. John Love Signs First Liberalized Abortion Law: 45 Years Ago Today," Colorado Right to Life, April 25, 2007, http://coloradortl.org/node/325, accessed March 13, 2019.

19 Sue Halpern, "How Republicans Became Anti-Choice," *New York Review of Books,* November 8, 2018, https://www.nybooks.com/articles/2018/11/08/how-republicans-became-anti-choice/, accessed March 13, 2019.

20 John D. Rockefeller III, quoted in Gary Allen, *The Rockefeller File* (Seal Beach, California: '76 Press, 1976), p. 135.

21 Ibid.

Commission also suggested that "federal, state, and local governments make funds available to support abortion services."[22]

In the summer of 1971, New York City opened its first abortion clinic, which would serve as the prototype of other clinics throughout the country. The facility was designed to perform more than 10,000 abortions a year with funds provided, in many cases, by Medicaid. The funding for the abortion mill came from the Rockefeller Brothers Fund.[23]

ROE V. WADE

On January 23, 1973, the Supreme Court in the case of *Roe v. Wade* by a 7–2 decision upheld the rights of women to terminate their pregnancies. The majority, led by Justice Harry Andrew Blackmun, determined that a woman's right to decide whether to have an abortion involved the question of whether the Constitution protected a right to privacy. The justices answered this question by asserting that the 14th Amendment, which prohibits states from "depriv[ing] any person of . . . liberty . . . without due process of law," protected a fundamental right to privacy." The Justices explained this position as follows:

> This right of privacy, whether it be founded in the Fourteenth Amendment's concept of personal liberty and restrictions upon state action, as we feel it is, or, as the District Court determined, in the Ninth Amendment's reservation of rights to the people, is broad enough to encompass a woman's decision whether or not to terminate her pregnancy. The detriment that the State would impose upon the pregnant woman by denying this choice altogether is apparent. Specific and direct harm medically diagnosable even in early pregnancy may be involved. Maternity, or additional offspring, may force upon the woman a distressful life and future. Psychological harm may be imminent. Mental and physical health may be taxed by child care. There is also the distress, for all concerned, associated with the

22 Ibid.

23 Ibid., p. 136.

KILLING INNOCENCE

unwanted child, and there is the problem of bringing a child into a family already unable, psychologically and otherwise, to care for it. In other cases, as in this one, the additional difficulties and continuing stigma of unwed motherhood may be involved."[24]

After considerable discussion of the law's historical lack of recognition of rights of a fetus, the justices further concluded "the word 'person', as used in the Fourteenth Amendment, does not include the unborn." The right of a woman to choose to have an abortion fell within this fundamental right to privacy, and was protected by the Constitution.[25]

SLAUGHTER OF THE INNOCENT

Now, by order of the Supreme Court, states were forbidden from outlawing or regulating any aspect of abortion performed during the first trimester of pregnancy. Abortions could only be regulated when related to maternal health in the second and third trimesters, and abortion laws protecting the life of the fetus could only be enacted in the third trimester. Even then, an exception had to be made to protect the life of the mother.[26]

In 1964, only two abortions per 10,000 live births took place in the United States. By 1974, that number had increased by over 140 percent, resulting in 284 abortions per 10,000 live births.[27] The total number of abortions in the United States between 1973 and 2014 was estimated at 56.5 million.[28]

24   "Roe v. Wade, 410 U.S. 113 (1973)," *Justia,* U.S. Supreme Court, https://supreme.justia.com/cases/federal/us/410/113/, accessed March 13, 2019.

25   Ibid.

26   "Roe v. Wade (1973)," *THE SUPREME COURT,* Thirteen/WNET New York, 2007, https://www.thirteen.org/wnet/supremecourt/rights/print/landmark_roe.html, accessed March 13, 2019.

27   William Robert Johnston, "United States Abortion Rates (1960–2013)" http://www.johnstonsarchive.net/policy/abortion/graphusabrate.html, accessed March 13, 2019.

28   "Abortion Statistics," American Life League, https://www.all.org/learn/abortion/abortion-statistics/, accessed March 13, 2019.

"REPRODUCTIVE JUSTICE"

Mainline Protestant churches weakened their stance against abortion after *Roe v. Wade* passed. As soon as the ruling was made, the United Methodist Church (UMC) began to support a woman's choice to abort under safe medical procedures. Over the next 40 years, the UMC continued to debate and reconsider their position on abortion. In 2018, the denomination proposed to amend their mission statement, to "recognize tragic conflicts of life that might justify abortion." Rather than using the word *abortion*, the UMC substituted the term "reproductive health." Additionally, the statement no longer discusses the sanctity of preborn life or the alarming recent increase in abortions.[29]

Similarly, the United Church of Christ (UCC) adopted the expression "reproductive justice" to describe its support of a woman's right to have an abortion. In 2016, UCC activists applauded the U.S. Supreme Court ruling to deny Texas limitations to abortion that would have shut down nearly 80 percent of abortion clinics in the state. The UCC Reverend Dr. John Dorhauer commended the ruling as follows: "As a longtime advocate for women's reproductive health, and now as the general minister and president of a denomination whose longstanding support for the same is deep and rich, I celebrate this decision. I recognize it as a crucial victory in the ongoing battle to protect a woman's Constitutional right to maintain control of her body and her reproductive health."[30]

"STEWARDSHIP RESPONSIBILITY"

Three years prior to *Roe v. Wade,* the Presbyterian Church (U.S.A.) published a study that described abortion as being a helpful aid for

---

29   Katie Anderson, "United Methodist Church New Belief: 'We Support Legal Access to Abortion,'" *Human Defense,* August 30, 2018, https://humandefense.com/united-methodist-church-proposes-new-belief-we-support-legal-access-to-abortion/, accessed March 13, 2019.

30   Ernest L. Ohlhoff, "Abortion: Where Do the Churches Stand?'" Pregnant Pause, September 2000, http://www.pregnantpause.org/people/wherchur.htm, accessed March 13, 2019.

unwanted pregnancies; phrases such as "personal choice" and "responsible decision" regarding abortion began to appear in ecclesiastical reports. In the early 1980s, Presbyterians approved a policy that asserted that abortion was a "stewardship responsibility."[31]

In 2012, a survey of Jewish values released by the Public Religion Research Institute (PRRI) recorded the opinions of American Jews on a wide variety of political, religious, and economic issues. According to the survey, 93 percent of all American Jews support some manner of legalized abortion. Ninety-five percent of Jewish Democrats support abortion; 77 percent of Jewish Republicans also favor legalized abortion in almost all cases. These large percentages far exceed the rate of any other group studied.[32]

THE CATHOLIC COLLAPSE

Historically, the Roman Catholic Church has maintained one of the strongest antiabortion stances, opposing the procedure under nearly all circumstances. Abortion is considered a sin, meriting excommunication, and pro-choice stances are rejected in many traditional Catholic communities. A large percentage of ordinary churchgoers and church officials, however, are willing to accept a more permissive attitude toward abortion. In the United States, many priests have been granted authority to give absolution, an act once reserved solely for bishops. Nearly half of the Catholics in America believe abortion should be legal in all or nearly all cases, according to data from a 2014 Pew Research Center study.[33]

---

31 "Abortion/Reproductive Choice Issues," Presbyterian Church U.S.A./Presbyterian Mission, February 23, 2016, https://www.presbyterianmission.org/blog/2016/02/23/abortion-issues-2/, accessed March 13, 2019.

32 Roger Price, "The Curious Consensus of Jews on Abortion," *Judaism and Science*, January 10, 2013, https://www.judaismandscience.com/the-curious-consensus-of-jews-on-abortion/, accessed March 13, 2019.

33 Weston Williams, "Has Pope Francis Softened the Catholic Stance on Abortion?" *Christian Science Monitor*, November 21, 2016, https://www.csmonitor.com/World/Europe/2016/1121/Has-Pope-Francis-softened-the-Catholic-stance-on-abortion, accessed March 13, 2019.

FROM ABORTION TO INFANTICIDE

On January 22, 2019, Governor Andrew Cuomo of New York passed the Reproductive Health Act (RHA), an alarming piece of legislation, pushing the "abortion envelope" even further than *Roe v. Wade*. The RHA allows for the following:

- Late-term abortions for the "life and health of the mother." The word *health* is now a subjective term, open to a wide variety of interpretations.

- The removal of the requirement that abortionists be licensed doctors. Now, nurse practitioners, physician assistants, and others are able to commit abortions.

- Taking away safeguards for accidental live births. An infant who has remained alive during an abortion can now be murdered outside the womb.

- Removing punishment for illegal and involuntary abortions, such as when a criminal attempts to cause a miscarriage by drugs or physical violence against a mother.[34]

The new law states: "The New York Constitution and United States Constitution protect a woman's fundamental right to access safe, legal abortion." The term "fundamental right" bears special significance in the philosophy of law. Naming abortion as "a fundamental right" could nullify an individual's right of conscience or religious freedom. This new protocol could be used as a tool to stifle pro-life and religious groups and to coerce physicians and health professionals to execute abortions despite their personal beliefs.[35]

---

34   "Cuomo, Hillary Clinton Push to Expand Late-Term Abortion in New York with State Legislature," Texas Right to Life, January 17, 2019, https://www.texasrighttolife.com/cuomo-hillary-clinton-push-to-expand-late-term-abortion-in-new-york-with-state-legislature/, accessed March 13, 2019.

35   Ibid.

Governor Andrew Cuomo of New York passed the Reproductive Health Act (RHA), an alarming piece of legislation, pushing the "abortion envelope" even further than *Roe v. Wade*. "Andrew Cuomo 2014" by Diana Robinson is licensed under CC BY 2.0

Shortly after the RHA bill was passed, abortion supporters in Virginia, Vermont, and Rhode Island began promoting comparable legislation. Governor Ralph Northam of Virginia declared that he would pass a bill that allows abortion even during the actual process of childbirth. By 2019, the following states had removed all gestational limits on abortion: Alaska, Colorado, New Hampshire, New Jersey, New Mexico, Oregon, Vermont, and New York, along with Washington, D.C.[36]

INSIDE PLANNED PARENTHOOD

According to the Family Research Council, Planned Parenthood Federation of America (PPFA) is the primary supplier of abortions in the U.S. From 2011–2017, Planned Parenthood committed more than 2.2 million abortions, and is responsible for over 30 percent of all abortions performed in the United States. Additionally, between 2011 and 2017, Planned Parenthood gave out an average of 1.79 million emergency contraception kits annually. Emergency contraception, such as Plan B, can kill a human embryo if fertilization has already occurred.[37]

In 2015, David Daleiden released videos showing Planned

36 Melissa Barnhart, "7 States Already Allow Abortion up to Birth—Not Just New York," *Christian Post*, January 30, 2019, https://www.christianpost.com/news/7-states-already-allow-abortion-up-to-birth-not-just-new-york.html, accessed March 13, 2019.

37 "The Real Planned Parenthood: Leading the Culture of Death—2019 Edition," Family Research Council, https://www.frc.org/issuebrief/the-real-planned-parenthood-leading-the-culture-of-death-2015-edition, accessed March 13, 2019.

Parenthood executives discussing fees for human fetal tissue and organs. By setting up a fictitious biomedical research company called Biomax Procurement Services, Daleiden and his associate, Sandra Merritt, posed as representatives of Biomax and secretly recorded a number of conversations.[38]

In the first interview, Dr. Deborah Nucatola of Planned Parenthood commented on baby crushing: "We've been very good at getting heart, lung, liver, because we know that, so I'm not gonna crush that part. I'm gonna basically crush below, I'm gonna crush above, and I'm gonna see if I can get it all intact." In the second video, Dr. Mary Gatter, who has served as a medical director for the organization's Los Angeles and Pasadena affiliates, jested: "I want a Lamborghini" as she haggled the optimum remuneration for dead baby parts.[39]

In a subsequent video, Holly O'Donnell, a former employee of StemExpress, recalled the remarks of her supervisor regarding a nearly intact late-term fetus aborted at a Planned Parenthood in San Jose, California: "You want to see something kind of cool?" O'Donnell recalled being asked by her supervisor, "And she just taps the heart, and it starts beating. And I'm sitting here; and I'm looking at this fetus; and its heart is beating; and I don't know what to think."[40] She also said that she was once asked to pierce through a baby's face in order to remove the brain—while the infant's heart was still pulsing.[41]

---

38 Matt Hamilton, "Two Anti-Abortion Activists behind Undercover Planned Parenthood Videos Charged with 15 Felonies," *Los Angeles Times,* March 28, 2017, https://www.latimes.com/local/lanow/la-me-ln-planned-parenthood-charges-activists-20170328-story.html, accessed March 13, 2019.

39 Steven Ertelt, "New Documents Prove Planned Parenthood Illegally Profited from Selling Aborted Baby Parts," *Lifenews.com,* April 20, 2016, https://www.lifenews.com/2016/04/20/new-documents-prove-planned-parenthood-illegally-profited-from-selling-aborted-baby-parts/, accessed March 13, 2019.

40 Ibid.

41 Jeremy Breningstall, Elizabeth D. Herman, and Paige St. John, "How Anti-Abortion Activists Used Undercover Planned Parenthood Videos to Further a Political Cause," *Los Angeles Times*, March 30, 2016, http://graphics.latimes.com/planned-parenthood-videos/, accessed March 13, 2019.

MONEY FOR BRAINS AND LIVERS

StemExpress is a biospecimen medical company, that used to work closely with Planned Parenthood. O'Donnell worked as a StemExpress procurement technician inside some of the biggest Planned Parenthood centers in Northern California. Her job was to draw blood and dissect organs from aborted fetuses, which StemExpress then shipped to research customers across the country. O'Donnell explained the close coordination between the two organizations:[42]

> At the beginning of the day, we would let them know what we were looking for. . . . We'd open up the Task Page, which, it shows you what the researchers want, how many specimens they want for that day or that week. We'd go to the head nurse, let the nurses know, hey this is what I'm looking for today. They'd give you a sheet of the appointments, which women were coming in, and it would tell you how many patients, what time they were coming in, their name, and if they knew how far along they were.[43]

O'Donnell said StemExpress staff, who worked inside Planned Parenthood clinics, were given bonuses for fetal body parts in "really high demand." More money was given for brains or livers, for example, as opposed to blood samples. She explained that different body parts were separated into different categories with corresponding pay.[44]

Documents released by U.S. House Select Panel on Infant Lives reveal one in five abortion clinics, whether they were affiliated with

---

42   Dorothy Cummings McLean, "Appalling New Video Shows Planned Parenthood Gave Patient Info to Baby Parts Harvesters," *Life Site,* November 1, 2017, https://www.lifesitenews.com/news/new-video-planned-parenthood-gave-out-patient-info-to-baby-parts-harvesters, accessed March 13, 2019.

43   Ibid.

44   "StemExpress Whistleblower Says Company Paid Bonuses for Organs That Were in 'Really High Demand,'" TheBlaze, November 14, 2017, https://www.theblaze.com/news/2017/11/14/stemexpress-whistleblower-says-company-paid-bonuses-for-organs-that-were-in-really-high-demand, accessed March 13, 2019.

Planned Parenthood or other abortion centers, were selling the body parts of aborted babies when David Daleiden began his investigation.[45] But the documents and the news investigations failed to state that the activities of Planned Parenthood had been funded by the Rockefellers.

45   Breningstall, Herman, and St. John, "How Anti-Abortion Activists Used Undercover Planned Parenthood Videos to Further a Political Cause."

28

KILLING MOTHER EARTH

Starting in 1965, India's Green Revolution transformed the country's few fertile regions into veritable breadbaskets, quadrupling India's output of wheat and rice. The revolution brought new irrigation techniques, hybrid seeds, fertilizers, pesticides, herbicides, and mechanization. Punjab's farmers became heroes of a self-sufficient India no longer dependent upon shipments of foreign grain and making a clean cut with a past full of mass starvation and food aid from the United States.

Times have changed, says Prof. R. K. Mahajan, an agricultural economist at Punjabi University. "The Green Revolution is not as green as it was earlier—it has now become brown and pale," he says. "The profit margins have skewed to the minimum."

The Green Revolution hardly seems to have made much of an impact in terms of well-being here. Rural poverty abounds, malarial mosquitoes breed in stagnant pools of water, and bullock carts far outnumber motor vehicles.

And behind the walls villagers speak of cancer, which they say is on the rise along with other ailments such as renal failure, stillborn babies, and birth defects that researchers attribute to the overuse and misuse of pesticides and herbicides.

—DANIEL PEPPER, "THE TOXIC CONSEQUENCES OF
THE GREEN REVOLUTION," 2008

IN 1943, Norman Borlaug, a Rockefeller University agronomist, and a team of Rockefeller-funded scientists arrived in northern Mexico to experiment with new agricultural techniques and petrochemical soil additives. The team created a genetically modified strain of wheat that proved resistant to the terrible blight of black stem rust that had destroyed wheat fields throughout the world. The new wheat could also withstand extreme weather conditions and grew on short stalks so that it could bear heavy seed heads. In the course of the experiments, pesticides, fertilizers, and soil enrichment chemicals were pumped into the barren fields. The new farms were operated by heavy machinery, including newly developed tractors and combine harvesters. Much of this equipment came from International Harvester, a company in which the Rockefellers maintained controlling interest.[1] By 1963, 95 percent of the Mexican wheat crop was Borlaug's variety. Mexico became a net wheat exporter, and the country's wheat yield was six times greater than it had been when Borlaug arrived.[2]

The hybrid seeds contained bacteria such as *Bacillus thuringiensis* within their DNA and were programmed by Borlaug and his fellow scientists to be sterile. They were called "terminator seeds," the implication being that they destroy themselves after producing one crop. For this reason, farmers were compelled to make yearly purchases of seeds in order to produce more produce. Moreover, the seeds were developed to pair with Monsanto's Roundup Ready, the most widely used herbicide in the world.[3] Monsanto possessed an interlocking directorate with the Rockefeller Groups, who controlled the direction of the world's largest agrochemical business.[4]

1   Gary Allen, *The Rockefeller File* (Seal Beach, California: '76 Press, 1976), p. 31.

2   "The Green Revolution—Norman Borlaug and the New Wheat," *Food Disruptors*, November 1, 2018, https://thefooddisruptors.com/the-green-revolution-norman-borlaug-and-the-new-wheat/, accessed March 28, 2019.

3   F. William Engdahl, "Bill Gates Talks about 'Vaccines to Reduce Populations,'" *Geopolitics— Geoeconomics*, March 4, 2010, www.engdahl.oilgeopolitics.net/Swine_Flu/Gates_Vaccines/ gates_vaccines.html, accessed March 28, 2019.

4   Allen, *The Rockefeller File*, p. 34.

The large plantation owners (*latifundistas*), who were able to afford the seeds, the Monsanto chemicals, and the machinery, became the sole beneficiaries of the so-called "Green Revolution." The small farmers were forced to liquidate their holdings to the new agricultural overlords, and thousands of unemployed Mexican workers were driven to the cities in search of employment. This development, for the Rockefellers and the money cartel, served as an additional benefit of the Revolution. A seemingly endless supply of cheap labor was now available for outsourcing and globalized manufacturing.[5]

THE SEED CARTEL

After the success of the Mexican experiment, Nelson Rockefeller founded the International Basic Economy Corporation (IBEC) in 1947. The purpose of the organization was to introduce "mass scale agricultural holdings in Latin America," where the CIA could be used to topple governments and set up puppet regimes. In Brazil, Nelson teamed up with the grain-trading giant Cargill to create genetically modified corn seed varieties with the intention of making the Latin American country "the world's third largest producer of [these] crop[s] after the U.S. and China."[6]

In 1954, JDR III set up his own branch of the Agricultural Development Council, and the two brothers initiated an effort to bring world agriculture and the planet's food supplies under their corporate hegemony.[7] The ABCD seed cartel of Archer Daniels Midland, Bunge, Cargill, and Louis Dreyfus now came into being. These companies,

---

5   "TMR 062: Transcript: F. William Engdahl: Seeds of Destruction—the GMO Hidden Agenda," interview between Julian Charles and William Engdahl, transcribed by Michael Cornelius, *The Mind Renewed*, June 15, 2014, https://www.themindrenewed.com/transcripts/107-int-43t, accessed March 28, 2019.

6   "Fateful War and Peace Studies," *Eugenics and Depopulation*, January 4, 2008, eugenicsanddepopulation.blogspot.com/2008/01/fateful-war-and-peace-studies.html, accessed March 28, 2019.

7   Ibid.

along with Monsanto and other Rockefeller-controlled petrochemical fertilizer plants, formed the hub of American "agribusiness," a concept that was developed at the Harvard Business School for the Rockefeller Foundation.[8]

FOOD FOR PEACE

The Green Revolution shifted into high gear during the tenure of Lyndon Baines Johnson (LBJ) in the White House. LBJ was a Rockefeller man, and his relationship with the family was so close that he wanted Nelson

CA17-1-63 November 27, 1963
Mr. Reuther of Food for Peace
with Pres. Johnson

Under his 1965 "Food for Peace" program, Johnson mandated the use of petrochemical-dependent agricultural technologies (fertilizers, tractors, irrigation, etc.) by aid recipients. In this way, the program guaranteed that the Rockefellers would become the world's new agricultural giants.

---

8   James Corbett, "How & Why Big Oil Conquered the World," *The Corbett Report,* October 6, 2017, https://www.corbettreport.com/bigoil/, accessed March 28, 2019.

to serve as vice president.[9] Under his 1965 "Food for Peace" program, Johnson mandated the use of petrochemical-dependent agricultural technologies (fertilizers, tractors, irrigation, etc.) by aid recipients. In this way, the program guaranteed that the Rockefellers would become the world's new agricultural giants. Unable to afford these new technologies themselves, the impoverished Third World "beneficiaries" of this program were forced to obtain loans from the International Monetary Fund and the World Bank. These loans were handled by the Rockefeller's own Chase Manhattan Bank and guaranteed by the U.S. government.[10]

With the Food for Peace program in place, the primary focus of the Rockefellers and their newly created food cartel became India, where the failure of the summer monsoons had produced a severe food shortage. With the specter of starvation hovering over the country, the government officials of India acquiesced to pressure from the Johnson Administration and the World Bank. The officials pared down government control of India's agriculture, liberalized the import restrictions, and devalued the rupee. In addition, the officials gave the Rockefellers permission to construct new fertilizer plants, to set their own prices, to handle their own distribution outside the normal channels of the rural cooperatives, and to maintain a greater share of management control than what had been allowed under Indian law. They further agreed to give greater emphasis to agriculture and to maintain high food prices as an incentive to growers.[11] Regarding this development, the *New York Times* said: "Call them 'strings', call them 'conditions,' or whatever one

---

9   Robert Morrow, "Lyndon Johnson Considered Putting Nelson Rockefeller on the 1968 Ticket as Vice President," *The Education Forum*, November 10, 2012, educationforum.ipbhost.com/topic/19670-lyndon-johnson-considered-putting-nelson-rockefeller-on-the-1968-ticket-as-vice-president/, accessed March 28, 2019.

10   Corbett, "How & Why Big Oil Conquered the World."

11   Steve Weissman, "Why the Population Bomb Is a Rockefeller Baby," *Ramparts*, 1970, reprinted by *Pulse*, October 2, 2009, https://pulsemedia.org/2009/10/03/why-the-population-bomb-is-a-rockefeller-baby/, accessed March 28, 2019.

likes. India has little choice now but to agree to many of the terms that the United States, through the World Bank, is putting on its aid. For India simply has nowhere else to turn."[12]

THE CANCER TRAIN

With the ground chemically saturated with fertilizers and pesticides, the genetically modified seeds grew beautifully. Once-barren land flowered. Indian farmers harvested 95 million tons of grain in 1967–1968, exceeding their previous top crop yields by 5 percent. The following year, they did almost as well.[13] Elated Indian officials predicted that their country would become self-sufficient in food production by 1971. "The Green Revolution," David Rockefeller proclaimed to the International Industrial Conference, "may ultimately have a cumulative effect in Asia, Africa, and Latin America such as the introduction of the steam engine had in the industrial revolution."[14]

But the elation was short-lived. Within a few years, Punjab, where the Green Revolution in India was initiated, saw a sharp rise in malignancies. Formerly known as the "food basket of India," Punjab now became known as the cancer state. In villages throughout Punjab, cancer deaths have occurred in every other home.[15] Every night at 9:30, Train No. 339, known as the cancer train, picks up at least 60 patients in the tiny farm village of Bathinda in northern Punjab for the overnight trek to the cancer treatment center in Bikaner.[16]

---

12   *New York Times*, quoted in ibid.

13   Ibid.

14   David Rockefeller, quoted in Ibid.

15   "Why India's Punjab State Has the Country's Highest Cancer Rates," *NBC News,* July 17, 2014, https://www.nbcnews.com/news/asian-america/why-indias-punjab-state-has-countrys-highest-cancer-rates-n158691, accessed March 28, 2019.

16   Daniel Zwerdling, "In Punjab, Crowding onto the Cancer Train," *All Things Considered*, National Public Radio, May 11, 2009, https://www.npr.org/templates/story/story.php?storyId=103569390, accessed March 28, 2019.

STILLBORN BABIES AND SUICIDE

The Indian state also witnesses a sharp rise in renal failure, stillborn babies, and birth defects. A Punjabi University study found a high rate of genetic damage among farmers, which the researchers attributed to pesticide use. The study further found DNA damage affecting a third of the sample group of 210 farmers spraying pesticides and herbicides, a level apparently unaffected by other factors such as age, smoking, and dietary habits. A second study discovered widespread contamination of drinking water with pesticide chemicals and heavy metals, all of which are linked to cancer and other life-threatening ailments.[17]

To make matters worse, yield growth across India and elsewhere actually slowed after the introduction of agribusiness.[18] The December 2000 edition of *Current Science* noted: "The green revolution has not only increased productivity, but it has also [produced] several negative ecological consequences, such as depletion of lands, decline in soil fertility, soil salinization, soil erosion, deterioration of environment, health hazards, poor sustainability of agricultural lands and degradation of biodiversity. Indiscriminate use of pesticides, irrigation and imbalanced fertilization has threatened sustainability."[19]

As in Mexico, the green revolution in India drove the small farmers out of business since they were unable to afford the required mechanization, the cost of fertilizers, pesticides, and herbicides, and the yearly supply of seeds. Faced with insurmountable debt and no income, many of the residents of the most fertile plains of Punjab had come to the end

---

17   Daniel Pepper, "The Toxic Consequences of the Green Revolution," *U.S. News & World Report*, July 7, 2008, https://www.usnews.com/news/world/articles/2008/07/07/the-toxic-consequences-of-the-green-revolution, accessed March 28, 2019.

18   Corbett, "How & Why Big Oil Conquered the World."

19   Ibid.

of the road. It is estimated that more than 125,000 farmers in one area of Punjab committed suicide within a time span of 15 years.[20]

THE MONSANTO MONOPOLY

As the Green Revolution spread throughout the Third World, Monsanto continued to tighten its grip over the food industry by purchasing nearly every seed company on the planet. By 2019, it controlled 95 percent of the cotton in India, 90 percent of the corn in Mexico, and 93 percent of the soy in the United States.[21]

The food giant also established a revolving door policy with the U.S. government. Dennis DeConcini, the former U.S. Senator from Arizona, became the legislative consultant for Monsanto; Mickey Kantor, who served on Monsanto's board of directors, emerged as the U.S. Secretary of Commerce under President Bill Clinton; Michael Taylor, Monsanto's former Vice President for Public Policy, was appointed Deputy Commissioner of the Food and Drug Administration by President Barrack Obama; Linda Fisher, who performed a five-year stint as Monsanto's Vice President of Government and Public Affairs, was named Deputy Administrator of the Environmental Protection Agency by President George W. Bush, and Clarence Thomas, one of Monsanto's corporate lawyers, ascended to the U.S. Supreme Court.[22]

These prominent government officials greased the way for the passage of the Monsanto Protection Act of 2013. This legislation granted companies dealing in modified organisms and genetically engineered seeds immunity from federal courts. It stipulated that even if future

---

20   Andrew Malone, "The GM Genocide: Thousands of Indian Farmers Are Committing Suicide after Using Genetically Modified Crops," *Daily Mail*, November 2, 2008, https://www.dailymail.co.uk/news/article-1082559/The-GM-genocide-Thousands-Indian-farmers-committing-suicide-using-genetically-modified-crops.html, accessed March 28, 2019.

21   Vandana Shiva, quoted in James Corbett, "Bayer + Monsanto = A Match Made in Hell," *Corbett Report*, June 23, 2018, https://www.corbettreport.com/bayer/, accessed March 28, 2019.

22   Ibid.

research shows that GMOs or GE seeds cause significant health problems, such as cancer, the federal courts no longer possess the power to stop their spread, use, or sale.[23] The legislation, which contained the Monsanto rider, had nothing to do with food, agriculture, or consumer health. It had been inserted within a spending bill by Senator Roy Blunt of Missouri, who possessed a history of working in tandem with Senator Jay Rockefeller of West Virginia.[24]

THE SECRET AGREEMENT

Before the Monsanto Protection Act, the giant agribusiness wielded its clout in a closed-door meeting with President George Herbert Walker Bush in 1992. The meeting resulted in Bush Sr.'s agreement to prevent the health and safety agencies of the government (like the Food and Drug Administration, the U.S. Department of Agriculture, Health and Human Services, and so forth) from authorizing any independent testing of any GMO products. The agreement, according to eco-scientist William Engdahl, "allowed Monsanto to do its own studies, give them to the government, say: 'This GMO soybean is completely healthy—no bad effects, etc.'" Engdahl adds: "So, after '92, GMO soybeans were sold to the American farmers as a solution to increase their profits in tough times."[25]

The momentousness of this agreement is impossible to understate. GMOs were to be treated like food that had not been modified by Rockefeller scientists. No one in America could know what they were buying at the supermarkets and what they were ingesting at the dinner table. The matter is critical since 93 percent of the soy crop has been genetically changed and soy is a ubiquitous additive. It is contained in

---

23   Ibid.

24   Ibid. See also "Senators Blunt, Rockefeller Introduce Legislation to Spur Investment, Jumpstart Job Creation in Low-Income Communities," Roy Blunt, US Senator for Missouri, June 11, 2013, https://www.blunt.senate.gov/news/press-releases/senators-blunt-rockefeller-introduce-legislation-to-spur-investment-jumpstart-job-creation-in-low-income-communities, accessed March 28, 2019.

25   "TMR 062: Transcript.

candy, baked goods (including Girl Scout cookies), peanut butter, mayonnaise, infant formula, protein bars, and salad dressings. Soy is fed to farm animals, and meat from soy-fed livestock lines the country's meat markets.

According to the nonprofit Pew Initiative on Food and Biotechnology, a project designed to facilitate dialogue about the pros and cons of genetic modification, "No single statute and no single federal agency govern the regulation of agricultural biotechnology products." And compared with the battery of tests demanded of chemical pesticides (evaluation of chronic exposure, carcinogenicity, etc.), the testing requirements for genetically altered crops, the Pew group contends, amount to "little more than a polite suggestion."[26]

THE RUSSIAN STUDIES

This lack of testing became alarming since independent scientists conducted studies that showed that GMOs produce disastrous effects on rats and other lab animals. In 2005, Irina Ermakova of the Russian National Academy of Sciences noted in her study that within three weeks, over half of the babies from mother rats fed GM soy died—over five times the mortality rate in the non-GMO soy control group. The pups from the GM group were also smaller. Later, Ermakova fed all the rats in her laboratory a GM soy diet. Two months later, the infant mortality rate reached 55 percent. The testicles of male rats fed a GM diet, which once were pink, turned blue.[27]

In 2012, Russian biologist Alexey V. Surov and a team of researchers fed three generations of hamsters varying diets: one without soy, one with non-GM soy, one with GMO soy, and the final with higher amounts of GMO soy. By the third generation, the pups from the

---

26   Amanda Kimble-Evans, "Genetically Modified Corn: Safe or Toxic?" *Mother Earth News,* April/
     May 2010, https://www.motherearthnews.com/nature-and-environment/environmental-policy/
     genetically-modified-corn-zmaz10amzraw, accessed March 28, 2019.

27   Lisa Garber, "GMO Soy Repeatedly Linked to Sterility, Infant Mortality, Birth Defects," *My
     Science Academy,* January 14, 2013, myscienceacademy.org/2013/01/14/gmo-soy-repeatedly-linked-
     to-sterility-infant-mortality-birth-defects/, accessed March 28, 2019.

fourth group suffered a high mortality rate, and most of the adults were infertile or sterile. Two years earlier, Surov had coauthored a research paper for *Doklady Biological Sciences*, in which he reported the incidence of hair growing in recessed pouches in the mouths of hamsters, most prominently in those of third-generation hamsters fed GM soy. "This pathology," Suroy wrote, "may be exacerbated by elements of the food that are absent in natural food, such as genetically modified (GM) ingredients (GM soybean or maize meal) or contaminants (pesticides, mycotoxins, heavy metals, etc.)."[28]

COLLAPSING COWS AND OTHER SORROWS

The American Academy of Environmental Medicine (AAEM) issued the following statement: "Several animal studies indicate serious health risks associated with GM food." The organization maintained that GM foods cause multiple adverse health conditions including "infertility, immune problems, accelerated aging, faulty insulin regulation, and changes in major organs and the gastrointestinal system." The AAEM further asked physicians to tell their patients to avoid GM foods.[29]

In addition to the genetically modified feed, the Green Revolution produced Bovine Growth Hormone for dairy cattle, which would increase milk yields by up to 30 percent for a given herd. The cattle lost most of their own natural nutrients and developed severe udder infections (mastitis) and such brittleness that they could no longer stand. Still and all, the Food and Drug Administration ruled that meat from cows that had been injected with such hormones was fit for human consumption.[30]

28   Ibid.

29   Christina Sarich, "GM Foods Are Inherently Unsafe, Warns American Academy of Environmental Science," *Natural Society*, October 4, 2015, naturalsociety.com/american-academy-of-environmental-medicine-warns-gm-foods-are-inherently-unsafe/, accessed March 28, 2019.

30   "Recombinant Bovine Growth Hormone," American Cancer Society, September 10, 2014, https://www.cancer.org/cancer/cancer-causes/recombinant-bovine-growth-hormone.html, accessed March 28, 2019.

CONTRACEPTIVE CORN

In 2001, Epicyte, a small California biotech company, with funding from the U.S. Department of Agriculture, developed a genetically modified strain of corn that acts as a spermicide. "We have a hothouse filled with corn plants that make anti-sperm antibodies," Mitch Hein, the president of Epicyte, announced to the press. He explained that his firm had taken antibodies from women with a rare condition known as immune infertility, isolated the genes that regulated the manufacture of those infertility antibodies; and using genetic engineering techniques, had inserted the genes into ordinary corn seeds used to produce corn plants. In this manner, they produced a concealed contraceptive embedded in corn meant for human consumption. "Essentially," Hein said, "the antibodies are attracted to surface receptors on the sperm. They latch on and make each sperm so heavy it cannot move forward. It just shakes about as if it was doing the lambada." The Epicyte president went on to say that the corn represented a possible solution to world "over-population."[31]

How much of the sperm-killing corn has been planted throughout the world remains unknown. Epicyte was purchased by Biolex in 2004, and Biolex filed for bankruptcy in 2012.[32] But these facts have come to light:

In 2001, Epicyte, a small California biotech company, with funding from the U.S. Department of Agriculture, developed a genetically modified strain of corn that acts as a spermicide.

---

31   William Engdahl, quoted in C. Stone, "GMOs Don't Qualify as Food," *Rense.com,* June 6, 2011, https://rense.com/general94/gmos.htm, accessed March 28, 2019.

32   Chris Bagley, "Biolex Therapeutics Files for $38M Bankruptcy," *Triangle Business Journal,* July 6, 2012, https://www.bizjournals.com/triangle/blog/2012/07/biolex-therapeutics-files-for-38m.html, accessed March 28, 2019.

1. Sperm counts among the world's male population have recently declined by 59.3 percent, according to researchers from Hebrew University-Hadassah Braun School of Public Health and Community Medicine in Jerusalem.[33]

2. Genetically modified corn purportedly containing spermicides has been distributed throughout the Third World by the Rockefeller and Bill Gates Foundations.[34]

3. Birth rates, in the United States reached an all-time low in 2017, bringing the general fertility rate to 62.0 births per 1,000 women ages 15 to 44.[35]

4. Although GM corn is outlawed in Mexico, a team of researchers from the National Autonomous University of Mexico discovered that over 90 percent of the tortillas contained traces of genetic modification, along with 82 percent of other corn products, such as tostadas, flour, cereals, and snacks.[36]

5. Genetically modified corn is used to create high fructose corn syrup, flavors, starches, flours, proteins, sugars, and most of the other ingredients that make up processed foods. The U.S. government, starting with George H. W. Bush, has adopted the policy that genetically

33 "Men's Sperm Counts Are Dropping, and Scientists Don't Know Why," *Yahoo Lifestyle*. March 3, 2018, https://www.yahoo.com/lifestyle/men-apos-sperm-counts-dropping-074720787.html, accessed March 28, 2019.

34 F. William Engdahl, "Bill Gates and Neo-Eugenics: Vaccines to Reduce Population," *Prison Planet*, March 5, 2010, https://www.prisonplanet.com/bill-gates-and-neo-eugenics-vaccines-to-reduce-population.html, accessed March 28, 2019.

35 Ariana Eunjung Cha, "The U.S. Fertility Rate Just Hit a Historic Low: Why Demographers Are Freaking Out," *Washington Post*, June 30, 2017, https://www.washingtonpost.com/news/to-your-health/wp/2017/06/30/the-u-s-fertility-rate-just-hit-a-historic-low-why-some-demographers-are-freaking-out/?noredirect=on&utm_term=.668428be2492, accessed April 8, 2019.

36 "GM Corn Found in Over 90% of Tortillas in Mx," *Mexico News Daily*, September 20, 2017, https://mexiconewsdaily.com/news/gm-corn-found-in-over-90-of-tortillas-in-mx/, accessed April 8, 2019.

modified foods are the same as unmodified ones. The sterility corn is, therefore, the same as natural corn in the United States.[37]

BABY KILLING VACCINES

In the 1970s, the UN's World Health Organization, an organization that works in tandem with the Rockefeller Foundation,[38] launched a campaign to vaccinate millions of women throughout the Third World with tetanus and diphtheria vaccines, containing the female hormone called human chorionic gonadotrophin (hCG). The human body treats hCG as an intruder and creates antibodies against it. This process results in the sterilization of girls and miscarriages by pregnant women who receive the vaccination.[39]

As soon as the antifertility vaccines were developed, they were delivered to countries that had been specifically targeted in the U.S. government's 1974 National Security Memorandum 200 for population reduction. Tens of millions of women received shots for tetanus laced with hCG. In 1995, this development became the subject of a BBC documentary called "The Human Laboratory." Within the program, Sister Mary Pilar Verzosa, founder of ProLife Philippines, gave this testimony:

> The women would say why is it that the tetanus shots that we've been getting have had effects on us? Our fertility cycles are all fouled up, some of the women among us have had bleedings and miscarriages,

---

37   Kevin Hayden, "Children of the Corn: GMO Sterility and Spermicides," *Salem News*, May 31, 2011, www.truthistreason.net/children-of-the-corn-gmo-sterility-and-spermicides, accessed April 8, 2019.

38   A. E. Birn, "Backstage: The Relationship between the Rockefeller Foundation and the World Health Organization, Part I: 1940s–1960s, *Public Health* 128, no. 2, (February 2014), https://www.sciencedirect.com/science/article/pii/S003335061300396X, accessed February 8, 2019.

39   Daniel Taylor, "Vaccinate the World: Gates, Rockefeller Seek Global Population Reduction," *Global Research,* September 7, 2010, https://www.globalresearch.ca/vaccinate-the-world-gates-rockefeller-seek-global-population-reduction/20942, accessed April 8, 2019.

some have lost their babies at a very early stage. The symptoms could come soon after their tetanus vaccination—some the following day, others within a week's time. For those who were pregnant on their first three or four months the miscarriage was really frightening . . .

I began to suspect that here in the Philippines that's exactly what's happening. They have laced the tetanus toxoid vials with the Beta hCG . . .

Oh boy that was really something when this came out of my fax machine. Report on HCG concentration in vaccine vials. Three out of those four vials registered positive for HCG, so my suspicions are affirmed that here in our country they are not only giving plain tetanus toxoid vaccination to our women, they are also giving anti-fertility.[40]

Within the Philippines, more than 3.4 million women were vaccinated.[41] In Thailand, pregnant women are forced to receive vaccines, including the contraceptive tetanus shots, in order to get ID cards for their children.[42] In Kenya, more than 1.3 million women were injected, thinking that they were receiving protection from lockjaw. None of the women were told that they were being sterilized. All 27 Roman Catholic bishops issued this statement in condemnation of the World Health Organization/Rockefeller Foundation tetanus vaccination campaign:

Dear Kenyans,

Due to the direction the debate on the ongoing Tetanus Vaccine campaign in Kenya is taking, we, the Catholic Bishops, in fulfilling our prophetic role, wish to restate our position as follows:

---

40   Mary Pilar Verzosa, quoted in ibid.

41   James A. Miller, "Were Tetanus Vaccines Laced with Birth-Control Drugs?" *ThinkTwice* (Global Vaccine Institute), June/July 1995, www.thinktwice.com/birthcon.htm, accessed April 8, 2019.

42   Taylor, "Vaccinate the World."

1. *The Catholic Church is NOT opposed to regular vaccines administered in Kenya, both in our own Church health facilities and in public health institutions.*

2. *However, during the second phase of the Tetanus vaccination campaign in March 2014, that is sponsored by WHO/UNICEF, the Catholic Church questioned the secrecy of the exercise. We raised questions on whether the tetanus vaccine was linked to a population control program that has been reported in some countries, where a similar vaccine was laced with Beta-HCG hormone which causes infertility and multiple miscarriages in women.*

3. *On March 26, 2014 and October 13, 2014, we met the Cabinet Secretary in charge of health and the Director of Medical Services among others and raised our concerns about the Vaccine and agreed to jointly test the vaccine. However the ministry did not cooperate and the joint tests were not done.*

4. *The Catholic Church struggled and acquired several vials of the vaccine, which we sent to Four unrelated Government and private laboratories in Kenya and abroad.*

5. *We want to announce here, that all the tests showed that the vaccine used in Kenya in March and October 2014 was indeed laced with the Beta-HCG hormone.*

6. *On 13th of October 2014, the Catholic Church gave copies of the results to the cabinet secretary and the Director of Medical Services. The same was emailed to the Director of Medical Services on October 17, 2014.*

Based on the above grounds, We, the Catholic Bishops in Kenya, wish to State the following:

1. *That we are shocked at the level of dishonesty and casual manner in which such a serious issue is being handled by the Government.*

2. That a report presented to the Parliamentary Committee on Health November 4, 2014 by the Ministry of Health, claiming that the Government had tested the Vaccine and found it clean of Beta- HCG hormone, is false and a deliberate attempt to distort the truth and mislead 42 million Kenyans.

3. That we are dismayed by attempts to intimidate and blackmail medical professionals who have corroborated information about the vaccine, with threats of disciplinary action. We commend and support all professionals who have stood by the truth.

4. That we shall not waver in calling upon all Kenyans to avoid the tetanus vaccination campaign laced with Beta-HCG, because we are convinced that it is indeed a disguised population control program.[43]

Suspicion about the vaccinations extended to Mexico, where Comite Pro Vida de Mexico, a Roman Catholic lay organization, had samples of the tetanus vaccines tested, after discovering that the shots were only being administered to women of childbearing age. The test confirmed that the vaccines being distributed by the World Health Organization contained human Chorionic Gonadotrophin and that thousands of Mexican women had been involuntarily sterilized. [44]

BILL GATES ARRIVES

The vaccination program received substantial funding from Bill Gates, the founder of Microsoft, who established the Bill and Melinda Gates Foundation. Gates teamed up with the Rockefellers and their foundation to finally put an end to the problem of human beings reproducing like rats. In a speech to the TED2010 Conference in Long Beach, California,

43   Letter of the Kenyan Bishops to the people of Kenya, in Steven Mosher, "Who's Behind the UN Sterilization Campaign Lacing Tetanus Vaccine with Drug to Cause Miscarriages?" *LifeNews*, November 17, 2014, https://www.lifenews.com/2014/11/17/whos-behind-the-un-sterilization-campaign-lacing-tetanus-vaccine-with-drug-to-cause-miscarriages/, accessed April 8, 2019.

44   William Engdahl, "Bill Gates and Neo-Eugenics."

Gates said: "First we got population. The world today has 6.8
billion people. That's headed up
to about 9 billion. Now if we
do a really great job on new vaccines, health care, reproductive
health services, we lower that by
perhaps 10 or 15 percent."[45] In
addition to making this statement, Gates pledged to donate
$10 billion from his founda-
tion to ensure the vaccination
of every newborn child in the
developing world.[46]

Gates teamed up with the Rockefellers and their foundation to finally put an end to the problem of human beings reproducing like rats. "Bill Gates—the Nuclear Future" by Steve Jurvetson is licensed under CC BY 2.0

THE AFRICAN ALLIANCE

Prior to making this commitment, Gates had united with David
Rockefeller to finance a project called the Alliance for a Green Revolution
in Africa (AGRA), which became headed by former UN chief, Kofi
Annan. Accepting the role as AGRA's chief executive, Annan expressed
his "gratitude to the Rockefeller Foundation, the Bill & Melinda Gates
Foundation, and all others who support our African campaign." As soon
as it was established, the AGRA board became dominated by representatives from both the Gates' and Rockefeller foundations. Monsanto,
du Pont, Dow, Syngenta, and other major GMO agribusiness giants
became primary movers and shakers behind AGRA, using the nonprofit organization as a back door to spread their patented GMO seeds
across Africa under the label of "bio-technology." By 2012, South Africa

45   Engdahl, "Bill Gates Talks about 'Vaccines to Reduce Populations.'"

46   Ibid.

became the eighth largest GMO producer, with 4.9 million acres of genetically modified maize, soybeans, and cotton.[47]

THE DOOMSDAY SEED VAULT

On a frozen island 800 miles from the North Pole, inhabited only by polar bears, Gates' and Rockefeller's foundations established a so-called "doomsday seed vault," in which more than 865,000 seeds from crops throughout the world are stored within the frozen tundra. The vault, which is secured by four sets of locks, remains protected by a small army of Norwegian security guards.[48]

This project got underway in 2008 and is currently operated by an organization called the Global Crop Diversity Trust (GCDT). Headquartered in Rome, GCDT is chaired by Margaret Catley-Carlson, who, until 1998, served as president of the Population Council, the organization that had been set up by JDR III to advance the family's interest in eugenics.

THE FINAL SOLUTION

Perhaps the seed vault is located in such a remote location because of the very real threat of global biological warfare, the outbreak of which would constitute the "final solution" of the eugenics program that has been fostered by the Rockefeller family through the decades. The seeds contained in the vault could be planted in the wake of such warfare to create the "brave, new world" envisioned by Aldous Huxley, or they could be modified and planted to wipe out vast sectors of the world's population.

The latter is the scenario advanced by F. William Engdahl, the

47 Zachary Stieber, "GMOs, a Global Debate: South Africa, Top GMO-Producer in Africa," *Epoch Times*, October 13, 2013, https://www.theepochtimes.com/gmos-a-global-debate-south-africa-top-gmo-producer-in-africa_323635.html, accessed April 8, 2019.

48 Elizabeth Palermo, "'Doomsday' Seed Vault: The Science Behind World's Arctic Storage Cube," *LiveScience*, September 24, 2015, https://www.livescience.com/52291-first-withdrawal-doomsday-seed-vault.html, accessed April 8, 2019.

world's leading expert on GMOs.[49] Francis Boyle of the University of Illinois College of Law and the author of the Biological Weapons Anti-Terrorism Act maintains that the Pentagon is "now gearing up to fight and win biological warfare" without public knowledge and review."[50] Rutgers University biologist Richard Ebright says that over 300 scientific institutions and some 12,000 American scientists and workers have access to pathogens suitable for biological warfare.[51] MIT Professor Jonathan King writes that the "growing bio-terror programs represent a significant emerging danger to our own population." He adds, "While such programs are always called defensive, with biological weapons, defensive and offensive programs overlap almost completely."[52]

But there remains another scenario. The Global Community Organization advocates sharp reductions in global population:

> The Global Community proposes a tight global policy, benignly implemented, or it will be very nasty indeed. In practice, a human population of 10 to 12 billion would be too uncomfortably high and would add a high strain on world resources. What kind of world population would be reasonable? What goal should we aim at? A population should be small enough to be sustainable indefinitely and still allow plenty of leeway for ourselves and other lifeforms. It should also be large enough to allow the formation of healthy civilizations. We propose a world population of 500 million.[53]

---

49   F. William Engdahl, "'Doomsday Seed Vault' in the Arctic: The Science Behind World's Arctic Storage Cube," *Global Research*, January 24, 2015, https://www.globalresearch.ca/doomsday-seed-vault-in-the-arctic-2/23503, accessed April 8, 2019.

50   Francis Boyle, quoted in ibid.

51   Richard Ebright, quoted in ibid.

52   Jonathan King, quoted in ibid.

53   Global Community, "Our Overpopulated Planet," GlobalCommunityWebNet.com, Global Dialog, 2007, http://globalcommunitywebnet.com/globalcommunity/overpopulatedplanet.htm, accessed April 8, 2019.

Given that such elitists openly assert that 500 million is their preferred world population, and the current world population approaches 7.7 billion people,[54] 15 of every 16 humans would have to be eliminated. This view is shared by media mogul Ted Turner, who says that a 95 percent reduction of world population to 225–300 million would be "ideal."[55] One way of achieving this result would be the cultivation and dissemination of seeds that would produce poisonous crops.

THE WORLD'S OVERLORDS

Within the decade, the Rockefellers, with the help of their new friend Bill Gates, will soon have total dominion over the earth's food supply. Genetically modified seeds are now being planted on every continent throughout the world. They are produced by massive agrichemical plants, such as Monsanto, DuPont, and Dow Chemical, all of which have interlocking directorates with the Rockefeller Groups.[56] Monsanto now holds world patent rights for the terminator seeds that have been programmed to produce only one crop. Every year, farmers throughout the world have to return to Monsanto and its sister companies to purchase the seeds necessary to produce corn, wheat, rice, soybeans, and other major crops for the marketplace. Should the seed companies decide not to provide seeds to a whole nation of farmers, the country will be faced with want and starvation. Never in the history of mankind has such power been wielded over the food chain. The Rockefellers who masterminded the production of genetically modified organisms and the birth of agribusiness had become the masters of the new feudal system and of the human race.

---

54   Worldometers, "Current World Population," http://www.worldometers.info/world-population/, accessed April 8, 2019.

55   Ted Turner, quoted in Engdahl, "Bill Gates Talks about 'Vaccines to Reduce Population.'"

56   Allen, *The Rockefeller File*, p. 34.

29

KILLING THE CLIMATE

From space, the masters of infinity would have the power to control the earth's weather, to cause drought and flood, to change the tides and raise the levels of the sea, to divert the gulf stream and change temperate climates to frigid.

In essence, the Soviet Union has appraised control of space as a goal of such consequence that achievement of such control has been made a first aim of national policy. [In contrast], our decisions, more often than not, have been made within the framework of the Government's annual budget. Against this view, we now have on record the appraisal of leaders in the field of science, respected men of unquestioned competence, whose valuation of what control of outer space means renders irrelevant the bookkeeping concerns of fiscal officers.

It lays the predicate and foundation for the development of a weather satellite that will permit man to determine the world's cloud layer and ultimately to control the weather; and he who controls the weather will control the world.

—VICE PRESIDENT LYNDON BAINES JOHNSON AT SOUTHWEST TEXAS STATE
UNIVERSITY (1962)

BY THE SECOND DECADE of the 21st century, the money cartel, led by the Rockefellers, stood accused of committing such horrendous acts against humanity that the fictional crimes of Professor James Moriarty were frivolous in comparison. The cartel had succeeded in stealing much of the world's wealth by manipulating paper currencies, seizing natural resources, and committing acts of grand theft, including the flagrant confiscation of America's vast gold reserves. They had spread the plague of heroin to the four corners of the globe, creating over 15 million addicts.[1] They had engaged in nefarious plots and false flag attacks that resulted in global conflagrations, the rise and fall of nations, and massive migration. They had caused the deaths of billions of people by war, pogroms, infanticide, abortion, and experiments in eugenics. They had perpetuated false events and fake news to manipulate the thought processes of the vast majority of mankind through their control of the media and educational systems. They had fostered social injustice and repression in courts throughout the world by their management of legal and political systems. They had spread poverty and want throughout creation by destroying the rights of national sovereignty and by the perpetuation of free trade. They had poisoned hundreds of millions of people through their pharmaceutical companies and agribusinesses that produced genetically modified foods. They had enslaved all of humanity to their demands by the institution of such global organizations and agencies as the United Nations, the World Bank, the International Monetary Fund, the Trilateral Commission, and the Bilderberg Group. The final means by which they sought to achieve their motive was the creation of a global crisis concerning climate change and the propagation of their fearmongering fiction that the world was melting into a putrid pool of toxic waste because of man-made carbon emissions.

CLIMATE CONTROL

Weather can be controlled by man. The only conspiracy regarding geo-engineering, as science writer Rady Ananda points out, is "that governments and industries refuse to publicly admit what anyone with eyes can see."[2]

---

1   "The Global Heroin Market," World Drug Report 2010, https://www.unodc.org/documents/wdr/WDR_2010/1.2_The_global_heroin_market.pdf, accessed April 11, 2019.

2   Rady Ananda, "Atmospheric Geoengineering: Weather Manipulation, Contrails and Chemtrails," *Global Research,* July 30, 2010, https://sbeckow.wordpress.com/2010/08/06/rady-ananda-atmospheric-geoengineering-weather-manipulation-contrails-and-chemtrails/, accessed April 11, 2019.

Indeed, the technology of cloud seeding dates back to 1915 when rainmaker Charles Hatfield produced downpours that destroyed much of San Diego.[3]

Environmental modification techniques had been used by the U.S. military in clandestine operations for more than half a century. In 1955, mathematician, meteorologist, and nuclear scientist John von Neumann wrote an article concerning his work with the Weapons Systems Evaluation Group of the U.S. Department of Defense in which he said:

Environmental modification techniques had been used by the U.S. military in clandestine operations for more than half a century. In 1955, mathematician, meteorologist, and nuclear scientist John von Neumann wrote an article concerning his work with the Weapons Systems Evaluation Group of the U.S. Department of Defense.

Let us now consider a thoroughly "abnormal" industry and its potentialities—that is, an industry as yet without a place in any list of major activities: the control of weather or, to use a more ambitious but justified term, climate. One phase of this activity that has received a good deal of public attention is "rain making." The present technique assumes extensive rain clouds, and forces precipitation by applying small amounts of chemical agents. While it is not easy to evaluate the significance of the efforts made thus far, the evidence seems to indicate that the aim is an attainable one.

But weather control and climate control are really much broader than rain making. All major weather phenomena, as well as climate as such, are ultimately controlled by the solar energy that falls on the earth. To modify the amount of solar energy, is, of course, beyond

---

3   Ibid.

human power. But what really matters is not the amount that hits the earth, but the fraction retained by the earth, since that reflected back into space is no more useful than if it had never arrived. Now, the amount absorbed by the solid earth, the sea, or the atmosphere seems to be subject to delicate influences. True, none of these has so far been substantially controlled by human will, but there are strong indications of control possibilities.[4]

THE GEOENGINEERING THESIS

Von Neumann's theory about reflecting sunlight back into space like a volcanic eruption was the first significant mention of the solar radiation management geoengineering thesis (SRM).[5] When he wrote this article for *Fortune* magazine, Von Neumann was a member of the Atomic Energy Commission, the group responsible for the Manhattan Project and the first atomic bomb.[6] He was also a chief consultant to the CIA and the recipient of funding from the Rockefeller Foundation.[7] Von Neumann noted that "either a general cooling or a general heating would be a complex matter. Changes would affect the level of the seas, and hence the habitability of the continental coastal shelves; the evaporation of the seas, and hence general precipitation and glaciation levels; and so on. . . . But there is little doubt that one *could* carry out the necessary analyses needed to predict the results, intervene on any desired scale, and ultimately achieve rather fantastic results."[8]

---

4   John von Neumann, "Can We Survive Technology?" *Fortune,* June, 1955, activistpost.net/Can-We-Survive-Technology.pdf, accessed April 11, 2019.

5   Markab Algredi, "The Strongest Evidence That 'Climate Change' Is a Strategy to Justify Spraying the Skies," *Nexus Newsfeed,* January 22, 2018, https://nexusnewsfeed.com/article/climate-ecology/the-strongest-evidence-that-climate-change-is-a-strategy-to-justify-spraying-the-skies/, accessed April 11, 2019.

6   Ibid.

7   Norman Macrae, *John Von Neumann: The Scientific Genius Who Pioneered the Modern Computer, Game Theory, Nuclear Deterrence, and Much More* (New York: Pantheon Books, 1992), pp. 350–51.

8   John Von Neumann, quoted in William H. Davenport and Daniel M. Rosenthal, *Engineering: Its Role and Function in Human Society* (Amsterdam: The Netherlands, Elsevier, 2016), p. 266.

THE SECRET CIA REPORT

In 1960, a CIA classified report entitled "The Need for a Climate Control Study Program" reads as follows:

> Much of the well justified skepticism about the feasibility of climate control has centered on the available human means for exercising necessary control. While there are many conceivable methods for the control of climate, all of them involve the expenditure of energy in one form or another. Even the vulnerable instabilities of the atmosphere which one would hope to uncover through a systematic program of climate control studies, the so-called "trigger mechanisms," will probably require access to energy sources of immense magnitude for proper exploitation. In this atomic age, we now have available truly immense potential sources of power, and it is highly likely that our lifetime will see the harnessing of hydrogen fusion power, which will provide almost limitless sources of energy. Thus it is no longer possible to relegate considerations of climate control to the fantasies of science fiction on this account. It has now become necessary for us to recognize the realities and potentialities of modern science for what they are and what they can mean for the possibilities of climate control. . . .
>
> The impact of the successful achievement of methods for the control of climate upon all types of human activities confounds the imagination. Slight amelioration of adverse precipitation or temperature regimes could result in the reclamation of vast territories for agricultural and many other types of human activities. Desert areas which cover a large fraction of the earth's surface are known in many cases to require only slight changes in moisture regimes to make them suitable for large scale agricultural production. Small changes in circulation regimes could bring about the moderation of severe temperature climates to yield additional areas suitable for human habitation. Such changes in circulation regimes can also affect the normal paths of destructive storms like hurricanes, such that their destructive energies could be dissipated in regions far removed from major human activities. Changes in atmospheric circulation regimes would have

marked effects upon oceanic circulations with consequent changes in the abundance and location of fertile fishing grounds. Moderate changes in climatic characteristics will have serious repercussions for all aspects of industrial activity.

Militarily, a climatic control capability raises the possibility of a totally new type of warfare. This type of warfare may be termed "Geophysical Warfare" in which our ability to control the weather environment can be used as a weapon. This geophysical weapon will be unique in character in that it can be used in both hot and cold struggles. It can be used to affect an enemy adversely or benefit a friend. As a function of the nature of the control capability, the use of such a weapon could be a determining factor in the success of national military operations.

As a hot war weapon it would be best to have strong control capability for specific areas and specific periods of time. Since we are talking about intermediate and long period climate control, this would imply a conflict of considerable duration. Specific military consequences of such a control capability would be in the potential for destruction of an enemy's food production capability thereby weakening his total military power, and also in the derangements of transportation systems and other industrial activities which might result from a marked change in climatic conditions.

As a cold war tool, the capability of climate control would place in the hands of this Government a tool for ameliorating the weather conditions in friendly and uncommitted nations as a means of strengthening bonds with this country. Conversely as a cold war weapon, a climate control capability provides for a unique surreptitious means for weakening a potential enemy so that he does not have the capability to wage a hot war.[9]

---

9   "Memorandum for: General Charles B. Cabell. Subject: Climate Control," November 22, 1960, declassified CIA document, https://www.cia.gov/library/readingroom/docs/CIA-RDP78-03425A002100020014-2.pdf, accessed April 11, 2019.

THE ROCKEFELLER CONNECTION

This internal report was prepared not by CIA technicians but rather scientists employed by the Travelers Weather Research Center, a branch of the Travelers Insurance Company. This revelation raises the question: Why was such a CIA top secret report about climate change written by one of America's insurance companies?[10] The answer resides in the fact that the Travelers Weather Research Company was headed by J. Doyle Dewitt, president of the Travelers Insurance Company and a director of the Chase Manhattan Bank.[11]

OPERATION POPEYE

By 1966, President Lyndon Baines Johnson's prediction that he who controls the weather will control the fate of mankind had come to fruition.[12] Specially configured WC-130 aircraft equipped with dry ice crushers and dispensers were deployed to alter the climate in Vietnam. On a typical mission, such an aircraft would fly a seeding pattern consisting of between five and 30 parallel lines, each five to six miles long and 0.5 to 1.5 miles apart. This pattern would be flown above the fog at a distance between 45 and 60 minutes upwind of the area where clearing was desired, with the machine generally dispensing 15 pounds of crushed dry ice per minute. Clouds of rain then would drift over the desired area at the desired time to extend the monsoon season and to cripple the Viet Cong. This undertaking became known as Operation Popeye. It was approved by the Joint Chiefs of Staff on September 1, 1966, and implemented by President Johnson in his Executive Order

---

10 VT Editors, "CIA 1960: Memorandum for Climate Control," *Veterans Today*, August 11, 2018, https://www.veteranstoday.com/2018/08/11/cia-1960-memorandum-for-climate-control/, accessed April 11, 2019.

11 "J. Doyle Dewitt, 70; Led Insurance Firm," *New York Times,* December 28, 1972, https://www. nytimes.com/1972/12/28/archives/j-doyle-dewitt-70-led-insurance-firm.html, accessed April 11, 2019.

12 Lyndon Baines Johnson, Graduation Address, Southwest Texas State University, 1962, https:// www.texasarchive.org/library/index.php/2010_00003, accessed April 11, 2019.

of September 17, 1966. Monsoon season over Laos was subsequently extended as a means of denying the enemy vehicular lines of communication. Intelligence sources had verified a significant movement of Viet Cong supplies and personnel through the Se Kong watershed and the adjoining mountainous areas. After three weeks of steady downpours, the Viet Cong supply trucks and other vehicles became completely immobilized by the poor road conditions caused by inclement weather.

"HOW TO WRECK THE ENVIRONMENT"

In the wake of the success of the first phase of Operation Popeye, other climate change techniques were developed by the Naval Ordnance Test Station in China Lake, California, which came to include the movement of rain clouds over the ocean to reduce precipitation on U.S. troops and friendly forces, dissipation of clouds by over-seeding to improve visibility of enemy territory, and other applications based on tactical operations. These activities continued throughout the course of the Vietnam War. In 1971, Popeye may have been a major contributor to the catastrophic 1971 floods in North Vietnam, which inundated over 10 percent of the country.[13] By this time, the covert program to control the climate remained under the complete control of Henry Kissinger, the Rockefellers' closest lackey.[14]

With insider knowledge, geophysicist Gordon J. F. MacDonald, a member of President Johnson's Science Advisory Committee, wrote "How to Wreck the Environment," an essay that contained the following observation: "The key to geophysical warfare is the identification of the environmental instabilities to which the addition of a small amount of energy would release vastly greater amounts of energy." MacDonald, a close Kissinger associate and a prominent member of the Council

---

13   "The Limits of Inside Pressure: The US Congress Role in ENMOD," *Archives Today*, January 20, 2014, archive.is/9rxM3, accessed April 11, 2019.

14   New York Times News Service, "Rainmaking Used as Weapon in SE Asia," *Daytona Beach Sunday News Journal*, May 19, 1974.

on Foreign Relations, predicted that climate modification, earthquake and tsunami generation, and mass behavior control via electromagnetic manipulation of the ionosphere would be developed by the 21st century.[15]

POPEYE BECOMES PUBLIC

When the weather modification operations initiated by Operation Popeye were uncovered by the press in 1972, they came to an immediate end. Seymour Hirsh now wrote an investigative report for the *New York Times* entitled "Rainmaking Is Used as Weapon by U.S." In the report, Hirsh wrote:

> The United States has been secretly seeding clouds over North Vietnam, Laos and South Vietnam to increase and control the rainfall for military purposes.
>
> Government sources, both civilian and military, said during an extensive series of interviews that the Air Force cloud seeding program has been aimed most recently at hindering movement of North Vietnamese troops and equipment and suppressing enemy antiaircraft missile fire.
>
> The disclosure confirmed growing speculation in Congressional and scientific circles about the use of weather modification in Southeast Asia. Despite years of experiments with rainmaking in the United States and elsewhere, scientists are not sure they understand its long-term effect on the ecology of a region.[16]

15   Gordon J. F. MacDonald, quoted in Rady Ananda, "Planetary Weapons and Military Weather Modification: Chemtrails, Atmospheric Geoengineering and Environmental Warfare," *Global Research,* October 19, 2017, https://www.globalresearch.ca/military-weather-modification-chemtrails-atmospheric-geoengineering-and-environmental-warfare/5356630, accessed April 12, 2019.

16   Seymour Hirsch, "Rainmaking Is Used as Weapon by U.S.," *New York Times,* July 2, 1972, https://www.nytimes.com/1972/07/03/archives/rainmaking-is-used-as-weapon-by-us-cloudseeding-in-indochina-is.html, accessed April 12, 2019.

Responding to this news, Gilbert Gude, a Congressman from Maryland, provided the following testimony before the U.S. Senate Subcommittee on Oceans and the International Environment on July 27, 1972:

> Why should we be so alarmed about a technique that it is not nearly as lethal as other forms of warfare? There are several reasons. First, there are distinct command and control problems associated with geophysical warfare and weather modification in particular. We simply do not have the effective short or long term control over the climates of the world. We can create disturbances, but as civilian experiments have shown, control is not very precise. In a military environment, control over the results of weather experimentation is even more uncertain.
>
> The command problem is not less acute. Since the technology to date does not involve great expense or sophisticated equipment, it is not difficult to imagine the use of weather modification by many different military subunits. In fact, there have been reports that we have trained the South Vietnamese to use weather modification. There are no double-key safe mechanism here, no exclusive possession as with nuclear weapons.
>
> We must also consider that the use of weather modification is potentially indiscriminate. Unlike other weapons, the winds and seas are not so directable that we can discriminate between one target and another. By their nature, they are areawide weapons. We cannot flood only military targets or cause droughts in areas producing only military rations. The technology will be used against people regardless of their uniform or occupation. Weather modification will inevitably strike civilians harder than nearby military objectives. Will rain along the Ho Chi Minh Trail succeed where years of bombing has not? And what will it exact from agrarian societies along its path, both friend and foe?
>
> The issues of command and control, and the discrimination highlight another disturbing characteristic of weather modification, the

difficulty of detection. Unlike other weapons, it may be possible to initiate military weather modification projects without being detected. In other words, the military results may not be visibly tied to the initiating party. This raises the possibility of clandestine use of geophysical warfare where a country does not know if it has been attacked. The uncertainty of this situation, the fear of not knowing how another country might be altering your climate is highly destabilizing.[17]

The fact that weather could be controlled escaped the attention of environmental activists, funded by the Rockefellers, who planned the first Earth Day.

EARTH DAY

On April 22, 1970, Earth Day, inaugurated by a massive media blitz, was held throughout the United States with teach-ins, demonstrations, and rock concerts. In accordance with the event, Governor Nelson Rockefeller of New York established a state Environment Department. Governor William T. Cahill of New Jersey signed a bill creating an Environmental Protection Department. Lieutenant Governor Paul Simon of Illinois proposed the creation of an environmental institute at one of his state universities.[18] An estimated 20 million people took part in the activities. So many politicians took part in the festivities that the United States Congress shut down.[19]

It was a triumph for the Rockefellers who planned, promoted, and funded the event, especially since they were keenly aware that environmental issues were closely connected to eugenics.

Earth Day participants were given copies of the *Environmental Handbook*. In his introduction to this work, Garrett De Bell said that the time of the earth's demise was so imminent that the contributing

---

17 Congressman Gilbert Gude, quoted in "The Limits of Inside Pressure."

18 Richard Harwood, "Earth Day Stirs the Nation," *Washington Post*, April 23, 1970, college.cengage. com/history/primary_sources/us/earthday_1970.htm, accessed April 12, 2019.

19 Ibid.

writers to the handbook were given a 30-day deadline. De Bell wrote: "We thought that the one-month deadline for the writing was impossible, that we could easily spend a year on it. But a year is about one-fifth of the time we have left if we are going to preserve any kind of quality in our world."[20] De Bell went on to say that, after halting population growth, "we must work toward reducing the current three and a half billion people to something less than one billion people . . . . This number, perhaps, could be supported at a standard of living roughly similar to that of countries such as Norway and the Netherlands at the present time."[21]

THE END OF DAYLIGHT

The handbook contained this vision of future life on planet Earth by Paul Ehrlich, author of *The Population Bomb*: "By September 1979, all important animal life in the sea was extinct. Large areas of coastline had to be evacuated, as windrows of dead fish created a monumental stench."[22] The cause of the problem, Ehrlich maintained was "too many cars, too many factories, too much detergent, too much pesticide, multiplying contrails, inadequate sewage treatment plants, too little water, too much carbon dioxide—all can be traced easily to too many people."[23]

University of California professor Kenneth E. F. Watt offered the following information on an Earth Day gathering at Swarthmore College: "If present trends continue, the world will be about four degrees colder for the global mean temperature in 1990, but eleven degrees colder in the year 2000. This is about twice what it would take to put us into an ice age." Watt explained that this problem of dropping temperatures is being caused by "the constantly increasing mass of

20 Garrett De Bell, quoted in Gary Benoit, "'Earth Day'—the Greatest Sham on Earth," *New American*, April 21, 2016, https://www.thenewamerican.com/tech/environment/item/23011-earth-day-the-greatest-sham-on-earth, accessed April 12, 2019.

21 Ibid.

22 Paul Ehrich, quoted in ibid.

23 Ibid.

smog-produced clouds all over the world."[24] Watt further predicted the world would run out of oil by the year 2000 and that humans would emit so much nitrogen that sunlight would actually be filtered out of the atmosphere.[25]

LIBERTY OR DEATH

Norman Cousins, CFR stalwart and *Saturday Review* editor, now called for the creation of a new world government that could impose international law in order to prevent Mother Earth from dying. He wrote: "Humanity needs a world order. The fully sovereign nation is incapable of dealing with the poisoning of the environment." He argued that "management of the planet . . . requires world government."[26]

Echoing this call for world government, John Fischer, a contributing editor of *Harper's* magazine, penned an article for the *Handbook* in which he dismissed the U.S. Constitution as a "political artifact" and proposed that all Americans be subjected to a comprehensive environmental education, which he called "Survival U." At Survival U, Fischer wrote that Americans would be required to answer the following questions: "Are nation-states actually feasible now that they have power to destroy each other in a single afternoon? What price would most people be willing to pay for a more durable kind of human organization—more taxes, giving up national flags, perhaps the sacrifice of some of our hard-won liberties?"[27] The environmentalists were championing the cause of a one-world government that consumed the lives of John D. Rockefeller Jr. and his four sons.

---

24   Kenneth E. F. Watt, quoted in ibid.

25   Kenneth Watt, quoted in Michael Bastasch, "Flashback 1970: Earth Day Prof. Predicted a Super Ice Age Would Engulf the World," *Daily Caller*, April 22, 2015, https://dailycaller.com/2015/04/22/flashback-1970-earth-day-prof-predicted-a-super-ice-age-would-engulf-the-world/, accessed April 12, 2019.

26   Norman Cousins, quoted in Benoit, "'Earth Day'—the Greatest Sham on Earth."

27   John Fischer, quoted in ibid.

THE ENVIRONMENTAL PROTECTION AGENCY

On July 9, 1970, less than three months after Earth Day, President Richard M. Nixon, under the guidance of his National Security Advisor, Henry Kissinger, brought the Environmental Protection Agency (EPA) into being by executive order. This massive government agency was staffed by 9,000 government workers, who wielded absolute power to eliminate the causes of pollution, including the emissions from the country's manufacturing plants. In accordance with the dictates of the EPA, America's automobile manufacturers were compelled to attach gas-eating gadgets to their cars and trucks. The net result of these measures was a 20 percent decline in mileage and a windfall of profits for the Rockefeller oil companies. Throughout the United States, 300,000 additional gallons of gas were being consumed because of the gadgets.[28] In addition, the EPA demanded the elimination of lead from gasoline, a measure that reduced the efficacy of new vehicles by an additional 20 percent.[29]

"WHO NEEDS MORE GAS?"

Coupled with the creation of the EPA and the new measures to eliminate carbon emissions from cars and trucks came the manufactured news that the earth was running out of oil and other fossil fuels. This myth was perpetuated by leading journalists under Rockefeller control, including prominent CFR member James Reston of the *New York Times*. In a 1973 article entitled "Who Needs More Gas?," Reston wrote:

> The craziest notion that has hit this country in a long while—and we've had quite a few nutty notions lately—is that shortages of gas, beef and a lot of other things are bad for the American people.
>
> What America really needs is more shortages. It is not our shortages but our surpluses that are hurting us. . . .

---

28   Gary Allen, *The Rockefeller File* (Seal Beach, California: '76 Press, 1976), p. 144.

29   Ibid.

We need to cut down, slow up, stay home, run around the block, eat vegetable soup, call up old friends and read a book once in a while. Americans have always been able to handle austerity and even adversity. Prosperity's what's been doing us in.

For most of this century, we have been told by our leaders that it was our right and destiny to have two cars and a boat for Sundays. The more we consumed, the more the nation would prosper. The Voice of America was the voice of the hawker, the prevalent melody of America was the singing commercial. Buy more, consume more, get more things, even if you can't afford them. The sky's the limit, and happiness is acquisitiveness, getting more things. . . .

Nobody suggested that the nation's resources were finite or that our power was limited. We thought money tells and the big guns win. The biggest is the best. We are No. 1. But lately, it appears that No. 1 is running out of gas, that the big money and the big guns didn't win in Vietnam or in the Middle East, and that we might be a little cold here and there in America this winter.[30]

The Zero Population Growth, expounded by the Rockefellers was now combined with the notion of Zero Economic Growth. With this issuance of Newspeak, Americans were now assured that they would be better off deprived of their possessions. It was a new bottle of Rockefeller snake oil, and the public drank it.

THE FIRST INTERNATIONAL CONFERENCE

Earth Day succeeded in convincing world leaders that they must unite in an effort to save the world from carbon emissions and unbridled childbirth. With funding from the Rockefeller dynasty, the United Nations organized the first International Conference on the Human Environment. The event was held in Stockholm, Sweden, from June 5

---

30 James Reston, "Who Needs More Gas?" *New York Times,* November 11, 1973, https://www.nytimes.com/1973/11/11/archives/who-needs-more-gas-washington.html, accessed April 12, 2019.

to June 16, 1972. It was attended by 1,200 official delegates from 11 countries. Maurice Strong, a trustee of the Rockefeller Foundation and the chairman of the conference, commissioned the publication of a paper entitled "Only the Earth" to serve as the basis of the summit. The text promoted the global management of natural resources through the United Nations Environmental Program (UNEP), a new global bureaucracy, which named Strong as its first director.[31]

UNEP began to churn out news release after news release about the pollution of the air by carbon emissions and of water by industrial waste. It manufactured studies to show that the planet's oil reserves were being depleted and perpetuated by the hoax of a world shrouded in carbon flumes that could not be penetrated by the rays of the sun.

NEWS FROM WALTER CRONKITE

On September 11, 1972, CBS news anchorman Walter Cronkite warned of global cooling and ended his report with these words of comfort: "But then there is some good news, that while the weather may be just a little colder in the immediate years to come, the full extent of the new ice age won't be reached for 10,000 years. And if you can stand any more good news, even then it won't be as bad as the last ice age 60,000 years ago. Then New York, Cincinnati, St. Louis, were under 5,000 feet of ice. Presumably no traffic moved and school was let out for the day. And that's the way it is, Monday September 11, 1972."[32] Cronkite neglected to say that climate control had become a matter of human engineering and that such control was now wielded by Kissinger and the CIA.

ANOTHER ICE AGE

In 1974, the editors of *Time* ran a story called "Another Ice Age" in which they wrote: "When meteorologists take an average of temperatures

---

31   James Corbett, "How & Why Big Oil Conquered the World," *The Corbett Report,* October 6, 2017, https://www.corbettreport.com/bigoil/, accessed April 12, 2019.

32   Walter Cronkite, quoted in Jeff Poor, "Flashback: In 1972, Cronkite Warned of 'New Ice Age,'" *Breitbart,* March 5, 2015, https://www.breitbart.com/clips/2015/03/05/flashback-in-1972-cronkite-warned-of-new-ice-age/, accessed April 12, 2019.

around the globe, they find that the atmosphere has been growing gradually cooler for the past three decades. The trend shows no indication of reversing. Climatological Cassandras are becoming increasingly apprehensive, for the weather aberrations they are studying may be the harbinger of another ice age."[33] Peter Gwynne of *Newsweek* in a 1975 article entitled "The Cooling World" said: "Meteorologists disagree about the cause and extent of the cooling trend. . . . But they are almost unanimous in the view that the trend will reduce agricultural productivity for the rest of the century."[34]

A CALL FOR AUTHORITATIVE CONTROL

In an article that appeared in the February 1976 *Reader's Digest*, Laurance Rockefeller Jr., president of the American Conservation Association, warned that the climate change was becoming so intense that people throughout the planet were obliged to adopt "a simpler lifestyle." He warned that if individuals persisted in their present pattern of consuming resources, "authoritative controls" would have to be imposed on all of mankind.[35]

In 1977, the Rockefeller Brothers Fund sponsored a task force report entitled *The Unfinished Agenda: The Citizen's Policy Guide to Environmental Issues*. The report described itself as a "consensus document" that reflected the "collective thinking of the participating environmental leaders . . . about a world transition from abundance to scarcity, a transition that is already well underway." It called for the implementation of the following measures:

33 "Another Ice Age?" *Time*, April 24, 1974, https://nationalcenter.org/Time-Ice-Age-06-24-1974-Sm.jpg, accessed April 12, 2019.

34 Peter Gwynne, "The Cooling World," *Newsweek*, April 28, 1975, www.denisdutton.com/newsweek_coolingworld.pdf, accessed April 12, 2019.

35 Laurance Rockefeller Jr., quoted in Benoit, "'Earth Day—the Greatest Sham on Earth.'"

1. "Continuation and increased funding of family planning programs."

2. "[A] progressively increasing gasoline tax, the proceeds of which should be used to begin reducing the ill effects of automobiles."

3. "An escalating tax on natural gas consumption. . . . A similar tax should be applied to all fossil fuels."[36]

PHILANTHROPY AND PROPAGANDA

The Rockefellers, through their philanthropies, now proceeded to provide massive funding for agencies involved in the environmental movement, including the Environmental Law Institute, the World Resources Institute, the NRDC (Natural Resources Defense Council), the American Environment, the Conservation Fund, the American Conservation Association, the National Audubon Society, the Environment Policy Institute, and Friends of the Earth Foundation. Since such organizations came to depend upon the Rockefeller foundations and funds to maintain their staff and operations, they came under the direct control of the Rockefeller money cartel, which proceeded to invest heavily in green energy. The Sierra Club, one of the principal recipients of the Rockefeller largesse, became the most effective organization in promoting Zero Economic Growth by blocking the construction of refineries, airports, shopping centers, apartment buildings, and every other form of development. Hundreds of thousands of workers in the United States lost their jobs because of this one agency.[37] The Rockefeller fortune now flowed from the fossil fuel companies that they created into green energy companies and mutual funds with an "environmental" focus. By 2018, the family had divested itself of its oil interests. Such a move was prudent since the companies the Rockefellers had

---

36   Ibid.

37   Allen, *The Rockefeller File*, pp. 146–47.

created were now faced with increased regulatory and litigation risk.[38]

Through their highly complex integration of hedge funds, inter-locking board positions, and nonprofit organizations, the Rockefellers were able to steer public policy on green energy issues, to obtain fore-knowledge of emerging markets, and to gain access to the developing world's natural resources.[39]

GREASING THE WHEELS

The Rockefellers established an intermediary nonprofit (501[c][3]) organization—the Energy Foundation—to conceal their donor intent and to push their climate agenda at both the state and federal levels of government. In accordance with IRS regulations, wealthy individuals can fund a 501(c)(3) organization (such as the Energy Foundation), and direct it to transfer large sums of money to 501(c)(4) organizations, which can legally fund political campaigns and lobby for public policy. With this loophole, the Rockefellers shelled out tens of millions of dollars to the Energy Foundation, wrote off their expenditures as charitable contributions, and channeled the money into the campaign coffers of politicians who were willing to do their bidding.[40]

The wheels of academia were also greased. Since universities and colleges throughout the country also relied on Rockefeller funding, environmental courses became mandatory, and students became indoctrinated into believing that they must take an active part in combating capitalism, since the American form of economies was transforming the globe into a fetid cesspool.

---

38 Philip van Doorn, "How to Invest Like a Modern-Day Rockefeller," *Market Watch*, September 23, 2014, https://www.marketwatch.com/story/how-to-invest-like-a-modern-day-rockefeller-2014-09-23, accessed April 12, 2019.

39 "The Rockefeller Way: The Family's Covert 'Climate Change' Plan," Energy & Environmental Legal Institute, December 2016, https://eelegal.org/wp-content/uploads/2016/12/Rockefeller-Way-Report-Final.pdf, accessed April 12, 2019.

40 Allen, *The Rockefeller File*, pp. 146–47.

George Soros, a protégé of the Rothschilds, joined the Rockefellers in funding the green energy scam. Through his Open Societies Foundations, Soros funneled billions of dollars to major green activist foundations such as the Aspen Institute, Defenders of Wildlife, Earthjustice, Green for All, the New America Foundation, Presidential Climate Action Project, the Tides Foundation, ClimateWorks Foundation, the Global Green Grants Fund, and the Natural Resources Defense Council.[41]

THE GEORGIA GUIDESTONES

In 1979, the environmental mania resulted in the erection of a granite monument in Elbert County, Georgia, that stands on a hilltop 750 feet above sea level. Designed to resemble Stonehenge, the "Georgia Guidestones" are over 19 feet tall and weigh 237,746 pounds. Their construction was commissioned by a mysterious man who assumed the pseudonym of Robert C. Christian. Christian shelled out the money for the monument—estimated at $250,000—to the Elberton Granite Finishing Company on behalf of "a small group of loyal Americans." Christian ordered the company to inscribe ten commandments on the four pillars, in eight different languages: English, Spanish, Swahili, Hindi, Hebrew, Arabic, traditional Chinese, and Russian. The commandments were as follows:

1. Maintain humanity under 500,000,000 in perpetual balance with nature.

2. Guide reproduction wisely—improving fitness and diversity.

3. Unite humanity with a living new language.

4. Rule passion—faith—tradition—and all things with tempered reason.

5. Protect people and nations with fair laws and just courts.

---

41   "The Rockefeller Way."

6. Let all nations rule internally resolving external disputes in a world court.

7. Avoid petty laws and useless officials.

8. Balance personal rights with social duties.

9. Prize truth—beauty—love—seeking harmony with the infinite.

10. Be not a cancer on the earth—Leave room for nature.[42]

WORLD WILDERNESS CONGRESS

In 1987, another international summit, called the World Wilderness Congress, was con-

In 1979, the environmental mania resulted in the erection of a granite monument in Elbert County, Georgia, that stands on a hilltop 750 feet above sea level. Designed to resemble Stonehenge, the "Georgia Guidestones" are over nineteen feet tall and weigh 237,746 pounds. "Georgia Guidestones" by Gr8full1 is licensed under CC BY-SA 4.0

vened by the Rockefellers in Denver, Colorado. It brought together David Rockefeller, Edmund de Rothschild, and a host of other representatives of the money cartel for the purpose of addressing the growing "environmental crisis." The discussion centered on the problem of the people multiplying like rats. At the summit, David Lang, a Canadian banker, spoke of the need of all the representatives at the summit to adopt an "elitist" attitude. Lang said: "I suggest therefore that this be sold not through a democratic process. That would take too long and devour far too much of the funds to educate the cannon fodder,

---

42 "The Georgia Guidestones Mystery," *The Secret Truth About . . .* , n.d., https://thesecrettruthabout. com/the-georgia-guidestones-mystery/, accessed April 12, 2019.

unfortunately, that populates the earth. We have to take almost an elitist program, [so] that we can see beyond our swollen bellies, and look to the future in time frames and in results which are not easily understood, or which can be, with intellectual honesty, be reduced down to some kind of simplistic definition."[43]

The gathering resulted in the formation of "wilderness areas," vast expanses of land from which the public was excluded. These areas were patrolled by the International Union for the Conservation of Nature, a branch of the United Nations Educational, Scientific and Cultural Organization (UNESCO). The Rockefeller Brothers Fund financed these ventures, and Stephen Rockefeller, Nelson's son, became integrally involved with their operations.[44]

The Congress also created the World Conservation Bank, a supranational organization for the development of projects for ecological and environmental protection. In establishing this bank, Edmond de Rothschild said: "The international bank must know no frontiers, no boundaries."[45] All of creation was now to be subjected to its demands. What the Rothschilds and the Rockefellers once sought to accomplish by a network of central banks was now being advanced by the World Conservation Bank and the money cartel's demand for global legislation to protect the earth's ecosystem.

SLEIGHT OF HAND

In the wake of the conference, a significant development occurred. By a sleight of hand that remained unnoticed by the mainstream media, the notion of global cooling was replaced with global warming and the news that Mother Earth soon would become a vast, uninhabitable desert. The first mention of the new theory came on June 23, 1988, when James E. Hansen of the National Aeronautics and Space Administration

---

David Lang, quoted in Corbett, "How & Why Big Oil Conquered the World."

44 "Conservation and the Environment," Rockefeller Brothers Fund, 2019, https://www.rbf.org/75/essay-environmental-grantmaking, accessed April 12, 2019.

45 Edmond de Rothschild, quoted in Corbett, "How & Why Big Oil Conquered the World."

told a Congressional committee that it was 99 percent certain that the planet was warming due to the buildup of carbon dioxide and other artificial gases in the atmosphere. Hansen said there was no "magic number" that showed when the greenhouse effect was actually starting to cause changes in climate and weather. But he added, "It is time to stop waffling so much and say that the evidence is pretty strong that the greenhouse effect is here."[46] In 1971, this same esteemed scientist said that the world would fall into a deep freeze within 50 years.[47] His change of mind was precipitated by the fact that 1987 was the warmest year on record.

The weather alarmists performed the about-face without a blush of embarrassment or hint of apology. They recited the new scenario without reference to their statements in the past. In turn, the environmental activists expressed neither surprise nor alarm and proceeded to act as though there was little difference between fire and ice.

46   Philip Shabecoff, "Global Warming Has Begun, Expert Tells Senate," *New York Times*, June 24, 1988, https://www.nytimes.com/1988/06/24/us/global-warming-has-begun-expert-tells-senate.html, accessed April 12, 2019.

47   Noel Sheppard, "NASA Scientists Predicted a New Ice Age in 1971," *MRC Newsbusters*, September 19, 2007, https://www.newsbusters.org/blogs/nb/noel-sheppard/2007/09/19/nasa-scientists-predicted-new-ice-age-1971, accessed April 12, 2019.

30

KILLING RATIONAL THOUGHT

Despite efforts to poison public discourse the world agreed to a plan, in 2015, which might give humanity a fighting chance to avoid catastrophic climate change.

To undo this progress now, while time is running out and physics is managing the clock, is to risk sentencing countless people to death via extreme weather, depleted resources, and associated political instability. We know the human consequences of our policies and the casual acceptance of those consequences incriminate us morally. . . .

The climate policies of the Trump administration, backed by many Republican leaders, are rooted in culpable ignorance and transparent corruption. And they place us all at risk on a scale that previous crimes against humanity never have.

Civility and fair mindedness do not require hospitality to policies that hasten the destruction of a livable planet. We don't depend on hindsight to recognize the moral gravity of our current situation.

We will search in vain for a better reason to depose elected officials. Every legal resource to remove such leaders is justified. We can't pretend we don't know the nature of what is unfolding. We are witnessing a crime against humanity—and the potential prelude to future genocide.

We are the bystanders who must choose to intervene or be defined by our failure.

—LAWRENCE TORCELLO, ASSISTANT PROFESSOR OF PHILOSOPHY, ROCHESTER INSTITUTE OF TECHNOLOGY, APRIL 29, 2017

IN 1992, the first Earth Summit was convened in Rio de Janeiro. On the eve of the event, a midnight-to-dawn homage to the "Female Planet" was held on Leme Beach. After dancing all night, the worshipers followed a Brazilian high priestess to the water's edge, where they offered flowers and fruits to the Voodoo mother goddess, "Iemanje, mae orixa, mother of the powers, queen of the seas," and then invoked the blessings of the sea goddess upon the summit's deliberations. At the culmination of the pseudo-religious service, a group calling itself the "Sacred Drums of the Earth" performed a ceremony by which they would "maintain a continuous heartbeat near the official site of the Earth Summit, as part of a ritual for the healing of our Earth to be felt by those who are deciding Earth's fate."[1]

The summit attracted representatives from 166 countries, 130 heads of state, and 150,000 executives of nongovernmental organizations. The new religion of Mother Earth permeated the proceedings. In his opening address, Maurice Strong directed the assembly to the Earth Charter and said: "The changes in behavior and direction called for here must be rooted in our deepest spiritual, moral, and ethical values. The [ecological] crisis transcends all national, religious, cultural, social, political and economic boundaries. . . . The responsibility of each human being today is to choose between the force of darkness and the force of light. We must therefore transform our attitudes and values, and adopt a renewed respect for the superior laws of Divine Nature."[2]

THE EARTH CHARTER

The Earth Charter to which Strong alluded was a "spiritual" declaration penned by Steven Rockefeller. In its preamble, the Charter declared: "The protection of Earth's vitality, diversity, and beauty is a sacred trust."

---

1   William F. Jasper, "The New World Religion," *New American*, September 23, 2002, https://www. thenewamerican.com/culture/faith-and-morals/item/15091-the-new-world-religion, accessed April 12, 2019.

2   Maurice Strong, quoted in ibid.

However, "an unprecedented rise in human population has overburdened ecological and social systems. The foundations of global security are threatened." Therefore, the Charter maintained, "we urgently need a shared vision of basic values to provide an ethical foundation for the emerging world community."[3]

The Charter stated that all of humanity must adopt the following steps in order to save Mother Earth from a poisonous death:

- "Recognize that all beings are interdependent and every form of life has value." (Despite the fact that the Charter was drafted by Rockefeller in accordance with the United Nations, no mention was made of the fact that unborn children are not included in the UN's definition of "every form of life." Moreover, Earth Summit II documents support the UN's pro-abortion measures.)

- "Affirm faith in the inherent dignity of all human beings." (The Charter failed to note that UN agencies endorse policies of euthanasia for those determined not capable of living a "quality" life.)

- "Adopt at all levels sustainable development plans and regulations." (This statement represented a prescription for global socialism in a super-regulated global state where all human activity would be monitored by climate-control cops.)

- "Prevent pollution of any part of the environment." (Enforcing this dictum would entail putting an end to all forms of human and animal activity.)

- "Internalize the full environmental and social costs of goods and services in the selling price." (This seemingly innocuous demand would grant the new superstate the power to price, tax, and regulate all production and consumption.)

---

3 Steven Rockefeller, "The Earth Charter," 1992, http://earthcharter.org/invent/images/uploads/echarter_english.pdf, accessed April 12, 2019.

- "Ensure universal access to health care that fosters reproductive health and responsible reproduction." (This dictate called for universal socialized medicine that would include abortion and presumably infanticide since both procedures could be classified under "responsible reproduction.")

- "Eliminate discrimination in all its forms, such as that based on race . . . [and] sexual orientation." (Enforcing this provision would require the incarceration and possible execution of those who refuse to accept homosexuality as positive and good.)

- "Promote the equitable distribution of wealth within nations and among nations." (Although penned by Steven Rockefeller, this proviso appeared to have been lifted from *The Communist Manifesto*.)[4]

THE ONE-WORLD RELIGION

After the Earth Charter was revealed at the Earth Summit, it was placed in an Ark of Hope for transportation from place to place. The Ark of Hope was designed to resemble the Ark of the Covenant. Moreover, the principles contained in the Charter were venerated as sacred. "The real goal of the Earth Charter," Strong announced to the Summit, "is that it will become like the Ten Commandments."[5] This sentiment was later echoed as follows by former Soviet premier Mikhail Gorbachev, who was one of the organizers of the gathering in Rio: "My hope is that this charter will be a kind of Ten Commandments, a 'Sermon on the Mount,' that provides a guide for human behavior toward the environment in the next century and beyond."[6] The one-world religion had come into being, and the object of worship was no longer the transcendent God of the Old and New Testaments but rather Mother Earth.

---

4   Jaspers, "The New World Religion."

5   Maurice Strong, quoted in ibid.

6   Mikhail Gorbachev, quoted in ibid.

THE RIGGED REPORTS

Out of this summit came the debt-for-nature swap, whereby Third World countries were granted debt relief in exchange for opening their lands to environmental protection projects. As a result of this project, the aborigines of Palawan island were kicked off their land and wiped off the face of the earth.[7]

The Earth Summit also gave rise to the Intergovernmental Panel on Climate Change, which was to compile monthly reports for the United Nations Convention on Climate Change. These reports were rigged from the get-go. Only human causes of climate change were to be taken into consideration. Natural causes were to be ignored.[8] The public was now swamped with stories that carbon emissions were melting ice caps, raising sea levels, and starving polar bears.

THE KYOTO PROTOCOL

Throughout the 1990s, the Rockefeller Brothers Fund spent a significant portion of its financial resources to advance the global adaptation of the Rio Treaty, which obligated complicit countries to reduce greenhouse gas emissions by an average of 5.2 percent from the 1990 levels by 2012. In 1997, with the assistance of Al Gore, the Rockefeller Brothers Fund helped promote and orchestrate the Kyoto Protocol with Japan.[9]

The Kyoto Protocol, as adopted on December 11, 1997, and enacted on February 16, 2005, is an international environmental treaty between the United Nations and 187 nations to effect the "stabilization of greenhouse gas concentrations in the atmosphere at a level that would prevent dangerous anthropogenic interference with the climate

7   James Corbett, "How & Why Big Oil Conquered the World," *The Corbett Report*, October 6, 2017, https://www.corbettreport.com/bigoil/, accessed April 12, 2019.

8   Ibid.

9   "The Rockefeller Way: The Family's Covert "Climate Change Plan.""

system."[10] The treaty stipulates that its ratifiers can purchase "carbon credits" from other participating countries in order to offset their carbon emissions.[11] In this one clause lay the possibility of untold wealth for the money cartel and the means by which they could forge a new world economy based not on gold or petroleum but rather carbon.

THE CARBON ECONOMY

The carbon economy, when fully implemented in accordance with the Kyoto Protocol, will require the implementation of an annual carbon allowance for every inhabitant of planet Earth. Such an allowance would be stored electronically in chips or energy debit cards; and points would be deducted every time someone purchased or used nonrenewable energy. Deductions would be made for electrical usages, the purchase of gas for a vehicle or an airplane ticket, and the heating and cooling of homes. Energy would evolve into a new monetary system based not on dollars and cents but on energy certificates. The industries capable of accumulating the most certificates will emerge as the masters of life on the planet, and the Rockefellers already control the lion's share of these companies.

With the implementation of the Protocol, trading in emissions of pollutants as sulphur dioxide and nitrogen oxide ("cap and trade") got underway in Australia, New Zealand, Japan, the European Union, and the United States.[12]

KILLING BIRDS

In keeping with the Kyoto Protocol, Spain created 50,000 green jobs

---

10   Alex Schenker, "The Kyoto Protocol Summary," *Earth's Friends*, September 10, 2014, https://www. earthsfriends.com/kyoto-protocol-summary/, accessed April 12, 2019.

11   Ibid.

12   Oliver Deschênes, Michael Greenstone, and Joseph S. Shapiro. 2017. "Defensive Investments and the Demand for Air Quality: Evidence from the NOx Budget Program." *American Economic Review*, 2017. DOI: 10.1257/aer.20131002

and became a beacon of the environmental movement. But reports of Spain's embrace of green energy failed to say that the cost of the subsidy for every new green job was $756,000, and the new jobs destroyed 110,000 old jobs. As a result of its embrace of the environmentally friendly measures, Spain became shackled with high-cost "green" electricity that hobbled its economy, increased burdensome debt, and produced high unemployment.[13]

Similarly, the government of Queensland, Australia became persuaded that global warming was producing a drought that would linger for decades and decided not to build dams or other flood control systems. When heavy rains pounded Queensland in 2010, the terrible flooding killed dozens of people and caused billions in property losses.[14]

With the development of wind energy, in keeping with the Protocol, the American Bird Conservancy estimated 100,000 to 300,000 birds were killed each year in the United States by wind farms. This figure is roughly equal to the estimated 250,000 birds killed in 1989 by the Exxon *Valdez* oil spill.[15]

ENRON'S END

Enron, a Texas-based company with a staff of 9,000 workers, became the largest trader in such emissions and was named "America's Most Innovative Company" for six consecutive years by *Fortune* magazine.[16] Enron was joined in the energy market by Goldman Sachs, the Wall Street investment bank, who set up the Chicago Climate Exchange as

---

13   Charles Kadlec, "The Goal Is Power: The Global Warming Conspiracy," *Forbes*, July 25, 2011, https://www.forbes.com/sites/charleskadlec/2011/07/25/the-goal-is-power-the-global-warming-conspiracy/#354a82cd7c08, accessed April, 12, 2019.

14   Ibid.

15   Ibid.

16   "Enron," *Fortune 500*, 2001, archive.fortune.com/magazines/fortune/fortune500_archive/snapshots/2001/478.html, accessed April 12, 2019.

the first North American emissions trading platform.[17] By 2000, Enron boasted assets of $101 billion and became a principal contributor to the presidential campaign of George W. Bush.[18]

It was all smoke and mirrors. The assets had been cooked by Enron accountants to cause investors to believe that it was making money hand over fist, while the company was actually hemorrhaging hundreds of millions of dollars. When the fraud was revealed in December 2001, shares in Enron fell from $90.15 to $0.26 and the company filed for bankruptcy.[19]

BLOOD AND GORE

In 2004, Al Gore, who has spent over two decades lobbying for the creation of a carbon trading market, established Generation Investment Management, an investment management partnership to sell carbon offsets. His partner was David Blood, the CEO of Goldman Sachs Asset Management, who stepped down from his position with Goldman to enter the energy trading business with Gore.[20] By 2010, Gore, according to financial experts, was on his way to become the world's first carbon billionaire.[21]

NO ANGEL'S HAARP

Along with the plans for the new economic order, Project Popeye re-emerged as the U.S. High-Frequency Active Auroral Research Project (HAARP). The research for the project was conducted by Advanced

---

17   Corbett, "How & Why Big Oil Conquered the World."

18   "Bush and Enron's Collapse," *Economist,* January 11, 2002, https://www.economist.com/ unknown/2002/01/11/bush-and-enrons-collapse, accessed April 12, 2019.

19   Troy Segal, "Enron Scandal: The Fall of a Wall Street Darling," *Investopedia,* February 9, 2019, https://www.investopedia.com/updates/enron-scandal-summary/, accessed April 12, 2019.

20   Corbett, "How & Why Big Oil Conquered the World."

21   Ibid.

Power Technologies, Inc. (APTI), a subsidiary of the Rockefeller-owned Atlantic Richfield.[22] In 1992, ATPI was sold to E Systems (a CIA front).[23] Two years later, E Systems was acquired by Raytheon, one of the four pillars of the military-industrial establishment.[24]

Constructed in Gokona, Alaska, HAARP was funded by the U.S. Air Force, the U.S. Navy, and the Defense Advanced Research Projects Agency (DARPA). According to its official website, HAARP was designed "to induce a small, localized change in ionospheric temperature so physical reactions can be studied by other instruments located either at or close to the HAARP site." But Rosalie Bertell, president of the International Institute of Concern for Public Health, took stock with this statement of purpose. She maintained that HAARP was set up to operate as "a gigantic heater that can cause major disruptions in the ionosphere, creating not just holes, but long incisions in the protective layer that keeps deadly radiation from bombarding the planet."[25] Similarly, physicist Bernard Eastlund, who worked on the project, called it "the largest ionospheric heater ever built," stating that it was constructed to "induce ionospheric modifications" in order to alter weather patterns.[26]

22   "BP Is Actually a Rockefeller Enterprise," *Above Top Secret,* July 13, 2010, http://www.abovetopsecret. com/forum/thread593375/pg1, accessed April 12, 2019.

23   Winfred Richardson, "E-Systems," Institute for the Study of Globalization and Covert Politics," June 28, 2002, https://isgp-studies.com/DL_E_Systems, accessed April 12, 2019.

24   Mark Rich, 'Weather War," *New World War,* 2011, www.newworldwar.org/weatherwar.htm, accessed April 12, 2019.

25   Rosalie Bertell, quoted in Michel Chossudovsky, "Weather Warfare: Beware the US Military's Experiments with Climatic Warfare," *Global Research,* October 27, 2018, https://www.globalresearch. ca/weather-warfare-beware-the-us-military-s-experiments-with-climatic-warfare/7561, accessed April 12, 2019.

26   Bernard Eastlund, quoted in ibid.

A SINISTER PURPOSE

Regarding the sinister nature of HAARP, Michel Chossudovsky of *Global Research* wrote:

> An analysis of statements emanating from the US Air Force points to the unthinkable: the covert manipulation of weather patterns, communications and electric power systems as a weapon of global warfare, enabling the US to disrupt and dominate entire regions. Weather manipulation is the pre-emptive weapon par excellence. It can be directed against enemy countries or "friendly nations" without their knowledge, used to destabilize economies, ecosystems and agriculture. It can also trigger havoc in financial and commodity markets. The disruption in agriculture creates a greater dependency on food aid and imported grain staples from the US and other Western countries.[27]

In May 2013, the HAARP site in Alaska was abandoned. All technicians and workers vanished from the military installation. The buildings were locked, and the power was shut off.[28] The experiments were successful, and the HAARP patent was acquired by Raytheon.[29] By this time, China and Russia became actively involved in cloud-seeding for military and agricultural purposes, and Monsanto shelled out a billion dollars for the Climate Corporation. According to *Forbes*, this acquisition would permit Monsanto "to sell more services to farmers who already buy Monsanto seed and chemicals." These services could

---

27   Ibid.

28   "HAARP Is Shut Down," *Unknown Country*, July 18, 2013, http://www.unknowncountry.com/news/haarp-shut-down#ixzz5k5Og5ctY, accessed April 12, 2019.

29   Rady Ananda, "Atmospheric Geoengineering: Weather Manipulation, Contrails and Chemtrails: A Review of the 'Case Orange' Report." *GeoEngineering Watch*, July 11, 2013, https://www.geoengineeringwatch.org/atmospheric-geoengineering-weather-manipulation-contrails-and-chemtrails-2/, accessed April 12, 2019.

include the guarantee for good growing seasons for all those willing to come up with the required cash.[30]

Recognizing the potential of climate control, Bill Gates joined the Rockefellers and George Soros in shelling out millions of dollars on geoengineering research. Gates' top science advisor soon unveiled a plan to expand solar radiation management "one hundred" fold from $10 million to $1 billion over the course of 10 years.[31] The future of man's life on the planet was now in the hands of a small group of billionaires.

MAN-MADE CLOUDS

Adding pollutants to the upper atmosphere to create climate change produced a proliferation of chemtrails across the sky. Unlike the contrails caused by normal aircrafts, chemtrails did not dissipate within a matter of minutes but remained visible for hours. At an international symposium held in Ghent Belgium May 28–30, 2010, aerospace engineer Dr. Coen Vermeeran presented a 300-page report called "CASE ORANGE: Contrail Science, Its Impact on Climate and Weather Manipulation Programs Conducted by the United States and Its Allies" in which he said: "We also know that chemtrails do exist because we do spraying; for crops, for example, and we know that they have been spraying for military purposes. So, chemtrails is nothing new. We know about it. Weather manipulation through contrail formation . . . is in place and fully operational."[32]

---

30 Rady Ananda, "Planetary Weapons and Military Weather Modification: Chemtrails, Atmospheric Geoengineering and Environmental Warfare," *Global Research,* October 19, 2017, https://www.globalresearch.ca/military-weather-modification-chemtrails-atmospheric-geoengineering-and-environmental-warfare/5356630, accessed April 12, 2019.

31 Ananda, "Atmospheric Geoengineering."

32 Coen Vermeeren, quoted in ibid.

Adding pollutants to the upper atmosphere to create climate change produced a proliferation of chemtrails across the sky. Unlike the contrails caused by normal aircrafts, chemtrails did not dissipate within a matter of minutes but remained visible for hours.

THE PARIS ACCORD

The Paris Accord of 2015 was forged by the United Nations Framework Convention on Climate Control to deal with "greenhouse emissions, mitigation, adaptation, and finance." It was signed by the leaders of 195 countries and amassed over $10 billion in pledges from developed nations such as the United States, France, and Japan, and developing countries, including Mexico, Indonesia, and Vietnam.[33]

In accordance with the terms of this agreement, Third World countries would receive $100 billion a year, beginning in 2020, to cut

---

33   Gwynne Taraska, "The Paris Climate Agreement," Center for American Progress, December 15, 2015, https://cdn.americanprogress.org/wp-content/uploads/2015/12/15030725/ParisClimateAgreement .pdf.

their carbon emissions. This stipulation mandated a massive transfer of wealth from wealthy to impoverished nations, which would become obliged to purchase green energy equipment and technology from companies owned by the Rockefellers and other members of the money cartel. For some strange reason, the agreement gave China and India a pass to reduce their carbon emissions, even though China consumed half of the world's coal and remained the planet's leading polluter. As soon as the measure was passed, French President Emmanuel Macron proposed the imposition of a stiff new fuel tax that brought angry mobs to the heart of Paris. In the words of Pat Buchanan, these mobs "battled police, burned cars, looted, smashed show windows of elite stores such as Dior and Chanel, and desecrated the Arc de Triomphe."[34]

JAIL FOR DISSENTERS

The hysteria over global warming also caused political leaders and spokesmen throughout the United States to demand an end to free speech and the incarceration of anyone who dared to challenge the claim that Mother Earth would soon melt under clouds of carbon pollution. Robert Kennedy Jr. declared that those who denied global warming should be treated as war criminals. Bill Nye, "the Science Guy," in support of Kennedy's position, said that those who dissented from the teachings of global warming warranted a stay in a jail cell since their expressions of doubt, if unchecked, could result in a disastrous effect upon the general public.[35]

During her appearance before the Senate Judiciary Committee in March 2016, Attorney General Loretta Lynch said that she asked the

---

34 Patrick J. Buchanan, "Massive Riots in Paris Threaten Climate Accord," *American Conservative,* December 4, 2018, https://www.theamericanconservative.com/buchanan/massive-riots-in-paris-threaten-climate-accord/, accessed April 12, 2019.

35 Valerie Richardson, "Bill Nye, the Science Guy, Is Open to Criminal Charges and Jail Time for Climate Change Dissenters," *Washington Times,* April 14, 2016, https://www.washingtontimes.com/news/2016/apr/14/bill-nye-open-criminal-charges-jail-time-climate-c/, accessed April 12, 2019.

FBI to examine whether the federal government should take legal action against so-called climate change deniers. Ms. Lynch was not responding to any criminal acts by global warming dissenters but rather her fear that such dissention would block the creation of a national consensus on the "environmental crisis."[36]

THE NEW GREEN DEAL

When President Donald Trump opted to pull out of the Paris Accord, his decision was met by new cries for environmental control and the formation of the New Green Deal. Developed by Representative Alexandria Ocasio-Cortez and Senator Edward Markey, the New Green Deal contained a list of goals for America to achieve with a span of 10 years. They included (1) a ban on all fossil fuel; (2) the elimination of nuclear energy; (3) the outlawing of combustion-engine vehicles, such as gasoline fueled cars, trucks, and airplanes; (4) the replacement of air travel with railroad service; (5) the guarantee of jobs that would provide a "family-sustaining wage, family and medical leave, vacations, and a pension" for all Americans; and (6) a ban on beef, since "farting cows" represented a health hazard; (7) and free college education for all, even those who lack an aptitude for academics. The authors of the plan added a final codicil, stating that this proposed legislation represented a means of "stopping current, preventing future, and repairing historic oppression of indigenous peoples, communities of color, migrant communities, deindustrialized rural communities, the poor, low-income workers, the elderly, the unhoused, peoples with disabilities and youth."[37] At a Martin Luther King Day event at Riverside Church in New York City (an imposing religious facility that had been built by John D. Rockefeller

---

36 Ron Paul, "Loretta Lynch Wants to Censor Climate Skeptics," *Newmax*, March 15, 2016, https://www.newsmax.com/RonPaul/Loretta-Lynch-Climate-Global-Warming/2016/03/15/id/719204/, accessed April 12, 2019.

37 Patrick J. Buchanan, "The Green New Deal Is a Suicide Note for Democrats," *American Conservative*, February 12, 2019, https://www.theamericanconservative.com/buchanan/the-green-new-deal-is-a-suicide-note-for-democrats/, accessed April 12, 2019.

Jr.), Ocasio-Cortez warned: "The world is gonna end in 12 years if we don't address climate change."[38]

The New Green Deal was endorsed by leading Democratic presidential candidates, including Cory Booker, Kamala Harris, Elizabeth Warren, Kirsten Gillibrand, Julián Castro, Beto O'Rourke, and Bernie Sanders.[39] The age of reason and human progression had come to an end. The calls for such a deal were echoed by financial, political, and spiritual leaders throughout the world, including German Chancellor Angela Merkel, Canadian Prime Minister Justin Trudeau, UN Secretary General Ban Ki-Moon, World Bank head Jim Yong Kim, Ecuadorian President Rafael Correa, Juan Hernandez of Honduras, Finland's Sauli Ninisto, Robert Mugabe of Zimbabwe, and Pope Francis.[40] Decades of media hype and the "philanthropic" financing of environmental organizations and educational institutions produced a vast sector of humanity who called for the institution of the world order envisioned by John D. Rockefeller and his progeny—a socialist order, free of competition, where all human thought and action remained under tight control.

GLOBAL COOLING

In the midst of the hysteria over global warming and the threats to jail anyone who challenged its existence, NASA scientists made the startling discovery that the world was not warming but rather cooling. Dr. Martin Mlynczak of NASA's Langley Research Center told reporters:

---

38   Alexandria Ocasio-Cortez, quoted in Kristinn Taylor, "Alexandria Ocasio-Cortez: 'The World Is Gonna End in 12 Years If We Don't Address Climate Change,'" *The Gateway Pundit*, January 21, 2019, https://www.thegatewaypundit.com/2019/01/alexandria-ocasio-cortez-the-world-is-gonna-end-in-12-years-if-we-dont-address-climate-change/, accessed April 12, 2019.

39   David Harsanyi, "The 10 Most Insane Requirements of the New Green Deal," *The Federalist*, February 7, 2019, https://thefederalist.com/2019/02/07/ten-most-insane-requirements-green-new-deal/, accessed April 12, 2019.

40   Alister Doyle, "Eighteen Quotes from World Leaders on Climate Change," *World Economic Forum*, December 1, 2015, https://www.weforum.org/agenda/2015/12/18-quotes-from-world-leaders-on-climate-change/, accessed April 12, 2019.

"We see a cooling trend. High above the earth's surface, near the edge of space, our atmosphere is losing heat energy. If current trends continue, it could soon set a Space-Age record for cold."[41]

These findings came from the SABER instrument onboard NASA's TIMED satellite. SABER monitored infrared emissions from carbon dioxide and nitric oxide, two substances that play a key role in the energy balance of air 100 to 300 kilometers above the earth's surface. By measuring the infrared glow of these molecules, SABER could assess the thermal state of gas at the very top of the atmosphere, a layer researchers call "the thermosphere." To track what was happening in the thermosphere, Mlynczak and colleagues developed the "Thermosphere Climate Index," which showed how much heat nitric oxide molecules was being dumped into space. During Solar Maximum, the Thermal Climate Index is high ("Hot"); during Solar Minimum, low ("Cold").

"Right now, it is very low indeed," Mlynczak, the associate principal investigator for SABER, said. "SABER is currently measuring 33 billion Watts of infrared power from NO. That's 10 times smaller than we see during more active phases of the solar cycle." He added: "The thermosphere always cools off during Solar Minimum. It's one of the most important ways the solar cycle affects our planet."

THE POLAR BEARS ARE HAPPY

The findings of the NASA scientists are verified by the fact that Greenland's Jacobshavn Glacier, once the fastest shrinking ice and snow melt on the planet, has been rapidly growing for the past two years.[42] Even worse news for the global warming hysterics comes from Antarctica (the South Pole), where scientists have reported the following finding:

41 Martin Mlynczak, quoted in Dr. Tony Phillips, "The Chill of Solar Minimum," *Space Solar Archive*, September 27, 2018, https://spaceweatherarchive.com/2018/09/27/the-chill-of-solar-minimum/, accessed April 12, 2019.

42 Seth Borenstein, "One of the Fastest Shrinking Greenland Glaciers Is Growing Again, NASA Says," *National Post*, March 29, 2019, https://nationalpost.com/news/big-u-turn-key-melting-greenland-glacier-is-growing-again, accessed April 12, 2019.

The Antarctic Peninsula (AP) is often described as a region with one of the largest warming trends on Earth since the 1950s, based on the temperature trend of 0.54 °C/decade during 1951–2011 recorded at Faraday/Vernadsky station. Accordingly, most works describing the evolution of the natural systems in the AP region cite this extreme trend as the underlying cause of their observed changes. However, a recent analysis . . . has shown that the regionally stacked temperature record for the last three decades has shifted from a warming trend of 0.32 °C/decade during 1979–1997 to a cooling trend of −0.47 °C/decade during 1999–2014. While that study focuses on the period 1979–2014, averaging the data over the entire AP region, we here update and re-assess the spatially-distributed temperature trends and inter-decadal variability from 1950 to 2015, using data from ten stations distributed across the AP region. We show that Faraday/Vernadsky warming trend is an extreme case, circa twice those of the long-term records from other parts of the northern AP. Our results also indicate that the cooling initiated in 1998/1999 has been most significant in the N and NE of the AP and the South Shetland Islands (> 0.5 °C between the two last decades), modest in the Orkney Islands, and absent in the SW of the AP. This recent cooling has already impacted the cryosphere in the northern AP, including slow-down of glacier recession, a shift to surface mass gains of the peripheral glacier and a thinning of the active layer of permafrost in northern AP islands.[43]

The same cooling has been evidenced in the Arctic (the North Pole), where cold summers have left 533,000 miles of the ocean covered with ice, an increase in ice formation of 29 percent in one year. The unbroken ice sheet stemming from the Arctic covers an area more than half the size of Europe and already extends from the Canadian islands

---

43   M. Oliva et al., "Recent Regional Climate Cooling in the Antarctic Peninsula and Associated Impacts on the Cryosphere," *Science of the Total Environment*, February 2017, https://www.sciencedirect.com/science/article/pii/S0048969716327152?via%3Dihub, accessed April 12, 2019.

to Russia's northern shores. This development completely negates the 2007 BBC report that global warming would leave the North Pole ice-free in summer by 2013.[44]

THE LOSS OF HOPE

This second about-face regarding climate change was ignored by the mass media, educational institutions, and environmental groups who had been brainwashed to believe that the carbon emissions were causing ice caps to melt, the sea to rise, the polar bears to starve, and the earth to croak. People throughout the world had been conditioned to believe that they must cease and desist from breeding like rats, from promoting consumerism and capitalism, and from burning fossil fuels to heat their homes and to drive their cars. The money cartel, having succeeded in killing truth, now succeeded in killing hope. In his op-ed piece of July 26, 2018 for the *New York Times*, Roy Scranton reflected this development by writing:

> I cried two times when my daughter was born. First for joy, when after 27 hours of labor the little feral being we'd made came yowling into the world, and the second for sorrow, holding the earth's newest human and looking out the window with her at the rows of cars in the hospital parking lot, the strip mall across the street, the box stores and drive-throughs and drainage ditches and asphalt and waste fields that had once been oak groves. A world of extinction and catastrophe, a world in which harmony with nature had long been foreclosed.
>
> My partner and I had, in our selfishness, doomed our daughter to life on a dystopian planet, and I could see no way to shield her from the future.[45]

---

44   David Rose, "And Now It's Global Cooling! Return of Arctic Ice Cap as It Grows by 29% in a Year," *Daily Mail* (UK), September 7, 2013, https://www.dailymail.co.uk/news/article-2415191/And-global-COOLING-Return-Arctic-ice-cap-grows-29-year.html, accessed April 12, 2019.

45   Roy Scranton, "Raising My Child in a Doomed World," *New York Times*, July 16, 2018, https://www.nytimes.com/2018/07/16/opinion/climate-change-parenting.html, accessed April 12, 2019.

31

A DIRGE

The way I look at technocracy, there's two levels operating at the same time. There's the operational side of it that has to do with things like smart grid. That have to do with things like various technocratic innovations, surveillance and other big hot-button [issues] for technocracy. These are operational issues. From a strategic point of view, which is where the Rockefeller-type people operate, it's a different view of where it's headed. On an operational level it's headed towards a scientific dictatorship and you don't have to be a visionary to figure that one out really anymore. You don't. It's there.

But on a strategic basis, what's happening is that there's a massive resource grab going on all over the planet. And when I say resource grab, you have to put yourself in Rockefellers' shoes—the bankers' shoes and the Rothschilds' shoes or whatever—and say, "What do you do when money runs out? What do you do? When you suck all of the value that you can out of the monetary systems you've created, what's left?"

Well, you and I don't think about those sort of things because we don't have that much money, but these people at the top, especially the bankers, I'm sure they stay up at night thinking, "What's after money? What comes after money?" The Rockefeller family especially has always been a resource intensive family. That's what oil was all about in the first place. It was a resource and they understood that energy would be the most important factor in the world over any other type of resource. They understood that, that's why they wanted to create a monopoly over energy.

Well, today as money has been sucked dry, the only thing left to do is to make a grab for the resources themselves and that's what sustainable development is all about. It's taking the resources of the world away from you and me, away from private companies that aren't part of the clique,

if you will, and putting them into a global common trust that will be managed by them for their benefit. This is really nothing more than neo-feudalism again where the resources are owned by a few and everybody else gets to operate with those resources at their pleasure and discretion.
—PATRICK WOOD, "HOW AND WHY BIG OIL CONQUERED THE WORLD,
OCTOBER 6, 2017

THE MASTER PLAN of Cecil John Rhodes and his Society of the Elect was a success. Their vision of a world united under the rule of a "synarchy"—an elite and enlightened group of bankers, industrialists, and businessmen who would meet in secret to chart the course of history—was now a reality.[1] They had risen above the masses through good breeding and could not allow their future to be determined by random affairs or the cries from the rabble.

Members of the Society quickly rose to positions of power and eminence. Lord Reginald Baliol Brett came to serve as Queen Victoria's closest advisor; Lord Archibald Primrose and Arthur James Balfour became British Prime Ministers; Lord Alfred Milner was appointed the High Commissioner of the Colony of South Africa and later Britain's Secretary of War.[2] Lord Nathan Rothschild, the most powerful member of the Society, continued to work with his family in establishing an international banking system. The Society proved that a small cadre of powerful men can change the course of world events by instigating the Second Boer War, which resulted in the institution of death camps and the incorporation of the Transvaal and the Orange Free State into the British Empire.[3]

---

1   Cecil John Rhodes, "Confession of Faith," June 2, 1877, https://publicintelligence.net/cecil-rhodes-confession-of-faith/, accessed April 12, 2019.

2   William T. Stead, *The Last Will and Testament of Cecil John Rhodes* (London: Review of Reviews Office, 1902), p. 108.

3   Thomas Pakenham, *The Boer War* (New York: Random House, 1979), p. 115.

After Rhodes died in 1902, a host of other powerful men joined the secret society, including Sir Philip Duncan, governor general of South Africa; Philip Henry Kerr, 11th Marquess of Lothian and the British ambassador to the United States; 1st Baron Robert Henry Brand, managing director of the House of Lazard in England; George Geoffrey Dawson, editor of the *London Times*; John Buchan, 1st Baron Tweedsmuir, governor general of Canada; T. E. Lawrence, who became known as "Lawrence of Arabia;" Leo Amery, Britain's colonial secretary; Stanley Baldwin, First Earl Baldwin of Bewdley, who would serve as prime minister of England under three monarchs; Sir Edward Peacock, a director of the Bank of England; and Rudyard Kipling, the first English-language writer to receive the Nobel Prize for Literature.

THE AMERICAN ELITE

Lord Rothschild became instrumental in establishing a chapter of the Society of the Elect in New York. Known as the Pilgrim Society, this group met each month in a private dining room within the Waldorf Astoria Hotel. Its members were America's new aristocracy—the Morgans, the Astors, the Vanderbilts, the Schiffs, the Mellons, and the Carnegies.[4] At these meetings, the American "pilgrims" drafted political and economic policies that would further their mutual interests.[5]

At these gatherings was a gaunt figure with a funeral manner and the appearance of Nosferatu, since he suffered from alopecia, a disease that had left him hairless. Reticent by nature, John D. Rockefeller lacked the gregariousness of J. P. Morgan and the social grace of Vincent Astor, but he shared their desire for increased wealth, political power, and international expansion. Moreover, he had developed close ties to Jacob Schiff, whose bank had funded his first oil refinery.[6]

---

4   G. Edward Griffin, *The Creature from Jekyll Island* (Westlake Village, CA: American Media, 2008), p. 5.

5   Joël van der Reijden, "The Pilgrim Society," *Journal of History*, September 21, 2005, http://www.truedemocracy.net/hj31/37.html, accessed April 12, 2019.

6   Ron Chernow, *Titan: The Life of John D. Rockefeller, Sr.* (New York: Vintage Books, 1998), p. 377.

From this group came the Federal Reserve, which would control America's money supply and its prevailing interest rate. This central bank was privately owned by representatives of the world's leading banking/business consortium: the Morgans, the Rothschilds, the Warburgs, the Schiffs, and the Rockefellers. These families represented a classic cartel. Through the Federal Reserve, they could join forces to create depression or prosperity.

Through the machinations of the Pilgrim Society, Woodrow Wilson ascended to the Oval Office in Washington, DC, and America entered World War I. In the wake of the war, the Society of the Elect morphed into the Royal Institute of International Affairs (the Chatham House) in London, and the Pilgrim Society transformed into the Council of Foreign Affairs (the Pratt House) in New York. By this time, John D. Rockefeller Jr. had assumed control of his father's oil business. Unlike his father, Junior had been educated at proper schools, including Brown, accepted into polite society, and became cosmopolitan in manner and outlook.

JUNIOR'S GENEROSITY

During the 1920s, Junior became a fixture at the Pratt House, where he oversaw the development of position papers on political, social, and economic issues. Eventually, he became the clandestine club's gate-keeper. No one passed through its portals without his approval. Under Junior's direction, the Council on Foreign Relations became the most powerful organization in the country.

The true genius of Junior resided in his use of "philanthropies" to extend his own sphere of power and influence. He shelled out millions to America's leading educational institutions that soon became reliant on his annual gifts to balance their budgets. Junior was ready to open his wallet if the institutions agreed to his demands, which came to include the manner in which they became politically, socially, and religiously indoctrinated. Junior's "generosity" was soon extended to legal and medical institutions and organizations, which, too, became subservient to the demands of his foundations.

Through the Council on Foreign Relations, Rockefeller gained control of America's newspapers.[7] What the people read was what Junior wanted them to read. And the events that captured the headlines were the events, in many cases, that had been manufactured or contrived.

PECUNIAE OBEDIUNT OMNIA

Junior now set his sights on world conquest. He donated the land for the construction of the United Nations and became instrumental in establishing its agenda. With the means of creating a global government in place, Junior went on to play a strategic role in the formation of the World Bank, the International Monetary Fund, and the World Trade Organization. Several scholars, including Emanuel Josephson, attribute the Rockefellers' lust for world control to their fear of poverty—a fear that plagued John D. Rockefeller Jr. to the end of his days. But, perhaps, the real reason resides in psychological egoism and the assertion, set forth by Herbert Spencer, Sigmund Freud, and Andrew Carnegie, that every creature acts to further and protect its own self-interest.[8]

After World War II, the Council on Foreign Relations, now headed by David Rockefeller, Junior's youngest son, gave rise to the Central Intelligence Agency. The original funding for the CIA came from the Rockefeller Foundation. Throughout the second half of the 20th century, the CIA engaged in operations to safeguard the holdings of the Rockefeller family. These operations came to include the toppling of democratically elected governments in Iran, Guatemala, Brazil, and Chile.[9]

---

7   Gary Allen, *The Rockefeller File* (Seal Beach, CA: '76 Press, 1976), p. 66.

8   Jim Powell, "Spontaneous Progress: A Biography of Herbert Spencer," Libertarianism.org, July 4, 2000, https://www.libertarianism.org/publications/essays/spontaneous-progress-biography-herbert-spencer, accessed April 12, 2019.

9   Eric Dubay, *The Atlantean Conspiracy* (Durham, NC: Lulu, 2009), pp. 76–77.

FROM RHODES TO ROCKEFELLER

Realizing, like Rhodes, that the creation of a New World Order was not a pipedream but a possibility, the Rockefellers perpetuated warfare, mass migration, and the breaking down of borders as a means of destroying nationalism, furthering free trade, and confiscating natural resources. The key to global control was fear—fear caused by external bogeymen that they propped up from time to time, including Osama bin Laden and Saddam Hussein. But such control also necessitated the creation of internal fear, including reports that the resources of the world were being depleted and that the problem of overpopulation had placed planet Earth in meltdown.

Global regimentation required monitoring, and monitoring required the surrender of individual rights and liberties. Such a surrender could only be brought about by an enormous catastrophe that would cause people to seek security for themselves and their loved ones. On September 11, 2001, under very mysterious circumstances, Islamic terrorist hijacked four American airliners; two crashed into the World Trade Center; one into the Pentagon in Arlington County, Virginia; and a fourth in a field near a reclaimed coal strip mine in Shanksville, Pennsylvania. Fear of another terror attack led to the Patriot Act of 2001 by which Americans surrendered their freedom of association, freedom of speech, freedom from unreasonable searches, and their right to legal representation and a speedy and public trial for the sake of security.

ENDLESS SURVEILLANCE

After 9/11, monitors were installed on the street corners of every major American city, at the entranceway to schools, workplaces, banks, theaters, and sporting arenas, and within public parks and places of public recreation. No dog could urinate on a fire hydrant and no rat could emerge from a sewer without being caught on camera. All ports of entry, including bus, train, and plane terminals, were kept under constant surveillance. Few developments could be of greater benefit to the money cartel who were intent upon controlling all human activity.

In 1973, David Rockefeller and Zbigniew Brzezinski created the Trilateral Commission with the goal of creating "a new international economic order" based on technocracy. In *Between Two Ages: America's Role in the Technocratic Era,* Brzezinski had written: "[The technocratic era] involves the gradual appearance of a more controlled and directed society. Such a society would be dominated by an elite whose claim to political power would rest on allegedly superior science know-how. Unhindered by the restraints of traditional liberal values, this elite would not hesitate to achieve its political ends by using modern techniques for influencing public behavior and keeping society under close surveillance and control."[10] He added: "[The] nation state as a fundamental unit of man's organized life has ceased to be the principal creative force. International banks and multinational corporations are acting and planning in terms that are far in advance of the political concepts of the nation state."[11]

TRILATERALISM AND TECHNOCRACY

The Trilateral Commission, under Rockefeller and Brzezinski, became one of the most powerful organizations on the planet. By 1976, its members included U.S. President Jimmy Carter, Vice President Walter Mondale, Secretary of State Cyrus Vance, Secretary of Defense Harold Brown, Secretary of the Treasury W. Michael Blumenthal, National Security Advisor Brzezinski, Deputy Secretary of State Warren Christopher, Secretary of Energy James Schlesinger; Ambassador to the UN Andrew Young; World Bank President Robert McNamara, Federal Reserve Chairman Arthur Burns, *Time* magazine editor-in-chief Hedley Donovan, and former Secretary of State Henry Kissinger.[12] Future Trilateral members would be George H. W. Bush, William Jefferson Clinton, Albert

---

10   Zbigniew Brzezinski, *Between Two Ages: America's Role in the Technocratic Era* (New York: Viking Press, 1970), p. 97.

11   Ibid., p. 246.

12   Patrick M. Wood, *Technocracy Rising: The Trojan Horse of Global Transformation* (Mesa, AZ: Coherent Publishing, 2015), pp. 48–59.

Gore, A. W. Clausen, Barber Conable, James Wolfenson, Paul Wolfowitz, Robert Zoellick, Alexander Haig, George Schultz, Lawrence Eagleburger, Madeleine Albright, Paul Volker, Allan Greenspan, *New York Times* columnist Nicholas Kristof, *Washington Post* columnist David Ignatius, Michael Bloomberg, NBC Foreign Affairs correspondent Andrea Mitchell, John Negroponte, and Richard "Dick" Cheney.[13]

Regarding the Rockefeller/Brzezinski organization, Senator Barry Goldwater in his 1979 book *With No Apologies* wrote: "The Trilateral Commission is international and is intended to be the vehicle for international consolidation of the commercial and banking interests by seizing control of the political government of the United States. The Trilateral Commission represents a skillful, coordinated effort to seize control and consolidate the four centers of power—political, monetary, intellectual and ecclesiastical."[14]

To effect such control and consolidation, the Trilaterals, under Rockefeller, turned to the concept of technocracy that had been in vogue during the Great Depression. As conceived by Howard Scott and M. King Hubbert, technocracy represented an attempt to impose scientific control over all aspects of human society. In their newsmagazine the *Technocrat,* Scott and Hubbert defined their movement:

> Technocracy is the science of social engineering, the scientific operation of the entire social mechanism to produce and distribute goods and services to the entire population of this continent. For the first time in human history it will be done as a scientific, technical, engineering problem. There will be no place for Politics or Politicians, Finance or Financiers, Rackets or Racketeers. Technocracy states that this method of operating the social mechanism of the North American Continent is now mandatory because we have passed from a state of actual scarcity into the present status of potential abundance in which we are now held to an artificial scarcity forced upon us in order to

---

13   Ibid.

14   Barry Goldwater, *With No Apologies* (New York: William Morrow, 1979), p. 280.

continue a Price System which can distribute goods only by means of a medium of exchange. Technocracy states that price and abundance are incompatible; the greater the abundance the smaller the price. In a real abundance there can be no price at all. Only by abandoning the interfering price control and substituting a scientific method of production and distribution can an abundance be achieved. Technocracy will distribute by means of a certificate of distribution available to every citizen from birth to death. The Technate will encompass the entire American Continent from Panama to the North Pole because the natural resources and the natural boundary of this area make it an independent, self-sustaining geographical unit.[15]

A SCIENTIFIC WORLD ORDER

In his *Technocracy Study Course* of 1934, Hubbert wrote that exact conditions would have been developed by global engineers before the scientific control of all human action could take place. These requirements were set forth as follows:

- A means must be developed to calculate and register all energy usage on a continuous and instantaneous basis.

- A system must be in place for the provision of a minute-by-minute inventory of all production and consumption.

- A central registry must be capable of listing all products available for sale, where they were produced, how much energy was expended in their production, and where and when they were sold.

- A device must be created to gather "specific registration of the consumption of each individual, plus a record and description of the individual.[16]

---

15   Howard Scott and M. King Hubbert, "What Is Technocracy?" *The Technocrat*, September, 1937, https://archive.org/details/TheTechnocrat-September1937, accessed April 12, 2019.

16   James Corbett, "How & Why Big Oil Conquered the World," *The Corbett Report*, October 6, 2017, https://www.corbettreport.com/bigoil/, accessed April 12, 2019.

Once these conditions were met, energy would become the basis
of the monetary system. For this reason, all forms of energy would be
controlled by a cadre of elite scientists and bankers, who would distribute Energy Certificates—the new money—to nations based on their
net energy expenditures. The nations, in turn, would distribute these
Certificates, in denominations of Joules, to their citizens. The citizens
would use the Joules to make their purchases. The information about
these purchases would be conveyed to the central governing system
so that they (in the words of one technocrat) could "create a thermo-
dynamically balanced load of production and consumption, thereby
doing away with unemployment, debt, and social injustice."[17]

The technocrats believed that it would be possible for manufacturers and industrialists by monitoring the actions of their employees
to establish work schedules with the goal of uninterrupted production,
maximum efficiency, and a sharp rise in profit. According to their cal-
culations, an average factory worker should work four hours a day for
four days and take the rest of the time off.

EX MACHINA
They held that humanism, freedom, and democracy were worthless in a
technological civilization since they were not directly indispensable for
rationality and efficiency. Why should man, a mere animal composed
of atoms, the technocrats argued, need freedom and democracy? Man,
they insisted was "an engine taking potential energy and converting it
into heat, work, and body tissue." They claimed that while technocracy,
ruled by engineers and scientists, would mean a dictatorship, it would be
a dictatorship not of an individual but of science. From such a system,
people should expect only peace and comfort, for this dictatorship
would be totally objective and free of any preferences or mistakes.[18]

---

17   Ibid.

18   Eduard Batalov, *The American Utopia*, translated by Dimitry Belyavsky (Moscow: Progress Press,
     1985), pp. 102–9.

During the 1930s, the technocrats' vision was of a totalitarian society in which every action and interaction of every person on the planet would be watched and reported to a central authority. To those who lived during the Great Depression, this smacked of insanity since the world remained without the internet and high-speed computers, let alone cell phones and power grids. The Continental Committee on Technocracy collapsed in 1937, and the movement came to an end.[19] W. King Hubbert, however, did not disappear. He accepted a position with Shell Oil. In this way, Hubbert's notion of a technocracy fell into the hands of the Bilderberg Group and ultimately the founders of the Trilateral Commission, who realized that the idea of a scientific dictatorship, controlled by a power elite, was no longer a pipedream but a distinct possibility.[20] Their realization intensified in the remaining decades of the 20th century with the advent of home computers, quantum dots, satellite television, the World Wide Web, test-tube babies, the wireless internet, cellphones, nanotechnology, and quantum computing.

THE INTERNET OF THINGS

After the attacks of 9/11, the "Internet of Things" (IoT) was brought into being for the sake of "security." Now any electric or electronic device can be connected to the internet and with each other. This includes cell phones, television sets, coffee makers, washing machines, lamps, stoves, toasters, and vacuum machines. It also applies to the components of machines, such as the jet engine of an airplane, the drill of an oil rig, or the ignition of an automobile. Gartner Research predicts

19   Howard P. Segal, *Technological Utopianism in American Culture* (Syracuse, NY: Syracuse University Press, 2005), p. 123.

20   M. King Hubbert, "On the Nature of Growth," National Energy Conservation Policy Act of 1974, Hearings before the Subcommittee on the Environment of the Committee on Interior and Insular Affairs House of Representatives, June 6, 1974, www.hubbertpeak.com/hubbert/onthenatureofgrowth.pdf, accessed April 12, 2019.

that by 2020, 26 billion devices will be connected and interconnected.[21] In his explanation of the Internet of Things for *Forbes* magazine, Jacob Morgan writes:

> The new rule for the future is going to be, "Anything that can be connected, will be connected." But why on earth would you want so many connected devices talking to each other? There are many examples for what this might look like or what the potential value might be. Say for example you are on your way to a meeting; your car could have access to your calendar and already know the best route to take. If the traffic is heavy your car might send a text to the other party notifying them that you will be late. What if your alarm clock wakes up you at 6 a.m. and then notifies your coffee maker to start brewing coffee for you? What if your office equipment knew when it was running low on supplies and automatically re-ordered more? What if the wearable device you used in the workplace could tell you when and where you were most active and productive and shared that information with other devices that you used while working?[22]

THE BIRTH OF BIG BROTHER

Smart houses, in which all appliances are interconnected, will be linked to a central 5G grid. In computer terminology, 5G stands for the fifth generation of mobile technology. The first generation was the original cellular networks of the 1990s; the second the advent of text messaging; the third the ability to access the internet on mobile devices; and the fourth the expansion of speed of internet access. The fifth generation will deliver speeds 200 times faster than the fourth and on a much wider

---

21   Jacob Morgan, "A Simple Explanation of the Internet of Things," *Forbes*, May 13, 2014, https:// www.forbes.com/sites/jacobmorgan/2014/05/13/simple-explanation-internet-things-that-anyone-can-understand/#1eb8872e1d09, accessed April 12, 2019.

22   Ibid.

broadband. It will (1) transmit airwaves that can penetrate thicker walls and structures; (2) require the erection of radiating towers throughout the globe, adding new meaning to the concept of electromagnetic soup; and (3) share frequencies with the military, meaning that 5G technology is weapons-grade and that microwaves can be deployed as miniature cannons to address any suspicious activity.[23] The smart grid can be used to track people, to disable them, and to see if they are carrying money or a weapon.[24] A law was recently passed in Australia that allows cops to tune into the microchips implanted in appliances (such as refrigerators) and to listen to conversations taking place within private residences.[25]

Verizon, the electronics giant, has staked much of its fortune in the creation of 5G technology and will own and operate the smart grids. It is no small surprise that the Rockefellers are principal Verizon shareholders.[26] The dream of their patriarch to forge a world that would operate under his supervision had finally come to pass.

THE PUBLIC HEALTH

Even before the 5G rollout, more than 230 scientists from 41 countries expressed their "serious concerns" about the ubiquitous and increasing exposure to electromagnetic frequencies (EMFs) generated by electric and wireless devices throughout the world. They referred to studies which showed that exposure to EMFs produce increased cancer risk, genetic damages, structural and functional changes of the reproductive system, learning and memory deficits, and neurological disorders.

---

23   "What Is 5g?" *The Motley Fool,* n.d., https://www.fool.com/knowledge-center/what-is-5g.aspx, accessed April 12, 2019.

24   Kevin Jessup, "5G, AI, and the New World Order Internet of Things," *Prophecy Investigators,* December 17, 2018, https://prophecyinvestigators.org/5g-ai-microwave-weapons-and-the-new-world-order-internet-of-things/, accessed April 12, 2019.

25   Ibid.

26   Rockefeller Core Taxable Bond Fund, Schedule of Investments, December 31, 2018, www.rockefellerfunds.com/media/pdfs/RCFIX_Holdings.pdf, accessed April 12, 2019.

In 2015, the National Toxicology Program conducted a $25 million study which linked 4G cellphone usage to brain and heart cancer in animals. The "EUROPAEM EMF Guideline 2016" maintained that "long-term exposure to certain EMFs is a risk factor for diseases such as certain cancers, Alzheimer's disease, and male infertility." Despite the fact that 5G met with the approval of the Federal Communications Commission in 2017, no tests were conducted on the health effects that the vastly increased electromagnetic airwaves will have on the general public.[27] The eugenics movement, advanced by John D. Rockefeller Jr., couldn't have imagined that the problem of overpopulation could be solved through air waves.

THE DIGITAL PRISON

Within the world of a 5G smart grid, future generations will eke out their existence in a digital prison under constant supervision and control. The information obtained from the monitors in their homes, vehicles, and workplaces will be transmitted to insurance companies so that premiums can be readjusted and to businesses so that new customers can be targeted. It will be conveyed to employers the personal beliefs of their employees and to law enforcement officials so that criminals can be arrested before they commit a crime. It will be sent to the money cartel, who own and oversee the new technology, so they will be able to access the value of every person's life.

It all began with snake oil and the awareness that people remain ready to buy it and drink it, thinking it might improve their well-being.

And it came to an end with the preparation of the rise of a one world leader, who, in accordance with Scripture, will be the Antichrist.

The road to Armageddon had been paved with asphalt.

---

27   Josh del Sol, "FCC Intimidates Press and Evades Questioning about Wireless and Cancer at 5G Rollout," *Global Freedom Movement*, 2019, https://globalfreedommovement.org/fcc-approves-rollout-5g-technology-evades-questioning-wireless-dangers/, accessed April 12, 2019.

Within the world of a 5G smart grid, future generations will eke out their existence in a digital prison under constant supervision and control.

EPILOGUE

IN CONCLUSION

BETWEEN THIS BOOK AND THE FIRST BOOK, *The Killing of Uncle Sam*, there is so much information to share. So many things are wrong in this world today. Can anything even be done? Where do we even start? How do we go about making the changes that are needed?

There are many questions that arise; however, there is one question we should each ask ourselves.

What can I do?

I need one thing I can do to make a difference in this world.

If everyone reading this book can find that ONE THING to do and to do it with all their might, we could see a change. To spend their life, their talents and their resources—making a difference; then the tide of evil could be rolled back and evil will be overcome with good.

I believe that we have one more hour of daylight, even as the sun is fast setting on the horizon of time. I believe that the preaching of the Good News of the Gospel of Jesus Christ will make the difference.

This is my life's purpose.

"Joy to the world, the Lord is come. I bring you glad tidings of great joy."

As far as I am concerned, this is the only hope for the nations of the earth. As of this writing, I have been privileged to have traveled to, and ministered in, seventy-eight nations of the earth. People are the same everywhere: they want freedom; they want to be loved; they want to do something with their life. They have dreams—all put there by their Creator. And God has a plan for each one of them.

According to God's Word, we are heading toward a one-world government, one money system, and the rise of a one-world leader—the coming of the Antichrist. However, let's not go hide in a mountain somewhere, or merely stand on the sidelines and watch. Let's stand up, as others have, and join the fight.

Down through the centuries and down through the years, those who stood up became the reformers. They made a difference. Come on, let us rise up and make a difference. The world is waiting.

I want to thank my co-author, Dr. Paul Williams. Thank you for helping me get this information out to the masses. We encourage every reader to also read *The Killing of Uncle Sam* and then get ready for the third book in the trilogy, which should be out in 2020.

To all those who have gone before us and paid the price, we will not fail. By God's divine grace we will accomplish His purpose and His plan until our work is done!

APPENDIX A

From: Luis Florez

Date: 22 November 1960

MEMORANDUM FOR: GENERAL CHARLES P CABELL

SUBJECT: Climate Control

Attached is a paper prepared by the Research Division of the Travellers Insurance Company on the need for climate control study program after discussions with Dr. Thomas Malone (Chief of the Division) and his staff. I trust you will find it interesting.

LUIS de FLOREZ

Research Chairman

Attachment: (1)

As Noted

CONFIDENTIAL

Declassified in Part—Sanitized Copy Approved for Release 2013/08/06: CIA-RDP78-03425A002100020014-2

THE NEED FOR A CLIMATE CONTROL STUDY PROGRAM

1. Introduction

Control of the weather environment involves the complete spectrum of weather phenomena. As a function of the time and space scale associated with such weather phenomena, different types of human activities are affected ranging from those of the individuals, through the complex operation of large industrial and military organizations and the activities of entire societies. The concept of weather control has meaning only when it is discussed in terms of the specific operations for which it is to be used. The techniques which are and can be used for control of the weather environment vary with the scale of the operation considered and with the specific goals which are to be achieved by such weather control.

Large scale climate control requires the modification of the global weather patterns by altering and interferring [*sic*] with the large-scale physical processes which are associated with the characteristic motions on the scale of the general circulation of the atmosphere. Many proposals have been made regarding means of altering the various physical processes in the atmosphere which might affect these large-scale atmospheric circulations. Most of these proposals have never been subjected to detailed scientific feasibility analyses.

These proposals fall into several general categories. In general they can be categorized by whether they seek to alter processes associated with the energy and momentum or moisture balance of the atmosphere. For example, proposals have been made to alter the energy balance of large areas by altering the surface albedo. Proposals of this nature involve changing surface albedos by the use of substances of appropriate absorptive or reflective characteristics which differ from the natural surface. An example is the proposal that polar areas be covered with layers of soot. Other proposals are made to alter the energy balance of the atmosphere by injecting dust and other particulate matter into the high atmosphere. Proposals for altering the normal energy cycle of the atmosphere extend also to the alteration of the chemistry of atmospheric substances especially in the high atmosphere which might also effect [*sic*] the radiational balance.

Proposals are made to alter the moisture balance of the atmosphere by the alteration of the evaporation mechanisms. These proposals suggest spreading various kinds of film upon large bodies of water thus cutting down evaporation and interferring [*sic*] with the moisture cycle of the atmosphere. Furthermore, when films are spread upon surfaces to alter their evaporation potential the mechanical effects of the surface are also altered, which might affect the momentum balance of the atmosphere. Proposals are also made for altering the momentum balance of the atmosphere. These proposals generally involve a modification of the surface frictional stresses by changing the frictional drag coefficients over large areas of surface.

2. The Technological Basis for the Reexamination of the Feasibility of Climate Control

Technological developments of the past two decades have provided the understanding, the techniques, and the means necessary for an assault on the problems of climate control. Control of any kind requires capabilities in all three of these areas. Meteorology is just now beginning to acquire such capabilities.

Achievement of an understanding of the large-scale physical processes of the atmosphere has been a continuing process over many decades. However, during the past several years the systematic exploitation of observational information on a global scale has led to a coherent description of the manner in which the large-scale physical processes in the atmosphere operate to provide for the maintenance of the global circulations against the dissipative effects of friction, and the manner in which they operate to transform the solar energy into the kinetic energy of the organized large-scale atmospheric circulations. Theoretical studies have led to an understanding of the reasons why the atmospheric physical processes operate in the observed manner. In combination these studies have led to the formation of the first consistent rudimentary theories for the causes of the fluctuations of the large-scale atmospheric circulations.

The attainment of such a theory holds broad implications for the manner in which climate control studies should be conducted. Much as the biologist must first achieve an understanding of the causes and processes involved in the generation and communication of diseases before he can consider the problem of disease control, so the meteorologist must achieve an understanding of the causes and processes involved in the fluctuations of the atmospheric circulations which control the regional and global climate. While the meteorologists' understanding is by no means perfect, and much remains to be done, at least the first and most necessary level of the understanding has been reached.

Given such understanding the meteorologist must have the capability of simulating and testing the natural phenomena he must control. In other physical sciences this is a relatively straightforward matter of laboratory simulation. The circulation phenomena of relevance in global climate are not so readily amenable to laboratory simulation. Fortunately, simple models of the atmospheric circulations of a mathematical nature can and have been intensively studied by meteorologists in connection with theoretical studies of the general circulation and in connection with the problems of numerical weather forecasting. The indispensible tool which has generated such intensive interest in such mathematical formulations of atmospheric models has been the high speed electronic computer, which has become the laboratory of the meteorologist. Rapid technological advances in the data processing and computing art now make it feasible to consider the treatment of simple mathematical models of the atmosphere of considerable sophistication in which important physical processes can be simulated. Such computing machines now place the meteorologist in the enviable position of other scientists in that the effects of various physical processes can be studied under controlled conditions. In particular, it has now become feasible not only to speculate about the consequences of human intervention in the atmospheric processes but also to simulate, test and study these consequences.

The meteorologist has also attempted to imitate his more fortunate scientific brethren by constructing laboratory models of large-scale atmospheric and oceanic circulations. He has been able to attain considerable success in producing reasonable hydrodynamic analogues of these large-scale atmospheric motions which are also amenable to study under controlled laboratory conditions. This second tool for simulation and test purposes provides the meteorologist with another indispensible capability which was unavailable to him just one decade ago.

Much of the well justified skepticism about the feasibility of climate control has centered on the available human means for exercising necessary control. While there are many conceivable methods for the control of climate, all of them involve the expenditure of energy in one form or another. Even the vulnerable instabilities of the atmosphere which one would hope to uncover through a systematic program of climate control studies, the so-called "trigger mechanisms," will probably require access to energy sources of immense magnitude for proper exploitation. In this atomic age, we now have available truly immense potential sources of power, and it is highly likely that our lifetime will see the harnessing of hydrogen fusion power, which will provide almost limitless sources of energy. Thus it is no longer possible to relegate considerations of climate control to the fantasies of science fiction on this account. It has now become necessary for us to recognize the realities and potentialities of modern science for what they are and what they can mean for the possibilities of climate control.

3. Civil and Military Implications

The impace [*sic*] of the successful achievement of methods for the control of climate upon all types of human activities confounds the imagination. Slight amelioration of adverse precipitation or temperature regimes could result in the reclamation of vast territories for agricultural and many other types of human activities. Desert areas which cover a large fraction of the earth's surface are known in many cases to require only slight changes in moisture regimes to make them suitable for large scale agricultural production. Small changes in circulation regimes could bring about the moderation of severe temperature climates to yield additional areas suitable for human habitation. Such changes in circulation regimes can also affect the normal paths of destructive storms like hurricanes, such that their destructive energies could be dissipated in regions far removed from major human activities. Changes in atmospheric circulation regimes would have marked effects upon oceanic circulations with consequent changes in the abundance and location of fertile fishing grounds. Moderate changes in climatic characteristics will have serious repercussions for all aspects of industrial activity.

Military, a climatic control capability raises the possibility of a totally new type of warfare. This type of warfare may be termed "Geophysical Warfare" in which our ability to control the weather environment can be used as a weapon. This geophysical weapon will be unique in character in that it can be used in both hot and cold struggles. It can be used to affect an enemy adversely or benefit a friend. As a function of the nature of the control capability, the use of such a weapon could be a determining factor in the success of national military operations.

As a hot war weapon it would be best to have strong control capability for specific areas and specific periods of time. Since we are talking about intermediate and long period climate control, this would imply a conflict of considerable duration. Specific military consequences of such a control capability would be in the potential for destruction of an enemy's food production capability thereby weakening his total military power, and also in the derangements of transportation systems and other industrial activities which might result from a marked change in climatic conditions.

As a cold war tool, the capability of climate control would place in the hands of this Government a tool for ameliorating the weather conditions in friendly and uncommitted nations as a means of strengthening bonds with this country. Conversely as a cold war weapon, a climate control capability provides for a unique surreptitious means for weakening a potential enemy so that he does not have the capability to wage a hot war.

The general study of the feasibility of climate control independent of the use of this capability in either hot or cold conflicts provides necessary national insurance if other nations achieve a control capability. Such a capability in either friendly or unfriendly hands represents a threat of weather conditions which might adversely affect the welfare of our nation. As an absolutely necessary countermeasure, this country must have within its scientific arsenal, the knowledge of how to combat any such attempts at control by other nations. Failure to undertake a consistent program at this time which might provide the knowledge necessary to combat such climate control operations on the part of other nations could lead to another "Sputnik" situation.

4. General Outline of a Technical Program for Investigating the Feasibility of Climate Control

4.1 Principle areas of technical activity.

Those items marked with asterisks are considered to be long range continuing activities of prime importance.

4.1.1 Complete literature survey especially focused upon Russian work.

4.1.2 A detailed scientific analysis of all proposals made to date for controlling climate with an evaluation of the economic feasibility as well as the possible scientific consequences, if any.

*4.1.3 An expanded effort to collect, systematize, and analyze observational material for the entire globe extending to the highest accessible levels to obtain a more detailed and clearer description of the fundamental physical processes operating in the earth's atmosphere.

*4.1.4 An expanded effort to develop mathematical models of the atmosphere capable of including those pertinent physical processes which are felt to be important in the fluctuations of the large-scale atmospheric motions.

*4.1.5 A consistent long range program of comparative numerical integrations of mathematical models to determine the consequences of interferring [sic] with any physical processes in the atmosphere.

4.1.6 A much expanded program in associated sciences, especially in the field of numerical analysis to enable us to conduct extended numerical integrations.

*4.1.7 An extended effort to undertake studies of radiational processes in the atmosphere which will provide necessary information for incorporation into mathematical models suitable for numerical integrations.

*4.1.8 An expanded effort to establish experimental laboratory facilities for the construction of experimental models suitable for simulating and testing various theories about atmospheric circulations which may be important for climate control.

4.1.9 A long range program of investigations of the interactions between ocean and atmosphere to determine the nature of these interactions.

4.1.10 A program of investigation into pertinent micrometeorological processes especially as they refer to the fictional dissipation of kinetic energy and the transfer of momentum and energy at the earth-atmosphere interface.

A Possible Program for the Study of Climate Control Problems

1.0 Introduction

It is proposed that a group of scientists be assembled to conduct experiments on the feasibility of climate control. The objective of this research will be to develop methods necessary to analyze and test the theoretical and economic feasibility of ideas which have been and will be proposed to control climate.

There is a clear need to undertake the following types of studies on a systematic long range basis.

a. The evaluation of present knowledge which may be pertinent to the problem.

b. The supplementary research not adequately being performed be [*sic*] present research organizations.

c. Theoretical climate control experiments as justified by the state of the art.

It should be clearly emphasized that the chances of attaining feasible climate control methods are extremely small. The potential value to the nation is so great, however, as to warrant the initiation of the activities proposed below.

2.0 Surveillance and Evaluation of the Existing State of the Art.

There are many research efforts in this country and abroad which have important bearing on the problems of climate control. This research encompasses numerical general circulation and short range forecast experiments, observational studies of the large scale atmosphere physical processes involving momentum, energy and moisture exchanges, experimental research on laboratory atmospheric analogues, and pertinent technological advances in non meteorological sciences concerned with the availability of energy sources, delivery and distribution systems, and materials.

An active program of surveillance and evaluation of the existing state of the art as represented by the research described above for its applicability to climate control problems is required. This work should commence with a literature survey of pertinent and related research. This surveillance program will permit the isolation of promising developments which require further engineering and testing and will define any supplementary research required to further climate control objectives. This should be a continuing effort to monitor all pertinent research so that at all times the state of the art is fully exploited for purposes of examining the feasibilities of climate control.

3.0 Supplementary Research

It is envisioned that the activities of the group will include research necessary to supplement the work of other groups. Additional research may be required to describe more fully the climatology of certain pertinent physical processes in the atmosphere. Information on space and time spectra will be required of the various atmospheric energy and momentum exchange processes. This research will aid in the formulation of realistic physical models of the atmosphere. It is likewise needed to test the suitability of various models for the purpose of numerical climate control experiments.

Extensive research into the formulation of mathematical models of the atmosphere which are suitable for long period integrations will be required. These models will be integrated numerically on an electronic computer and tested for agreement with the climatology of pertinent physical processes. Depending upon the test results, the numerical integration methods and the mathematical models may require modification in order to achieve a formulation which is suitable to numerical climate control experiments.

4.0 Climate Control Experiments

A series of systematic numerical climate control experiments will be performed with suitable atmospheric models to analyze and test the theoretical and economic feasibility of ideas which have or will be proposed to control climate. These experiments will be designed to assess the climatic change which would result from changes due to artificially introduced energy and momentum sources and sinks. Innumerable ways have been proposed for varying these sources and sinks, such as changing radiation absorptions and reflection characteristics controlling evaporation from free water bodies, altering surface stresses, etc.

5.0 Personnel and Program Costs

Until such time as it is clear that the state of the art can permit extensive climate control numerical experimentation, the research effort should be concentrated on items 2.0 and 3.0. When the model development under item 3.0 has progressed to a satisfactory point, a large increase in electronic computer time would be required for item 4.0.

Personnel required to pursue this program would be:

2 Senior Research Associates (dynamic meteorology)

1 Senior Research Associate (physicist)

1 Senior Research Associate (mathematician)

2 Research Associates (dynamic meteorology)

3 Research Associates (mathematician, analysists, and programmers),

plus supporting help.

Total salary support and overhead costs estimated on the basis of $25,000.00 per professional would be $225,000/year. Initially, computer rental for 200 hours/year would total approximately $75,000/year. Computer costs would greatly increase for any substantial effort under item 4.0.

APPENDIX B

BY KRISANNE HALL, JD

THE DECLARATION OF INDEPENDENCE lays before us the basis for all governments—past, present, and future. It states:

> *We hold these truths to be self-evident, that all men are created equal, that they are* endowed by their Creator *with certain unalienable Rights, that among these are Life, Liberty and the pursuit of Happiness.*—That to secure these rights, *Governments are instituted among Men, deriving their just powers from the consent of the governed* (emphasis mine).

The entire purpose of any form of government is to secure the rights of individual citizens. The rights that our foundational document refers to are classified as "inherent rights," and they consist of life, liberty, property, and the right to personally secure them in the best manner possible. The most basic of natural rights is the right to self-preservation to which the natural right to secure property is connected. Government is instituted to protect property of every sort, even that property which lies in the various rights of individuals. This being the end of government, that alone is a just government, which impartially secures to every man, whatever is his own.

Our constitutional republic was designed with three branches of government. Their specific powers were delegated for this one just cause: to secure all the rights of the individual. Even so, that delegation of power to the federal government is specifically defined and very limited. James Madison, the Father of the Constitution and fourth president of the United States, said, "The powers delegated to the federal government are few and defined." He lists them in *Federalist* No. 45 as war, peace, negotiations, and foreign commerce. In other words, our founders believed in and intended limited government—very limited.

In a 1792 debate in Congress, then congressman James Madison said,

> *I, sir, have always conceived—I believe those who proposed the Constitution conceived—it is still more fully known and more material to observe, that those who rarified the Constitution conceived—that it is* not an indefinite government...*but* a limited Government. *The Powers delegated to the federal government are few and defined...war, peace negotiations, and foreign commerce.* (emphasis mine)

However, our governments have been infected by federal supremacists. They often assert that all federal law is superior to state laws and constitutions. Yet the Constitution itself denies that false ideology in Article 6 clause 2 where it declares that only laws made by Congress "in pursuance" to the Constitution are supreme and that when they are not, the judges in the States are not bound by them. Alexander Hamilton offers great clarity on this subject in *Federalist* Paper No. 78:

> There is no position which depends on clearer principles, than that every act of a delegated authority, contrary to the tenor of the commission under which it is exercised, is void. No legislative act, therefore, contrary to the Constitution, can be valid.

These same federal supremacists commonly assert that the Supreme Court has the power to ultimately interpret the Constitution through judicial review and therefore sovereignly determine the limits of the power delegated to itself as well as the other branches of the federal government. To allow Congress to enforce any law as supreme means that the Constitution has no meaning and the government has no limit. In that same vein, the Supreme Court, being part of the federal government and possessing the power to define the federal government, voids the entire purpose for a written Constitution and negates any established limit of power whatsoever.

Alexander Hamilton again shows us the simplicity of this limited power principle in *Federalist* No. 83: "An affirmative grant of special powers would be absurd as well as useless, if a general authority was intended." Basically, Hamilton was saying, "Why did we make a specific list of powers, if the power existed to do whatever they can imagine or get a majority vote upon?"

Most federal supremacists and every judicial supremacist will assert that the judicial system not only carries a general, also known in the legal field as "plenary" power, but also defines it. This self-defined and ever-expanding federal power, being rewritten every day through errant judicial precedent, is power stolen from the people and their states. It is power neither authorized nor delegated. Friends, this is *not* what a constitutional republic looks like. This is a *kingdom* of stolen power by an oligarchy of thieves.

What every American must understand is that if the federal government exercises a power that is not specifically, by name, delegated to the federal government, that exercise of power is completely unconstitutional. One may ask, "What about the checks and balances?" James Madison argued in 1789 that the judiciary was established to provide an important internal check and balance on federal power, not to increase it, not to alter it, but to enforce its limits to guard the rights of the people when the other two branches of government violated their boundaries. He said the judiciary would

> consider themselves in a peculiar manner the guardians of those rights; they will be an impenetrable bulwark against every assumption of power in the legislative or executive; they will be naturally led to resist every encroachment upon rights expressly stipulated for in the constitution by the declaration of rights.

However, the judiciary has become just another head of the federal behemoth, consuming and sanctioning every power imaginable. Thomas Jefferson somehow feared that this would be the fate of our federal judiciary. He described it as his greatest fear:

> The great object of my fear is the federal judiciary. That body, like gravity, ever acting, with noiseless foot, and unalarming advance, gaining ground step by step, and holding what it gains, is ingulfing insidiously the special governments into the jaws of that which feeds them . . . government will become as venal and oppressive as the government from which we Separated.

What those who ratified the Constitution wanted us to know is that they knew the institutions of the federal government could fail in spite of the specific limitations created through the Constitution. James Madison refers to the Constitution as a "parchment barrier," a mechanism of mere ink and paper. He knew that the Constitution had no power of its own and therefore could not limit the power of the government over the citizenry nor could it prevent the branches of government from expanding their own power beyond the grant of the Constitution or from taking power from other branches that was delegated. Our problem is not with the way the Constitution created our federal government, but how the Constitution is enforced today!

Elections are not corrupted because the Constitution failed. Politicians are not immoral and dishonest because the Constitution failed. We do not have trillions of dollars in debt because the Constitution failed. We are not in a perpetual state of war because the Constitution failed. Our rights and liberties are not being trampled upon by agencies and agents because the Constitution failed. The Constitution cannot fail. The Constitution cannot succeed. The Constitution is an inanimate object, mere ink and paper.

When any or all of the branches of the federal government fail to follow the law of the land; when government becomes a tool of destruction of individual rights instead of their defense; when the individuals and branches of federal government exceed the limited and defined boundaries as established within the Constitution, it is not the document's fault. It is the fault of the people who do not require their government to be limited and defined by the document that created it. Samuel Adams summed it up quite precisely when he wrote:

> No people will tamely surrender their Liberties, nor can any be easily subdued, when knowledge is diffused and virtue is preserved. On the Contrary, when People are universally ignorant, and debauched in their Manners, they will sink under their own weight without the Aid of foreign Invaders.

Ignorance of the people must end regarding the limited nature of their government and their personal responsibility to confine that government within its designed limited capacity. We the people must reassert ourselves as the master of our government if we want our children to be free. We must put the federal government back in its limited and defined box, and we must stop accepting the programming that we have been taught and start refusing the asserted "plenary powers." We must start demanding that our government be specifically limited and defined as our Constitution and those who ratified it demand.

To restore proper government, we do not need to change or get rid of the Constitution. We must get educated! God gave us rights, not government. A government that operates contrary to our rights is not a just government. The only reason government exists is to secure our rights, not to regulate, control, or deny them. The purpose of this book is dedicated to that specific education, but it is not just to equip people with knowledge. It is to ignite that understanding into wisdom that inspires the reader to stand up and say: "I will be the check and balance."

BIBLIOGRAPHY

Ahamed, Liaquat, *Lords of Finance: The Bankers Who Broke the World*, New York: Penguin Books, 2009.

Allen, Gary, *None Dare Call It Conspiracy*, San Diego, CA: Dauphin Publications, 1971.

———. *The Rockefeller File*, Seal Beach, CA: '76 Press, 1976.

Ayers, Bradley, *The War That Never Was: An Insider's Account of CIA Covert Operations against Cuba*, New York: Bobbs Merrill, 1976.

Bailey, Alice A., *Ponder on This: A Compilation*, Washington, D.C.: Lucis Publishing, 2003.

Baker, James C., *The Bank for International Settlements: Evolution and Evaluation*, Santa Clara, CA: Quorum, 2002.

Baratta, Joseph Preston, *The Politics of World Federation: United Nations, UN Reform, Atomic Control*, New York: Praeger, 2004.

Batalov, Eduard, *The American Utopia*, translated by Dimitry Belyavsky, Moscow: Progress Press, 1985.

Bergen, Peter L., *Holy War, Inc.: Inside the Secret World of Osama Bin Laden*, New York: Simon and Schuster, 2002.

Bernard, Raymond W., *The Revolt against Chemicals*, Whitefish, MT: Kessinger Publishing, 2010.

Best, Gary Dean, *Pride, Prejudice, and Politics: Roosevelt Versus Recovery, 1933–1938*, New York: Praeger, 1991.

Bodley, John H., *Cultural Anthropology: Tribes, States, and the Global System*, Lanham, MD: Rowan and Littlefield, 2016.

Brodsky, Melvin I., *Division and Discord: The Supreme Court under Stone and Vinson, 1941–1953*, Columbia, SC: University of South Carolina Press, 1997.

Brown, Robin, *The Secret Society: Cecil John Rhodes's Plan for a New World Order*, Cape Town, ZA: Penguin Books, 2015.

Brzezinski, Zbigniew, *Between Two Ages: America's Role in the Technetronic Era*, New York: Viking, 1970.

———. *The Grand Chessboard: American Primacy and Its Geostrategic Imperatives*, New York: Basic Books, 1998.

Buchanan, Pat, *Suicide of a Superpower*, New York: Thomas Dunne Books, 2011.

Cannon, Barry, *Hugo Chavez and the Bolivian Revolution: Populism and Democracy in a Globalized Age*, Manchester, UK: Manchester University Press, 2010.

Cassell, Gustav, *The Downfall of the Gold Standard*, New York: Augustus Kelly, 1966.

Chambers, John Whiteclay, *The Oxford Companion to American Military History*, New York: Oxford University Press, 2000.

Chernow, Ron, *The House of Morgan: An American Banking Dynasty and the Rise of Modern Finance*, New York: Grove Press, 1990.

————. *Titan: The Life of John D. Rockefeller, Sr.*, New York: Vintage Books, 2004.

Chossudovsky, Michel, *America's "War on Terrorism,"* Montreal, Quebec: *Global Research*, 2005.

————. *The Globalization of Poverty and the New World Order*, Montreal: *Global Research*, 2003.

————. *The Globalization of War: America's "Long War" against Humanity*, Montreal: *Global Research* 2015.

Clark, Wesley, *Winning Modern Wars*, New York: Public Affairs, 2003.

Cockburn, Alexander, and Jeffrey St. Clair, *Whiteout: The CIA, Drugs and the Press*, New York: Verso, 1998.

Coetzer, Owen, *Fire in the Sky: The Destruction of the Orange Free State*, Johannesburg: Covos Day, 2000.

Corbin, Jane, *Al Qaeda: In Search of the Terrorist Network That Threatens the World*, New York: Thunder Mouth Press, 2003.

Critchlow, Donald T., *Intended Consequences: Birth Control, Abortion, and the Federal Government in Modern America*, New York: Oxford University Press, 2001.

Davenport, William H., and Daniel M. Rosenthal, *Engineering: Its Role and Function in Human Society* (Amsterdam: The Netherlands, Elsevier, 2016),

Dall, Curtis B., *FDR: My Exploited Father-in-Law*, Washington, D.C.: Action Associates, 1970.

DeSocio, Richard James, *Rockefellerocracy: Assassinations, Watergate, and Monopoly of "Philanthropic" Foundations*, Bloomington, IN: Author's House, 2013.

Dickinson, Robert Latou, and Louise Stevens Bryant, *Control of Conception: An Illustrated Medical Manual*, Baltimore: The Williams & Wilkins Company, 1938.

Dowd, Kevin, and Richard Henry Timberlake, *Money and the Nation State: The Financial Revolution and the World Monetary Systems*, Oakland, CA: Independent Institute, 1998.

Dubay, Eric, *The Atlantean Conspiracy*, Durham, NC: Lulu, 2009.

du Randt, Charl, *Demonised Doctoring: Exposing the Occultic Mission of the Medical Industry*, Cape Town, ZA: Rapture Publications, 1999.

Eichengreen, Barry J., *Gold Fetters: The Gold Standard and the Great Depression*, New York: Oxford University Press, 1992.

Engdahl, F. William, *Gods of Money: Wall Street and the Death of the American Century*, San Diego, CA: Progressive Press, 2011.

Estulin, Daniel, *The True Story of the Bilderberg Group*, 2nd ed., Walterville, OR: Trine Day, 2009.

Felix, David, *Biography of an Idea: John Maynard Keynes and the General Theory of Employment, Interest, and Money,* Piscataway, NJ: Transaction, 1955.

Flynn, John Thomas, *The Roosevelt Myth*, Auburn, AL: Ludwig von Mises Institute, 2008.

Fosdick, Raymond E., *John D. Rockefeller, Jr.: A Portrait*, New York: Harper and Brothers, 1958.

Gates, Jr., Robert, *The Conspiracy That Will Not Die: How the Rothschild Cartel Is Driving America into One World Government*, Oakland, OR: Red Anvil Press, 2011.

George, Susan, *A Fate Worse Than Debt: The World Financial Crisis and the Poor*, New York: Grove Press, 1990.

Goldberg, Michelle, *The Means of Reproduction: Sex, Power, and the Future of the World,* New York: Penguin, 2009.

Goldwater, Barry, *With No Apologies*, New York: William Morrow, 1979.

Goodson, Stephen Mitford, *A History of Central Banking and the Enslavement of Mankind*, London: Black House, 2014.

Griffin, G. Edward, *The Creature from Jekyll Island: A Second Look at the Federal Reserve*, 5th ed., Westlake Village, CA: The Reality Zone, 2010.

Gunaratna, Rohan, *Inside Al Qaeda: Global Network of Terror*, New York: Berkeley Books, 2002.

Harr, John Ensor, and Peter J. Johnson, *The Rockefeller Century: Three Generations of America's Greatest Family*, New York: Scribner's, 1988.

Higham, Charles, *Trading with the Enemy: An Expose of the Nazi-American Plot, 1933–1949*, New York: Delacorte Press, 1983.

Hoar, William P., *Architects of Conspiracy: An Intriguing History*, Appleton, WI: Western Islands, 1985.

Hoover, Herbert, *Memoirs of Herbert Hoover, 1929–1941: The Great Depression*, New York: Macmillan, 1952.

Howells, Robert, *The Illuminati: The Counterculture Revolution from Secret Societies to Wikileaks and Anonymous*, London: Watkins, 2016.

Irons, Peter H., *The New Deal Lawyers*, Princeton: Princeton University Press, 1993.

Johnson, Hugh, *The Blue Eagle from Egg to Earth*, New York: Doubleday, 1935.

Johnson, Paul, *Modern Times: The World from the Twenties to the Nineties*, rev. ed., New York: Harper Collins, 1992.

Jones, Eliot, *The Trust Problem in the United States*, New York: Macmillan, 1923.

Jones, Geoffrey, *Multinationals and Global Capitalism: From the Nineteenth to the Twenty-First Century*, New York: Oxford University Press, 2005.

Josephson, Emanuel M., *Rockefeller "Internationalist:" The Man Who Misrules the World*, New York: Chedney Press, 1952.

———. *The "Federal" Reserve Conspiracy and Rockefellers: Their "Gold Corner,"* New York: Chedney Press, 1968.

———. *The Truth about Rockefeller: "Public Enemy No. 1," Studies in Criminal Psychopathy*, New York: Chedney Press, 1962.

Josephson, Matthew, *The Robber Barons*, San Diego: Harvest Books, 1934.

Keynes, John Maynard, *The Collected Writings of John Maynard Keyes*, vol. 5, New York: Macmillan, 1971.

Kim, Yong-jin, *Major Powers and Korea*, Silver Spring, MD: Research Institute on Korean Affairs, 1973.

Klein, Henry H., *Dynastic America and Those Who Own It*, New York: Henry Klein, 1921.

Klos, Felix, *Churchill on Europe: The Untold Story of Churchill's European Project*, London: I. B. Tauris, 2016.

Koss, Peter, *Carnegie*, New York: John Wiley and Sons, 2002.

Kruger, Henrik, *The Great Heroin Coup: Drugs, Intelligence and International Finance*, Boston: South End Press, 1980.

Labeviere, Richard, *Dollars for Terror*, New York: Algora Press, 2000.

Lader, Lawrence, *Abortion*, Indianapolis: Bobbs-Merrill, 1966.

Larson, Erik, *Dead Wake: The Last Crossing of the Lusitania*, New York: Crown, 2015.

Lebor, Adam, *Tower of Basel: The Shadowy History of the Secret Bank that Runs the World*, New York: Public Affairs, 2013.

Lernoux, Penny, *In Banks We Trust*, New York: Penguin Books, 1984.

Lewis, Charles, *935 Lies: The Future of Truth and the Decline of America's Moral Integrity*, New York: Public Affairs, 2014.

Lewis, Frederick Allen, *The Lords of Creation*, New York: Harper and Brothers, 1935.

Low, Sidney, "Some Conversations in London," in *The Nineteenth Century and After*, vol. 51, New York: Leonard Scott, 1902.

Lundberg, Ferdinand, *America's Sixty Families*, New York: Vanguard Press, 1938.

Macrae, Norman, *John Von Neumann: The Scientific Genius Who Pioneered the Modern Computer, Game Theory, Nuclear Deterrence, and Much More*, New York: Pantheon Books, 1992.

Manchester, William, *A Rockefeller Family Portrait: From John D. to Nelson*, New York: Little Brown, 1959.

Marrs, Jim, *Rule by Secrecy*, New York: HarperCollins, 2001.

McCoy, Alfred W., *The Politics of Heroin: The CIA's Complicity in the Global Drug Trade*, Chicago: Lawrence Hill Books, 2003.

———. *The Politics of Heroin in Southeast Asia*, New York, Harper & Row, 1972.

Meredith, Martin, *Diamonds, Gold, and War: The British, the Boers, and the Making of South Africa*, New York: Public Affairs, 2008.

Michell, Sir Lewis, *The Life of Rt. Hon. C. J. Rhodes, 1853–1902*, vol. 1, London: Edward Arnold, 1910.

Mira Williams, *The History of Foreign Investments in the United States, 1914 to 1945*, Cambridge, MA: Harvard University Press, 2004.

Mullins, Eustace, *Secrets of the Federal Reserve*, New York: Kasper and Horton, 1982.

———. *The World Order*, New York: Modern History Project, 1983.

Norgren, Susan, *When the Golden Egg Cracks*, Carlsbad, CA: Balboa Press, 2012.

Pelton, Robert Young, *The World's Most Dangerous Places*, 4th ed., New York: HarperCollins, 2000.

Perloff, James, *The Shadows of Power: The Council on Foreign Relations and the American Decline*, Appleton, Wisconsin: Western Islands, 2005.

Bergen, *Holy War, Inc.: Inside the Secret World of Osama Bin Laden*, New York: Simon and Schuster, 2002.

Petersen, James, *The Century of Sex*, New York: Grove Press, 1999.

Phillips, Kevin, *American Dynasty: Aristocracy, Fortune, and the Politics of Deceit in the House of Bush*, New York: Viking, 2004.

Quigley, Carroll, *Tragedy and Hope: A History of the World in Our Time*, San Pedro, CA: GSG & Associates, 2004.

Reeve, Simon, *The New Jackals: Ramzi Yousef, Osama bin Laden, and the Future of Terrorism*, Boston: Northeastern University Press, 1999.

Rich, Mark M., *The Hidden Evil: The Financial Elite's Covert War against the Civilian Population*, Raleigh, NC: Lulu Press, 2009.

Rivers, Charles, *Robber Barons: The Lives and Careers of John D. Rockefeller, J. P. Morgan, Andrew Carnegie, and Cornelius Vanderbilt*, Scotts Valley, CA: Createspace Publishing, 2016.

Rockefeller, David, *Memoirs*, New York: Random House, 2002.

Roosevelt, Franklin D., *The Public Papers and Addresses of Franklin Roosevelt*, New York: Random House, 1938.

Rosen, Christine, *Preaching Eugenics*, New York: Oxford University Press, 2004.

Rotberg, Robert I., *The Founder: Cecil Rhodes and the Pursuit of Power*, New York: Oxford University Press, 1988.

Rothbard, Murray N., *The Case against the Fed*, Auburn, AL: Ludwig von Mises Institute, 2007.

Sanger, Margaret, *The Pivot of Civilization*, New York: Bretano's, 1922.

Scott, Peter Dale, *American War Machine: Deep Politics, the CIA Global Drug Connection, and the Road to Afghanistan*, Washington, D.C.: Rowman and Littlefield, 2010.

———. *Drugs, Oil, and War: The United States in Afghanistan, Colombia, and Indochina*, Lanham, MD: Rowman and Littlefield, 2004.

Schlafly, Phyllis, and Chester Ward, *Kissinger on the Couch*, New Rochelle, NY: Arlington House, 1975.

Segal, Howard P. *Technological Utopianism in American Culture*, Syracuse, NY: Syracuse University Press, 2005.

Segall, Grant, *John D. Rockefeller: Anointed with Oil*, New York: Oxford University Press, 2001.

Shoup, Laurence H., *Wall Street Think Tank: The Council on Foreign Relations and the Empire of Neoliberal Geopolitics, 1976–2014*, New York: Monthly Review Press, 2014.

Smith, G. Vance, and Tom Gow, *Masters of Deception: The Rise of the Council on Foreign Relations*, Colorado Springs: First Freedom Society, 2012.

Smith, Richard Norton, *Nelson Rockefeller: On His Own Terms*, New York: Random House, 2014.

Stead, William T., *The Last Will and Testament of Cecil John Rhodes*, London: Review of Reviews Office, 1902.

Stephenson, Nathaniel Wright, *Nelson W. Aldrich: A Leader in American Politics*, Port Washington, NY: Kennikat Press, 1971.

Sterling, Claire, *Octopus: How the Long Reach of the Sicilian Mafia Controls the Global Narcotics Trade*, NY: Simon and Schuster, 1990.

Stern, David L., *Rockefeller Philanthropy and Modern Science*, Abingdon, UK: Routledge, 2015.

Stone, Oliver, and Peter Kuznick, *The Concise Untold History of the United States*, New York: Gallery Books, 2014.

Sutton, Antony C., *Wall Street and the Bolshevik Revolution: A Remarkable True Story of the American Capitalists Who Financed the Russian Revolution*, London: Clairview, 2011.

Taylor, S. J., *Stalin's Apologist: Walter Duranty, the "New York Times" Man in Moscow*, New York: Oxford University Press, 1990.

Thomas, Evan, *The Very Best Men: Four Men Who Dared*, New York: Touchstone, 1985.

Titus, Herb, *The Common Law*, Chapel Hill, NC: Professional Press, 1998.

Trento, Joseph, *Prelude to Terror: The Rogue CIA, the Legacy of America's Private Intelligence Network*, New York: Carroll and Graf, 2005.

Thomas, Ken, and David Hatcher Childress, *Inside the Gemstone File: Howard Hughes, Onassis, and JFK*, Kempton, IL: Adventures Unlimited Press, 1999.

Unger, Craig, *House of Bush, House of Saud*, New York: Scribner's, 2004.

Warburg, James, *Testimony, Revision of the United Nations Charter: Hearings before a Senate Subcommittee on Foreign Relations*, Washington, D.C.: U.S. Government Printing Office, 1950.

Webster, Nesta H., *The Surrender of an Empire*, London: Bowell, 1933.

Weinberg, Robert, *The Revolution in 1905 in Odessa: Blood on the Steps*, Bloomington, IN.: Indiana University Press, 1993.

Williams, Mira, *The History of Foreign Investments in the United States, 1914 to 1945*, Cambridge, MA: Harvard University Press, 2004.

Wood, Patrick M., *Technocracy Rising: The Trojan Horse of Global Transformation*, Mesa, AZ: Coherent Publishing, 2015.

Wrigley, E. A., ed., *Nineteenth-Century Society: Essays in the Use of Quantitative Methods for the Study of Social Data,* Cambridge: Cambridge University Press, 2008.

Yergin, Daniel, *The Prize: The Epic Quest for Oil, Money and & Power*, New York: The Free Press, 2008.

Ziegler, Philip, *Legacy: Cecil Rhodes, the Rhodes Trust, and Rhodes Scholarships*, New Haven, CT: Yale University Press, 2008.